INTERCULTURAL AND INCLUSIVE EDUCATION IN LATIN AMERICA

INTERNATIONAL PERSPECTIVES ON INCLUSIVE EDUCATION

Series Editor: Chris Forlin

Recent Volumes

Volume 1:	Emotional and Behavioural Difficulties in Mainstream Schools – Edited by John Visser, Harry Daniels and Ted Cole
Volume 2:	Transforming Troubled Lives: Strategies and Interventions for Children with Social, Emotional and Behavioural Difficulties – Edited by John Visser, Harry Daniels and Ted Cole
Volume 3:	Measuring Inclusive Education – Edited by Chris Forlin and Tim Loreman
Volume 4:	Working with Teaching Assistants and other Support Staff for Inclusive Education – Edited by Dianne Chambers
Volume 5:	Including Learners with Low-Incidence Disabilities – Edited by Elizabeth A. West
Volume 6:	Foundations of Inclusive Education Research – Edited by Phyllis Jones and Scot Danforth
Volume 7:	Inclusive Pedagogy Across the Curriculum – Edited by Joanne Deppeler, Tim Loreman, Ron Smith and Lani Florian
Volume 8:	Implementing Inclusive Education – Edited by Amanda Watkins and Cor Meijer
Volume 9:	Ethics, Equity and Inclusive Education – Edited by Agnes Gajewski
Volume 10:	Working with Families for Inclusive Education: Navigating Identity, Opportunity and Belonging – Edited by Dick Sobsey and Kate Scorgie
Volume 11:	Inclusive Principles and Practices in Literacy Education – Edited by Marion Milton
Volume 12:	Service Learning: Enhancing Inclusive Education – Edited by Shane Lavery, Dianne Chambers and Glenda Cain
Volume 13:	Promoting Social Inclusion: Co-Creating Environments That Foster Equity and Belonging – Edited by Kate Scorgie and Chris Forlin
Volume 14:	Assistive Technology to Support Inclusive Education – Edited by Dianne Chambers

Volume 15: Resourcing Inclusive Education – Edited by Janka Goldan, Jennifer Lambrecht and Tim Loreman

Volume 16: Minding the Marginalized Students Through Inclusion, Justice, and Hope: Daring to Transform Educational Inequities – Edited by Jose W. Lalas and Heidi Luv Strikwerda

Volume 17: Instructional Collaboration in International Inclusive Education Contexts Edited by Sarah R. Semon, Danielle Lane, and Phyllis Jones

Volume 18: Transition Programs for Children and Youth with Diverse Needs – Edited by Kate Scorgie and Chris Forlin

Volume 19: Reading Inclusion Divergently: Articulations from Around the World – Edited by Bettina Amrhein and Srikala Naraian

Volume 20: Interdisciplinary Perspectives on Special and Inclusive Education in a Volatile, Uncertain, Complex & Ambiguous (Vuca) World – Edited by Pennee Narot and Narong Kiettikunwong

Volume 21: Progress Toward Agenda 2030: A Mid Term Review of the Status of Inclusive Education in Global Contexts. – Edited by Danielle Lane, Nicholas Catania, and Sarah Semon

Volume 22: Contextualizing Critical Race Theory on Inclusive Education from A Scholar-Practitioner Perspective: Does It Really Matter? – Edited by Jose W. Lalas and Heidi Luv Strikwerda

Volume 23: Including Voices: Respecting the Experiences of People from Marginalised Communities – Edited by Richard Rose and Michael Shevlin

INTERNATIONAL PERSPECTIVES ON INCLUSIVE
EDUCATION   VOLUME 24

INTERCULTURAL AND INCLUSIVE EDUCATION IN LATIN AMERICA: TRAJECTORIES, PERSPECTIVES AND CHALLENGES

EDITED BY

SILVIA ROMERO-CONTRERAS
Universidad Autónoma de San Luis Potosí, México

ISMAEL GARCÍA-CEDILLO
Universidad Autónoma de San Luis Potosí, México

AND

LUZ MARÍA MORENO-MEDRANO
Universidad Iberoamericana, México

United Kingdom – North America – Japan
India – Malaysia – China

Emerald Publishing Limited
Emerald Publishing, Floor 5, Northspring, 21-23 Wellington Street, Leeds LS1 4DL

First edition 2024

Editorial matter and selection © 2024 Silvia Romero-Contreras, Ismael García-Cedillo and Luz María Moreno-Medrano.
Individual chapters © 2024 the authors.
Published under exclusive licence by Emerald Publishing Limited.

Reprints and permissions service
Contact: www.copyright.com

No part of this book may be reproduced, stored in a retrieval system, transmitted in any form or by any means electronic, mechanical, photocopying, recording or otherwise without either the prior written permission of the publisher or a licence permitting restricted copying issued in the UK by The Copyright Licensing Agency and in the USA by The Copyright Clearance Center. Any opinions expressed in the chapters are those of the authors. Whilst Emerald makes every effort to ensure the quality and accuracy of its content, Emerald makes no representation implied or otherwise, as to the chapters' suitability and application and disclaims any warranties, express or implied, to their use.

British Library Cataloguing in Publication Data
A catalogue record for this book is available from the British Library

ISBN: 978-1-83753-141-7 (Print)
ISBN: 978-1-83753-140-0 (Online)
ISBN: 978-1-83753-142-4 (Epub)

ISSN: 1479-3636 (Series)

Corrigendum: It has come to the attention of the publisher that the chapter del Valle, S.S. (2024), "The Implications of Epistemic Justice for Intercultural and Inclusive Education", Romero-Contreras, S., Garcìa-Cedillo, I. and Moreno-Medrano, L.M. (Ed.) Intercultural and Inclusive Education in Latin America (International Perspectives on Inclusive Education, Vol. 24), Emerald Publishing Limited, Leeds, pp. 227–240. https://doi.org/10.1108/S1479-363620240000024015, incorrectly listed the author Sylvia Schmelkes del Valle as del Valle, S.S.; the correct author information is as follows: Schmelkes, S. This has been amended in both the published version and metadata. The author sincerely apologizes for this mistake.

Printed and bound by CPI Group (UK) Ltd, Croydon, CR0 4YY

INVESTOR IN PEOPLE

CONTENTS

About the Editors	*ix*
About the Contributors	*xi*
Series Editor Preface	*xxi*
Preface	*xxv*
Acknowledgments	*xxix*

Context and Sociocultural Determinants of Inclusion and Interculturality in Latin America   *1*
Ismael García-Cedillo and Silvia Romero-Contreras

Opportunities for People With Special Educational Needs in Higher Education in Chile: An Analysis of Educational Trajectories   *15*
Ernesto Treviño Villarreal and Eugenia Victoriano Villouta

Inclusive Education in Brazil: The Potential of Technology to Facilitate Inclusive Practice   *33*
Dianne Chambers and Rodrigo Hübner Mendes

Education for All From the Early Years: Inclusive Experience in Chile   *45*
Paula Tapia Silva, Patricia Soto de la Cruz and Yarela Muñoz López

Inclusive Education in the Plurinational State of Bolivia: From Decolonisation to Inclusion   *67*
Chris Forlin, Luis Adolfo Machicado Pizarro and Gisselle Gallego

Training Teachers for Inclusive Education in Colombia: From Policy to Practice   *81*
Gloria Calvo

Teacher Training as a Mediator of Change Towards Inclusive Education in Costa Rica 97
Lady Meléndez Rodríguez, Rocío Deliyore Vega and Mario Segura Castillo

Inclusion of Families in Basic Education in Mexico: Policies, Practices and Cultures 113
Cristina Perales Franco

Teachers' Scientific Explanation Practices: Opportunities for Equity 127
Valeria M. Cabello and David Geelan

Interculturality and Educational Inclusion in Brazil and Mexico: A Comparative Analysis 141
Stefano Claudio Sartorello and Alexandre Ferraz Herbetta

Interculturality In and Out of the Classroom: Indigenous Voices and Knowledge About Equity 155
Laura Alicia Valdiviezo, Rukmini Becerra Lubies and Dayna Andrea Moya Sepulveda

Inclusion and Equity in Higher Education: The Case of Ecuador, a Plurinational and Intercultural Country 175
Pilar Samaniego-Santillán, Verónica Gabriela Maldonado-Garcés and Mónica Delgado-Quilismal

The Rural Education Model With Escuela Nueva and the Universidad en el Campo in Colombia 197
Diego Juárez Bolaños

Schools as Learning Communities: Critical Interculturality and Inclusion in Action 215
Luz María Moreno-Medrano

The Implications of Epistemic Justice for Intercultural and Inclusive Education 227
Sylvia Schmelkes del Valle

Index 241

ABOUT THE EDITORS

Silvia Romero-Contreras, Universidad Autónoma de San Luis Potosí, Mexico, is a Research Professor at the Faculty of Psychology at the Universidad Autónoma de San Luis Potosí, México (UASLP). She holds Doctorate in Education from Harvard University and is National Researcher Level II in Humanities and Social Sciences in Mexico. She is the Founder of the Degree in Psychopedagogy at the UASLP and Coordinator of the Catherine E. Snow LabLit Literacy Lab at the Faculty of Psychology-UASLP. She was an advisor to the National Project for Educational Integration in Mexico and academic coordinator of the Postgraduate Programme for Teacher Training in Inclusive Education in Paraguay. She has adapted and developed culturally appropriate intervention models of oral language, reading and writing for typical and atypical students. Her research interests focus on language assessment and intervention, inclusive education policy and practice, teacher preparation and sustainable community education.

Ismael García-Cedillo, Universidad Autónoma de San Luis Potosí, Mexico, is a Research Professor at the Faculty of Psychology at the Universidad Autónoma de San Luis Potosí, México (UASLP). He gained his Bachelor, Master and Doctorate in Psychology from the National Autonomous University of Mexico (UNAM); is National Researcher Level II in Humanities and Social Sciences in Mexico. He directed the National Project of Educational Integration in Mexico and the Postgraduate Programme in Teacher Training in Inclusive Education in Paraguay. His research interests focus on national and comparative studies on special and inclusive education policies and teacher preparation. He is the first author of three national courses and a diploma course on inclusive education for Mexican teachers. His publications include the book chapters Understanding the Mexican paradox on inclusive education: Continuities and discontinuities between public policy and educational practices. Routledge and Where Does Mexico Stand Regarding the Agenda 2030 Goals for Inclusive Education? Emerald.

Luz María Moreno-Medrano, Universidad Iberoamericana, Mexico City, holds Doctorate in Education from the Cambridge University, Director of the Research Institute for the Development of Education at the Universidad Iberoamericana (INIDE), Mexico City. She teaches in the PhD in Critical Gender Studies, the Inter-institutional PhD in Education and the MA in Research for the Development of Education. Her research interests focus on intercultural education from the anti-racist and feminist agenda and the search for educational alternatives from the movements for the rights of indigenous peoples in urban contexts. She has experience in teacher professional development from collaborative perspectives and learning communities. Her recent research includes the articles The Otomí autonomous educational project: supporting children's literacy and agency. *Journal for Critical Education Policy Studies*, and Avances y retos para desarrollar investigaciones comprometidas con la justicia educativa, *Revista Latinoamericana de Estudios Educativos.*

ABOUT THE CONTRIBUTORS

Rukmini Becerra Lubies, Pontificia Universidad Católica de Chile, has extensive experience in intercultural and childhood issues in educational centres. She has developed the Fondecyt de Iniciación 11160746 "Construir, aprender y compartir un lugar: el desafío de la educación intercultural bilingüe para jardines infantiles y comunidades mapuche en la Región de la Araucanía" (Building, learning and sharing a place: the challenge of intercultural bilingual education for Mapuche kindergartens and communities in the Araucanía Region). She has directed the Explora project 'Huerteando cultivo mi cultura'. She is currently directing the Fondecyt Regular 'Repairing relationships'. In these projects, she has mainly used qualitative and ethnographic methodologies in educational centres to understand and analyse the experiences, practices and perceptions of pedagogical teams. In her work, she has collected the voices, opinions and experiences of school actors. This work has created instances of dialogue between schools, families and community actors. Recently, she has specialised in research methodologies for implementation with diverse children, especially children under 10 years of age from minority groups, including Indigenous peoples, migrants, foreigners and gender-differentiated groups.

Valeria M. Cabello, Pontificia Universidad Católica de Chile, is an Associate Professor, Faculty of Education at the Pontificia Universidad Católica de Chile (UC Chile). Her experience combines teaching and research in learning and development with focus in science in the lifespan. She has worked in public and private organisations aimed at improving teaching skills. As her background is in educational psychology, her interests focus on peer learning, discursive practices for teaching in diverse settings and assessment for learning, which can promote high order thinking and social skills. She was Vice-president of the Chilean Society for Science Education (SCHEC) and served as a head of the PhD in Education program at UC Chile.

Gloria Calvo, National Pedagogical University, Bogotá, Colombia, is a Honorary Professor at the Universidad Pedagógica Nacional in Bogotá, Colombia (1983–2006). Her basic training is in Philosophy and Psychology. She has more than 30 years of experience in educational research on topics such as teacher training, equity and educational policies, educational reform, systematisation of pedagogical experiences, citizenship education and the use of information. She is a consultant for international organisations such as UNESCO, IDB, EUROSOCIAL, OEI and PREAL. She has several publications – articles, book chapters and books – in her fields of research. Her most recent article, published

xi

in the June 2023 issue of Aula Pyahu, is based on the coordination of the IIEP/ UNESCO team to advise the National University of Asunción on a project supported by the European Union for the transformation of teacher education in Paraguay in the year 2022.

Dianne Chambers, Hiroshima University, Japan, has been working in inclusive education for 25 years and has published broadly in this area. She has a special passion for assistive technology, particularly after seeing the changes it made to so many children in their ability to access the classroom. For 18 years Dianne was the coordinator of Special and Inclusive Education at the University of Notre Dame Australia, Fremantle. She is now starting a new role as Professor in the Institute for Diversity and Inclusion at Hiroshima University in Japan, where she will continue to teach, research and publish in the field. Previous publications can be found in the areas of inclusion, assistive technology, service learning, initial teacher training and transition. She has worked as a consultant with UNESCO and the Commonwealth of Learning (COL).

Mónica Delgado-Quilismal, Independent consultant – Ecuador, has a degree in Psychology with a major in Education, a degree in Primary Education and is currently studying for a master's degree in Educational Administration. She is the author of school textbooks. In 18 years of professional experience in educational institutions, both urban and rural, she has worked as a teacher, academic coordinator and director of primary education centres. As an independent consultant, she develops social projects and interventions in children and adolescents' mental health. She does voluntary work and gives free advice in charitable and social aid institutions.

Rocío Deliyore Vega, Universidad de Costa Rica-Instituto de Investigación en Educación (INIE)-Observatorio Nacional de Educación Inclusiva (ONEI), Costa Rica, is a Research Professor at the Faculty of Education and at the Institute for Research in Education at the University of Costa Rica, and also a member of the National Observatory of Inclusive Education (ONEI), of the Ibero-American Network of Intercultural and Interdisciplinary Studies and of the Research Team on Equity, Diversity and Inclusive Education at the Autonomous University of Madrid. She has worked as Coordinator of the Special Education Major at the University of Costa Rica. She holds a PhD in Education from the Universidad Nacional en Educación a Distancia of Spain, a master's degree in Psychopedagogy from the Universidad Estatal a Distancia of Costa Rica, and also in Pedagogy with emphasis in Early Childhood Care from the Universidad Nacional de Costa Rica, with a Post doctorate in Education from the Universidad Autónoma de Madrid. She is the author of the book ' Alternative and Augmentative Communication. Actions and reflections to break the silence in the classroom' (2018), and several articles on this topic.

Chris Forlin, The University of Notre Dame Australia, is a Professorial Research Fellow. She has extensive consultancy, research and publications over the past 40+ years with a strong focus on equity and diversity; inclusive education;

ABOUT THE CONTRIBUTORS

change paradigms in education; systemic support for children and youth with disabilities; education policy and practice; along with curricula and pedagogy for teacher education. She has led innovative research in working with systems, governments and schools to establish sustainable inclusive education. Professor Forlin is the Series Editor of the *International Perspectives on Inclusive Education* which has published over 20 volumes. She has also published more than 120 articles, papers and books about inclusive education. She has been the principal/co-investigator of numerous research projects and Government and NGO tenders for 20+ years, and a consultant on government and Australian funded projects providing systematic reviews, data collection, analysis, report writing and recommendations about inclusive education.

Gisselle Gallego, The University of Notre Dame Australia, is a Senior Research Fellow and health professional educator at the School of Medicine Sydney at the University of Notre Dame Australia. Her research and teaching focus on the experiences of marginalised populations. This includes the experiences of culturally and linguistically diverse (CALD) people and those living with disability as well as the intersection of these. She also utilises innovative mixed-methods approaches and interdisciplinary perspectives to support multidimensional understandings of the lived experience, health outcomes and ways to improve well-being. Dr Gallego's expertise in the area of marginalisation and health is also recognised by the publication of her research in journals and national policy documents. Dr Gallego's achievements include building productive research collaborations with international, national and local community partners, demonstrated by her record of grant funding, publications and presentations. She has authored over 200 research papers, reports and conference papers.

David Geelan, The University of Notre Dame Australia, is the National Head of the School of Education at the University of Notre Dame Australia. His research interests span science education, educational research methods and educational technology, with a particular focus on the ways in which science teachers explain concepts to students. David has been a teacher educator in Papua New Guinea and Canada and led professional development for teachers in South Africa and Philippines. He is past-President of the Australian Science Education Research Association and has active research collaborations with colleagues in Germany and Chile. David's published books (some co-authored with colleagues) include 'Simplicity and Complexity in Science Education', 'Theorising Personalised Education', 'Connected Science: Strategies for Integrative Learning in Science' and 'Weaving Narrative Nets to Capture Classrooms: Multimethod Qualitative Approaches for Research in Education'.

Alexandre Ferraz Herbetta, Universidade Federal de Goiás (UFG) (Brazil), is an Associate Professor at the Federal University of Goiás (UFG). He is an anthropologist at the *Takinahaky Nucleus of Indigenous Higher Education*

xiv   ABOUT THE CONTRIBUTORS

(NTFSI) and at the Postgraduate Programme in Social Anthropology (PPGAS). He is a researcher at the Centre for Decolonial Practices and Knowledge/NTFSI and at IMPEJ – Nucleus of Indigenous Ethnology/PPGAS/UFG. He is the Vice-coordinator of the Takinahaky Nucleus, Coordinator of the Programme of Supervised Teaching Studies of the Intercultural Indigenous Education Course (NTFSI/UFG) and member of the Latin American Society of Intercultural Studies. He has experience and publications in the area of Critical Interculturality, Anthropology, Politics and Education, with emphasis on Decoloniality, Participatory Methodologies and Indigenous Ethnology, as highlighted in the project Alfabecantar: cantando el Cerrado Vivo (www.alfabecantar.com.br).

Diego Juárez Bolaños, Universidad Iberoamericana Mexico City, Mexico, is a Full-time Academic at the Research Institute for the Development of Education (INIDE). He has doctoral studies in Social Sciences in the area of Rural Studies at El Colegio de Michoacán. He is a member of the National System of Researchers (SNI) and responsible for the Thematic Research Network on Rural Education. His research interests are rural and multigrade education.

Luis Adolfo Machicado Pizarro is the Principal of the Unidad Educativa Sagrada Familia school of the Mecapaca District in Bolivia. He has been teaching for over 26 years and the Principal at the school for the last 12 years. Prior to this he was a teacher for 14 years. He is Aymara and was born in the Manco Kapac Province, Copacabana community on the shores of Lake Titicaca. He migrated to La Paz when he was five-years old. He trained as a mathematics and computer teacher at the Simón Bolívar teacher training school. He has a degree in education administration and a master's degree in teacher training policies.

Verónica Gabriela Maldonado-Garcés, Pontificia Universidad Católica del Ecuador – Ecuador, is an Educational Psychologist and holds a master's degree in Early Childhood Education and Special Education. She is currently doctoral candidate in Psychology. She has extensive experience in educational institutions at all levels. She is a Lecturer and researcher at the Faculty of Psychology of the Pontificia Universidad Católica del Ecuador. Her line of research and publications is related to the areas of education, educational psychology, disability and inclusion of people in vulnerable situations. She leads the research group Psychology, inclusion and coexistence (PSICO).

Lady Meléndez Rodríguez, University of Costa Rica-Instituto de Investigación en Educación (INIE)-Observatorio Nacional de Educación Inclusiva (ONEI), Costa Rica, is the member of the National Accreditation Council of SINAES, of the National Observatory of Inclusive Education (ONEI), Professor at the University of Costa Rica (UCR) and at the State Distance University of Costa Rica (UNED). She is a Research professor of Doctorate in Education at the UCR, tutor of the Doctoral Program in Education at the Don Bosco University in El Salvador. She has worked as National Advisor on Special Education for the Ministry of Public Education, as a coordinator of the Special Education Programme at UNED, as a researcher for the State of Education Programme in

ABOUT THE CONTRIBUTORS

Costa Rica and also as a University Lecturer for more than 30 years. She is a national and international consultant and speaker. She is the author of 'La inclusión escolar del alumno con discapacidad intelectual' (2000), 'Inclusión educativa: una perspectiva de la Didáctica de las Ciencias Naturales' (2013), 'Fundamentals and evolution of Special Education in Costa Rica' (2016), Inclusive Education in Latin America' (2016) and 'Education and Inclusion in Pandemic' (2021).

Rodrigo Hübner Mendes, Instituto Rodrigo Mendes, Brazil is the Founder and the CEO of the Rodrigo Mendes Institute, a non-profit organisation (NGO) whose mission is to guarantee that every child with disability has access to quality education. The institute develops research and teacher training programs in several countries aiming to transform the public education systems into environments that respect and value human diversity. Hübner Mendes began his career in 1998 as a business consultant at Accenture. In 2004, he decided to dedicate his efforts for the social sector, assuming the management of the Rodrigo Mendes Institute. He holds a bachelor's degree in Business Administration and a master's degree in Human Diversity Management from the Getulio Vargas Foundation. Hübner Mendes is a Young Global Leader (World Economic Forum) and a fellow of Ashoka. He has received numerous awards and serves on the board of several Brazilian organisations.

Dayna Andrea Moya Sepulveda, Pontificia Universidad Católica de Chile, has a background in early childhood education and a PhD in Neuroscience and Education. This interdisciplinary training has allowed her to move between different perspectives and methodologies of analysis, from educational applications with evaluation consultancies to foundations in methodological proposals. She uses her experience to teach courses on the use of media and data collection at a distance. She has experience in intervention analysis, considering inclusion from the development of research with autistic population and its neuromarkers. She has international partnerships that have allowed her to analyse different educational realities in Latin America, such as Colombia and the Dominican Republic, and in the United States, especially in early childhood. She has published in the SCOPUS journal and in books on interculturality and inclusion. She is currently involved in projects in the intercultural area in early childhood, educators training and neuroscience and education.

Yarela Muñoz López, Universidad Finis Terrae, Chile, is a Differential Educator with a Bachelor's Degree in Education from the Metropolitan University of Education Sciences (UMCE), Master in Neurosciences applied to Education at the Universidad Finis Terrae (UFT) and Diploma in Early Intervention Strategies at the Universidad del Desarrollo (UDD). She has more than 10 years of classroom experience in special schools, schools with integration projects, nursery schools and kindergartens, both public and private, as well as the management and coordination of inclusive projects and work with families. In 2015, she started teaching in the UFT's Early Childhood Education course and currently works as an Academic and Coordinator of the students' area in the same course.

xvi

Her interests are mainly focused on quality education for all, diversity in the classroom, initial teacher training and continuing education.

Cristina Perales Franco, Instituto de Investigaciones para el Desarrollo de la Educación, Universidad Iberoamericana Mexico City, Mexico. PhD in Education from the Institute of Education, University College London, UK. She holds a degree in Educational Sciences from ITESO and a master's degree in Social Sciences from FLACSO-Mexico. Her research interests are school *convivencia*, inclusion and educational equity, peace building and the relationships between schools, their communities and environments. She also works on qualitative methodologies in education. She has been a middle-school teacher, undergraduate and graduate level professor and has created teacher professional development processes. She has collaborated with the Mexican Ministry of Public Education in the curricular design of the Civic and Ethics Education curriculum. Two recent publications are the article 'School and community relationships in Mexico. Researching inclusion in education from a critical and decolonial perspectives' published in 2023 in the *British Journal of Sociology of Education,* and the book *School-community relationships* published by the Universidad Iberoamericana in 2022.

Pilar Samaniego-Santillán, Independent consultant – Ecuador, is the author of studies and publications related to human rights, education, disability and public policies for national, regional and multilateral organisations. The Ministry of Labour of Ecuador awarded her the national decoration 'Labour Merit' for 'studies that have contributed to the development and strengthening of social peace'. She has taught in universities in Ecuador, Spain, Nicaragua and Panama. She has directed primary and secondary schools and promoted and led associative movements in favour of the rights of people with disabilities at national and Ibero American. http://orcid.org/0000-0002-5266-3928

Stefano Claudio Sartorello, Iberoamerican University of Mexico City (Mexico), is a Political scientist from the Università degli Studi di Milano (Italy). He holds Master in Social Anthropology from the Centro de Investigaciones y Estudios Superiores en Antropología Social (CIESAS) and PhD in Education from the Universidad Iberoamericana in Mexico City. Since August 2015, he has been working at INIDE-IBERO as a researcher in the line: 'Interculturality, power and diversities'. He currently conducts studies on intercultural relations and intersectional dynamics in a private university. From 2004 to date, he has been collaborating in intercultural educational projects with a critical and decolonial approach with the community educators of UNEM AC (Unión de Maestros de la Nueva Educación para México) and the teachers of REDIIN AC (Red de Educación Inductiva Intercultural). The project 'Milpas Educativas para el Buen Vivir' (Educational Milpas for Good Living) (https://inide.ibero.mx/assets_front/assets/libros/2020/milpas-educativas-para-el-buen-vivir-nuestra-cosecha.pdf) stands out as a product of this international collaboration.

ABOUT THE CONTRIBUTORS

Sylvia Schmelkes del Valle, Universidad Iberoamericana, Mexico, is a Sociologist with a master's degree in Educational Research and Development from the Universidad Iberoamericana. She has published more than 400 papers on the topics of quality education, adult education, values education and intercultural education. She founded and was General Coordinator of Intercultural and Bilingual Education at the Ministry of Public Education. She received the Joan Amos Comenius Medal, awarded by the Czech Republic and UNESCO, in 2008. She holds Honorary doctorates from the Autonomous University of Baja California in 2017, from Concordia University in Montreal, Canada in 2019 and from the University of Colima in 2023. She was the first president of the National Institute for the Evaluation of Education. She was Academic Vice-Rector of the Universidad Iberoamericana Cd. de México until February 2022. She is a retired researcher at the Research Institute for the Development of Education at the Universidad Iberoamericana.

Mario Segura Castillo, University of Costa Rica – Instituto de Investigación en Educación (INIE)-Observatorio Nacional de Educación Inclusiva (ONEI), Costa Rica, is a National advisor of the Department of Educational Support for Students with Disabilities of the Ministry of Public Education of Costa Rica, Professor at the School of Orientation and Special Education of the University of Costa Rica, member of the National Observatory of Inclusive Education (ONEI). He has worked as national advisor of Educational Evaluation of the Ministry of Public Education of Costa Rica and is also a Professor. He holds a PhD in Education with emphasis in Pedagogical Mediation from La Salle University of Costa Rica, master's in Educational Evaluation from the University of Costa Rica, master in Democracy and Values from the University of Barcelona, bachelor's in Educational Administration and bachelor in Teaching of Social Studies from the University of Costa Rica.

Patricia Soto de la Cruz, Universidad Finis Terrae, Chile, is an Early Childhood Educator, Licentiate in Education and Psychopedagogue from the Pontificia Universidad Católica de Chile. She holds Magister in Cognitive Development from the Diego Portales University, Magister in University Teaching from the Finis Terrae University and Doctor in Social Sciences, Latin American Faculty of Social Sciences, FLACSO, Argentina. In addition to her educational experience, she has more than 10 years of classroom experience in national and international contexts and seven years of experience in the management of public and private educational spaces. In 2014, she took over the direction of the Early Childhood Education degree at the Universidad Finis Terrae. Her research interests are mainly focused on the training of future kindergarten educators, early childhood education, in the areas of justice and diversity.

Paula Tapia Silva, ANADIME, Chile, is a Specialised Dance Teacher at the University of Chile. She holds Bachelor in Aesthetics at the Pontificia Universidad Católica de Chile and Master in Liberal Arts in the field of Cultural Anthropology at Harvard University. Her training has allowed her to move through various professional spaces, teaching, nationally and internationally, with a focus on aesthetic and artistic education and the development of critical thinking. Within the field of pedagogical management she has worked in managerial and advisory roles. She currently works as a researcher for ANADIME (National Association of the Mentally Disabled) and teaches in Chilean universities. Her research interests focus on inclusive education, educational innovation and reflection on corporal expression and its aesthetic connotations, taking the body-culture relationship as a fundamental axis.

Ernesto Treviño Villarreal, Faculty of Education, Pontificia Universidad Católica de Chile, gained Doctorate in Education from Harvard University. He is a Professor at the Faculty of Education of the Pontificia Universidad Católica de Chile, director of the Centro UC para la Transformación Educativa (CENTRE UC) and principal researcher at the Centro de Justicia Educacional. He has collaborated with UNESCO, UNICEF, OEI, OAS and other international organisations.

His research includes the project 'Good citizenship around the world: Using IEA data to understand the next generation of citizens' for which he was responsible, and his most recent publications include the book chapter 'Segregation of Indigenous Students in the Chilean School System', the book Ciudadanías, educación y juventudes. Investigaciones y debates para el Chile del futuro (2021); and the articles 'Effects of Between-Class Ability Grouping on Secondary Students' Academic Achievement: Quasi-experimental evidence from Chile'.

Laura Alicia Valdiviezo, University of Massachusetts-Amherst, USA, began as a classroom educator at the secondary level in a public school in Peru and then in public primary and secondary schools in the United States, where she taught in bilingual and Spanish programmes, respectively. For more than two decades she has been an ethnographer dedicated to researching educational policies, programmes and actors in state institutions implementing intercultural bilingual education curricula in Peru and, more recently, in ethnic studies programmes in the United States. Her work focuses on the analysis of state discourses, actions and initiatives created to serve minority populations such as Indigenous communities in South America, and Latino, Native American and African American students in the United States. She analyses ideologies of power and inequity at the macro level and alternatives generated from local action by historically marginalised actors. She publishes her work in English and Spanish in academic journals, books and educational documentaries.

Eugenia Victoriano Villouta, Mis Talentos Foundation, Chile, holds Doctorate in Education from the Pontificia Universidad Católica de Chile, Master in Educational Psychology from the same institution and Psychologist from the Universidad de Concepción.

She has taught in various higher education institutions, currently works as a diversity analyst at the Quality Education Agency of the Chilean Ministry of

ABOUT THE CONTRIBUTORS

Education and provides consultancy services to Fundación Mis Talentos, an institution that works for inclusion.

Her publications include the article 'University access policies for persons with disabilities: Lessons from two Chilean universities' published in the International Journal of Educational Development.

SERIES EDITOR PREFACE

The adoption internationally of inclusive practice as the most equitable and all-encompassing approach to education and its relation to compliance with various international Declarations and Conventions underpins the importance of this series for people working at all levels of education and schooling in both developed and less developed countries. There is little doubt that inclusive education is complex and diverse and that there are enormous disparities in understanding and application at both inter- and intra-country levels. A broad perspective on inclusive education throughout this series is taken, encompassing a wide range of contemporary viewpoints, ideas and research for enabling the development of more inclusive schools, education systems and communities.

Volumes in this series on *International Perspectives on Inclusive Education* contribute to the academic and professional discourse by providing a collection of philosophies and practices that can be reviewed by considering local, contextual and cultural situations to assist governments, educators, peripatetic staffs and other professionals to provide the best education for all children. Each volume in the series focuses on a key aspect of inclusive education and provides critical chapters by contributing leaders in the field who discuss theoretical positions, quality research and impacts on school and classroom practice. Different volumes address issues relating to the diversity of student need within heterogeneous classrooms and the preparation of teachers and other staffs to work in inclusive schools. Systemic changes and practice in schools encompass a wide perspective of learners to provide ideas on reframing education to ensure that it is inclusive of all. Evidence-based research practices underpin a plethora of suggestions for decision-makers and practitioners, incorporating current ways of thinking about and implementing inclusive education.

While many barriers have been identified that may potentially constrain the implementation of effective inclusive practices, this series aims to identify such key concerns and offer practical and best practice approaches to overcoming them. Adopting a thematic approach for each volume, readers will be able to quickly locate a collection of research and practice related to a topic of interest. By transforming schools into inclusive communities of practice all children can have the opportunity to access and participate in quality and equitable education to enable them to obtain the skills to become contributory global citizens. This series, therefore, is highly recommended to support education decision-makers, practitioners, researchers and academics, who have a professional interest in the inclusion of children and youth who are potentially marginalising in inclusive schools and classrooms.

SERIES EDITOR PREFACE

Volume 24 in the *International Perspectives on Inclusive Education* series offers a unique opportunity to explore different aspects of intercultural inclusive education, specifically within the Latin America region. This is the first book in the IPIE series to focus on one region and in addition, to publish the book both in English and in Spanish. This convergence of perspectives provides an exclusive chance to delve in greater depth across the Latin America region. Being bilingual, it also gives access to this information in the local language, thus allowing a greater number of people to benefit from the shared research and perspectives about inclusion across eight countries.

The collection of distinguished authors has presented detailed information on their countries' context and status regarding implementing inclusive educational practices. These highlight the enormous variety in how inclusion is enacted within the region and some of the distinctive issues and challenges that they face. While all countries are aiming for equity in education, the additional challenges encountered by indigenous populations, large numbers of immigrants, those living in rural areas, culturally diverse families and those who experience disadvantage results in different opportunities for establishing effective inclusive schools. Many countries are aiming to better include families in partnership in education decision-making, to support more inclusive communities. Teacher training is also considered critical as a mediator of change towards inclusion across all jurisdictions, with an emphasis on ensuring teachers have the necessary knowledge and skills to translate policy into practice.

Advances in education and the use of technology are evidenced across all regions. The authors report that many countries have implemented inclusive legislation or policy, but that competences to promote and implement effective inclusive practices are still underdeveloped. The authors all provide a realistic critique of how their countries have sought to adopt a more inclusive approach, often within difficult political changes, with many providing effective examples of how this is occurring. Although these positive outcomes allow for other countries to reflect on whether these findings can help them to better facilitate inclusion in their own region, examples of highly effective practices are still seen to be in the minority.

Though this book focuses on a specific region, there are few similarities in how individual countries are working towards implementing inclusion in practice. Education across the region is highly complex, very diverse and manifold. What each country has in common though, is a clear understanding of what needs to be done with a strong focus on equity. To do this the challenges vary both across and within nations, but by providing examples of how each country is meeting some of these challenges enables the astute reader to gain insights into practices that may be appropriate for responding to some of their own challenges.

I strongly recommend Volume 24 in the *International Perspectives on Inclusive Education* series as essential reading for anyone interested in reflecting upon how the unique regions across Latin America are moving towards establishing sustainable inclusive educational practices. The editors are to be commended on being able to bring together such an eclectic group of authors able to provide detailed and considerate information about such diverse countries; and the

SERIES EDITOR PREFACE

xxiii

chapter authors on their sincerity in reporting practices that aim to enhance an equitable educational approach for all. So many pertinent issues are raised and treated with genuineness, thoughtfulness and integrity. This gives readers a range of perspectives to utilise to reflect upon their own regions, with a critical review of how these ideas may help them in their own goals to achieve effective, equitable and sustainable intercultural inclusive educational practices.

Chris Forlin
Series Editor

PREFACE

In the panorama of inclusion and interculturality in 21st century Latin America, political, economic, social and epistemological tensions and conditions converge and interact at different levels and in different educational spaces in complex ways. The study of these manifestations is the subject of this volume in which renowned researchers participate to offer an overview of these processes – inclusion and interculturality – necessarily imbricated in education with a human rights perspective in the Latin American region.

This book is composed of 15 chapters written by 30 authors, who present different facets of inclusive education and intercultural education in Bolivia, Brazil, Chile, Colombia, Costa Rica, Ecuador, Mexico and Peru.

The first chapter is an initial approach offered by two of the editors, Silvia Romero-Contreras and Ismael García-Cedillo, regarding the current contexts and determinants of inclusive and intercultural education in Latin America. Next, regarding inclusive education, issues related to its implementation at the basic and higher education levels and teacher education and training for inclusion are addressed; the relationship between families and schools is also analysed from the perspective of inclusion and the role of explanation in science education in promoting equity. In relation to intercultural education, the evolution of interculturality in Brazil, Mexico, Chile, Peru and Ecuador is presented. In addition, the implementation of the rural education model with escuela nueva in Colombia and the study of lessons through learning communities in rural Mexico are discussed. The final chapter is on the promotion of epistemic justice and intercultural learning communities.

In relation to the chapters related to inclusive education, Ernesto Treviño Villarreal and Eugenia Victoriano Villouta analyse educational opportunities at higher education level for students with special educational needs associated with disabilities in Chile. Through the educational trajectories in higher education of students with disabilities, they report on the barriers they face in transition (low expectations and insufficient guidance in their entry process), access (they are not selected through an exam, like other applicants) and permanence (they face physical, social and academic barriers).

Dianne Chambers and Rodrigo Hübner Mendes analyse the situation of persons with disabilities and the inclusive education process in Brazil. They highlight advances in legislation to promote inclusion. The authors analyse the progress and challenges facing inclusive education in the country, particularly in relation to students with disabilities and the provision of technological support.

Paula Tapia Silva, Patricia Soto de la Cruz and Yarela Muñoz López describe the experience of the ANADIME-CEA Educational Centre, located in a disadvantaged neighbourhood of Santiago, Chile, which aimed to provide quality learning spaces for all its students. It was ensured that 12% of its enrolment was made up of students with disabilities, although the space was also opened to immigrant students and students from different sociocultural backgrounds, and a transdisciplinary work team was formed. The community participated very actively.

Chris Forlin, Luis Adolfo Machicado Pizarro and Gisselle Gallego describe how, despite advances in education in Bolivia, persons with disabilities face many challenges. Five-year-old children with disabilities start school in regular schools, but without accessibility and inclusion-oriented training for their teachers, who lack the fundamentals to implement inclusive education.

Gloria Calvo reports how, despite the fact that inclusive education has a solid legal basis in Colombia, teacher training needs to be improved, because although topics related to diversity and inclusion are reviewed, competencies to promote inclusive education are not developed. However, she documents several valuable experiences in her chapter: the experience of a teacher training school (Escuela Normal) where, among others, Braille and sign language strategies to manage indiscipline and pedagogy for peace are taught; a school that seeks to recover students who have dropped out of school and; a higher level pedagogical proposal that addresses initial teacher training with an innovative perspective and high social commitment.

Also, in the context of teacher training, Lady Meléndez Rodríguez, Rocio Deliyore Vega and Mario Segura Castillo describe successful experiences of teacher training for inclusion in Costa Rica. They identify the features of an inclusive school and its curricular dimesion, and describe research conducted by the National Observatory for Inclusive Education to identify good practices in training for implementing inclusive education.

Cristina Perales Franco presents research on the role of families in the inclusion of their children in Mexico. She analyses the school–family relationship under an inclusion approach, i.e. the possibilities and barriers for the participation of all families. She reviews the three main practices linking school and families: firstly related to participation in parents' associations; secondly related to cultures, for example in the construction of gender roles; and thirdly related to families' contributions: economic and cooperative through manual work or food preparation.

Valeria M. Cabello and David Geelan report a study in which they analyse the ways in which science is taught, particularly in relation to the explanations of teachers in Australia, Canada and Chile. The explanations offered in class can be emancipatory when they are done as intentional teaching, which requires a deep knowledge of the students and not just a focus on correct answers. They found that there is a relationship between the type of explanations and socio-economic status.

In relation to intercultural education, the chapter by Stefano Claudio Sartorello and Alexandre Ferraz Herbetta provides the context in which intercultural education has evolved in Mexico and Brazil. They consider the substitution of the paradigm of critical interculturalism for that of inclusive education to be harmful for

PREFACE

xxvii

the indigenous population, given the deficient nature of the population served by the latter. They consider that it remains to be seen whether recent political changes in these countries will lead to the development of intercultural and inclusive policies that are also critical and decolonial.

Laura Alicia Valdiviezo, Rukmini Becerra Lubies and Dayna Andrea Moya Sepulveda point out that the Peruvian state has dismantled intercultural bilingual education and describe how the Chilean state has failed to implement the legislative framework that protects the rights of minority groups. In their work, they address the experience of the Quechua and Mapuche populations.

Pilar Samaniego-Santillán, Verónica Gabriela Maldonado-Garcés and Mónica Delgado-Quilismal mention that, especially in higher education, there is still a long way to go to achieve the goals set years ago, as Indigenous and Afro-descendant populations show interrupted educational trajectories and much higher poverty rates than the general population.

Diego Juárez Bolaños analyses rural higher education in Colombia. He specifically describes the experience of implementing the Rural Education Model with Escuela Nueva in Caldas, Colombia, through the testimonies of graduates of the Universidad en el Campo; given the good results, he points out some recommendations for replicating the experience in other regions.

Luz María Moreno-Medrano, co-editor of this volume, points out, based on the framework of critical interculturality, that teachers must know their students in depth, so that they can perceive the dynamics of exclusion produced by differences of class, ethnicity, gender and disability in order to offer them a relevant education. In order to make these differences visible and overcome them, she proposes lesson study, a pedagogical approach that allows teaching collectives to reflect on how they learn, how to improve the classroom climate and how to promote collaborative learning not only among students, but also among teachers themselves, and presents an experience in which the proposal to create schools as learning communities is successfully implemented in a rural teacher training college on the southern border of Mexico.

For Sylvia Schmelkes del Valle, one of the strands of interculturality proposes that inclusive education should include minorities through an environment free of discrimination and prejudice and offer culturally and linguistically relevant educational content. She advocates for an education for indigenous peoples characterised by epistemic justice, i.e. that their knowledge and ways of constructing it should be given on an equal footing with Western knowledge and the scientific way of producing it, in order to achieve a more complete understanding of the world. She analyses some contributions of indigenous knowledge: the relationship with nature and the understanding of the cosmos, the conception of community, governance and the style of democracy, the containment of inequality and the conceptions of educating and learning.

Education in Latin America has made substantial progress, but major challenges remain related to inequality, poverty and, in some cases, the unwillingness of some governments to address and overcome them. The implementation of intercultural and inclusive education will allow the education offered to all students to be of progressively higher quality. When 'all' is mentioned, it means that the personal, social, family and school conditions in which children live should not be used as an excuse to avoid offering them a quality education, as this is precisely what they need most to transcend these conditions. For indigenous children, moreover, an intercultural and critical education is required.

As can be seen, the contributions presented in this book reflect a multifaceted picture of inclusive education and critical interculturality in Latin America. In all the texts, the difficulties of Latin American students are made visible and successful experiences or strategies for overcoming difficulties are outlined.

We are grateful for the enthusiastic and generous collaboration of all the authors. We believe that reading these works will bring about changes that will benefit the people of the region, particularly those living in vulnerable conditions.

Silvia Romero-Contreras
Ismael García-Cedillo
Luz María Moreno-Medrano
Mexico, 2024

ACKNOWLEDGMENTS

EDITORIAL BOARD

All chapters in the text have been peer reviewed by two academics or practitioners in the field of intercultural and inclusive education. The reviewers formed the editorial board of this text.

Alexis Céspedes Quiala	Centro de Estudios Pedagógicos Manuel F. Gran. Universidad de Oriente	Cuba
Ana Laura Gallardo Gutiérrez	Instituto de Investigaciones sobre la Universidad y la Educación UNAM	Mexico
Ana María Elisa Espinosa Marroquin	Universidad UTE Quito	Ecuador
Araceli Camacho Navarro	Universidad Autónoma de San Luis Potosí	Mexico
Blanca Araceli Rodríguez Hernández	Universidad Autónoma de San Luis Potosí	Mexico
Christoph Kulgemeyer	University of Bremen	Germany
Dora Yolanda Ramos Estrada	Instituto Tecnológico de Sonora	Mexico
Diana Cecilia Rodríguez Ugalde	Conahcyt- ENES Morelia de la UNAM	Mexico
Gabriela Silva Maceda	Universidad Autónoma de San Luis Potosí	Mexico
German Treviño	Consultor	Ecuador
Gloria Elena Gómez Martinez	Universidad Autónoma de San Luis Potosí	Mexico
Ivette Flores Laffont	Universidad de Guadalajara	Mexico
Kelly Kathleen Metz		U.S.A.
Libia Vélez Latorre	Universidad Pedagógica Nacional	Colombia
María de Lourdes Vargas Garduño	Universidad Michoacana de San Nicolás de Hidalgo	Mexico
Melva Marlene del Pilar	Universidad Nacional de Chimborazo	Ecuador
Nicholas Timothy Kaufmann	Universidad Autónoma de San Luis Potosí	Mexico
Norma Guadalupe Márquez	Universidad de Colima	Mexico

Pilar Arnaiz Sánchez	Universidad de Murcia	España
Rodolfo Cruz Vadillo	Universidad Popular Autónoma del Estado de Puebla	Mexico
Sebastián F. Galán Jiménez	Universidad Autónoma de San Luis Potosí	Mexico
Tamara Cristina Espinosa Guzmán	Consultora y Docente de Educación Superior	Ecuador
Ulrike Barbara Ingeborg Keyser	Universidad Pedagógica Nacional	Mexico
Vashti Jocabed Barrera Flores	Universidad Autónoma de San Luis Potosí	Mexico
Yaneth Fabiola Yolima Aglaya Daza Paredes	Fundación Universitaria Agraria de Colombia	Colombia

CONTEXT AND SOCIOCULTURAL DETERMINANTS OF INCLUSION AND INTERCULTURALITY IN LATIN AMERICA

Ismael García-Cedillo and Silvia Romero-Contreras

Universidad Autónoma de San Luis Potosí, México

ABSTRACT

This chapter presents an overview of the main structural challenges facing the Latin American region, as well as the characteristics of its education systems, to provide a contextual framework for the theme of this book, intercultural and inclusive education.

Keywords: Inclusive education; intercultural education; Latin America; human rights; Indigenous people; people with disabilities

INTRODUCTION

Latin America is a region consisting of the following countries: Argentina, Brazil, Bolivia, Chile, Colombia, Costa Rica, Cuba, Dominican Republic, Ecuador, El Salvador, Guatemala, Haiti, Honduras, Mexico, Nicaragua, Panama, Paraguay, Peru, Puerto Rico, Uruguay and Venezuela (Liferder, 2022); depending on the source, there may be differences in this list.

The official languages in the region are derived from Latin, and are Spanish, Portuguese and French, which is related to the fact that the countries were conquered mainly by Spain, Portugal and France (Enciclopedia Humanidades, n.d.). The cultural and natural heritage of Latin America is of enormous richness (UNESCO, n.d.a). The region has a great biological diversity, although in recent years it is being lost due to changes in land use, which is being devoted to food production. This situation is representing 'a very high cost for the well-being of the planet and humanity' (Troya, 2020, n. p.).

Intercultural and Inclusive Education in Latin America
International Perspectives on Inclusive Education, Volume 24, 1–13
Copyright © 2024 Ismael García-Cedillo and Silvia Romero-Contreras
Published under exclusive licence by Emerald Publishing Limited
ISSN: 1479-3636/doi:10.1108/S1479-363620240000024001

Its total population is 665 million people, of which 30.5% live in poverty and 11.3% live in extreme poverty (CEPALSTAT, 2021). One out of every three inhabitants does not have access to adequate food, which has repercussions on the development of overweight and obesity problems. In rural areas, children are stunted (FAO et al., 2020). The population grows annually by 0.8%, currently 81.5% live in urban areas (CEPALSTAT, 2021).

In 2021, life expectancy for the inhabitants of Latin America was 72 years; in the same year, 273,494 people migrated mainly from Central America and Mexico to the United States (World Bank, n. d.). Particularly complex is the situation in Venezuela; according to the World Bank (4 April 2023), from 2015 to date, due to economic and political issues, seven and a half million Venezuelans have emigrated, mostly to countries in the region (Colombia, Peru, Chile and Ecuador, but also to the United States) (United Nations Refugee Agency [UNHCR] and the Universidad Católica Andrés Bello [UCAB], n.d.). The World Bank (4 April 2023) considers that Latin America is going through the worst migration crisis in its history.

The unemployment rate in 2022 was 7% (World Bank, n. d.). According to the Economic Commission for Latin America and the Caribbean (ECLAC, 2019): 'Latin America is sadly known as the most unequal region in the world' (p. 21). UNESCO (2020) reiterates what ECLAC says, and notes that in Latin America 'the Gini coefficient of income inequality fell from 0.527 in 2003 to 0.456 in 2018, but remains the highest in the world.[1] The richest 10% have 30% of total income, while the poorest 20% have only 6%' (p. 3).

According to 2015 figures, there is a large number of young people in Latin America, almost 166 million between the ages of 10 and 24 (Pan American Health Organization [PAHO], 2018); of these, 30 million were not studying, not working and not receiving training, most of them women (76%). Girls and women face a further problem: their future employment does not depend to a large extent on their education, with only 20% of those with an education managing to get a job (United Nations Development Programme [UNDP], 2019).

Ten percent of the total population of Latin America is indigenous (UNESCO, 2023b). In recent years, the situation of this indigenous population has improved. In Peru and Bolivia, the percentage living in poverty has decreased; in Bolivia, Brazil, Chile, Ecuador and Peru, extreme poverty has also decreased. There has been progress in education (for example in primary education, the gender gap has been reduced in some countries), and access to electricity, water and sanitation services has improved. However, these improvements have been differentiated. A child born into an indigenous household will be more likely to be poor, regardless of other variables such as parental education (World Bank Group, 2015).

The countries with the largest populations of indigenous people are Mexico, Guatemala, Peru and Bolivia. Almost half of this indigenous population lives in rural areas. Those who have migrated to urban areas face slightly less difficult conditions than those in rural areas: a higher percentage have access to electricity and water; they are 1.6% more likely to complete primary school, 3.6% secondary school and 7.7% tertiary school; however, this population living in an urban environment is highly vulnerable compared to the non-indigenous population. For example a higher proportion has less access to electricity and drinking water, their houses have dirt floors and they live in unsafe places (World Bank Group, 2015).

EDUCATION IN LATIN AMERICA

The Third Regional Comparative and Explanatory Study (TERCE) (UNESCO-OREALC, 2015a) assessed the academic level of Latin America students in the third and sixth grades of primary school in the areas of Mathematics, Reading, Writing and Science, for which tests were applied to measure learning achievements and, in addition, questionnaires were applied to provide context to these achievements. More than 67,000 students from 15 countries in the region participated. It was found that, with respect to the Second Regional Comparative and Explanatory Study (conducted in 2006), average achievement in TERCE improved in all grades and subject areas, but students continued to perform at levels considered low. Students at a higher level are in the minority.

Grouping the regional scores into three groups (significantly above average, at average and significantly below average), the countries were placed as follows: above average on all measures, Chile, Costa Rica and Mexico; above average on most measures, Argentina and Uruguay; below average on most measures: Guatemala, Honduras, Nicaragua, Panama, Paraguay and Dominican Republic; and on average, Brazil, Colombia, Ecuador and Perú.

In the case of reading, 61% of third graders and 70% of sixth graders reach performance levels I and II (of the four levels considered), which are the lowest. In mathematics, 71% of third graders and 83% of sixth graders are in the same levels. In science, 80% of students score at the same levels I and II. In writing (assessed in a different way), it was found that students are able to write coherent texts, although there is much room for improvement in the production of texts to make them suitable for communicative purposes.

In terms of factors associated with the level of student performance, it was found that there is a close relationship between learning achievement and the socio-economic level of families, parental support, the encouragement of reading at home and having attended pre-school. The achievement of indigenous students is lower than that of non-indigenous students.

In relation to classrooms, the factors associated with learning achievement are good teacher practice, in addition to high attendance and punctuality, and the availability of school materials (notebooks and books). In relation to schools, learning is influenced by school violence, poor infrastructure and low inclusiveness (UNESCO-OREALC, 2015b).

In the 2018 edition of the Programme for International Student Assessment, known as PISA, 10 Latin American countries participated in the assessment (Organization for Economic Co-operation and Development [OECD], 2019).

In that year, reading was predominantly assessed, while mathematics and science were assessed in a more cursory manner. Half of the Latin America countries were found to have improved in reading literacy, although growth was slowing in Argentina, Chile, Colombia, Peru and Uruguay. Half of the students tested showed that they have not developed basic reading skills (they have difficulties in identifying the main idea in a medium-length text or difficulties in connecting information from different sources). Meanwhile, young people in Brazil, Mexico and Panama show no significant improvement, and those in Costa Rica and the Dominican Republic have shown setbacks. All countries in the region ranked in the bottom half of the table. The best-ranked Latin America countries in PISA were Chile (43rd place), Uruguay (48th place) and Costa Rica (49th place). The worst performers were Panama (71st) and the Dominican Republic (76th). All countries in the region ranked at least one year of schooling below the OECD countries; Costa Rica, Mexico, Brazil, Colombia, Argentina and Peru were two years below. The Dominican Republic was at four years below (Bos et al., 2008).

In 2019, a new assessment of student learning was conducted in Latin America (Regional Comparative and Explanatory Study; UNESCO, 2021). Around 160,000 students in third and sixth grades of primary school in 16 countries participated (Bolivia and Chile did not participate, as they did not have the conditions to do so). The results indicate that student learning achievement in Latin America is stagnating. In reading and mathematics, in 16 countries in the region, 40% of third grade students and 60% of sixth grade students 'do not reach the minimum level of fundamental competencies' (UNESCO, 2023a, n. p.). In reading, in grade 6, only 17% of students reach level III; the highest scores are achieved by Peru, Mexico and Uruguay. In science, only 20% of students reach level III; Cuba and Costa Rica have the highest scores (UNESCO, 2021a).

In reading, girls generally score higher than boys, with the exception of Honduras, Peru, Nicaragua and Guatemala. In mathematics, there are no differences in girls' and boys' scores (with the exception of the Dominican Republic). In science, in seven of the 16 countries there are differences between girls' and boys' scores in favour of girls, although not significant (UNESCO, 2021a).

The socio-economic factors that most positively influence school trajectories are pre-school attendance, high parental expectations of future school performance, parental involvement in learning activities at home and time spent studying outside school. Grade repetition, school absenteeism and belonging to indigenous peoples have a negative influence.

With respect to teachers, their positive expectations, interest in students' well-being, pedagogical support and teaching organisation are associated with good results. On the other hand, classroom disruptions are associated with negative results (UNESCO, 2021a).

According to UNESCO (2020), among the educational challenges facing Latin America are the difficulties in accessing 'quality education, which are still too high for persons with disabilities, migrants and refugees, indigenous peoples and Afro-descendent populations, affecting girls from these population groups the most' (p. vi).

In the region, 12% of the school population has a disability, as assessed by the questions developed by the Washington Group (the six questions relate to different functions considered critical: hearing, vision, mobility, cognition, self-care and communication (UNESCO, 2020)). Students with disabilities are more likely to be out of school, particularly in Ecuador, Mexico and Trinidad and Tobago (p. 11). Another group living in unequal conditions is ethnic minority groups. The educational outcomes of indigenous language speakers are often worse than those of self-identified indigenous people who speak only Spanish (UNESCO, 2020).

Bolivia is the country that invests the highest percentage of its Gross Domestic Product (GDP) in education (more than 8%), while Haiti invests the least (less than 2%). The region has high literacy rates (over 98% among men and women), high primary (over 96%) and secondary enrolment rates (77.9% for men and 80.4% for women) (CEPALSTAT, n.d.).

As a result of the pandemic, the educational situation of students in Latin America worsened, with two-thirds of school days lost, equivalent to the loss of 1.5 years of learning, which is likely to translate into the loss of 12% of people's lifetime earnings (World Bank, 2023). In fact, it is estimated that globally, one in three countries that closed their schools did nothing to support students (UNESCO, 2021b).

On the other hand, ECLAC reports show that in Latin America there have been important educational achievements in terms of coverage, completion of studies, as well as a decrease in school dropout and backwardness; but there are many pending issues, for example those concerning the attention of the poorest young people (ECLAC, 2019). Another very important achievement is investment in education: in 2000 it was 3.9 of GDP, while in 2015 it reached 5.6 (UNESCO, 2020).

In conclusion, the region faces major educational challenges, particularly those related to offering quality and equitable education to disadvantaged groups. These challenges were exacerbated by school closures, which undeniably caused severe setbacks in student learning.

INCLUSIVE EDUCATION

In the words of the Committee on the Rights of Persons with Disabilities (CRPD, 2016), there are differences between exclusion, segregation, integration and inclusion, which correspond to the welfare, medical, interactive and social models of disability/diversity care. Exclusion corresponds to the stage when children with disabilities and other conditions were relegated to institutional care. Segregation implies that students with disabilities study in different spaces from their non-disabled peers, i.e. in special schools. Educational integration is a process of educational care in mainstream schools for students with special educational needs (not only those with disabilities), based on the interactive model, while inclusion involves educational care for all students in mainstream schools, based on the social model.

Integration implies the attention of students with special educational needs (SEN) in regular schools, for which a psycho-pedagogical evaluation is carried out to identify their SEN and the individual curricular adaptations they need to learn according to their learning potential are designed and put into practice. Strictly speaking, then, their entry or permanence in school does not modify it; it is the student who has to adapt to school conditions. Inclusion, on the other hand, implies the acceptance of all students, regardless of their personal, family or social characteristics; it requires an analysis of the barriers that could hinder the learning process of students, as well as the search for their elimination. It implies the possibility of identifying the reasonable adjustments that some students need in order to access school and the curriculum. Thus, it is the school that is modified; it is the school that must be transformed to accommodate all students (García, 2018).

Education systems around the world have responded to the challenge of providing quality education for all through inclusive education, which is why its implementation is considered the greatest challenge for education systems (Lewis & Norwich, 2015).

Inclusive education has been defined in different ways. For example, for UNESCO (2008), inclusion is: (a) a process; (b) seeks to identify barriers to learning and participation (BAP); (c) involves not only the presence but also the participation of all learners; and (d) requires specific attention to groups of learners considered to be at risk of exclusion, marginalisation or underachievement.

UNESCO (2017) notes that a hallmark of inclusion is the pursuit of equity, understood as 'ensuring that there is a concern for fairness, so that the education of all learners is considered of equal importance'. (p. 13). He points out that the main message of inclusion is that 'all learners count and count equally' (p. 12). Moreover, it must be recognised that students' difficulties arise from the education system itself (the way it is organised, the way it promotes teaching and the way students are supported and assessed). UNESCO (2017) mentions the principles of inclusive and equitable education:

- to value all students positively;
- to value diversity favourably;
- identify the BAPs faced by pupils, particularly those at risk of exclusion;
- to build consensus among participants on the notion that inclusive education systems improve education by promoting gender equality, enhancing teacher preparation and reducing inequalities;
- mobilising key actors to create the conditions for inclusive learning; and
- implement and evaluate actions in favour of inclusion.

In UNESCO (2020), the terms equality and equity have been sought to be defined more precisely. Equality is considered to be a *state of affairs* (what), i.e. an outcome that can be observed in resources, outputs or results, such as achieving gender equality. On the other hand, equity is a *process* (how), i.e. the actions that aim to ensure equality. Inclusion is more difficult to define. As used in the Education for All Global Monitoring Report (UNESCO, 2020), it reflects equity, which is a process made up of 'actions and practices that take into account diversity and create a sense of belonging, based on the belief that each person is valuable...' (p. 15). In addition, inclusion should also be seen as an 'outcome, with a multifaceted nature that makes it difficult to pin down' (p. 15).

UNESCO (n.d.b) also mentions that inclusive education aims to enable all learners, especially those who are excluded or belong to vulnerable groups, to access, participate and succeed.

One of the difficulties facing the implementation of inclusive education, according to UNESCO (2020), has to do with the fact that the Convention on the Rights of Persons with Disabilities did not define it precisely, so the term remains controversial; nor does it have a strict conceptual approach. An example of the latter is the lack of clarity regarding the role of special schools. 'Ultimately, the Convention gave governments carte blanche to shape inclusive education, which can be seen as an implicit recognition of the dilemmas and tensions in overcoming barriers to full inclusion' (UNESCO, 2020, p. 16). In other words, when defining where students should study, two positions emerge: one that advocates for increased interaction between students with disabilities and their non-disabled peers (all children study under the same roof), and one that defines that they should study in spaces that enhance their learning potential, even if they do not interact with everyone (placing them where they learn best) (Norwich, 2014).

On the other hand, insistence on mainstreaming children in regular schools those are under-resourced or unprepared to serve the whole student body 'can increase exclusion and hinder efforts to make schools and education systems more inclusive' (UNESCO, 2020, p. 16). Or, as Cigman (2007) points out, forcing children with disabilities to study in regular schools that do not have sufficient resources to serve them may constitute a violation of their human rights.

Dyson (2001) argues that inclusion was undoubtedly a real breakthrough for special education, but the insistence that all students must learn in the same school generates strong tensions not only at the practical level (not all teachers are prepared to cater for everyone, for example or there are pressures for schools to limit inclusion), but also at the theoretical level. In other words, as opposed to what some authors call radical or universal inclusive education (Florian, 2010), Dyson proposes to continue to cater for the individual needs of some students, while caring for the progress of the whole class, which he called responsible inclusive education (other authors, for example García (2018), call this moderate inclusive education). It will be evident, then, that the concept of radical inclusion constitutes an ideal of inclusion that is very difficult to achieve.

The aforementioned difficulties forced the CRPD (2016) to clarify that, despite the fact that inclusion is considered to seek the profound transformation of education systems, i.e. making very serious curricular changes in the content addressed, forms of teaching and assessment, approaches and strategies, which would allow 'overcoming barriers with the vision that all learners in relevant age groups have an equitable and participatory learning experience and in the environment that best corresponds to their needs and preferences' (p. 4), when students with disabilities are incorporated into mainstream schools, without the changes mentioned above, it cannot be considered as a process of inclusion, but of integration.

The different ways in which inclusion is conceptualised in different regions makes it difficult to assess its progress. As mentioned by different authors (e.g. Ainscow & Miles, 2008), each region, each country and even each school assumes inclusion according to its particularities, i.e. in a situated way. Therefore, the progress of inclusion has to be assessed in relation to each school, each country and each region. For example, according to UNESCO (2020), while 60% of countries have a definition of inclusive education in their laws, policies and practices, only 64% of them include multiple marginalised groups in their definitions. In 26% of countries, the definition of inclusive education only refers to persons with disabilities or special needs.

According to the CRPD (2016), some of the constraints that Latin America faces in promoting inclusive education include:

- The difficulty of understanding inclusive education from a human rights perspective.
- Insufficient budgets for education systems.
- Lack of accessibility of schools (which should also be in the place where the students live), facilities, classrooms, curricula, educational materials, etc.
- The difficulty in understanding that the implementation of Universal Design for Learning does not preclude making reasonable adjustments to support individual learners.
- Little understanding that reasonable accommodation relates to measures to ensure accessibility, but can also affect the curriculum, in that it can 'use alternative assessment methods and substitute an alternative for an element of the curriculum' (p. 10).
- The difficulty in considering that individualised curricula should be offered to learners who require it, indicating reasonable adjustments as well as technical and professional supports
- Curricula developed taking into account the European perspective and downplaying non-European knowledge.
- Emphasis on academic performance as measured by standardised PISA-type assessments
- The idea that inclusive education is necessary and appropriate for all.
- The fact that inclusive education is still at a very early stage of development in higher education.
- Lack of training for teachers with disabilities.
- Lack of comprehensive teacher training to implement inclusive education in their classrooms.

In relation to the latter point, the CRPD states that inclusion is hampered by 'lack of political will and lack of capacity and expertise to realise the right to inclusive education, including inadequate training of all teachers' (2016, p. 2).

Other considerations related to the implementation of inclusive education relate to how quickly systems can move towards the ideal and what happens during the transition (Stubbs, 2008). That is if change happens too quickly, it may become harmful to the children it is intended to protect.

It should also be added that not all those involved in the implementation of inclusive education are in favour of it. The deaf community, for example is against the idea of inclusion because they point out that deafness is not a disabling condition when the means of communication is manual, and they consider themselves organised as an ethnic group, with their own culture. They demand schools where teachers value their culture and teach using sign language. Similarly, it is thought that the process of inclusion seriously harms the indigenous student population because their difference is thought of from the point of view of deficit, when what this population needs is a respectful recognition of their language, their culture, their traditions, their epistemology, which may be different from those of the dominant group. Therefore, what this group needs is intercultural bilingual education.

INTERCULTURAL BILINGUAL EDUCATION

As a result of the conquest of different regions of the Americas, predominantly by the Spanish and also by the Portuguese, the indigenous people were forbidden to speak their own language and were forced to learn the new dominant languages. In the 19th century, indigenous people were accused of being a burden to the progress of the countries (Martínez, 2015). For example, in post-revolutionary Mexico, efforts were made to educate the indigenous population by assimilating them into the predominant culture, which resulted in contempt for their cultures. In Mexico, bilingual education was created in 1939, which consisted of educating Indians in their own language so that they could later acquire Spanish as a second language. Thanks to pressure from various indigenous organisations and bilingual teachers, the General Directorate of Indigenous Education was created in 1978. However, children continued to be educated in Spanish. It was not until 2000 that Intercultural Bilingual Education was instituted. In 2003, the General Law on the Linguistic Rights of Indigenous Peoples was published (Martínez, 2015).

Despite these advances, the indigenous population in the country is subject to discrimination and exclusion; for example 28% of the population over the age of 12 years say they have been discriminated against because of their appearance (skin tone, way of speaking and way of dressing) (Consejo Nacional para Prevenir la Discriminación [CONAPRED], 2023). Children in basic education experience this discrimination in schools, with their classmates and with teachers, so they try to make themselves invisible.

The basic education curriculum in Bolivia and Mexico has sought to recognise the richness of indigenous peoples. This curriculum focuses on 'decolonisation, community participation and productivity, which implies a response to indigenous, rural and Afro-descendent populations' (UNESCO, 2020, p. 55). In Mexico, the implementation of the New Mexican School is beginning, with a basic education curriculum that is characterised by avoiding the fragmented teaching of disciplines, replacing it with contextualised learning, centred on the community and respectful of the ancestral knowledge of the peoples. This has generated angry protests from powerful groups that seek to ridicule or caricature its main proposals, pointing out that the curriculum promotes communism, mediocrity, spurious knowledge, the absence of fundamental scientific knowledge, the neglect of technology, etc.

'Intercultural and bilingual education is understood as a set of intentional pedagogical processes aimed at training people capable of understanding reality from different cultural points of view and of intervening in processes of social transformation' (p. 49). To achieve this, knowledge of one's own cultural logic and the cultural logics of others is required (Coordinación General de Educación Intercultural y Bilingüe [CGEIyB, 2004, p. 49). In educational terms, this process is also marked by three spheres: epistemological, ethical-political or choice and linguistic or communication (CGEIyB, 2004).

According to Lara (2015), 'an intercultural educational proposal is the path to the (de) and (re)construction of a fragmented, unequal society with deep chasms between its inhabitants' (p. 226). Walsh (2012) warns that, despite its popularity, this term can be framed as functional to the dominant system or as a decolonial project of political, social and ethical transformation. For the same author, interculturality only has value when it is assumed in a critical way, that is when it implies an 'action, project and process that seeks to intervene in the refoundation of the structures and orders of society that racialise, inferiorise and dehumanise' (p. 62). Walsh (2012) conceptualises interculturality from three perspectives: the relational (which implies contact between different cultures), a perspective that hides conflicts and asymmetries in power; the functional (which promotes the recognition of diversity) but, by not taking into account the causes of this diversity, ends up being 'functional' to the dominant system, ending up controlling ethnic differences and favouring the capitalist system. This perspective is linked to cultural inclusion. The third perspective is critical interculturality, which 'deeply questions the irrational instrumental logic of capitalism' and aims at building 'different societies [. . .], another social order' (p. 65).

In relation to the school, critical interculturality seeks to turn it into a space of 'pluralities, where multiple voices, positions and experiences converge, where through education, different ways of being and inhabiting the world are strengthened and empowered' (Lara, 2015, p. 227).

Lara (2015) comments that critical interculturality, assumed by schools, implies the development of pedagogies that transcend single valid visions, abandoning exclusion, an education that truly values differences, that transforms the attitudes of the protagonists of education and the decolonisation of discourses.

As can be seen, the context in which inclusive education and critical interculturality are implemented in Latin America is very complex. In addition to the conditions of poverty, there are political conditions that do not always favour the reduction of, among others, the gap in access to education that is most relevant to each country, region and school. The pandemic caused by COVID-19 aggravated the situation, affecting even more children living in poverty and with disabilities, making their future even more uncertain. However, in spite of everything, there are advances that should be appreciated and should become a reference for the development of good practices. Thus, hope is still alive. Let us help to keep it alive through research, through better pedagogical practice and through political participation to improve the conditions of the region's inhabitants.

NOTE

1. In this index, 0 equals maximum equality, i.e. income is equal for all citizens, and 1 equals maximum inequality (one citizen has all the income) (Montero & López, 2020).

REFERENCES

Ainscow, M., & Miles, S. (2008). Making education for all inclusive. Where next? *Prospects, 37*(1), 15–34.

Bos, M. S., Viteri, A., & Zoido, P. (2028). *PISA 2018 in Latin America: How did we do in reading? IDB, CIMA.* https://publications.iadb.org/publications/spanish/viewer/Nota_PISA_18_PISA_2018_en_Am%C3%A9rica_Latina_C%C3%B3mo_nos_fue_en_lectura_es.pdf

CEPALSTAT. (2021). *2020, Statistical Yearbook for Latin America and the Caribbean.* https://repositorio.cepal.org/server/api/core/bitstreams/c858635c-4c08-41e4-b511-28ef46516f4d/content

CEPALSTAT. (n.d.). *Statistical databases and publications.* https://statistics.cepal.org/portal/cepalstat/index.html?lang=en&link=cepal

Cigman, R. (2007). A question of universality: Inclusive education and the principle of respect. *Journal of Philosophy of Education, 41*(4), 775–793. https://www.researchgate.net/publication/227734296_A_Question_of_Universality_Inclusive_Education_and_the_Principle_of_Respect

Committee on the Rights of Persons with Disabilities. (2016). *General Comment No. 4 (2016) on the right to inclusive education. Convention on the Rights of Persons with Disabilities.* United Nations.

CONAPRED. (2023). *2023 - 016. National survey on discrimination (ENADIS) 2022.* https://www.conapred.org.mx/index.php?contenido=boletin&id=1485&id_opcion=&op=213

Coordinación General de Educación Intercultural y Bilingüe. (2004). *Políticas y fundamentos de la educación intercultural bilingüe en México.* Ministry of Public Education. https://dgeiib.basica.sep.gob.mx/files/fondo-editorial/educacion-intercultural/cgeib_00002.pdf

Dyson, A. (2001). Special needs in the twenty-first century: Where we've been and where we're going. *British Journal of Special Education. 28*(1), 24–29.

ECLAC. (2019). *Social Panorama of Latin America.* https://repositorio.cepal.org/bitstream/handle/11362/44969/5/S1901133_es.pdf

Encyclopaedia Humanities. (n.d.). *Latin America.* https://humanidades.com/america-latina/

FAOIFADPAHOWFPUNICEF. (2020). *Panorama de la seguridad alimentaria y nutrición en América Latina y el Caribe 2020.* https://www.fao.org/3/cb2242es/cb2242es.pdf

Florian, L. (2010). Special education in an era of inclusion: The end of special education or a new beginning? *The Psychology of Education Review, 2*(34), 22–29. https://www.academia.edu/24487820/Special_education_in_an_era_of_inclusion_The_end_of_special_education_or_a_new_beginning

García, I. (2018). Inclusive education in Mexico's Education Reform. *National and International Journal of Inclusive Education, 11*(2), 49–62. https://revistaeducacioninclusiva.es/index.php/REI/article/view/373/359

Lara, G. (2015). Critical interculturality and education: An encounter and a wager. *Revista Colombiana de Educación, 69*, 223–235. http://www.scielo.org.co/pdf/rcde/n69/n69a11.pdf

Lewis, A., & Norwich, B. (2015). *Special teaching for special children?* Open University Press.

Liferder. (2022). *Nine characteristics of Latin America.* https://www.lifeder.com/caracteristicas-america-latina/

Martínez, E. (2015). Intercultural and bilingual education (IBE) in Mexico: The road to the construction of democratic citizenship? *Relaciones. Studies in History and Society, 36*(141), 103–131. https://www.scielo.org.mx/pdf/rz/v36n141/0185-3929-rz-36-141-00103.pdf

Montero, Y., & López, J. F. (2020). Gini index. *Economipedia.* https://economipedia.com/definiciones/indice-de-gini.html

Norwich, J. (2014). Recognising value tensions that underlie problems in inclusive education. *Cambridge Journal of Education.* https://doi.org/10.1080/0305764X.2014.963027

Organization for Economic Co-operation and Development (OECD). (2019). *PISA 2008 Results. Combined executive summaries* (Vol. I, II and III). https://www.oecd.org/pisa/Combined_Executive_Summaries_PISA_2018.pdf

Pan American Health Organization. (2018). *Profile of adolescents and young people in the Americas region.* https://www3.paho.org/informe-salud-adolescente-2018/part-one-a-profile-of-adolescents-and-youth-in-the-americas.html

Troya, R. (2020, September 9). *Latin America has the highest indicators of biodiversity loss in the world.* https://www.wwf.org.mx/?364705/Latinoamerica-tiene-los-mayores-indicadores-de-perdida-de-biodiversidad-en-el-mundo

UNDP. (2019). *Human Development Report 2019. Beyond income, beyond averages, beyond the present: Human development inequalities in the 21st century.* https://hdr.undp.org/system/files/documents/hdr2019espdf_1.pdf

UNESCO. (2008). *Inclusive education: The way of the future.* https://unesdoc.unesco.org/ark:/48223/pf0000180629

UNESCO. (2017). *A guide to ensuring inclusion and equity in education.* https://unesdoc.unesco.org/ark:/48223/pf0000248254

UNESCO. (2020). *Global education monitoring report 2020. Latin America and the Caribbean. Inclusion and education: All men and women without exception.* https://unesdoc.unesco.org/ark:/48223/pf0000374615

UNESCO. (2021a). *Fundamental learning in Latin America and the Caribbean. Assessment of student achievement.* Estudio Regional Comparativo y Explicativo (ERCE 2019). https://unesdoc.unesco.org/ark:/48223/pf0000380257

UNESCO. (2021b, July 13). *New UNESCO/UNICEF/World Bank/OECD report documents education responses to COVID-19 in 142 countries.* UNESCO. https://es.unesco.org/news/cada-tres-paises-no-esta-tomando-medidas-ayudar-estudiantes-ponerse-al-dia-aprendizaje-cierre

UNESCO. (2023a, April 20). *UNESCO warns that since 2013 there has been a lack of progress in fundamental learning in Latin America and the Caribbean.* Press release. https://www.unesco.org/es/articles/la-unesco-alerta-que-desde-2013-hay-lack-of-advances-in-fundamental-learning-in-america-0

UNESCO. (2023b, August 8). *Indigenous peoples of Latin America and the Caribbean.* https://www.unesco.org/es/node/83544#:~:text=Summary&text=M%C3%A1s%20of%20800%20ind%20ind%C3%ADgenous%20peoples,10%25%20of%20the%20total%20population

UNESCO. (n.d.a). *Latin America and the Caribbean.* https://whc.unesco.org/es/lac/

UNESCO. (n.d.b). *Education 2030. Incheon Declaration and Framework for Action for the Realization of Sustainable Development Goal 4.* https://uis.unesco.org/sites/default/files/documents/education-2030-incheon-framework-for-action-implementation-of-sdg4-2016-en_2.pdf

UNESCO-OREALC. (2015a). *TERCE results report: Learning Achievement Third Regional Comparative and Explanatory Study.* https://unesdoc.unesco.org/ark:/48223/pf0000243532

UNESCO-OREALC. (2015b). *TERCE results report: Factors associated with learning. Third Regional Comparative and Explanatory Study.* https://www.unesco.org/es/node/80221

UNHCR-UCAB. (n.d.). *Profile of recent migration reported from Venezuelan Households.* https://assets-global.website-files.com/5caccaedb32e39d3c7d6819e/64f87ad2706bfecbecf798f0_Proyecto%20ACNUR-UCAB%20Estudio%20migraci%C3%B3n%20basado%20en%20ENCOVI_light%20(1).pdf

Walsh, C. (2012). Interculturality and (de)coloniality. Critical and political perspectives. *Visão Global, Joaçaba, 15*(1–2), 61–74.

World Bank. (2023, April 4). *Latin America and the Caribbean: Overview* https://www.bancomundial.org/es/region/lac/overview

World Bank Group. (2015). *Indigenous Latin America in the 21st century.* https://documents1.worldbank.org/curated/en/541651467999959129/pdf/Latinoam%C3%A9rica-ind%C3%ADgena-en-el-siglo-XXI-primera-d%C3%A9cada.pdf

World Bank. (n.d.). *Latin America and the Caribbean.* https://data.worldbank.org/region/latin-america-and-caribbean

OPPORTUNITIES FOR PEOPLE WITH SPECIAL EDUCATIONAL NEEDS IN HIGHER EDUCATION IN CHILE: AN ANALYSIS OF EDUCATIONAL TRAJECTORIES

Ernesto Treviño Villarreal[a,1] and
Eugenia Victoriano Villouta[b,2]

[a]*Pontificia Universidad Católica de Chile, Chile*
[b]*Fundación Mis Talentos, Chile*

ABSTRACT

In Chile, there is clear progress in inclusion policies; however, during the last decade, there is a decrease in the participation of young people with special educational needs (SEN), especially in higher education. This chapter studies the factors that influence the educational trajectories of students with SEN and their entry into higher education using quantitative and qualitative methods. It shows both how trajectories of SEN students are shaped and the relationship of educational policies in such trajectories.

Keywords: Inclusion; special educational needs; disability; higher education; participation; Chile

INTRODUCTION

Relevance of Inclusion in Higher Education

Higher education brings enormous benefits for both social and personal development at both the pecuniary and non-pecuniary levels (Becker, 1964). In the social sphere, at the pecuniary level, higher education improves the level of productivity and growth of countries (Bernasconi & Rodríguez-Ponce, 2017). On the non-pecuniary level, it is related to greater development of knowledge and democratisation, reduction of crime, reduction of poverty and inequality.

In the personal sphere, at the pecuniary level, it is estimated that the higher the level of education, the greater the possibility of having a better paid job (Santiago et al., 2008). In terms of non-pecuniary benefits, higher education is associated with a better quality of life in general and greater development of cognitive skills (Santiago et al., 2008). In addition, higher education institutions are constituted as political groups where knowledge is produced, and participating in them may imply participating in decision-making to a certain extent (Collins & Buasuwan, 2017).

Higher education is fundamental for disadvantaged groups for three reasons. First, because this educational level is directly related to opportunities for future insertion in the labour market (Sachs & Schreuer, 2011). Second, because greater educational opportunities ensure social mobility and constitute a space for social encounter (Palma et al., 2016). And, thirdly, when access to education is limited access, particularly in early childhood and in higher education, this barrier plays a decisive role in the processes of social exclusion (Villafañe et al., 2016). This is reaffirmed by UNESCO (2017) stating that overcoming inequality and exclusion is the path towards sustainable development of societies and for the coexistence of humanity and its well-being, which is materialised by involving the diversity of the population in the educational, social, cultural and economic realms of life. In this line, overcoming inequality implies, first and foremost, making progress in inclusion and participation of diverse populations.

Within the context described above, policies have been promoted worldwide that tend to guarantee access to higher education with an emphasis on promoting equity for the most disadvantaged groups, through funding policies and support programmes that have resulted in increased participation rates for people from the most vulnerable sectors (Santelices et al., 2018). Despite this progress, challenges remain as discussed below.

Policy Challenges

Worldwide, there are undeniable advancements in the massification of higher education and the creation of opportunities for access for groups that were previously unrepresented in this level. However, disadvantaged groups, such as people with disabilities, show scarce participation. For example, in the United States, where 11.1% of those who attend university report having a disability (National Center for Educational Statistics [NCES], 2015) or Spain, where 4% of people with disabilities of higher education age have access to this level of education, compared to the general population, whose rate is 20% (Diez et al., 2011).

In response to this phenomenon, international organisations have provided guidelines and suggested regulations to avoid any kind of discrimination and promote inclusive higher education for people with disabilities. UNESCO proposes a set of strategies aimed at mitigating the impacts and overcoming the difficulties encountered in the higher education system. This is reflected in numerous policy documents and specialised analyses on the subject. Among them is the Framework for Action on Special Needs Education (UNESCO, 1994), which mentions that it is up to public agencies to find ways to ensure access for all. The document 'Overcoming Exclusion through Inclusive Approaches in Education' (UNESCO, 2003) stresses the need to develop inclusive education systems.

Also, in 1993 the United Nations presented the Standard Rules for the Equalisation of Opportunities, which affirms equal rights to education for children, youth and adults with disabilities (United Nations [UN], 1993). And in 2006, in the Convention on the Rights of Persons with Disabilities, the UN promotes, protects and ensures the full and equal respect of all human rights and fundamental freedoms for all persons with disabilities, promoting respect for their inherent dignity. The main principles declared in this convention are non-discrimination; full and effective participation and inclusion in society; respect for difference and acceptance of persons with disabilities as part of human diversity and humanity; equality of opportunity; and accessibility (UN, 2006). At the level of higher education, article 24 emphasises that 'States Parties shall ensure an inclusive education system at all levels, as well as lifelong learning' (UN, 2006, p. 19), specifying that 'States Parties shall ensure that reasonable accommodation is provided' for persons with disabilities (UN, 2006, p. 20).

Chile ratified the Convention on the Rights of Persons with Disabilities, and more recently, in 2010, enacted Law No. 20.422 (Ministry of Planning and Cooperation [MIDEPLAN], 2010) which establishes Rules on Equal Opportunities and Social Inclusion of Persons with Disabilities, stating that higher education institutions must have mechanisms to facilitate access for persons with disabilities, as well as adapt study materials and teaching aids so that such persons can pursue different careers. In the context of this same law, the National Disability Service (SENADIS) was created with the aim of contributing to educational inclusion and the effective exercise of the right to education for students with special educational needs (SEN) associated to disability, through the financing of interventions and projects related to the access and permanence of university students. Specifically, in the field of higher education, SENADIS has implemented measures to improve admission rates, as well as to provide economic support to institutions and students through competitive bids for funds, the creation of an Inclusive Education Network, the holding of regional meetings on inclusive higher education and the definition of continuity plans in higher education aimed at students with motor and hearing disabilities (Servicio Nacional de Discapacidad [SENADIS], 2021). Complementarily, the Department of Evaluation, Measurement and Educational Registry (DEMRE), since 2017, has offered adjustments to the University Selection Test for applicants with physical disabilities who request them. The adjustments consist of extended answer sheets and booklets, assistance from a teacher monitor and the use of a computer with *software* or an adapted room, among others. When the accommodations do not meet the special needs of the applicants, they have the option to enter through the Special Admission System, according to the regulations of each university (DEMRE, 2023).

As can be seen in the previous paragraphs, international and national policies have sought to promote the participation of people with disabilities in higher education, with some accessibility measures. However, judging by the low figures of participation in higher education for students with disabilities, there are still challenges ahead, probably because beyond the guidelines that are provided, there are shortcomings at the level of institutional practices that constitute barriers, as detailed below.

Challenges of Practice

From a practical perspective, there are some barriers that the literature has identified as obstacles for the participation of people with disabilities in higher education. These barriers can be organised into three phases, such as transition, access and retention.

With regard to the transition from secondary to tertiary education, some authors point out that while this is a complex process for any young person, it is intensified for those with disabilities. Firstly, teachers and school personal tend to have low educational expectations for students with disabilities regarding their chances of continuing their educational trajectory beyond school. This means that schools are not concerned about providing good preparation for the transition to higher education (Hewett et al., 2017). On the other hand, higher education institutions have offered insufficient guidance for students with disabilities in their university admission processes. Although the institutions know in advance that applicants have a disability, they do not contact them beforehand to offer them guidance in the process, such as offering guided visits and pointing students to the institutional support services they can access (López-Gavira & Moriña, 2014; Moriña, 2015; Vickerman & Blundell, 2010). In this sense, research recommends that universities provide the necessary information to adapt to this new stage.

In terms of access, some studies report that students with disabilities face a rather limited set of options when choosing their career. In many cases, they cannot base it on their vocation or aptitudes, because they look for careers and institutions where they may be better accepted or where they will face fewer barriers. In fact, few access their first career choice, and they must settle for the career they can study or choose the university that is closer to them or where they believe they will face fewer barriers (Babic & Dowling, 2017; Butler et al., 2016; Emong & Eron, 2016; Hopkins, 2011; Redpath et al., 2013). On the other hand, some research points out that access mechanisms are not always equitable. In the case of Chile, for example students with disabilities generally gain access through special admission mechanisms without taking the university access test as their peers. In the experience of students with disabilities, this implies inequity, since the pressure they point out that in interviews during the admission process they may feel more pressured in comparison to taking the test with adjustments, due in part to the perceived differing degree of objectivity between the admission test and interviews (Palma et al., 2016).

Research has found three types of barriers to educational performance of people with disabilities in higher education. First, physical barriers related to infrastructure and accessibility to buildings and spaces. These barriers pose difficulties for students when accessing the university in terms of transportation, wheelchair use and orientation for those with visual impairment (Babic & Dowling, 2017; Soorenian, 2013). Also, physical barriers limit the access to common spaces, such as dormitories, bathrooms, parking and accommodation, where students face difficulties in spaces where daily activities such as cooking and laundry are carried out (Babic & Dowling, 2017; Soorenian, 2013). The second type of barriers is social. In this regard, some studies have found negative attitudes of professors, for example by questioning the veracity of the disability when it is not visible, a situation which has a direct impact on the disclosure of the students' disability and, consequently, on the support provided to them (Mutanga & Walker, 2017; Arellano & Ortiz, 2022). Furthermore, professors may not be willing or able to make accommodations for students with disabilities because they may consider that this may offer unjust advantages to these students over the rest of their peers (Mullins & Preyde, 2013). Finally, academic barriers refer to obstacles that hinder learning, either by interfering with access to information or through teaching or assessment methodologies that impede equity of opportunity. Authors agree that this is due to two main reasons: negative teacher attitudes and poor teacher training for inclusion (Butler et al., 2016; Kendall, 2016; López-Gavira & Moriña, 2014; Molina et al., 2016; Morgado et al., 2016).

As noted in the previous paragraphs, although policies for the inclusion of people with disabilities in higher education have been promoted, they are still insufficient to guarantee inclusion. This chapter seeks to describe the situation regarding inclusion of people with disabilities in higher education in Chile. To this end, the first section of the theoretical framework addresses the issue of diversity in higher education, its relationship with social justice and how this is addressed in Chile. This section analyses the conceptualisation of disability from different models is presented and, in particular, how the term SEN is defined in this country. Finally, this first section describes Chilean public policies in relation to these issues. The second section focuses on the experiences of young people with disabilities in Chile in terms of their educational trajectories from the school stage, their situation when taking the university admission test, and, finally, the experiences when accessing higher education. The third section discusses Chilean public policies in the light of the data described. Finally, this chapter presents a section of conclusion, reflections and recommendations.

THEORETICAL FRAMEWORK

Diversity and Social Justice in Higher Education

In general terms, diversity refers to the variety of heterogeneous groups and the multiplicity of representations or manifestations within these groups, regardless of the source of this heterogeneity. Therefore, there would be diversity in a group associated with the age, interests, religion, abilities, skin colour, gender or social background of its members. In short, ethnicity, culture, social class, gender, religion, political ideology, different abilities and needs are elements to be taken into account when analysing heterogeneity among students in higher education institutions.

According to Booth and Ainscow (2015), diversity refers to all kinds of differences: obvious, non-palpable differences and similarities between subjects. Thus diversity is about dissimilarity within a common society and encompasses all individuals regardless of their status. However, these authors warn that when we do not accept others as they are, we generate non-recognition and denial of ourselves.

In order to respond to the diversity of needs, it is useful to resort to the Theory of Social Justice, which in its most classical perspective points out that all primary social goods (freedom, equality of opportunity, income and wealth) should be distributed equally, unless an unequal distribution of one or all of the goods implies a benefit for the less advantaged (Rawls, 1971). Along these lines, access to higher education should be an equally distributed good and special emphasis should be placed on measures that respond to the different needs of human diversity. According to Ávalos and Valenzuela (2016), in general, in the most vulnerable groups there are factors in the school trajectory that make a difference in terms of predicting access to university, such as gender (there are more possibilities of access in the case of women), having graduated from a public high school and high school grades.

In Chile, although higher education policies try to respond to the diversity of needs, they do so in an atomised manner, by type of diversity. For example, there are programmes associated with economic vulnerability, others focused on indigenous peoples, others related to gender and others associated with disability. However, although policies in Chile are disaggregated by type of diversity, there is a lack of a multifactorial attention in the case these disadvantages intersect in the same individual or group. Tenorio and Ramírez (2016), for example point out that the school of origin of a student with a disability is a relevant factor in predicting access to higher education, being a facilitator when it is a private school.

In the following, we present how disability is conceptualised in the Chilean education system.

Conceptualisation of Disability in the Chilean Context

Traditionally, the concept of disability has been contrasted from two perspectives: the medical model and the social model. The former focused on the deficit, arguing that those afflicted by the condition had limited autonomy and capacity for participation, and therefore needed to be rehabilitated (Bunbury, 2019). In contrast to this perspective, the social model posits that disabilities are the product of barriers created by society that affect the participation of people with disabilities. In a third perspective, the International Classification of Functioning, Disability and Health proposes a bio-psycho-social model of disability, which states that disability arises from the interaction of personal factors, environmental barriers and participation restrictions (WHO, 2001).

It is important to note that Chilean education policy uses the medical model as a conceptual and practical framework, although it is timidly moving towards a social model with the introduction of the Universal Design for Learning, included in decree number 83 of 2015 for preschools and schools (Ministerio de Educación de Chile [MINEDUC], 2015). However, school policy focuses on diagnosing disabilities in order to provide additional support to students with SEN (MINEDUC, 2013). In this sense, policies in higher education resemble those in the school system, where the discourse is based on the social model, but the specific mechanisms to promote inclusion are based on the medical model. This is reflected in the concept of SEN, which is detailed below.

Special Educational Needs (SEN)

In 1978, the Warnock Report (1978) coined the concept of SEN to refer to the situation of students who need help or support throughout their schooling. In Chile, although it is recognised that all students have their own specific educational needs in order to learn and, therefore, they all require personalised pedagogical attention, there are some students who also experience barriers (personal or contextual) to access, participate and progress in learning experiences. This means that students with special educational needs require, temporary or permanent, specific and specialised educational responses.

The incorporation of this concept sought a change of orientation in education in the face of the diversity of students, and in particular those who presented learning challenges. Thus, an attempt was made to surpass the deficit approach, which entailed understanding learning difficulties in the classrooms and schools related, not only to personal factors, but, to a great extent, to the educational responses offered to them in the school context, the characteristics of the school, the teaching styles and the support they receive from their family and environment. With these premises, the education policies of the last decade in Chile were born. The following is a detailed description of such policies.

Public Policy

Chile has systematically worked on policies to promote the learning of students with SEN. In the 1990s, there are four milestones that mark the beginning of the transition to more inclusive education policies. First, the enactment of the Decree No. 490 (MINEDUC, 1990) supporting the integration of students with disabilities in regular schools. Second, in 1994, the Law No. 19.284 on the Social Integration of Persons with Disabilities (MIDEPLAN, 1994) was enacted, which urges public and private schools to regulate and incorporate the necessary innovations and curricular adaptations to allow and facilitate access to existing courses or levels for persons with SEN. Thirdly, the promulgation of Decree 01 (MINEDUC, 1998), which regulated the access to education of the Law 19.284, establishing the procedures for carrying out school integration projects funded with public resources. Finally, the publication of the 2004 report of the commission of experts, entitled New Perspectives and Vision of Special Education (MINEDUC, 2004), which created a conceptual framework and recommendations that would initiate the transition from a model of integration to one of inclusion. In other words, a model in which it is not the individual who adapts to the environment, but rather the environment that breaks down barriers to respond to the needs of all people.

In the 2000s, the Ministry of Education enacted the National Policy on Special Education 2006–2010, which sought to improve school integration and the quality of learning of integrated students, without straining the regular education system, and to strengthen special schools. In 2008, Chile ratified the Convention on the Rights of Persons with Disabilities. And, in 2009, the implementation of Decree No. 170 (MINEDUC, 2013) began, which sets standards for identifying students with SEN and making them beneficiaries of the special education subsidy, regulating the professionals involved in their support.

In 2010, the Law No 20.422 (Government of Chile, 2010), which establishes rules on equal opportunities and social inclusion of persons with disabilities, began its implementation. During 2015, two policies that are essential for this issue were promoted. First, the enactment of Law 20.485 on School Inclusion (Republic of Chile, 2015), which based on the principle of 'no arbitrary discrimination' regulated three fundamental axes for school inclusion: a) the end of student selection; b) the elimination of school fees (or co-payment by parents to private subsidised schools); and c) the prohibition of profit-making in schools which receive public funding. In addition, Decree No. 83 (MINEDUC, 2015) was enacted that year, offering guidelines and criteria for curricular adaptation and the diversification of teaching for all students in kindergarten and basic education. It states that, regardless of the type of school, level or educational modality in question, any child or young person in the classroom, by virtue of their individual characteristics or the circumstances of their context, may at some point in their school career encounter barriers to learning, development or participation in the culture, curriculum and life of the school, and may require more or less specialised or personalised support. In addition to this, during 2018, Decree 67/2018 (MINEDUC, 2018) was enacted, providing guide for the students' assessment in the school, promoting the learning progress of all students, and considering diversity as an inherent aspect of all classrooms.

In higher education, 2018 saw the enactment of Law No. 21.091 (Library of the National Congress of Chile, 2018), which declares that higher education is a right, stating that the system will promote the inclusion of students in higher education institutions, ensuring the elimination and prohibition of all forms of arbitrary discrimination. Thus, it defined new admission processes and criteria that, among other aspects, consider the diversity of talents, abilities or previous trajectories of student. Furthermore, the law stresses that institutions must have special access programmes aligned with the principle of inclusion, aiming at promoting equity in the admission processes.

Finally, it is important to mention that in 2018 the Law on Labour Inclusion came into force in Chile (Library of the National Congress of Chile, 2018).

This law, although it does not directly guide educational actions, aims at promoting labour inclusion of persons with disabilities, both in the public and private spheres. The law has five main elements for enhancing job inclusion. First, it requires public bodies and private companies with 100 or more workers must hire at least 1% of persons with disabilities. Second, the law eliminates wage discrimination. Third, it sets the age limit for signing the Apprenticeship Contract with persons with disabilities at 26 years. Fourth, it prohibits any discrimination against persons with disabilities. Finally, it states that people with disabilities will have guarantees during the selection of personnel for public posts.

As reported, Chile has made progress in terms of inclusion policies and this has undoubtedly had an impact on practices. The following describes what is current landscape for education of people with disabilities at the secondary education level, their participation in the higher education admission test and their access to higher education.

EDUCATIONAL TRAJECTORIES

Students With Disabilities in School Establishments

In Chile, the study of academic trajectories has been restricted to the analysis of completion rates in the general student population (Treviño et al., 2016), which has recently reached 71.14%. However, this scenario is different when students have SEN. Below is an exploration using the enrolment databases provided by the Ministry of Education's Centro de Estudios, where students enroled in the education system are recorded. On this occasion, two cohorts are shown, firstly using the databases from 2004 to 2017 to observe students throughout their entire trajectory and then a focus on secondary education, following a cohort from 2014 to 2017.

Academic trajectories are understood as the paths taken by students in relation to the theoretical expectation of advancement implied by the design of the school system (Rumberger, 2003; Terigi, 2009) in which students continue their studies without experiencing grade retention and/or drop out. These trajectories can be distinguished between regular and non-regular (Terigi, 2007). The former are those where the student enters school at the age established by the rules and progresses through the education system in a continuous manner (remains in the education system in the grade that corresponds to his/her age and learns the content established in the curriculum). On the other hand, irregular trajectories are defined as those where the student moves through the system in a non-continuous manner.

In the first cohort, 261,249 students entered regular education in the first year of primary school in 2004. Within this universe of students, 23.5% had SEN and participated in the School Integration Programme (PIE). In terms of schools, 52% of them had a PIE or differential group to accommodate one or more integrated students for at least one year. When studying the trajectories of this group, using logistic regression, it was found that students with SEN are approximately 66% less likely to have a regular route compared to students without SEN. Thus, while

17.9% of students without SEN dropped out of the system, this situation occurred in 19.7% of the cases of students with transient SEN, and in about 32% of the cases of students with permanent or unidentified SEN. On the other hand, while 32.8% of students without SEN experienced grade retention, this figure reached 73.1% among students with temporary SEN and 79.5% for those with permanent SEN.

TRANSITION TO UNIVERSITY: PARTICIPATION IN THE ENTRANCE EXAMINATION

Students applying to most universities in Chile have to reach certain level of achievement in the university admission test. Most secondary school graduates participate in this test. Since 2017, although it is not regulated, access adjustments to this assessment have been made. In this context, Victoriano Villouta and Treviño Villarreal (2023) compared some cohorts of high school graduates (2015, 2016 and 2017) to analyse whether this policy had any impact on the participation of students with disabilities taking this exam. To this end, we used the Ministry of Education's databases on school enrolment and registration for the selection test and, considering students participating in the PIE, we ran a logistic regression to estimate whether accommodations are a factor affecting the likelihood of students with disabilities taking this assessment. The analysis found that of the students who were in their final year of secondary school in 2015, 2016 or 2017 ($n = 206,159$), 83.72% took the university selection test in 2016, 2017 or 2018, and of these, only 1.21% had a disability. Logistic regression with respect to accommodations showed that implementing accommodations in 2017 or 2018 increased the likelihood of a student with a disability taking the selection test by 1.23 times.

In addition, among the variables considered, physical disability (motor, visual and hearing), in contrast to intellectual disability, is the factor that most increases the probability that a student with a disability will take the assessment. Thus, a student with a physical disability is 2.09 times more likely to take the test than a student with an intellectual disability. Finally, when a student with a disability comes from a municipal school, the probability of taking the test decreases, and increases when the student is female.

As a conclusion of this work, it can be noted that access adjustments did indeed increase the participation rate of this group; however, it is still a very low participation rate (Victoriano Villouta and Treviño Villarreal, 2023). As you may have seen, adjustments to the admission test have increased participation in test-taking for entering higher education on behalf of people with SEN. However, there are other avenues to apply and access higher education for people with disabilities, which are analysed in the next section.

University Access Policies and Opportunities for People with Disabilities

According to the literature, institutional policies from higher education policies are key elements affecting the access of people with disabilities to this level (Lissi et al., 2013; Tenorio & Ramírez, 2016). This section reports on a study that investigated the characteristics of admission policies in two Chilean universities that have achieved access for a significant proportion of students with motor and sensory disabilities and are pioneers in allowing this access (Victoriano & Treviño, 2022). For this purpose, a qualitative methodology was used in which documentary analysis of admission policies was carried out, as well as interviews with academic authorities linked to the subject and with students with disabilities in the participant universities. The results show that the institutions offer facilitators and barriers which influence the access for students with disabilities.

Among the facilitators, the work done by the support programmes in each university studied stands out, both in terms of the resources they provide and the mediation they carry out to ensure that significant adjustments are made. Having support programmes in the institution represents an incentive for young people with disabilities to choose one institution over others. Another facilitator of access is the institutionalisation of inclusion policies, i.e. that these are known and shared by the whole community. This facilitates the provision of support and guidance, as well as an inclusive culture that enables these students to access and participate on an equitable basis.

The participants in this study highlight as barriers the scarce dissemination of the special admission processes and institutional support. Students with disabilities within this universities point out that information is not communicated in a timely manner to young people who wish to access these study institutions, so they do not know what support they could have or what the process is for accessing it, which discourages them for applying. Another obstacle, perceived mainly by the academic authorities, is the subjectivity of special admission, where in their opinion there is no clarity on the selection criteria, which as a consequence does not ensure that students have the necessary competences to excel in this educational level.

Finally, it is important to point out that recommendations proposed by academics and students themselves. On the one hand, they suggest the necessity of implement plans to support the transition of students from secondary education to higher education, with emphasis on vocational guidance, the timely dissemination of admission mechanisms and the kinds of support offered by the different institutions, as well as the development of certain key competences necessary for excelling in higher education.

As a conclusion of this study, it is possible to point out that, despite the advances in policies, it is necessary to continue working on promoting access for people with disabilities, and to reach a consensus among the different higher education institutions in order to offer equal opportunities through sound policies. In the following section, we focus on the participation of people with disabilities in vocational technical higher education in Chile.

Participation of People With Disabilities in Higher Vocational Technical Education

Internationally, vocational technical education is seen as a key component of the solution to slow growth, poverty, inequalities, unemployment (especially for youth and women) and as a means to address relevant social problems. In Chile, this type of higher education is divided between Professional Institutes (IP) and Technical Training Centres (CFT) and has steadily increased its enrolment over the last 15 years, receiving mainly students from lower socio-economic sectors (Droguett & Celis, 2018).

In view of these data, thanks to funding from the Public Policy Centre of the Pontificia Universidad Católica. Treviño et al. (2022) analysed the probability of a young people with disabilities gaining access to a CFT or IP. To do so, the study analysed the 2020 school enrolment and the 2021 higher education enrolment databases, considered those students with SEN who in their last school year participated in the PIE (n = 200,620) and analysed, through a logistic regression, and then a multinomial regression, which of them entered a technical education institution compared to a university. The analyses showed that students with SEN are more likely to enrol in an IP and a CFT than in a university. Specifically, the probability of being enroled in a Technical Training Centre and a Vocational Institute instead of a university is 1.6 and 1.3 times higher, respectively, for students with SEN than for students without SEN.

The above studies show that the trajectories of students with SEN differ from those of their peers. First, at school level, SEN students generally exhibit more irregular trajectories that their non-SEN peers, facing barriers to enter universities, and being more likely to access higher technical and vocational education institutions. This suggests that it is necessary to enhance the inclusion policies described in the previous sections of this chapter and analyse them in the light of these results.

Analysis of Existing Education Policies in Chile

In the light of the results described above, it is possible to point out that although from the 1990s to the present day in Chile there has been progress in how SEN are understood. However, the country still uses a disability framework underscoring students' deficits as the main barrier for inclusion, and inherently leaving all the responsibility for educational inclusion on them and their families instead of the context. For example, the PIE at schools has contributed to regulate and standardise support provided for students with SEN, but it is still not enough to ensure regular trajectories. In this regard, it is worth questioning whether other types of support will be necessary, especially in order to avoid drop out. Another regulation that seeks to promote inclusion is Decree 83; however, this is only compulsory until the end of basic education (eighth grade), which could be a decisive factor in the trajectories at secondary level, as this decree provides both pedagogical guidance and also raise awareness in educational communities about the relevance of inclusive pedagogical practices. In this sense, it would be of utmost relevance if it could be extended to secondary education.

Moving on to tertiary education, there has certainly been progress in terms of promoting the participation of diverse groups, as evidenced by the recently enacted Higher Education Act. However, although it indicates non-discrimination, it does not provide specific guidance on how this should be implemented, beyond the percentage of special admission quotas. Therefore, institutions continue to use free will in this regard.

Finally, in terms of the world of work, since 2018 the Law on Labour Inclusion has been implemented, opening opportunities for participation for this group. Unfortunately, this law seems decoupled with the laws and policies developed at the educational level. Therefore, although organisations often seek to hire people with disabilities, they are faced with the fact that they do not have the necessary training, since participation at the level of professional technical or university training is low.

Based on the results and these analyses, the following conclusion, reflections and some recommendations emerge from this chapter.

CONCLUSION, REFLECTIONS AND POLICY RECOMMENDATIONS

This chapter describes the educational policies that have been implemented in Chile to promote the participation of persons with disabilities in conditions of equity and contrasts such policies with evidence regarding the educational trajectories of cohorts of students in this country. The analysis suggest that Chilean educational inclusion policies have advanced in terms of promoting educational equity for people disabilities, but the latter is still a factor associated with more irregular educational trajectories in basic and secondary education. This means that, even though the progress registered, policies still do not necessarily guarantee the right to education for persons with disabilities in Chile.

Given the findings presented, we suggest a set of measures that could contribute to improving inclusion throughout the educational trajectories of students with disabilities. Firstly, it is necessary to reform legislation so that schools, school managers and education and social policies are responsible for protecting positive educational trajectories of students, a situation that is easily verifiable given the high level of computerisation of data per student in Chile. Secondly, it would be a contribution to extend the coverage of Decree 83 on inclusion of persons with disabilities beyond basic education to include secondary and higher education. This would open the door for schools to make adaptations and diversify strategies at all levels of education. Furthermore, in line with what is proposed in this regulation, we suggest that diversification guidelines be given to higher education.

Thirdly, the PIEs should be mandatory policy of all schools, instead of depending on the will of school leaders and their ability to organise support, regardless of whether they are financed with public or private resources, in order to guarantee access to school education for students with disabilities. In addition, it is necessary that PIEs contain technical guidelines to advance effective inclusion and favour positive and stable educational trajectories. Likewise, these programmes must ensure the funding of in-service training for teachers and specialists that can improve the inclusion of students with disabilities in schools.

Fourthly, and in relation to higher education, it is necessary that education policies identify and support students with SEN who participate at this level, particularly in higher technical-professional education. Thus, together with the extension of Decree 83, it is necessary to advance in the design of guidelines and orientations, as well as the provision of resources for higher technical-professional education institutions to offer the necessary support and adaptations in conditions of equity to people with SEN. As for the universities, it is necessary to guide and update special admission systems so that they have common admission requirements and a global policy which does not depend on each university (or each degree programme) to avoid arbitrariness.

Finally, and given the legislation on labour inclusion that requires companies to have at least one percent of their employees be persons with disabilities, it is essential to promote inter-sectoral instances so that secondary and higher education institutions can link their graduating students with employment opportunities in their contexts. In this way, the educational and life trajectories of people with disabilities can be protected.

In summary, although great progress has been made in Chile, there is still much to be done in the field of education so that the educational trajectories of children and young people with disabilities are equitable and allow for continuous development and effective inclusion throughout their educational and working lives.

NOTES

1. Ernesto Treviño acknowledges the support of ANID/PIA CIE, Chile 160007.
2. The authors acknowledge the support of the PIA CIE 160007 project from ANID-Chile for developing this publication.

REFERENCES

Arellano, C., & Ortiz, A. (2022). Educación media superior en México: abandono escolar y políticas públicas durante la covid-19. *Íconos. Revista de Ciencias Sociales, (74)*, 33–52.

Ávalos, B., & Valenzuela, J. P. (2016). Education for all and attrition/retention of new teachers: A trajectory study in Chile. *International Journal of Educational Development, 49*, 279–290.

Babic, M., & Dowling, M. (2017). Social support, the presence of barriers and ideas for the future from students with disabilities in the higher education system in Croatia. *Disability & Society, 30*(4), 614–629.

Becker, G. (1964). *Human capital: A theoretical and empirical analysis, with special reference to education*. National Bureau of Economic Research.

Bernasconi, A., & Rodríguez-Ponce, E. (2017). Exploratory analysis of perceptions of leadership styles, academic climate and quality of undergraduate education. *Formación universitaria, 11*(3), 29–40.

Booth, T., & Ainscow, M. (2015). *A guide to inclusive education. Developing learning and participation in schools* (adapted from the third revised edition of the Index for Inclusion). OEI, FUHEM.

Bunbury, S. (2019). Unconscious bias and the medical model: How the social model may hold the key to transformative thinking about disability discrimination. *International Journal of Discrimination and the Law, 19*(1), 26–47.

Butler, M., Holloway, L., Marriott, K., & Goncu, C. (2016). Understanding the graphical challenges faced by vision-impaired students in Australian universities. *Higher Education Research and Development, 36*(1), 59–72.

Chilean Ministry of Education (MINEDUC). (1990). *Normas para integrar alumnos discapacitados en establecimientos comunes.* Decreto No. 490. https://www.bcn.cl/leychile/navegar?idNorma=13743&idVersion=1990-09-03

Chilean Ministry of Education (MINEDUC). (1998). *Normas para la integración social de personas con discapacidad.* Decreto No. 1. https://www.bcn.cl/leychile/navegar?idNorma=120356

Chilean Ministry of Education (MINEDUC). (2013). *Technical guidelines for school integration programmes (PIE).* Government of Chile.

Chilean Ministry of Education (MINEDUC). (2015). *Decree N°83. Approves criteria and guidelines for curricular adaptation for students with special educational needs in kindergarten and basic education.*

Chilean Ministry of Education (MINEDUC). (2018). *Decreto Supremo 67 de Evaluación, Calificación y Promoción Escolar.* Ministry of Planning and Cooperation.

Collins, C., & Buasuwan, P. (Eds.). (2017). *Higher education access in the Asia Pacific Privilege or human right?* Springer.

DEMRE. Department of Evaluation, Measurement and Educational Registration. (2023). *Application for adjustments, adaptations or support for the participation of applicants with disabilities and/or special educational needs.* https://demre.cl/inclusion/solicitudAjustes

Diez, E., Alonso, A., Verdugo, M., Campo, M., Sancho, I., Sánchez, S., Calvo, I., & Moral, E. (2011). *European Higher Education Area: Standards and indicators of good practice for the care of university students with disabilities.* Inico.

Droguett, F., & Celis, S. (2018). Influencia del contexto institucional en el trabajo de los profesores de matemáticas en la educación superior técnico-profesional en Chile. *Estudios Pedagogicos, 44*(3), 235–252.

Emong, P., & Eron, L. (2016). Disability inclusion in higher education in Uganda: Status and strategies. *African Journal of Disability, 5*(1), 2–11.

Government of Chile. (2010). *Law No. 20.422. Establece Normas sobre Igualdad de Oportunidades e Inclusión Social de Personas con Discapacidad.* Ministry of Planning.

Hewett, R., Douglas, G., McLinden, M., & Keil, S. (2017). Developing an inclusive learning environment for students with visual impairment in higher education: Progressive mutual accommodation and learner experiences in the United Kingdom. *European Journal of Special Needs Education, 32*(1), 89–109.

Hopkins, L. (2011). The path of least resistance: A voice-relational analysis of disabled students' experiences of discrimination in English universities. *International Journal of Inclusive Education, 15*(7), 711–727.

Kendall, L. (2016). Higher education and disability: Exploring student experiences. *Cogent Education, 16.*

Library of the National Congress of Chile. (2018). *History of law No. 21.091.*

Lissi, M. R., Zuzulich, M. S., Hojas, A. M., Achiardi, C., Salinas, M., & Vásquez, A. (Eds.). (2013). *En el camino hacia una educación superior inclusiva en Chile. Fundamentos y adecuaciones curriculares para estudiantes con discapacidad sensorial o motora. PIANE-UC.* UC/SENADIS.

López-Gavira, R., & Moriña, A. (2014). Hidden voices in higher education: Inclusive policies and practices in social science and law classrooms. *International Journal of Inclusive Education, 19*(4), 365–378.

MIDEPLAN- Ministry of Planning. (1994). *Law 19.284 Social integration of persons with disabilities.* Ministry of Planning and Cooperation.

MIDEPLAN- Ministry of Planning. (2010). *Ley N° 20.422: Establece normas sobre igualdad de oportunidades e inclusión social de personas con discapacidad.* http://www.leychile.cl/Navegar%3FidLey%3D20422

Ministry of Education of Chile (MINEDUC). (2004). *Comisión de expertos en educación especial: nueva perspectiva y visión de la educación especial.* Author.

Molina, V., Perera, V., Melero, N., Cotan, A., & Moriña, A. (2016). The role of lecturers and inclusive education. *Journal of Research in Special Educational Needs, 16*, 1046–1049.

Morgado, B., Cortés-Vega, M., López-Gavira, R., Álvarez, E., & Moriña, A. (2016). Inclusive education in higher education? *Journal of Research in Special Educational Needs, 16*(S1), 639–642.

Moriña, A. (2015). We aren't heroes, we're survivors': Higher education as an opportunity for students with disabilities to reinvent an identity. *Journal of Further and Higher Education, 9486*(March), 1–12.

Mullins, L., & Preyde, M. (2013). The lived experience of students with an invisible disability at a Canadian university. *Disability & Society, 28*(2), 147–160.

Mutanga, O., & Walker, M. (2017). Exploration of the academic lives of students with disabilities at South African universities: Lecturers' perspectives. *African Journal of Disability, 30*(6), 316–325.

National Center for Educational Statistics. (2015). *Fast facts: Post-secondary students with disabilities.* Author, Washington: DC.

Palma, O., Soto, X., Barría, C., Lucero, X., Mella, D., Santana, Y., & Seguel, E. (2016). Qualitative study of the adaptation and inclusion process of a group of higher education students with disabilities at the University of Magallanes. *Magallania, 44*(2), 131–158.

Rawls, J. (1971). *A theory of justice.* Harvard University Press. [English translation (1978): Teoría de la Justicia, Mexico: FCE]

Redpath, J., Kearney, P., Nicholl, P., Mulvenna, M., Wallace, J., & Martin, S. (2013). Studies in higher education. *Studies in Higher Education, 38*(9), 1334–1350.

Rumberger, R. (2003). The causes and consequences of student mobility. *The Journal of Negro Education, 72*(1), 6–20.

Sachs, D., & Schreuer, N. (2011). Inclusion of students with disabilities in higher education: Performance and participation in student's experiences. *Disability Studies Quarterly, 31*(2), 1561–1593.

Santelices, V., Catalán, X., & Horn, C. (2018). *Equity in higher education, design and outcomes of access programs in selective universities.* Ediciones UC, Santiago.

Santiago, P., Tremblay, K., Basri, E., & Arnal, E. (2008). *Tertiary education for the knowledge society* (Vol. 1). OECD.

SENADIS. Servicio Nacional de Discapacidad (National Disability Service). (2021). *Programa de Apoyo a Estudiantes con Discapacidad en Instituciones de Educación Superior 202.* Support Programme for Students with Disabilities in Higher Education Institutions 202. https://www.senadis.gob.cl/pag/609/1959/programa_de_apoyo_a_estudiantes_con_discapacidad_en_instituciones_de_educacion_superior_2021

Soorenian, A. (2013). Housing and transport: Access issues for disabled international students in British universities. *Disability & Society, 28*(8), 1118–1131.

Tenorio, S., & Ramírez, M. (2016). Experience of inclusion in higher education of students with sensory disabilities. *Education and Educators, 19*(1), 9–28.

Terigi, F. (2007). *Los desafíos que plantean las trayectorias escolares. III Latin American Education Forum. Young people and teachers. La escuela secundaria en el mundo de hoy.* https://periferiaactiva.wordpress.com/wpcontent/uploads/2018/03/teriggi-los-desafios-que-plantean-lastrayectorias-escolares.pdf

Terigi, F. (2009). Urban segmentation and education in Latin America. Contributions of six studies on educational inclusion policies in six large cities in the region. *REICE: Revista Iberoamericana sobre Calidad, Eficacia y Cambio en Educación, 7*(4), 28–47.

Treviño, E., Victoriano, E., & Zúñiga, I. (2022). Support for students with special educational needs in higher vocational technical education: A pending challenge in Chile. *Temas de la Agenda Pública, 17*(161), 1–12.

Treviño, E., Villalobos, C., Vielma, C., Hernández, C., & Valenzuela, J. P. (2016). Students' school trajectories and grouping within the classroom in Chilean secondary schools. Analysis of academic heterogeneity within schools. *Pensamiento Educativo: Revista de Investigación Educacional Latinoamericana, 53*(2), 1–16. https://doi.org/10.7764/PEL.53.2.2016.5

UN - United Nations. (2006). *Convention on the Rights of Persons with Disabilities.* https://social.desa.un.org/issues/disability/crpd/convention-on-the-rights-of-persons-with-disabilities-crpd

UN-United Nations Organisation. (1993). *Standard rules on the equalization of opportunities for persons with disabilities*. UN General Assembly.

UNESCO. (1994). *Salamanca Statement. Framework for action on special needs education*. Author. http://www.unesco.org/education/pdf/SALAMA_S.PDF

UNESCO. (2003). *Overcoming exclusion through inclusive Approaches to education author*. http://unesco.org/educacion/inclusive

UNESCO. (2017). *A guide for ensuring inclusion and equity in education*. Author. https://unesdoc.unesco.org/ark:/48223/pf0000248254

Vickerman, P., & Blundell, M. (2010). Hearing the voices of disabled students in higher education. *Disability & Society, 25*(1), 21–32.

Victoriano, E., & Treviño, E. (2022). University access policies for persons with disabilities: Lessons from two Chilean universities. *International Journal of Educational Development, 91*, 102577. https://doi.org/10.1016/j.ijedudev.2022.102577

Victoriano Villouta, E., & Treviño Villarreal, E. (2023). Facilitan los ajustes a la prueba de selección universitaria en Chile la participación de estudiantes con discapacidad en esta evaluación? *Revista Española de Educación Comparada, 44*(44), 437–454. https://doi.org/10.5944/reec.44.2024.34276

Villafañe, G., Corrales, A., & Soto, V. (2016). Students with disabilities in a Chilean university. *Revista Complutense de Educación, 353*(1), 1130–2496.

Warnock, H. M. (1978). *Report of the committee of enquiry into the education of handicapped children and young people*. Her Majesty's Stationery Office.Special education needs.

World Health Organization (WHO). (2001). *The international classification functioning, disability and health*. https://www.who.int/standards/classifications/international-classification-of-functioning-disability-and-health

INCLUSIVE EDUCATION IN BRAZIL: THE POTENTIAL OF TECHNOLOGY TO FACILITATE INCLUSIVE PRACTICE

Dianne Chambers[a] and Rodrigo Hübner Mendes[b]

[a]Hiroshima University, Japan
[b]Instituto Rodrigo Mendes, Brazil

ABSTRACT

This chapter examines the current educational provision in Brazil, with a specific focus on inclusive education and how this is provided in the country. Students who experience disadvantage due to disabilities, living in poverty, gender and geographic isolation are often most at risk for not accessing education, or being provided with poor quality education which may not meet their needs. Supports and barriers to inclusive education are examined within Brazil's existing political and social context. The role of technology in supporting inclusion is also examined.

Keywords: Education in Brazil; inclusive education; educational technology; learning supports; barriers for learning and participation; assistive educational devices

INTRODUCTION

The international agenda focuses on increasing the inclusion of marginalised and disadvantaged people, particularly in education (Amor et al., 2019). The Convention on the Rights of Persons with Disabilities (CRPD) (United Nations, 2006) and the Sustainable Development Goals (United Nations, n.d.) call upon all countries to develop infrastructure, increase access to education and support inclusion in all aspects of life, including social and community activities for people with disabilities. It is based on the notion of human rights and respect for

---

Intercultural and Inclusive Education in Latin America
International Perspectives on Inclusive Education, Volume 24, 33–44
Copyright © 2024 Dianne Chambers and Rodrigo Hübner Mendes
Published under exclusive licence by Emerald Publishing Limited
ISSN: 1479-3636/doi:10.1108/S1479-363620240000024003

the dignity of the individual person. The CRPD Article 24 notes that students with disabilities should not be '...excluded from the general education system on the basis of disability' and should 'receive the support required, within the general education system to facilitate their effective education' (United Nations, 2006, p. 17). Countries which have ratified the CRPD, including Brazil, have pledged to initiate steps to address this article.

Sustainable Development Goal 4 summarises the intent of inclusive education by stating that countries will 'Ensure inclusive quality education for all and promote lifelong learning' (United Nations, n.d.). In elaboration, Target 4.5 suggests that 'By 2030, [countries will] eliminate gender disparities in education and ensure equal access to all levels of education and vocational training for the vulnerable, including persons with disabilities, indigenous peoples and children in vulnerable situations' (United Nations, n.d., para. 5). Increasing access to quality education reduces poverty, improves health outcomes, increases work opportunities and allows people to be full members of their community (UNESCO, 2020).

This chapter focuses on Brazil, the fifth largest country in the world, and will describe the current state of education, specifically inclusive education, to address disparities and disadvantage that may be experienced by students with disabilities. Additionally, the potential of technology to assist in meeting the inclusive educational needs of children with disabilities will be a focus. The questions that will be addressed are:

- What is the current state of inclusive education in Brazil?
- What factors are supports and barriers to inclusive education in Brazil?
- How can technology assist with overcoming barriers to successful inclusive education in Brazil?

SCHOOLING SYSTEM IN BRAZIL

The system of education in Brazil includes both public and private schooling options. The government requires all children to attend schooling between the ages of 6 and 14 (Brazil Ministry of Education, 2014), and that free public education is available. Pre-school education (*Educação Infantil*) is provided and there is a choice between *Maternal*, state run creches for children aged two to five, or *Jardim*, which cater for children aged three to six years of age and are privately run and more expensive (AngloInfo Brazil, 2023). There are two levels in the primary and lower secondary education (*Ensino Fundamental I* and *Ensino Fundamental II*), which comprise of the compulsory nine years of education required by the government. Students of all academic ability are mixed in one class and class sizes can be large due to the large population in the country. Exams are held each year, and students who have not made appropriate progress can be held back to repeat the year (AngloInfo Brazil, 2023). Upper secondary education (*Ensino Médio*) prepares students aged 15–18 years to enter university or provides professional training.

There are currently 46.7 million students enroled in basic education, with 8.3 million in pre-school, 26.5 million in elementary school and 7.7 million in high school (International Trade Administration, 2023). In addition, 4.1 million students are enroled in other training programs. Class sizes in compulsory education are often large and may consist of up to 40 students.

Within the country, 45 million people are said to have disabilities. Approximately 3.5 million are children with disabilities up to 14 years of age, who are expected to be attending school (Alana Institute, 2019). It is estimated that one in five children with disabilities are not attending school and many have never attended an educational setting (Garcia Mora et al., 2021). Only 42% of schools in 2022 were accessible for students with disabilities, which may help to explain the low level of school enrolment (QEdu, 2022). This accessibility refers to the physical school environment; however, the pedagogical environment, or lack of access to the content of the learning, must also be considered when examining the exclusion of students with disability.

INCLUSIVE EDUCATION IN BRAZIL

Many countries in Latin America have been struggling against the deep level of educational inequality faced by the persons with disabilities (Garcia Mora et al., 2021). People with disabilities are more likely to live in poverty, face challenges in obtaining employment and have limited ability to be involved in decision-making which affects their lives (Orsati et al., 2019; World Bank Group, 2021). Brazil, the largest nation in this region, represents an interesting source for the investigation of the supports and challenges related to the implementation of inclusive education principles in its schools.

Following the historical patterns of many other countries around the world, structured national policies regarding the education of persons with disabilities began to appear in the middle of the 19th century, as a response to civil society pressures around this topic (Baptista, 2019). Over decades, the state invested in the maintenance of special schools that offered segregated education to this segment of the population. In general, schooling services were provided by private institutions financed by public resources (Baptista, 2019; Melletti, 2008).

This context started to change after the publication of the Convention on the Rights of Persons with Disabilities (CRPD, United Nations, 2006). Brazil not only signed the Convention, but also incorporated it into the Brazilian Federal Constitution. This act was a turning point in the history of Special Education in the country, since it generated profound changes in laws and public policies (United Nations, 2015). The first milestone of this change process was the creation of a National Special Education Policy by the Ministry of Education, in 2008. This new regulation stated that all students with disabilities should not be enroled in segregated environments (special schools or special classes) but should be supported by mainstream schools, together with the rest of the students. In addition, all the public financial resources available to special education should be directed to mainstream schools in order to improve infrastructure, to support pedagogical teams and to promote all the other transformations needed (Brazil Ministry of Education, 2008).

Inspired by the CRPD, in 2015 the Congress approved a new federal law named the Brazilian Law on the Inclusion of Persons with Disabilities (Soares, 2015). This law introduced more explicit inclusion rules in the educational system. Schools were prohibited from denying the enrolment of persons with disabilities and to charge extra fees to families with children with any type of impairment. The law also stated that discriminating against a person due to their disability could lead to jail for the perpetrators, including school principals (Presidency of the Republic, 2015).

The implementation of all those regulations resulted in a drastic change in the landscape of Special Education in Brazil. Since 2018, 90% of the students with disabilities enroled in Basic Education – which encompasses Early Childhood Education, Primary Education, Secondary Education and Higher Education – have been served by inclusive schools. That scenario represented almost the opposite of the context observed before the publication of the CRPD. Moreover, the civil society opinion about inclusive education also changed radically, with many teachers, school principals and student parents in favour of the educational inclusion of students with disabilities in mainstream schools, after all the changes promoted by the new regulations. For example, research conducted by the Alana Institute (2019) in Brazil suggested that the majority of those surveyed believed that schools are better when children with disability are included and that their inclusion did not impact on the learning of children without disabilities. They also believed that teachers, while willing to support children with disabilities, had insufficient training to do so.

It is important to mention that all those advancements were put at risk after the election of the extreme right Federal Administration, in 2018. In September of 2020, President Jair Bolsonaro signed a Federal Decree that stated the re-establishment of the segregated special schools financed by public resources. The Brazilian civil society reacted fast creating a national coalition to defend the full inclusion of students with disabilities in mainstream schools. The case was judged by the Supreme Court which considered the decree unconstitutional. In January 2023, as one of the first acts of President Luiz Inácio Lula da Silva, elected in the previous year, that decree was revoked.

SUPPORTS AND BARRIERS TO INCLUSIVE EDUCATION IN BRAZIL

The impact of the inclusive education legislation in Brazil has supported increased numbers of students with disabilities included in general education classrooms, with an increase from 29% of students with disabilities in general classrooms in 2003 to 79% in general classrooms in 2014 (Orsati et al., 2019). While the political and legal will may be evident in supporting inclusive education in Brazil, there has been some criticism that it has become an administrative task, rather than the building of an inclusive culture (Voltolini, 2019), with placement in a classroom, rather than actual inclusion taking place. Schabbach and da Rosa (2021) state that there are two coalitions involved in supporting students with disabilities, which include those that believe in the provision of exclusive assistance, often related to disability type (i.e., vision impairment, hearing impairment), and those who advocate for inclusive education, as they believe all students can learn together. Barriers to the inclusion of students with disabilities may be evident because of poor understanding of disability/labelling, poor training in inclusive pedagogy, funding concerns or lack of respect for the dignity of the individual.

Many elements of society favour inclusive education as the way forward for the education of all students, including those with disabilities. There are, however, those who oppose this view and work against these efforts, continuing to promote a dual education system with students with disabilities excluded from general education classrooms and educated in special education settings (Queiroz & Guerreiro, 2019; Slee, 2018). Labelling students according to the disability they may have can also have negative consequences for inclusion of the student in the school and classroom, leading to low expectations from teachers and peers, and possibly inappropriate provision of curriculum (Manrique et al., 2019). These views may be historical or based upon existing educational structures. It may also be possible that people who hold positions in existing special education services seek to extend their authority. Mendes (2019) suggests that there is some concern about what to do with existing special education facilities, and ideas extend from extinction of these settings to a reconfiguration to support inclusion. Further discussion around how to utilise the resources of the special education settings within an inclusive education focus is warranted.

The recent COVID-19 pandemic impacted heavily on the access of students with disabilities to an appropriate education, particularly those who are living in poverty, or in geographical isolation (Garcia Mora et al., 2021). Many people with disabilities are living in poverty and have limited access to alternative means to access education, including electronic devices. In Brazil, many children did not receive any education during the pandemic. Costin and Coutinho (2021) state that the '...shocks on the educational system caused by COVID-19 have (and will) inequitably hinder growth and development in Brazil' (p. 41). Inequitable educational opportunities are experienced by those who are most impacted, including students with disability, those living in poverty and those in remote locations.

One persistent barrier to supporting inclusive education that has been commonly cited is funding, or the lack of appropriate resources. The OECD (2021) report *Education at a Glance* suggests that Brazil invests a high share of its gross domestic product (GDP) on education (approximately 4%) although this is lower than many other OECD countries. There is still room for additional support in inclusive education, including in resources and teacher training, and a level of 10% of GPD has been suggested as more appropriate. Investing in education for students with disabilities can result in economic returns up to three times higher than those without disabilities (World Bank Group, 2021).

Slee (2018) suggests 'that local action based on strong community partnerships' (p. 24) is needed to support countries to develop inclusive practice and to encourage a perspective that addresses the needs of all students, without excluding those who are disadvantaged. The examination of why and how students with disabilities are excluded from education in Brazil is necessary to determine how best to approach these barriers. Public education, private education and NGOs should work together to address access to educational facilities, appropriate training and support for teachers, and increase understanding of disability in the community. Training at a university level for new teachers should also consider the wide range of student needs within the classroom, which is currently not always evident, and the specific barriers that exclude students in the classroom (Forlin & Chambers, 2011; Manrique et al., 2019; Ordóñez Santos & Granja Escobar, 2023; Tomczyk et al., 2021).

In addition to the political approaches to inclusive education, there has also been some concern regarding teachers' perceptions of their ability to support students with disabilities in the regular classroom (Manrique et al., 2019). Manrique et al. (2019) studied teachers' perceptions on inclusion in basic school and found that teachers felt that they required additional training and assistance with developing or accessing appropriate support materials, such as software and assistive technology, to support student needs. Technology, as a support for teachers in the classroom, will be explored further.

TECHNOLOGY FOR INCLUSION

The world has, and still is, changing rapidly as a result of increasing advances in technology (OECD, 2015). Technology includes communication technology (i.e. phones and computers), construction technology (i.e. Computer-Aided Drawing and farm machinery), medical technology (i.e. MRI scanners and vaccines), information technology (i.e. Learning Management Systems and Wi-Fi routers), educational technology (i.e. electronic whiteboards and iPads) and assistive technology (i.e. wheelchairs and speech recognition programs) (Ramey, 2022). Of most relevance to inclusive education is educational and assistive technology.

While not focusing specifically on education, a recent European Commission (2020) publication on a digital future detailed the need for all members in society to be digitally literate and for the technology to be inclusive of all needs. Initiatives such as developing sustainable products, allowing consumers a role in determining digital tools that will be made available and development of a digital education action plan are a few that have been proposed. Digital technology has been widely described as being able to effectively support students with a range of disabilities to access the curriculum and culture of a school (Panesi et al., 2020). Panesi et al. (2020) suggest that ensuring digital technology supports inclusion requires the whole school community to come together. Technology use can assist in preparing students with disability to be active members of the classroom and school community, and to acquire skills which will support them in accessing the community.

In the classroom, technology can be leveraged to address the specific needs of students with disability and promote inclusive practice. Teachers may be required to differentiate instruction to create an inclusive environment and technology can play a role (Ayon & Dillon, 2021; Johler & Krumsvik, 2022). There are a number of considerations for teachers when using technology to support inclusion, including the need for a positive attitude, the use of multiple modes of instruction and assessment to address a wide variety of student needs, and knowledge of the technologies and pedagogical practices that are most appropriate for their setting. One-to-one technologies are increasingly available in the classroom and have the potential to support differentiation of curricula for students with disability (Johler & Krumsvik, 2022). Many of the one-to-one devices that are used, such as laptops and mobile phones, are available to all students, and have the added bonus of not highlighting any additional needs of the student with a disability.

Assistive technologies are devices and tools that support the needs of people with disability in many areas including learning, communication, social interaction and access to resources and collaborative processes (Chambers, 2020). There is a wide variety of assistive technology and it is often categorised as low, medium or high-tech, depending on the complexity and construction of the device/software/tool. Low or medium tech assistive technology is often more easily sourced and requires less training for the teacher (Chambers, 2019; Shaw, 2016). When considering what assistive technology can be used, educators should take the functional nature of any disability into account, and determine what assistive technology is best to address this functional need.

TECHNOLOGY USE IN BRAZIL

In Brazil, the formal organism of the Ministry of Education architecture responsible for offering education to persons with disabilities is named special education. This organism adopts the directions established by the Convention on the Rights of Persons with Disabilities. Therefore, it assumes that the disability is a social condition generated by the interactions between clinical long-term impairments, physical, mental, intellectual or sensory, and barriers imposed by the environment (Brazil Ministry of Education, 2008).

Based on the former definition, the *National Policy of Special Education in The Perspective of Inclusive Education*, launched by the Ministry of Education in 2008 suggests that the efforts of the schools in order to promote equal opportunities to students with disabilities should be driven by the search for the elimination of barriers. In this sense, the use of technology can play a decisive role as a mean to obliterate all kinds of barriers presented in the classrooms and in other educational environments of the schools (Tomczyk et al., 2021). Technology also allows flexibility and customisation of teaching. Digitals books, tablets, apps and other software designed for facilitating the learning process are concrete examples of how technology can collaborate to inclusive education.

The use of digital technologies in Brazilian schools has been regulated since the 1990s. The first actions of the Ministry of Education were generally dedicated to equipping schools with computers and multimedia equipment. In 1997, the National Educational Technology Programme (ProInfo) and the Interactive Virtual Education Network (RIVED) were created. However, it was not until 2005 that great incentives were given to digital technologies, through the regulation of distance higher education, the improvement of connectivity and the use of personal computers in schools. In that context, the Brazil Ministry of Education (2006) *Educational Technologies Guide* was produced and became a reference document aimed to assist managers in decisions regarding the acquisition of technological resources.

Despite the initiatives listed above, the reality of Brazilian schools is marked by connectivity and infrastructure challenges, which vary according to regional aspects and administrative levels (municipalities and states). Data from the School Census referring to the use of computers and internet by students indicate that only 45.6% of schools have a desktop computer in use by students. Regarding connectivity, 83.4% of Brazilian schools have a broadband internet connection but only 31.1% of schools offer internet access to students (Regional Centre for Studies on the Development of the Information Society, 2019). Data from the 2018 International Research on Teaching and Learning (TALIS) indicate that only 10.9% of the teachers express that there is no need to develop skills in teaching technologies, and 25.7% assess that there is a high level of need to develop such skills (OECD, 2019).

Even though teachers want to incorporate technology into their teaching practice, much of the public-school system still faces limitations related to infrastructure and availability (Tomczyk et al., 2021). With a view to overcoming these limitations in the future, the use of digital educational technologies at school must be ensured by effective, continuous and nationwide public policies. In addition, the delivery of assistive technology services requires further staff training and knowledge to be a focus, so that appropriate decision-making around assistive devices and other technology takes place (Maximo & Clift, 2016).

Teachers may think of high-tech devices when considering ICT or assistive technology to support students in the classroom; however, there are instances where low-tech assistive technology can be of benefit, as demonstrated by the research conducted in Brazil by da Silva et al. (2018). The research focused on the construction and trial of a low-tech device to support the education of students with cerebral palsy. Results showed that the device was effective at supporting communication and interaction for the students with cerebral palsy and the four participants of the study rated the use of the device as satisfactory on the QUEST questionnaire (Carvalho et al., 2014). Vize (2013) also suggests that a wide range of assistive devices including those that are low-tech, such as egg timers, picture cues and photographs, can be used to support student needs in the classroom. In support of the use of low-tech devices, Shaw (2016) stated that 'the simplicity and ready availability of low-tech devices should be explored in order to enable the student to learn to use the tools at an independent level within a variety of environments' (p. 40). It is not suggested that low-tech devices are the only assistive technology that is considered, rather that it is not forgotten. Further training and examination of a complete range of appropriate tools can be of great benefit for teachers to effectively support students' learning.

CONCLUSION

The historical evolution of Human Rights movements and findings generated by research in the contemporary pedagogy field promoted huge advancements in the education of students with disabilities in many parts of Latin America. Several countries signed the Convention on The Rights of Persons with Disabilities, including Brazil, and started large transformations in their education systems aiming to respond to the directions of this Convention, which recommends that persons with disabilities study in inclusive schools, regardless of the singularities of each person.

Brazil is one of the countries that is moving in that direction and has been investing significant efforts in order to ensure the right of inclusive education for everyone. The majority of children and teenagers with disabilities that are enroled in Basic Education are now studying in inclusive schools, together with all other students (Orsati et al., 2019). This context is the consequence of very robust legislation that was introduced after the publication of the CRPD, which proposes a new definition of disability. This new conception orients all professionals to focus their attention on the elimination of the barriers presented in the learning environments. The barriers that may be evident include limited understanding of the needs of people with disability, poor teaching training in inclusive pedagogy, funding concerns or lack of respect for the dignity of the individual. Many of the tools necessary in the process of eliminating the obstacles come from the area of digital technologies.

As a consequence of the exponential evolution of the digital technology industry, there are a wide range of resources that can be used in the classrooms as a means to leverage the learning process. These resources benefit all students, including the ones that historically have been left behind, like persons with disabilities, as they can support access to the curriculum, regardless of ability, socio-economic level or gender. In Brazil, the market for technology has been experiencing constant expansion. Big technology companies revealed a growing concern with accessibility, diversity and inclusion. Google, Apple, Meta and many others explicitly approach the issues of inclusion as part of their core values. Those organisations not only assumed commitments with the promotion of equality, but also invested in the creation of specific areas exclusively dedicated to this matter. The products and services offered by this industry can play a fundamental role in the process of supporting the transformations needed in schools so that their infrastructure can offer adequate resources to the pedagogical teams.

A set of factors influence the feasibility of those outcomes. First, Brazilian authorities need to work together in order to improve the connectivity to internet in all schools of the country. Second, equipment and software need to be provided by the education secretaries. And third, the digital technology developers, including start-ups, companies and other institutions, need to incorporate their responsibility in offering inclusive education to all, creating partnerships with the government and all entities involved in the promotion of the right to education for every Brazilian citizen.

REFERENCES

Alana Institute. (2019). *What Brazilians think about inclusive education.* https://alana.org.br/wp-content/uploads/2021/01/relatorio_educacao_inclusiva_INGLES.pdf

Amor, A. A., Hagiwara, M., Shogren, K. A., Thompson, J. R., Verdugo, M. A., Burke, K. M., & Aguayo, A. (2019). International perspectives and trends in research on inclusive education: A systematic review. *International Journal of Inclusive Education, 23*(12), 1277–1295. https://doi.org/10.1080/13603116.2018.1445304

AngloInfo Brazil. (2023). *The school system.* https://www.angloinfo.com/how-to/brazil/family/schooling-education/school-system

Ayon, V., & Dillon, A. (2021). Assistive technology in education: Conceptions of a socio-technical design challenge. *The International Journal of Information, Diversity and Inclusion, 5*(3), 174–184. https://doi.org/10.33137/ijidi.v5i3.36136

Baptista, C., & R. (2019). Public policy, special education and schooling in Brazil. *Education and Research, 45*(e217423), 1–17. https://doi.org/10.1590/S1678-4634201945217423

Brazil Ministry of Education. (2006). *Guia de tecnologias educacionais [Educational technologies guide].* http://portal.mec.gov.br/seb/arquivos/pdf/Avalmat/guia_de_tecnologias_educacionais.pdf

Brazil Ministry of Education. (2008). *Política nacional de educação especial na perspectiva da educação inclusiva [The national policy of special education on the perspective of inclusive education].* MEC/SEESP. http://portal.mec.gov.br/arquivos/pdf/politicaeducespecial.pdf

Brazil Ministry of Education. (2014). *National Education Plan: Law No. 13,005/2014.* http://pne.mec.gov.br/18-planos-subnacionais-de-educacao/543-plano-nacional-de-educacao-lei-n-13-005-2014

Carvalho, K. E. C. D., Gois Júnior, M. B., & Sá, K. N. (2014). Tradução e validação do Quebec User Evaluation of Satisfaction with Assistive Technology (QUEST 2.0) para o idioma português do Brasil. *Revista Brasileira de Reumatologia, 54*(4), 260–267. https://doi.org/10.1016/j.rbr.2014.04.003

Chambers, D. J. (2020). Assistive technology supporting inclusive education: Existing and emerging trends. In D. J. Chambers (Ed.), *Assistive technology to support inclusive education* (Vol. 14, pp. 1–16). International Perspectives on Inclusive Education. Emerald Publishing Ltd.

Chambers, D. J. (2019). *Assistive technology to enhance inclusive education.* Oxford Research Encyclopedia of Education. https://doi.org/10.1093/acrefore/9780190264093.013.155

Costin, C., & Coutinho, A. (2021). Experiences with risk-management and remote learning during the Covid-19 pandemic in Brazil: Crises, destitutions, and (possible) resolutions. In F. M. Reimers (Ed.), *Primary and secondary education during Covid-19 disruptions to educational opportunity during a pandemic* (pp. 40–41). Springer International Publishing AG.

da Silva, A. P., Bulle Oliveira, A. S., Pinheiro Bezerra, I. M., Pedrozo Campos Antunes, T., Guerrero Daboin, B. E., Raimundo, R. D., dos Santos, V. R., & de Abreu, L. C. (2018). Low cost assistive technology to support educational activities for adolescents with cerebral palsy. *Disability and Rehabilitation: Assistive Technology, 13*(7), 676–682. https://doi.org/10.1080/17483107.2017.1369590

European Commission. (2020). *Shaping Europe's digital future.* Publications Office of the European Union.

Forlin, C., & Chambers, D. (2011). Teacher preparation for inclusive education: Increasing knowledge but raising concerns. *Asia-Pacific Journal of Teacher Education, 39*(1), 17–32.

Garcia Mora, M. E., Orellanda, S. S., & Freire, G. (2021). *Disability inclusion in Latin America and the Caribbean: A path to sustainable development.* World Bank Group. https://documents1.worldbank.org/curated/en/099015112012126833/pdf/P17538305622600c00bf3f09659df1f2f79.pdf

International Trade Administration. (2023). *Brazil: Education and training.* https://www.trade.gov/country-commercial-guides/brazil-education-and-training

Johler, M., & Krumsvik, R. J. (2022). Increasing inclusion through differentiated instruction in a technology-rich primary school classroom in Norway. *Education 3-13,* 1–15. https://doi.org/10.1080/03004279.2022.2143721

DIANNE CHAMBERS AND RODRIGO HÜBNER MENDES

Manrique, A. L., Dirani, E. A. T., Frere, A. F., Moreira, G. E., & Arezes, P. M. (2019). Teachers' perceptions on inclusion in basic school. *International Journal of Educational Management, 33*(2), 409–419. https://doi.org/10.1108/IJEM-02-2018-0058

Maximo, T., & Clift, L. (2016). Assessing service delivery systems for assistive technology in Brazil using HEART study quality indicators. *Technology and Disability, 27*(4), 161–170.

Melletti, S. (2008). APAE educadora e a organização do trabalho pedagógico em instituições especiais [APAE educator and the organization of pedagogical work in special institutions]. In Presented at *Annual Meeting of the National Association of Post-Graduation and Research in Education (ANPED)*. https://www.anped.org.br/sites/default/files/gt15-4852-int.pdf

Mendes, E. G. (2019). A política de educação inclusiva e o futuro das instituições especializadas no Brasil [The policy of inclusive education and the future of specialized institutions in Brazil]. *Education Policy Analysis Archives, 27*, 22. https://doi.org/10.14507/epaa.27.3167

OECD. (2015). *Students, computers and learning: Making the connection.* PISA, OECD Publishing. https://www.oecd-ilibrary.org/education/students-computers-and-learning_9789264239555-en

OECD. (2019). *TALIS 2018 Results (Volume I): Teachers and school leaders as lifelong learners.* OECD Publishing. https://doi.org/10.1787/1d0bc92a-en

OECD. (2021). *Education at a glance 2021: OECD indicators: Brazil.* OECD Publishing. https://www.oecd-ilibrary.org/sites/d8d547f5-en/index.html?itemId=/content/component/d8d547f5-en#section-d12020e24197

Ordóñez Santos, M. A., & Granja Escobar, L. C. (2023). Factores de exclusión al interior de las instituciones educativas: Una revisión necesaria [Exclusion factors within educational institutions: A necessary review]. *Revista Conrado, 19*(91), 270–279.

Orsati, F. T., Lowenthal, R., & Nikaedo, C. C. (2019). Possibilities and challenges of inclusive education in Brazil: Understanding the role of socioeconomic factors. In *The Sage handbook of inclusion and diversity in education* (pp. 431–445). Sage Publications Ltd. https://doi.org/10.4135/9781526470430.n36

Panesi, S., Bocconi, S., & Ferlino, L. (2020). Promoting students' well-being and inclusion in schools through digital technologies: Perceptions of students, teachers, and school leaders in Italy expressed through SELFIE piloting activities. *Frontiers in Psychology, 11*, 1–17. https://doi.org/10.3389/fpsyg.2020.01563

Presidency of the Republic. (2015). *Law No. 13.146. Brazilian law for the inclusion of persons with disabilities (statute of persons with disabilities).* http://planalto.gov.br/ccivil_03/_Ato2015-2018/2015/Lei/L13146.htm

QEdu. (2022). *Brazil: Basic education schools: Infrastructure.* https://qedu.org.br/brasil/censo-escolar/infraestrutura

Queiroz, J. G. B. D. A., & Guerreiro, E. M. B. R. (2019). Education and pedagogical policy of special education in the perspective of inclusive education in the public education network of Manaus-Brazil. *Revista Brasileira de Educação Especial, 25*(2), 231–246. https://doi.org/10.1590/s1413-65382519000200004

Regional Center for Studies on the Development of the Information Society [CETIC]. (2019). *Executive summary: ICT in education survey – 2019.* https://www.cetic.br/media/docs/publicacoes/1/20201123093020/executive_summary_ict_education_2019.pdf

Ramey, K. (2022). *What is technology: Meaning of technology and its use.* https://useoftechnology.com/what-is-technology/

Schabbach, L. M., & da Rosa, J. G. L. (2021). Segregate or include? Advocacy coalitions, ideas, and changes in special education in Brazil. *Revista de Administração Pública, 55*(6), 1312–1332. https://doi.org/10.1590/0034-761220210034

Shaw, A. (2016, September). *Low tech tools of empowerment.* Exceptional Parent. http://www.eparent.com/education/low-tech-tools-of-empowerment/

Slee, R. (2018). *Defining the scope of inclusive education: Think piece prepared for the 2020 global education monitoring report inclusion and education.* Report No. ED/GEMR/MRT/2018/T1/1. UNESCO. https://unesdoc.unesco.org/ark:/48223/pf0000265773

Soares, E. (2015). Brazil: Senate passes new law regulating inclusion of persons with disabilities [Web Page]. https://www.loc.gov/item/global-legal-monitor/2015-06-17/brazil-senate-passes-new-law-regulating-inclusion-of-persons-with-disabilities/

Tomczyk, L., Martins, V. F., de la Higuera Amato, C. A., Eliseo, M. A., & Silveira, I. F. (2021). The use of technology on inclusive education in Brazil: A discussion on the teacher and student views. In T. Antipova (Ed.), *Advances in digital education* (pp. 105–115). Springer.

UNESCO. (2020). *Global education monitoring report: Latin America and the Caribbean inclusion and education: All means all*. Author. https://unesdoc.unesco.org/ark:/48223/pf0000374614

United Nations. (2006). *Convention on the rights of persons with disabilities*. https://www.ohchr.org/en/instruments-mechanisms/instruments/convention-rights-persons-disabilities

United Nations. (2015). *Concluding observations on the initial report of Brazil*. Committee on the Rights of Persons with Disabilities. https://digitallibrary.un.org/record/811092?ln=en

United Nations. (n.d.). *Sustainable development goals*. https://sdgs.un.org/goals/goal4

Vize, A. (2013). Using assistive technology. *Practically Primary, 18*(1), 37–39, 41.

Voltolini, R. (2019). Ethical interpellation to inclusive education. *Educação e Realidade, 44*(1), 1–18. https://doi.org/10.1590/2175-623684847

World Bank Group. (2021). *Disability inclusion in Latin America and the Caribbean: A path to sustainable development*. Author. https://openknowledge.worldbank.org/handle/10986/36628

EDUCATION FOR ALL FROM THE EARLY YEARS: INCLUSIVE EXPERIENCE IN CHILE

Paula Tapia Silva[a], Patricia Soto de la Cruz[b] and Yarela Muñoz López[b]

[a]ANADIME, Chile
[b]Universidad Finis Terrae, Chile

ABSTRACT

Over the last decade, the discourse of inclusive early childhood education has been actively promoted in Chile. However, the implementation of appropriate models has been slow and challenging. The purpose of this study is to assess users' perceptions of the inclusive service they received in an early childhood education centre. In addition, it seeks to obtain the ex-post perspective of the education professionals who participated in this intervention, with the aim of providing information for similar proposals in the future. This study explores the fundamental characteristics of the implementation of the inclusive-ecological model in a kindergarten located in a vulnerable area of the city of Santiago, analysing the results of an opinion survey of families and the testimony of educational agents. The research findings suggest a positive perception by family members and neighbours with respect to people with disabilities; they also underline the importance of continuous training of educational staff and collaboration in networks, and show that the model implemented had a favourable impact on the early detection of educational support needs.

Keywords: Early childhood; inclusive education; early detection; early childhood education; educational research; barriers to learning and participation (BAP)

Intercultural and Inclusive Education in Latin America
International Perspectives on Inclusive Education, Volume 24, 45–65
Copyright © 2024 Paula Tapia Silva, Patricia Soto de la Cruz and Yarela Muñoz López
Published under exclusive licence by Emerald Publishing Limited
ISSN: 1479-3636/doi:10.1108/S1479-363620240000024004

INTRODUCTION

In 1990, Decree 490 established rules for integrating students with disabilities into regular schools. Since then, the principles of integration and inclusive education have been timidly and progressively introduced into Chilean legislation. Specifically, in kindergarten education these ideas take shape through a discourse that considers that in education for diversity each child 'is a unique being with characteristics, needs, interests and strengths that must be known, respected and effectively considered in every learning situation' (Ministry of Education [MINEDUC], 2005 in Devia, 2017, p. 17). This approach has had an impact at the theoretical and practical level on state institutions in charge of early childhood.

At a theoretical level, the discourse of attention to diversity strained the integration and inclusion models. The integrative model was a major breakthrough in the late 1980s because it posed the challenge of including all children in regular education, and generated support for them to adapt to schools that 'fit', but without considering their individual characteristics, language, culture and abilities. The inclusive approach proposed a much more structural change, targeting institutional culture to ensure the right to equitable and quality education for each student, respecting their abilities, but also their sociocultural identity, sexual orientation or other conditions. Under this paradigm, the education system should be mobilised as a whole, changing the curriculum and forms of assessment, promoting a universal learning design that favours everyone, so that it is the school that adapts to the children. In this model, it is essential to provide support for teachers and families so that they can respond to diversity and to generate collaboration and exchange with other professionals, community networks, social, educational and state organisations (López, 2018).

The new approach also had an impact at a practical level. In Chile, educational programmes that considered education for diversity were implemented and lines of action were defined even before the enactment of Law No. 20.845 (2015), which emphasises school inclusion.[1] Subsequently, state institutions (Junta Nacional de Jardines Infantiles and Integra) created departments or units specifically aimed at implementing this orientation in their kindergartens and/or nursery schools (Devia, 2017).

This action shows a clear intention to improve access to early childhood education, promoting equity, reducing inequalities and removing barriers that limit the learning options of disadvantaged groups. However, it looks like that at the level of legal regulation, inclusive education is simple, but in practice its implementation is complex (Duk & Murillo, 2018), and the reality is that, in Chile, access to education for the most vulnerable groups remains low. For example the Junta Nacional de Jardines Infantiles (JUNJI) in its 2019 Characterisation Report states that, '[a]ccording to institutional records, a total of 1,166 infants have some kind of disability, a figure that reaches 1.4% of the total enrolment of directly administered kindergartens' (JUNJI, 2020, p. 23). Although this is a significant figure, it is not representative of the national reality, as the III Disability Study-2022 indicates that the population of children between 2- and 5-

years old with disabilities is 12.72% (Servicio Nacional de la Discapacidad [SENADIS], 2022). On the other hand, although enrolment has increased, the permanence of these students in nurseries and kindergartens are lower than that of children who are not disabled. JUNJI assumes this reality and establishes that one of the reasons for the withdrawal of infants from its educational centres is related to the 'lack of professionals to address SEN' (JUNJI-Galerna Consultores, 2017, p. 110), a situation that educators indicate as a critical issue given that they do not feel prepared 'to focus' on the education of these students, the study concludes that there is 'a lack of procedures to support these processes' (JUNJI-Galerna Consultores, 2017, p. 31).

The case of Chile is not isolated; in Latin America there is a clear intention to implement more inclusive models. And, although there are examples of good practices, it is necessary to strengthen schools at a systemic level, so that each level is provided with structure/regulations and procedures that ensure equity and continuity.

Taking into consideration the above information and with the aim of contributing to the discussion, the experience of the ANADIME Educational Centre (CEA), which operated between 2010 and 2012 in a vulnerable neighbourhood of Santiago de Chile, is presented in this chapter.[2] In this educational space an inclusive-ecological model was installed that showed very favourable effects with respect to the relevance of the continuous training of the educational team, the work in networks, the early research and the perceptions of the family and the community.

Specifically, to assess the impact of the CEA, the data collected through two studies are concisely examined:

(1) First study: report on the results of a survey commissioned by ANADIME to find out how families and caregivers perceived disability. The instrument was applied in the CEA and in another kindergarten in the sector in order to compare the families' appreciation of a traditional educational space versus the impressions of those who participated in the inclusion model.

   The research tool had the following characteristics:

   • The data collection instrument used was a structured survey.
   • The instrument was applied during the second half-yearly parents' meeting, specifically at the end of 2011.
   • The sample universe in both centres was 104 families, 40 at the nursery level (3 months–2 years) and 64 at the middle level (2–4 years). The confidence level was 95% in CEA and 93% in the other centre; the margin of error was 5% and 7%, respectively.

(2) The second study: is based on the analysis of the autobiographical accounts of key informants who provide the perspective of those who were protagonists in the implementation of the educational centre (educational team, neighbourhood leader and supervisor of the National Disability Service). The purpose of these data collection is to provide a retrospective view that can

provide information about lessons learnt for the planning of similar projects in the future. Distinctive aspects of the testimony gathering were:

- The process was carried out in 2023, almost 10 years after the implementation of the project, firstly because it was an investigative projection of the first stage of the project and, secondly, because the aim was for the actors to have the opportunity to live other educational experiences, considering that for many it was their first experience either as parents or as an educational team.
- The sample sought to represent different roles within the process, so four educational agents (educator, technician, student in practice and art teacher), a kinesiologist, the president of the neighbourhood council and the SENADIS coordinator at the time were selected.
- As a selection criterion for the informants of the educational team and the kinesiologist, it was determined that the persons had been active in the educational field in similar roles.
- The autobiographies were conducted independently by each actor, under the guidance of one of the researchers.

Taking into consideration the background provided by these studies, this chapter presents the main characteristics of the inclusive classroom model and then reviews its implementation and effect on the educational population of CEA.

THE CHALLENGE OF THE INCLUSIVE MODEL IN CHILE

Inclusion policies in kindergarten education in Chile are part of national and international regulatory frameworks that encourage all children to have access to, participate in and progress towards the learning objectives of the national curriculum, on equal terms and with a focus on disadvantaged contexts (Government of Chile, 2015; Subsecretaría de Educación Parvularia, 2018). At its core, the legal framework challenges the traditional pedagogical approach based on the clinical diagnosis of cognitive deficiencies or gaps to move towards one that values diversity as an enriching element of the learning process (Dueñas Buey, 2010). Inclusion strategies in preschools consist fundamentally of curricular innovations and adaptations aimed at guaranteeing the necessary conditions for the equitable use of learning opportunities and participation in the school community. In this sense, these strategies are understood as relevant and contextualised modifications to the programming and implementation of classroom pedagogical work, with the aim of adapting the curriculum to the needs and responses of individual children, and not the other way around. This inclusive perspective is based on empirical evidence that differentiating children's school socialisation processes between those with 'deficits' and those 'without' substantially limits the learning opportunities of the former and lowers the standard and expectations of pedagogical practices (Ainscow, 2001;

Blanco, 1997; Blanco et al., 2003). This approach aims to increase participation in regular contexts and consciously reduce exclusion from community culture (Parrilla, 2002).

The inclusive approach requires a multi-professional, collaborative and informed approach that simultaneously addresses the child's community, social, psychoeducational and health development contexts (Government of Chile, 2015) and allows for the early detection and intervention of barriers to learning and participation and/or disability, 'to provide them in a timely manner with the stimuli and experiences they require to achieve the maximum development of their potential capacities' (Ministry of Education, 2018, p. 19). These stimuli consist fundamentally in providing support and necessary resources for the optimisation of the pedagogical process of children who face barriers to learning, with the aim of favouring their access, participation and effective progress in the education system. The nature of these interventions is decided according to the warning signs or precursor signs in the student's psycho-evolutionary developmental history. These warning signs are understood as biopsychosocial indicators that may signal a maladjustment or dysfunction in the predictable sequence of development and mastery of cognitive, socio-affective, motor or linguistic skills and abilities (National Institute for Comprehensive Early Childhood Care, 2017).

The assessment and early detection of alterations in the precursor signs allows for the recovery of diverse neuropsychological functions based on the progressive acquisition of a repertoire of elementary cognitive skills. These are defined as the level of basic and foundational skills, from which the child can begin to construct and perform the intellectual behaviours and operations required for learning to read, write and calculate. The literature recommends that, in these cases, the psycho-pedagogical intervention strategy should be deployed in four fundamental areas of action: (1) the differential and individualised assessment of the specific manifestations of alterations in the neuropsychological functions of the child's development, (2) the evaluation of the family, environmental and socio-educational variables that may be influencing the dysfunctional realisation of the precursor signs, (3) the programming and sequencing of the psycho-pedagogical action and technique appropriate to the case and (4) the periodic and systematic monitoring of the general efficacy and incremental results of the strategy (Arbones, 2005). In the context of early childhood education, the early intervention approach articulates these four areas by supporting the child and his/her context (Federación de Organizaciones en Favour de las Personas con Retraso Mental de Madrid [FEAPS], 2001, p. 47).

Based on the above definition, one of the fundamental characteristics of the inclusive approach in pre-primary education is that it should be understood as a 'multi-centred participatory experience' (United Nations Educational, Scientific and Cultural Organization [UNESCO], 2014, p. 12), and requires the active participation of family and community agents to increase learning opportunities and accompany students in their comprehensive development (Rubilar & Guzmán, 2021). In this same sense, Dueñas Buey (2010, p. 362) has pointed out that inclusive education is a social process rather than a solely educational one, where families and communities reinforce and provide feedback on pedagogical decisions in pursuit of the effective improvement of the quality of education that children receive. The emphasis on psycho-pedagogical intervention is key to the effectiveness of the strategy. When families and communities are engaged, a virtuous circle is generated in which environments conducive to learning and development are reinforced and consolidated. Inclusion in preschool education is not only done by the special educator in charge of the child. An appropriate psychoeducational intervention goes beyond the classroom and incorporates an interdisciplinary group of professionals and the people who are committed to the student, 'parents (first and foremost) or guardians, the educational community (everyone, from the management to the cleaning staff), professionals who attend or have attended the child; psychologist, psychopedagogue, social worker and teachers who will be with the child, among others' (Ministry of Education of Costa Rica, 2010, p. 26).

Finally, this interdisciplinary team must be in constant reflection and training, considering the challenges of professional development and updating of pedagogical standards contextualised to the reality in which the school is inserted (López, 2018).

As mentioned above, it is relevant to present the example of the CEA for discussion, as many of the issues that have been made explicit in this document were discussed and addressed in its implementation. However, after a decade of implementation, problems continue to be detected with the installation of the inclusive model in Chile. For example, the recent study by Rubilar and Guzmán (2021), which recovers the testimony of educational agents about the implementation of the inclusive education model in the Atacama region, indicates that, although it is possible to identify a series of learning methodologies with the aim of promoting participation in the classroom, 'there is a lack of conceptual knowledge of inclusive education [...] there is evidence of little training on disability, insufficient teaching materials, outdated professional training' (p. 23). As a result, the use of inappropriate language is detected, for example the use of the labels 'handicapped or normal', and the replication of prejudices, myths and overprotection (Rubilar & Guzmán, 2021).

Taking into consideration the above, the following is a description of how the inclusive model was approached in CEA, from a participatory, psychoeducational and community perspective.

ANADIME-CEA EDUCATIONAL CENTRE INCLUSIVE MODEL

The CEA is the result of a partnership between ANADIME, JUNJI (Junta Nacional de Jardines Infantiles) and the Municipality of Peñalolén.

ANADIME is a non-profit civil society organisation dedicated to the education and training of people with intellectual disabilities. Since its beginnings in 1966, it has promoted initiatives to raise barriers and break the reality of reclusion and exclusion in which these people had to live. Its actions are aimed at facilitating channels of real participation, while educating the population in the value of respect for diversity. However, although there has been progress, people with intellectual disabilities continue to live a reality of greater marginalisation and vulnerability than those who are not in this condition or who have other types of disabilities. That is why, at the time of focusing its attention on early childhood, ANADIME proposed an educational project that would ensure a percentage (reflecting the census data of the time) specifically for people with intellectual disabilities.

JUNJI is an institution of the State of Chile, which is responsible for early education. One of its operating modalities is the allocation of resources to public and/or private non-profit organisations for the implementation of educational centres, preferably oriented towards the care of children under four years of age in vulnerable situations. The establishments that operate under this modality are called via transfer of funds (VTF).

The objective of the alliance between these two institutions was to implement an early childhood education project aimed at educating in diversity through the construction of a quality social and pedagogical context for children with different conditions and/or disabilities.

For its implementation, an alliance was created with the Municipality of Peñalolén and the Neighbourhood Council of the La Faena sector. This neighbourhood organisation donated the land on which the CEA was built and played a special participatory role from the outset.

Methodological Characteristics

Taking into consideration the inclusive approach, the central objective of the CEA was to promote the valuing and respect for children, through quality pedagogical spaces based on the interests and needs of all children, in their different family and sociocultural contexts, to address their needs and difficulties, not only cognitive but also affective and emotional. Its central axes were equal opportunities and the diversity of people (pupils, families and educational team).

In order to carry out the project, the following guidelines in Table 1 were intended in the CEA:

In summary, the most relevant aspects of the model were associated with: (1) an enrolment that ensured a percentage of 12% for people with disabilities (with a diagnosis). But, assuming that the term diversity considered the particular characteristics of each child, the space was also opened to those who faced temporary barriers to learning and participation, as well as to immigrant students and those from different sociocultural contexts. (2) Transdisciplinary professional team. In terms of staffing, the most relevant action was the incorporation of a full-time special needs educator (funded by the JUNJI subsidy) who followed up on each student included. In addition, art professionals were in charge of outlining the guidelines for aesthetic education, working in coordination with the educators. On the other hand, the management work carried out by the management team made it possible to establish alliances that provided support professionals in the area of health, whose intervention both inside and outside the

Table 1. Guidelines for Promoting an Inclusive Model in CEA.

Dimension	Action	Relevant Aspects
Staffing	Professional and technical coefficient in accordance with the law, plus a full-time special needs educator. Part-time teachers of visual arts, dance, music therapy and theatre.	Inclusion-sensitive plant and equipment.
Registration	Consider the representativeness of 'all' in the classroom. Approximate 12% of children diagnosed with a disability.	The first study on disability, carried out in 2004, indicated that the population with disabilities in Chile was 2,068,072, equivalent to 12.93% (Fondo Nacional de la Discapacidad [FONADIS], 2005).
Multidisciplinary Health Support	Active participation, inside and outside the classroom, of multidisciplinary teams (kinesiologist, speech therapist, neurologist, occupational therapist and psychologist).	External teams were managed through partnerships with rehabilitation centres and universities. Of particular relevance is the collaborative relationship with the Peñalolén Community Rehabilitation Centre (CCR).
Educational methodologies	Active participation, inside and outside the classroom, in multidisciplinary teams in the field of the arts.	Aesthetic Education is the fundamental pillar of all ANADIME's educational and training spaces.
	Active methodologies that allow the inclusion, development and pedagogical empowerment of ALL.	Reggio Emilia methodology. Project Method.
Learning Community	Ongoing training for the whole team according to the challenges presented by the diagnoses (also including family members and community).	Training managed through the National Training and Employment Service. Duration between 10 and 30 chronological hours. Example of courses held: • Challenges for the care of children with intellectual disabilities in kindergarten. Rapporteur: Lucía Margarita Vivanco Muñoz. • References for an update in didactics and evaluation. Rapporteur: Silvia Hirmas Ready. • Teaching activities for children with sensory-integrative dysfunctions. Rapporteurs: Enrique Henny – Fresia Vargas
	Raise awareness among the community and parents.	Home visits. Coordinated work with the Neighbourhood Council.
Continuous Assessment	Ongoing evaluation of the inclusive model.	Systematisation of internal and external evaluations. Implementation of continuous improvement strategies. Agreements and internships with universities. Presentation of the project at various seminars. Application to competitive funds.

PAULA TAPIA SILVA ET AL.

classroom facilitated early detection and provided the teaching and para-teaching staff with the necessary rudiments to strengthen educational interventions.

In addition to the staffing, it is important to highlight the intentional actions to foster learning communities, facilitate cooperation, and instal a continuous improvement approach. The CEA was a participatory experience in which the educational community as a whole, the neighbours of La Faena and the communal mechanisms became relevant to expand learning and development opportunities from an integral perspective, with emphasis on the idea that inclusive education is a social process in which families and the community provide feedback and give shape to pedagogical decisions, with a view to ensuring the quality of the education that children receive.

This collaborative work yielded different results and one of them was the relevance of early detection, which was achieved thanks to the support of kine-siologists and occupational therapists, whose intervention in the classroom facilitated, firstly, that the specialists could observe all children and, secondly, that these professionals guided the work of educators to detect warning signs that allowed them to suggest to parents the relevance of a referral for professional evaluation.

Collaborative Work and Early Detection

To approach the work, the educational team began with an early assessment of the needs and support required by the children who already had a previous diagnosis. Based on these diagnoses, a strategy of articulation and alliance was established with the Peñalolén CCR and/or the neurologist who provided medical services at ANADIME. The special educator operated as the main interlocutor and mediator between the support networks and the educational team at the CEA. Her role was fundamental in the institutional circuit of implementation and operational improvement of the strategy.

The ecological and community model of intervention was structured on two pillars: family interviews and home visits. Both processes were carried out in psychosocial pairs according to the taxonomy of the diagnosis received by the child. In the case of those who did not have a previous differential diagnosis, the pair was made up of the kindergarten educator and one of the kindergarten technicians in the classroom. In the case of children with a previous diagnosis, the professional dupla consisted of the classroom kindergarten educator and the special educator in charge of the intervention strategy. These two intervention devices also informed the nature of the training provided by the professionals of the support networks for the educational team and the service team.

For students with a clinical diagnosis, the special educator prepared a report that brought together the main clinical and pedagogical intervention strategies proposed by professionals from the support networks (neurologist from ANA-DIME, occupational therapist, speech therapist and kinesiologist from the Community Rehabilitation Centre [CCR]) and passed this information to the educational team in the classroom who, after a period of implementation, returned a technical report on the evaluation and results obtained with the strategy.

Subsequently, the special educator reported this information back to the medical team and specialists in charge and the strategy was reviewed, thus forming a virtuous circle of feedback and continuous improvement of intervention opportunities.

In the case of children without a differential diagnosis, an institutionalised process of early detection and warning signs was generated, in which the educators and nursery technicians of each classroom, the differential educator, the management team and the support professionals participated. The basis of the warning signs was the behaviour of the students in and outside the classroom. Based on this institutionalised diagnosis, a family interview was called again, in which a possible need for referral to the CCR was explained, for professional assistance from occupational therapists, speech therapists or kinesiologists, or, if neurological support was required, to ANADIME. In both cases, the special educator completed a referral form based on what she and the educational team observed. After the visit to the CCR or ANADIME, the professionals issued a diagnostic report that gave an account of the professional assessment of the existence of the clinical condition, which required intervention based on the warning signs of the CEA team. The results of this circuit demonstrated the validity of the warning signs. It is worth mentioning that most of the presumptions about the need for intervention were medically confirmed.

Both for children with and without diagnosis, a strategy of educating families about the nature of interventions and clinical diagnoses was deployed, with a focus on diversity, inclusion and respect for individual differences. Generally, these workshops took place in the CEA and were led by support professionals, by the same educational team in the classroom or by the special educator.

The pedagogical intervention work was optimised with the help of students in the process of professional practice in special education, kindergarten education, kinesiology, occupational therapy and speech therapy. The support of these students focused on strengthening the team in the classroom and, in some cases, the improvement and alignment of the pedagogical planning.

Evolution of Student Enrolment in CEA's Inclusion Project

Below is a breakdown of enrolment associated with permanent or transitory diagnoses and its evolution over time. Table 2 summarises the total enrolment of the CEA by educational level. It can be seen that approximately one hundred

Table 2. Annual Enrolment, by Level of Education.

	2010	2011	2012
Classroom 1 (3 months–1 year old)	22	20	19
Classroom 2 (1–2 years old)	22	22	19
Classroom 3 (2–3 years old)	34	32	32
Classroom 4 (3–4 years old)	34	32	30
Total	112	106	100

Note: Prepared by the authors, based on systematised data from the intervention.

PAULA TAPIA SILVA ET AL.

students per year were served by the Centre, concentrated in the lower secondary and upper secondary levels. In order to promote healthy inclusion, the number of students per classroom was reduced from the second year onwards.

Table 3 shows the number of students participating in the inclusion project by level. It also shows the number of subsequent diagnoses identified through the early screening model, and the percentage they represent in relation to the total enrolment of the educational level per year of the Centre. It is necessary to clarify that in some cases the screening indicates a new diagnosis for students who already had a previous condition.

The indicator % of early detection shows the effectiveness of the intervention model. In the second year the screening was higher, possibly due to the experience acquired by the educational team, and then in the third year it decreased because when passing from one year to the next, students were reported with a previous diagnosis (from the previous year). Another interesting aspect is that the enquiries detected educational support needs, largely associated with the areas of language and psychomotor skills, which, when dealt with in a timely manner, made it possible to define specific treatments, which were applied as part of the school routine and after which the students were discharged. This may possibly explain

Table 3. Students Included With Previous Diagnosis and Subsequent Diagnosis by Early Screening Model, 2010–2012.

	2010	2011	2012
Enrolment Total Enrolment Classroom 1	22	20	19
N students in inclusion project	7	4	3
N students with previous diagnosis	4	3	2
N of subsequent diagnoses CRC and/or ANADIME	6	4	1
Early detection	27%	20%	5%
Enrolment Total Classroom 2	22	22	19
N students in inclusion project	6	7	5
N students with previous diagnosis	4	2	2
N of subsequent diagnoses CRC and/or ANADIME	5	6	3
Early detection	23%	27%	16%
Total Enrolment Classroom 3	34	32	32
N students in inclusion project	8	10	6
N students with previous diagnosis	2	3	3
N of subsequent diagnoses CRC and/or ANADIME	7	9	3
Early detection	21%	28%	9%
Total Enrolment Classroom 4	34	32	30
N students in inclusion project	6	13	6
N students with previous diagnosis	1	2	2
N of subsequent diagnoses CRC and/or ANADIME	6	13	4
Early detection	18%	41%	13%

Note: Prepared by the authors, based on systematised data from the intervention.

why in 2012, the percentage of screening decreased as most of the children remained at the centre and had been diagnosed and/or treated the previous year.

At the beginning of the CEA, in 2010, the main previous diagnosis was Down Syndrome. Subsequently, as a result of the early screening model, language disorders (such as language delay and expressive difficulties) and motor, kinesthetics or musculoskeletal disorders (such as limb rotation) were detected. Most of the diagnoses found as a result of the early screening model were made at the lower middle and upper middle levels.

The implementation of this inclusive model allowed for early research and the installation of continuous improvement practices that showed, in the short term, a positive impact on the community, making it possible to plan real actions of articulation with community services (CCR) in order to optimise resources and facilitate opportunities for inclusion and development from early childhood onwards.

Impact of CEA at the Community Level

CEA implemented an ecological model of intervention, which had an impact on the educational community, the community environment and the supervising state institutions. In order to make the significance of the project visible, the results of the survey comparing the perception of inclusion and disability among CEA's user families and those of another kindergarten in the sector are briefly analysed. We also examine the testimonies of key informants who provide the perspective of those who were protagonists in the implementation of the educational centre.

User Families' Perceptions of Inclusion

As part of the policy of periodic evaluation of its educational projects, and as a way to know the impact of the new inclusive model that was being implemented, ANADIME requested the assessment of the project through the application of a survey that compared the understanding of disability among the families of the CEA and those of another centre with similar characteristics. The opinion survey, carried out in December 2011 (Ávila, 2011), yielded interesting results regarding perceptions of inclusion and disability in these VTF kindergartens. Although the study is not generalisable, as it only covers and compares two centres, it provides strong information regarding the impact of the inclusive model on families. The study was authorised in both schools, but for confidentiality reasons the name of the second school evaluated is not given.

When analysing the results of both kindergartens, it can be seen that there are no major differences in terms of perceptions of quality, be it infrastructure, centre-proxy interaction, quality of the staff, etc. However, there are differences in perceptions of inclusion and acceptance of diversity.

In response to the statement, 'My child's education is negatively affected by sharing with children with special needs', the results in Fig. 1 suggest that in CEA a large majority of parents do not believe that their children's education will be

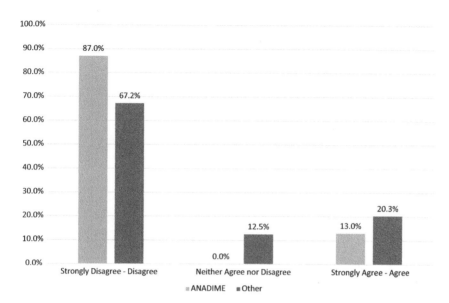

Fig. 1. My child's Education is Negatively Affected by Sharing With Children With Special Needs. *Source:* Ávila (2011) with permission from the author.

negatively affected by sharing with people with disabilities. In contrast, in the other centre, although a large number disagree with the statement, the discrepancy is smaller compared to CEA.

Fig. 2 shows that in CEA 96.2% believe that sharing with children with disabilities will make their children more caring in the future. In the other centre 80.3% share this opinion. Despite the variation in the results, the figures show a positive assessment of the incorporation of students who face barriers to learning and participation in the classroom. And although the trend is slightly higher in CEA, it is clear that parents in both schools appreciate this aspect.

However, when asked directly whether they would prefer their child to be in a kindergarten without children with disabilities or who present barriers to learning and participation, there is a clear difference (Fig. 3). 84.6% of CEA parents said they disagreed with the statement, while only 28.8% of the other centre said they disagreed and 36.5% agreed that they would prefer their children to participate in an educational space without children with disabilities. This result is an indicator that the CEA parents were more aware of the concept of inclusion, its benefits and above all the absence of negative externalities of having a child with SEN in the same room with a child who does not have SEN.

The following question (Fig. 4) is a clear reflection of the reality of the schools as the percentage of inclusion in the other school is very low. It is therefore obvious that children with greater exposure to inclusion are likely to show more sensitive and humane treatment.

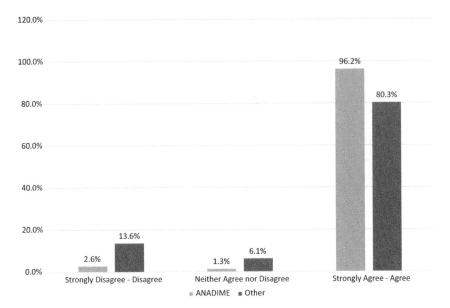

Fig. 2. Sharing With Children With Special Needs Will Make My Child More Empathetic and Caring in the Future. *Source:* Ávila (2011) with permission from the author.

In the case of two schools with similar characteristics, the evaluation indicated greater empathy and acceptance towards children with disabilities and/or who face barriers to learning and participation in the inclusive school model.

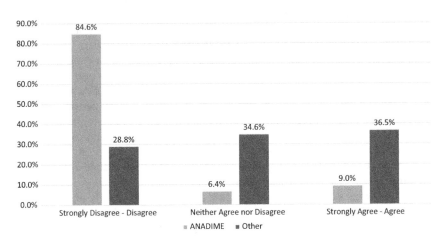

Fig. 3. I Would Prefer My Child to Be in a School Without Children With Special Needs. *Source:* Ávila (2011) with permission from the author.

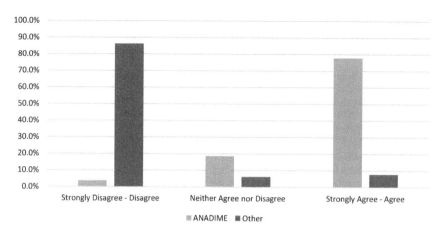

Fig. 4. My child is Concerned About Helping Children With Special Needs.
Source: Ávila (2011) with permission from the author.

Perception of the Protagonists
In order to get the community's perspective, testimonies were collected from key agents, under a qualitative interpretative approach, which from a retrospective perspective (10 years later) seeks to obtain relevant information about the lessons learnt that can guide the planning of future similar projects. Due to the limited length of the text, only a synthesis of the results of this research is presented.

The educational agents (kindergarten educator, kindergarten technician, student in practice and art teacher) agree in highlighting: the participation of a special educator; the presence of health professionals in the classroom; the role given to self-education and continuous training; the pedagogical approach based on observation and documentation of processes; the intervention strategies and open doors; and the establishment of a learning community with transdisciplinary teams that shared knowledge and where each person played an important role in the children's education, from the 'lady who made the food to the headmistress'.

Kinesiologist Susana Matzner emphasises the interdisciplinary work and the willingness of the educational team to learn to detect warning signs and apply the necessary treatments in the classroom.[3]

> The focus of the interventions was to improve the quality of life of the children and their families within the school context. While the intervention was initially individual, it then moved to the needs of each child in the classroom where he or she spends most of his or her time, where his or her adaptation and group behaviour with peers was re-evaluated.
>
> A number of simple modifications were made, which helped to improve the quality and time of care, as well as educators and technicians were trained if they required any assistance.

The testimony of neighbourhood leader Mitchel Varas is full of pride and commitment.[4] It was his idea that the neighbourhood council requested the municipality to build a kindergarten on the vacant land, and for this reason the community took part, prevented theft, looked after and beautified the surrounding area. But for him this was not a kindergarten like others and in his speech the word integration is constantly reiterated: integration of children, nationalities, families, neighbours and the community as a whole with the focus on creating opportunities.

> [...] and this issue of vulnerable children, with problems, came up, which was like a second project because it was never thought of in that sense [...] so a very good association was formed, it was nice, I didn't think that could happen. And to see children coming out of there makes me feel a horrible pride to think that little children are being educated thanks to an idea, an idea as simple as this space, it makes me proud [...] and to know that the community was so strongly integrated into the kindergarten project was the beauty of it.

> I always heard that poor children start about five metres further back than a child with money, and I assimilated that this made them start from the same line. Because the children brought with them an educational background that was not so different from that of a child with money, and I liked that a lot, because it put them on the same footing. I don't know what elementary school they went to, but at least they left here with a basis of education, a basis, I don't know, a way of doing things, a basis of respect.

Mónica Apablaza coordinated, in 2010, the SENADIS Early Attention Programme in charge of the design, implementation and monitoring of inclusive projects in public kindergartens.[5] Her view of CEA highlights the institutional culture of inclusion, approached not as a disability issue but as a rights issue.

> The culture of inclusion that was lived inside was consistent with the rights of the children and their families, and also with the rights of the people who worked there.

> I was struck by the 10% that ensured the right to education, and I was also struck by how they built all the disciplines in an educational space while maintaining that essence [...] that the children remained in the routine, they were not taken out, as in the famous integration projects that we still have today in the regular system in basic education [...].although it is true that we as educators are very afraid of the inclusion of children with disabilities because they do not prepare us, I saw that their culture as a centre was very collaborative because they had a common objective, which was the wellbeing and development of the children and their learning, there was a culture of collaborative work.

Another characteristic that Apablaza highlights is the use of the support networks offered by the context, mainly the articulation with the CCR, but also with other health centres.

> This was not copied from abroad, it was adjusted to the reality of the environment, to the culture and also to the existence of the resources at their disposal.

> They had a very good articulation with the CCR, which is where the specialists were. Observing this articulated work was an important experience for me because we have to try to turn good practices into public policies. I proposed to SENADIS to carry out a nationwide survey of where the CCRs are located so that they could be linked to the kindergartens in the neighbourhoods, because we do not have reference centres or centres for rehabilitation and support for families. In the CEA I saw that it was possible to articulate the networks because it contributed in every sense, from direct intervention with children and support for families. But it also contributed to the continuous training of the educational team. Obviously, SENADIS did not carry out the survey, but it is something for which I continue to advocate.

The testimonies of those who participated or were involved with CEA highlight some of the aspects that stand out as strengths of the model implemented.

From the point of view of the educational team, the methodological approach, ongoing training, staffing and transdisciplinary teams, both internal (special educator and art teachers) and external (therapists), are highlighted. At the same time, the culture of collaboration installed in the CEA is highlighted by the SENADIS supervisor, who emphasises the importance of generating care networks that can support children within their educational spaces, without separating them from their peers and usual environment. Furthermore, she is emphatic in highlighting that the alliance between the CEA and the Community Rehabilitation Centre is a practice that should be promoted and ensured by State Policies. Unfortunately, although Apablaza proposed to promote the relationship between RCCs and kindergartens, to date there has been no progress in this regard.

Finally, the words of the neighbourhood leader highlight the quality education that the CEA children received as a way to bridge the social gap and instal a culture of respect and tolerance for diversity.

FINAL CONSIDERATIONS

The following considerations summarise the main lessons learnt from the CEA experience and then hypothesise about the threats faced by projects of this nature.

This chapter described the implementation of a VTF kindergarten under the ANADIME Corporation, which applied an inclusive-ecological model based on work with educational communities, families and specialised professionals. It is important to note that the subsidy provided by the state through JUNJI made it possible to finance almost in its entirety an establishment with these characteristics. The school had the professional and technical coefficient established by legislation, including, in addition, a full-time special educator. The provision of specialised staff was achieved thanks to the management of strategic alliances with health institutions. However, aspects such as the limitations for the payment of settlements or the subsidy associated with attendance became inhibitors for the permanence of this initiative and led to the closure of the establishment after three years of operation.

Despite its short duration, the CEA experience contributes to the reflection on future educational projects, especially if one takes into consideration that the Chilean regulatory frameworks show a spirit of inclusion in early education, especially ensuring quality education respectful of individual differences for the most vulnerable groups of the population. However, despite the promotion of inclusive education in legal regulations, there are shortcomings in its implementation.

The starting point of CEA's educational project was established on the basis of an institutional culture based on commitment, respect and appreciation of differences. For this reason, the continuous training of the team as a whole was a cornerstone to unify criteria in order to provide the educational support that all children required. As an integral part of the educational community, families and some community representatives also received support and guidance to address diversity and encourage collaboration.

The external support required for a model of this nature was managed through strategic alliances: the CCR of Peñalolén, next to the garden, provided therapeutic treatment for those who required it; ANADIME, as an institution focused on the care of people with intellectual disabilities with a focus on aesthetic education, provided neurological and kinesiological advice and art teachers; not least the support provided by universities that distinguished the CEA as a centre of practice.

Although specialised care was initially provided at the CCR, over time, health professionals began to validate the leadership of the educator and, therefore, accepted intervention in the school context as a way of strengthening rehabilitation work, reducing exclusion from the community culture and ensuring the fulfilment of the educational objectives defined for each child. Although staff and parents were trained or oriented, the specialist's visit to the classroom was still carried out due to its relevance and, in addition, it allowed for the detection of new cases that required assistance. Finally, the on-site intervention of transdisciplinary teams helped to foster constant reflection and exchange of knowledge.

The management of strategic and collaborative alliances between civil society groups and state institutions dedicated to the service of intellectual disabilities in Chile was a big step to break with the traditions and beliefs installed with respect to the incorporation of people with disabilities into the educational system. The change in institutional culture focused on tackling the barriers to learning and participation that exist in the country, making a coordinated use of public and private resources. On the other hand, thanks to transdisciplinary collaboration and internal management, the school's management was able to instal a work philosophy centred on the continuous evaluation of the inclusive-ecological approach, which became a valuable source of information and rectifications.

In terms of teaching-learning strategies, active methodologies were used to promote the inclusion and pedagogical development of all. Specifically, the Reggio Emilia methodology, the project method and aesthetic education were implemented, focusing on providing, in a timely manner, stimuli and experiences that optimise the pedagogical process of boys and girls, favouring access, participation and progress in the educational system.

Finally, it is crucial to highlight the impact of the project on its environment, especially with regard to perceptions of inclusion and acceptance of diversity. The latter are the basis for generating real and significant changes in the attitudes of all those who are part of a community and are fundamental for the transformation of educational spaces and the co-construction of an inclusive culture.

Considering the lessons learnt, two hypotheses are put forward with regard to the threats that projects of this nature face, since 10 years after their closure, work such as that of CEA continues to be informal efforts that come up against state bureaucracy and the slow response of the institutions, which still look at the child as an entity that requires health on the one hand and education on the other in a fragmented manner.

The sustainability of kindergartens with these characteristics is likely to remain a long-term challenge unless public policies are coherent in aligning the discourse of regulatory frameworks with the implementation of educational models. Currently, although government institutions promote a message of inclusion, the allocation of budgets reveals an orientation towards a care policy with a welfare perspective rather than an educational or social inclusion policy. In this context, it is hypothesised that a shift in focus is essential to emphasise the importance of close collaboration between the education and health sectors, supported by a financial subsidy to ensure the technical, skilled and transdisciplinary level required for the inclusive-ecological model. Such a measure could be crucial to successfully address the challenges.

The second hypothesis proposes that fragmented initial teacher education, which lacks an emphasis on interdisciplinary dialogue and collaboration with professionals from diverse disciplines, such as the arts, special education and occupational therapy, hinders the effective implementation of inclusive models in the school environment. The success of inclusive approaches in education depends to a large extent on the promotion of collaborative work, continuous training and the construction of a common language among the various participants in the educational process. In this context, it is imperative to challenge and dismantle the implicit theories rooted in initial training that perceive diversity as a threat rather than a richness, as they act as obstacles when attempting to carry out projects of this type. Unfortunately, in Chile, in general terms, the idea still prevails that children with diagnoses of intellectual disabilities cannot be integrated into regular classrooms, reflecting a lack of understanding of diversity as a valuable resource and a lack of recognition that we are all diverse.

Quality, inclusive education is an achievable reality in early childhood, although it faces significant challenges in terms of institutional biases, funding and teacher training. It is crucial to recognise that, despite these obstacles, inclusive education is presented as a social rather than a purely educational process in which families and communities play a key role in reinforcing and feeding back into pedagogical decisions.

NOTES

1. Law No. 20.845 – On school inclusion that regulates the admission of students, eliminates shared financing and prohibits profit-making in educational establishments that receive state contributions.
2. ANADIME started as the National Association of the Mentally Handicapped, nowadays, it is only known as ANADIME.
3. Testimony used with permission of Susana Matzner.
4. Testimony used with permission of Mitchel Varas.
5. Testimony used with permission of Mónica Apablaza.

REFERENCES

Ainscow, M. (2001). *Desarrollo de escuelas inclusivas: Ideas, propuestas y experiencias para mejorar las instituciones escolares.* Narcea.

Arbones, B. (2005). *Detection, prevention and treatment of learning difficulties.* Ideaspropias Editorial.

Ávila, P. (2011). *User satisfaction and inclusion of children with special educational needs-N.E.E. in two educational centres in La Faena* [unpublished document]. ANADIME.

Blanco, R. (1997). *Integration and educational possibilities. A right for all.* Bulletin 44, Major Project on Education in Latin America and the Caribbean.

Blanco, R., Duk, C., Benteri, B., & Pérez, L. (2003). *Every school is a world, a world of diversity. HINENI Foundation.* OREALC/UNESCO.

Decree 490 Establishes rules for integrating disabled pupils into mainstream schools. (1990, September 3). https://www.bcn.cl/leychile/navegar?idNorma=13743&idVersion=1998-06-23&idParte=

Devia, S. (2017). *Particularidades de la Educación Parvularia. Intendencia de Educación Parvularia.* Superintendencia de Educación/MINEDUC. https://bibliotecadigital.mineduc.cl/bitstream/handle/20.500.12365/17218/Particularidades-Educaci%C3%B3n-Parvularia.pdf?sequence=1

Dueñas Buey, M. L. (2010). Inclusive education. *Revista Española de Orientación y Psicopedagogía, 21*(2), 358–366.

Duk, C., & Murillo, J. (2018). The message of inclusive education is simple, but its implementation is complex. *Latin American Journal of Inclusive Education, 12*(1), 11–13. https://doi.org/10.4067/S0718-73782018000100001

FEAPS. Federación de Organizaciones en Favor de las Personas con Retraso Mental de Madrid. (2001). *Study of reality and proposals for the future of the Feaps-Madrid Early Intervention Centres.* https://plenainclusionmadrid.org/wp-content/uploads/2017/12/EstudioRealidadAtencionTemprana.pdf

FONADIS. Fondo Nacional de la Discapacidad. (2005). *Primer Estudio Nacional de la Discapacidad en Chile. ENDISC - CIF Chile 2004.* Santiago de Chile.

Government of Chile. (2015). *Decree N°83. Aproueba Criterios y Orientaciones de Adecuación Curricular para Estudiantes con Necesidades Educativas Especiales de Educación Parvularia y Educación Básica.* Ministry of Education, Division of General Education. https://especial.mineduc.cl/wp-content/uploads/sites/31/2016/08/Decreto-83-2015.pdf

JUNJI-Galerna Consultores. (2017). *Estudio Sobre Factores Asociados a la Permanencia de los Párvulos en Programas Educativos de la JUNJI - 2017.* https://www.junji.gob.cl/wp-content/uploads/2020/11/eye02.pdf

JUNJI. Junta Nacional de Jardines Infantiles. (2020). *Characterisation Report 2019.* Departamento de Planificación Junta Nacional de Jardines Infantiles (JUNJI). https://www.junji.gob.cl/wp-content/uploads/2020/11/Informe-de-caracterizacion_2019.pdf

Law 20.845 of 2015 on school inclusion that regulates the admission of students, eliminates shared financing and prohibits profit-making in educational establishments that receive state contributions. (2015, June 8). https://www.bcn.cl/leychile/navegar?idNorma=1078172

López, A. L. (2018). *The inclusive school. The right to equity and educational excellence.* Universidad del País Vasco/Euskal Herriko Unibertsitatea, Argitalpen Zerbitzua = Editorial Service. https://addi.ehu.es/bitstream/handle/10810/26837/USPDF188427.pdf?sequence=1&isAllowed=y

Ministry of Education. (2018). *Introductory guide. Educational responses to diversity and special educational needs.* https://especial.mineduc.cl/wp-content/uploads/sites/31/2016/08/201305151517130.GuiaIntroductoria.pdf

Ministry of Education of Costa Rica. (2010). *Abordaje de las Necesidades Educativas Especiales en el aula de Preescolar.* Instituto de Desarrollo Profesional Uladislao Gámez Solano. https://www.mep.go.cr/sites/default/files/recursos/archivo/antologia_necesidades_educativas_especiales_preescolar.pdf

National Institute for Comprehensive Early Childhood Care. (2017). *Identification of warning signs in child development.* Ministry of Education of the Dominican Republic. United Nations Children's Fund (UNICEF).

Parrilla, A. (2002). About the origin and meaning of inclusive education. *Revista de Educación, 327,* 11–29.

PAULA TAPIA SILVA ET AL.

Rubilar, F., & Guzmán, D. (2021). Procesos inclusivos de la educación parvularia desde la mirada de agentes educativas. *Revista Actualidades Investigativas en Educación, 21*(1), 1–28. https://doi.org/10.15517/aie.v21i1.42517

SENADIS. Servicio Nacional de la Discapacidad. (2022). *III Estudio Nacional de la Discapacidad.* https://www.senadis.gob.cl/pag/693/2004/iii_estudio_nacional_de_la_discapacidad

Subsecretaría de Educación Parvularia. (2018). *Bases Curriculares Educación Parvularia.* Ministry of Education of Chile. https://parvularia.mineduc.cl/wp-content/uploads/2019/09/Bases_Curriculares_Ed_Parvularia_2018-1.pdf

UNESCO. (2014). *Parent, family and community involvement in inclusive education.* Booklet 13. https://www.unicef.org/lac/media/7446/file/13.%20Participaci%C3%B3n%20de%20familia%20y%20comunidad.pdf

INCLUSIVE EDUCATION IN THE PLURINATIONAL STATE OF BOLIVIA: FROM DECOLONISATION TO INCLUSION

Chris Forlin[a], Luis Adolfo Machicado Pizarro[b] and Gisselle Gallego[a]

[a]University of Notre Dame Australia, Australia
[b]Unidad Educativa Sagrada Familia, Ecuador

ABSTRACT

This chapter presents a compilation of the historical approach towards inclusive education in the Plurinational State of Bolivia. It describes the regulatory framework, the evolution and status of inclusive education in Bolivia. Consideration is given to legal implications and research that highlights inclusion in practice. A brief case study is provided of how a high school manages inclusion. While the substantial focus in Bolivia has been on the inclusion of indigenous peoples to address prior discrimination and exclusion, limited attention has been given to the inclusion of learners with disability and other special educational needs. The discussion focuses on future directions that need to address more equitable approaches for all learners.

Keywords: Inclusive education; disability; Bolivia; indigenous; diversity; equity

INTRODUCTION

The 2009 Constitution defined Bolivia as a plurinational state and the name of the country was officially changed to the 'Plurinational State of Bolivia' (hereinafter referred to as Bolivia). This was a way of recognising the country's sociocultural diversity and acknowledging the indigenous rights (Tockman & Cameron, 2014). The Constitution also established that the educational system

---

Intercultural and Inclusive Education in Latin America
International Perspectives on Inclusive Education, Volume 24, 67–79
Copyright © 2024 Chris Forlin, Luis Adolfo Machicado Pizarro and Gisselle Gallego
Published under exclusive licence by Emerald Publishing Limited
ISSN: 1479-3636/doi:10.1108/S1479-363620240000024005

should be plurilingual and inter and intracultural. The new constitution was led by the country's first indigenous president, Evo Morales. This saw the beginning of a new political, social and economic direction for the Andean nation (Radhuber, 2012). Bolivia is a multicultural South American country with a population of 12 million (The World Bank, 2021b); it is one of the most multi-ethnic countries worldwide (Klein, 2022). Almost half (41%) of the population over 15 years of age is of indigenous origin. It is also one of the least developed countries in the region with one of the highest levels of income inequality in Latin America (Bohoslavsky, 2020; Carvajal et al., 2019). Bolivia also has high levels of poverty, six out of 10 Bolivians (about 5.8 million people) are poor and four out of 10 (3.9 million people) people live below the poverty line (UNDP, 2022). In 2021, Bolivia had a gross domestic product (GDP) of US $40,408 million (The World Bank, 2021a).

Discrimination and exclusion have been commonplace in the history of Bolivia (Callisaya Argani, 2021; Lopes Cardozo, 2012). Education during colonial times was used as a method of subordination and control. It excluded indigenous people and promoted discrimination against cultures and languages (Lopes Cardozo, 2012). The 2010 (Law No. 70) Avelino Sinani Elizardo Perez (ASEP) education reform (Ministerio de Educación -Estado Plurinacional de Bolivia, 2010) has been described as a step to end centuries of inequitable education and cultural colonialism (Cajías de la Vega, 2013). The Law recognised and included indigenous languages, knowledge and values (Lopes Cardozo, 2012). It also highlighted the need for education to be 'inclusive' for all Bolivians. Furthermore, it aimed to satisfy the interests and expectations of every citizen, including people with disability.

EDUCATION IN BOLIVIA

In 2020, 6.1% of Bolivia's GDP was allocated to education (World Data Atlas, n.d.). In that same year, it was reported that approximately 95% of Bolivian children aged 6–11-years old were enroled in primary school (Andersen et al., 2020). Irrespective of their ethnicity, income and gender, it appears the Avelino Siñani Elizardo Pérez' (ASEP) education reform has been successful at getting most children (not necessarily those with disabilities) through primary and secondary education (Andersen et al., 2020). Over the past three decades, there have been huge improvements in a number of education areas in Bolivia. For example, in 1976, the illiteracy rate was 36.21% but by 2015 that figure had fallen to 7.54% of the population (Muyor-Rodríguez et al., 2021). The ASEP education reform also established the Plurinational Education System (SEP for its acronym in Spanish); this system is divided into three subsystems: the regular 'mainstream', the alternative and special education and the vocational higher education (Ministerio de Educación -Estado Plurinacional de Bolivia, 2018).

Despite the success of the education reform at improving access to education to make it more equitable, inclusive and collaborative, the quality of Bolivian education is uncertain. In many ways, this is due to the lack of statistical data on education outcomes. For the last two decades, Bolivia has not taken part in any of the international standardised tests, usually conducted by organisations like the Organisation for Economic Co-operation and Development's Programme for International Student Assessment (PISA) or the International Energy Agency's Trends in International Mathematics & Science Study (TIMSS). Bolivia last participated in an international education achievement test in 1997. Furthermore, it is one of the few countries in the Americas that has not been included in the World Bank's new Human Capital Index or the Global Database on Education Quality, 1965–2015 (Andersen et al., 2020).

THE NATIONAL PLAN FOR EQUALITY AND EQUALISATION OF OPPORTUNITIES FOR PERSONS WITH DISABILITIES (PNIEO)

The recognition of the rights of people with disability and the first laws and regulations against exclusion were recognised in April 2006, with establishing the National Plan for Equality and Equalisation of Opportunities for Persons with Disabilities (PNIEO for its acronym in Spanish). This plan focused on equal opportunity and conditions for people regardless of their gender, ethnicity or disability (Stang Alva, 2011). The decree specifically stated that children and young people with disability (it did not include adults) should be able to attend their local mainstream school.

PEOPLE WITH DISABILITY

According to the Bolivian Constitution, people with disability have the right to comprehensive and free health care and education. The state should guarantee and promote education for children and adolescents with a disability, or gifted students under the same principles, structure and values of the education system (UN Committee on the Rights of Persons with Disabilities [CRPD], 2011). In 2012, the General Law for Persons with Disabilities (Supreme Decree No. 1893) defined inclusive education as one that '... responds to diversity through physical and curricular adaptations and support personnel, seeking greater participation in learning, cultures and communities to reduce exclusion from education' (Estado Plurinacional de Bolivia. Asamblea Legislativa Plurinacional, 2012, p 11.)

While the exact number of people with disabilities in Bolivia is unknown, the latest available national census undertaken in 2012 identified 342.929 people, which equates to around 3.4% of the Bolivian population as living with a disability (Ministerio de Salud y Deportes [MSyD], 2012). To address this issue, between 2006 and 2011 the Ministry of Health, with support from the Japan International Cooperation Agency (JICA), implemented the Single National Registry of People with Disabilities (PRUNPCD for its name in Spanish).

People with disability in Bolivia face several specific challenges, including social and economic exclusion. They have higher levels of poverty and experience widespread prejudice (Murillo Lafuente & Sherry, 2021; Muyor-Rodríguez et al., 2021). There are minimal efforts being made to eliminate social (in education and employment) and physical or structural (roads, buildings and lighting) barriers (Murillo Lafuente & Sherry, 2021; Ramírez et al., 2020). In 2021, attitudes towards people with disability in Bolivia were still considered to be negative, with continued stigmatisation and discrimination (Muyor-Rodríguez et al., 2021).

When a child with a disability turns five (the age at which compulsory education begins in Bolivia), they should have access to a place in a public mainstream school. According to research by the Bolivian Ombudsman's Office in 2020, however, the learning environments are not suitable for the needs of students with disabilities. The research found that 69% of the mainstream schools do not have ramps, 72% lack pedestrian crossings at the entrance of the buildings, 82% do not have adequate bathrooms for students with disability and 92% do not have support rails. They also identified that there was a lack of appropriate accommodations or effectively trained staff (Defensoría del Pueblo Bolivia, 2022). There are many structural barriers, including a lack of inclusive policies, a lack of trained teachers, a lack of infrastructure, and very limited economic and teaching resources (Defensoría del Pueblo Bolivia, 2022). A further 2022 report from the Ombudsman's Office of Bolivia found that only 65% of the 90,631 people with disabilities registered in the PRUNPCD (shows that only a small percentage of people identified in the census with disability are enroled in the PRUNPCD), did not have access to education or only accessed education at primary levels. Based on these data, 27,025 people, who represent 30% of registered people with disabilities, do not have any degree of educational instruction. Further, 31,507, who mean 35%, only attended primary level of schooling. In addition, of the total, only 13,310 or 15% reached secondary school (Defensoría del Pueblo Bolivia, 2022). Since only a small percentage of people with disabilities are registered in the PRUNPCD the numbers could potentially be lower.

In 2019, it was reported that children aged 6–11 years with a disability were less likely to attend school (Hincapié et al., 2019). This report also found that children with a disability have difficulties staying in school and completing their education. An investigation carried out by the Bolivian Ombudsman's Office showed that the current education system segregates and excludes people with disability. It does so by allowing the coexistence of two subsystems, one for regular mainstream education and the other for alternative and special education. The latter is exclusive for people with disability, which seems to imply that segregation against this population group is legitimised (Defensoría del Pueblo Bolivia, 2022). Discrimination and lack of access to education indicate children with disability are trapped in a loop of inequality; when they reach adulthood they also have fewer employment opportunities, and are further discriminated, which leads to poverty. This creates a circle between education and poverty with persistent inequalities and inequities (World Bank, 2018)

SPECIAL EDUCATION CENTRES IN BOLIVIA

The alternative and special education subsystem is the educational response to students with disability, learning difficulties and those with extraordinary talent, whose education can be provided directly by special education centres and indirectly by supporting inclusive education institutions, multi-sector integral centres or mainstream schools (de la Cruz Aliaga, 2021). In this subsystem special education target populations are people with disability who require permanent or temporary support in the educational processes, students with learning difficulties and students with extraordinary talent (Ministerio de Educación -Estado Plurinacional de Bolivia, 2012). The Vice Ministry of Alternative and Special Education oversees this subsystem.

In 2020, there were 178 public and 35 private special education centres in Bolivia (Ministerio de Educación -Estado Plurinacional de Bolivia, 2020). These centres were financed by the government through taxes. In 2020, the alternative and special education system was standardised by the Ministry of Education Ministerial Resolution No. 001. The main goal was to include privately run special education centres (18% of the total centres) in the main education system. This was seen as a mechanism to ensure the quality of the services provided by the centre and to mandate that once a student is enroled in an inclusive education unit, they are simultaneously enroled in a special education centre where they will receive support from a technical/pedagogical support teacher (Ministerio de Educación -Estado Plurinacional de Bolivia, 2020).

Some special education centres in Bolivia are operated by non-government organisations (NGOs) (de la Cruz Aliaga, 2021). Besides providing services, NGOs also serve as training institutions for therapists, especially in rural areas (Kindernothilfe, 2022). Some special education centres also provide other services such as physiotherapy, psychology, speech pathology, and rehabilitation. Some of the students attending these centres also attend mainstream schools (Ministerio de Educación -Estado Plurinacional de Bolivia, 2012).

EDUCATION REFORM TOWARDS INCLUSION

Following the PNIEO, in 2010, the ASEP education reform was established. This Law acknowledged the diversity of the population that lives in Bolivia. It stated that inclusive education was to be based on recognising Bolivian diversity (intracultural, intercultural and multilingual), and referred to the right of all people to access education, regardless of their condition and situation. The reform focused on timely access to education based on people's needs and expectations.

The ASEP education reform recognised that there were several disadvantaged groups in terms of access to education. This included indigenous people, people with disability and people living in rural areas. One of the main pillars of this reform was decolonising education (Lopes Cardozo, 2012; Muyor-Rodríguez et al., 2021), and not leaving anyone behind. The ultimate aim was seen to be peoples 'living well' ('vivir bien'). This was described in Article 13.3 (Ministerio de Educación -Estado Plurinacional de Bolivia, 2010) as '...the values of unity, equality, inclusion, dignity, freedom, solidarity, reciprocity, respect, complementarity, harmony, openness, balance, equal opportunities, social and gender equity in participation, welfare, responsibility, social justice, distribution and redistribution of social goods and products to live well.' (p 7)

While expecting that students '... learn, to appreciate, and to respect the myriad forms of diversity present in the classroom among teachers, professors, and their peers' (Cortina & Earl, 2020, p. 3), diversity remains mainly considered from the perspective of cultural differences; with little recognition of other forms of diversity such as disability. The term disability is usually represented with the presentation of a person in a wheelchair or with Down syndrome and seen in a negative or derogatory light.

Despite the Law promoting inclusive education and supporting children to be enroled in mainstream schools (Ministerio de Educación -Estado Plurinacional de Bolivia, 2010), what has been reported is that schools still segregate students with disability. They are taught at different times and as a separate group (Defensoría del Pueblo Bolivia, 2022). The appropriate accommodations are not provided, and schools are not prepared to include students with disability in mainstream classrooms (Cordeiro et al., 2021).

ACCESS TO HIGHER EDUCATION

In 2009, to promote access to university by potentially vulnerable groups, Resolution no. 9/09 of the National Congress of Universities established a direct admission option. For students with disabilities, and members of identified socioeconomic or ethnic groups, access was allowed without the need for admission tests. Although such policies in education have significantly improved access to higher education in recent years, access to university education for those with functional diversity remains difficult (Muyor-Rodríguez et al., 2021). Students with disabilities identified '... a persistent lack of practical implementation of the education policies' (p. 13), as presenting a major challenge to their inclusion in higher education. Conclusions draw by the research of Muyor-Rodríguez et al., 2021 was that: 'The theoretical construction of the diversity paradigm does not embrace multiple realities but rather a particular and limited vision of those oppressed groups that have had greater political protagonism' (p. 15).

Disability in Bolivia remains as a negative and limiting condition for many people. Whereby the underlying principles of a truly inclusive society relate to equity and equality for all, these concepts do not seem to apply to people with disabilities seeking to attend higher education in Bolivia (Muyor-Rodríguez et al., 2021).

TEACHER PREPARATION FOR INCLUSION

In earlier years, teacher education in Bolivia was completely foreign-driven (Lopes Cardozo, 2012, 2013). A transition to a Bolivian directed teacher training programme in the 1990s resulted in greater clarity and expected consistency of approaches. In supporting the socio-educational change following the ASEP, a further crucial step has been seen as the transformation of pre-service teacher education in Bolivia's Normales. There are four types of recognised teachers in Bolivia: normal teachers (normalistas), senior teachers (titulares por antigüedad), interim teachers (interinos) and graduate teachers (egresados). Normal teachers have a professional certificate that allows them to teach at all levels in the school system and they receive their pedagogical training in higher education normal institutes (INS, Institutos Normales Superiores) (Bürgi, 2019).

Teacher education was first established under the 1994 reform with the consistency expected of training being six semesters long, organised in both urban and rural Normales and with a concentration of decision-making power at the Ministry of Education (Lopes Cardozo, 2012, 2013). Since 2006, a further radical restructuring of Bolivian society occurred. As part of this process, education was reorganised around four pillars (Lopes Cardozo, 2012, 2013):

(1) decolonisation,
(2) intra- and inter-culturalism together with plurilingualism,
(3) productive education, and
(4) communitarian education.

The General Law for Persons with Disabilities (Article 11) established that the Ministry of Education would ensure that teachers were trained with a focus on inclusive education, giving priority to the Braille system, alternative language, Bolivian Sign Language and curricular adaptations to accommodate students with disability (Estado Plurinacional de Bolivia. Asamblea Legislativa Plurinacional, 2012). The state was also required to ensure that there were multidisciplinary teams for the support and inclusion of people with disability in the education system.

Initially, this involved training provided by NGOs and international agencies. For example, between 2010 and 2013 the JICA and the Ministry of Education conducted the 'Teachers Training in Special Needs Education' project. In many ways this mimicked colonial ways as overseas based NGOs as well as donor agencies would send high-income country 'experts' to low-income countries to offer 'technical assistance' when they might know little about the problems around inclusion or attitudes towards people with disability. An analysis of 17 universities that offered education in 2022 found that offering teacher training for 'special education' (educacion especial) and special inclusive education (educacion especial inclusive) varied. One university offered a six semester Higher Technical Diploma (Diploma de Técnico Superior) for teachers, and another offered a nine semester Bachelor's degree (Licenciatura). In addition, private colleges offered a variety of courses as complementary training programs for pre- and in-service teachers in practice (Cursos de especialidad).

Due to the nature of the students attending schools in Bolivia, where almost half of the population is of indigenous origin, the needs of teachers providing an inclusive approach to education remains focused on this one diverse group. Much of the professional development offered for teachers by the universities, therefore, concentrates on the preparation of indigenous teachers to support the inclusion of bilingual children learning in their own local languages (Cortina & Earl, 2020). Research by the Bolivian Ombudsman's Office concluded that educators do not have the necessary foundations to implement an inclusive education, so much so that many of them believe that including is the same as integrating (Defensoría del Pueblo Bolivia, 2022).

THE CASE OF UNIDAD EDUCATIVA 'SAGRADA FAMILIA' HUAJCHILLA PRINCIPAL MR LUIS ADOLFO MACHICADO PIZARRO (MR LUIS M)

The second author of this chapter, Mr Luis M, is a principal of a school in the Municipality of Mecapaca (La Paz Department), in the town of Huajchilla, in Bolivia. This brief example highlights inclusion from the perspective of his school.

Mr Luis M has been at this school for 26 years. He was a teacher for 14 years and has been a principal for the last 12 years. The school population is made up of long-term settlers and new arrivals who come because of the good climate and availability of work. As the area has begun a trend of having large houses there is a new group of migrants coming from the nearby city of El Alto. Most of the population has an Aymara background. The Aymara ('Aimara') are a group of indigenous people who live mostly in the Andean highlands of Bolivia and Peru. They are the second largest indigenous group in Bolivia.

The children come from 18 different communities within the Mecapaca municipality. The school has Pre-Kinder, Kinder, primary and secondary levels. In 2022, the approximate number of students was 779 with 105 in kinder, 350 in primary and 320 in secondary. Due to the progressive diversity of the population, the social structure of the community is changing. While grandparents/parents may retain the customary modes of the Aymara, the children mainly speak Spanish and no longer follow the traditions. Their parents work in a range of sectors such as transport, agriculture, floriculture and increasingly in commercialisation. Locally grown products, such as vegetables, especially corn, and flowers, are sold in the city markets. Locally mined aggregates, such as sand, gravel, and stone, are transported to supply centres.

There is a small number of students with disability in his school. Some are registered and thus can receive free health care and 50% discount on transport, whereas others are not. To be registered means that the child has a clinical certificate stating the type of disability and then receives a 'Disability ID'. The children have different types of disabilities such as autism, physical disability including paraplegia and traumatic brain injury. At present, following extensive coordination between the school and the District Directorate of Education, the school is hoping to open a Special Education Centre in Yupampa also in the Municipality of Mecapaca. While there is now a dedicated space, as yet they do not have any staff to work there, or any resources. All students with disability attending his school are, therefore, integrated into the regular education classes. To assist the teachers to support these students, they have received some orientation training in developing a complementary curriculum that provides adaptations to meet the student's specific needs. The principal reports several success stories where the students have been included in regular classrooms and continue with their studies with support from teachers.

Developing and maintaining a sense of community has been of critical importance to becoming an inclusive school. The cooperation between teachers and parents, without competition, is allowing the school to develop a complimentary approach for supporting the diverse nature of the school and its students. The focus on sustaining this over time has been achieved through consistency in the type of activities the school provides and the actions they take. According to the principal, the school's vision for enacting this complimentary approach to inclusion is through a cooperative style '. . . having an opportunity, making our students, parents, our teachers themselves glimpse that opportunity in that horizon of life. We are Aymaras, there are principles that we already have through the oral tradition of our elders, the experiences within our families'. The school principal provides five levels which he referred to as 'moments' for their aspiration to become inclusive:

(1) There is a moment of awakening.
(2) There is a second moment where everyone searches.
(3) A third moment where one appropriates it.
(4) A fourth moment where one begins to act upon all that they have awakened and begins to live it.
(5) A fifth moment is when one communicates from experience, from their continuous and permanent doing and articulates this for others to understand.

Needless, the principal highlights several key challenges presented by inclusive education in his school. The first is to be able to harmonise and balance life consensus by nurturing life and letting oneself be nurtured by it. The second is to support the Aymara concept of 'Good Living' (the suma qamaña) and to maintain a passion for what we do. He likens this to the following Aymara analogy:

Walking all these years, we have not planted, we have not done, we have not contributed a grain of sand because we have passed through the Atacama Desert, and there are many grains of sand and there is not a single plant. But we have seen the Altiplano that there is green, then we have provided a seed so that it falls on fertile ground, and we know that in some places it will grow.

76   *Education in the Plurinational State of Bolivia*

A further challenge was that once classes enroled students with disabilities some were subject to bullying. This has represented a big learning curve for the regular students and the teachers have worked hard to explain that all students can learn from each other. Based upon a sense of community, and the concepts of family in the Aymara way of life, they have been able to develop a sense of belonging and acceptance for them.

An essential component of becoming an inclusive school is seen as the need for having and expressing affection. And through being empathetic with all students and their families, the school's philosophy is to understand and relate to all students and their parents as human beings, so they can join and through words of encouragement feel accepted. Through this they aim to include all learners so they can complete their study with their peers. The principal's concluding comment summed up for him and his school what inclusive education means in Bolivia:

> I would like to be able to share this message with you. It comes from our elders and says *"Jan p'iqi amtasa, chuyma thakhin sarantanani"* (translated this means *without losing our reason let's walk the path of the heart*). This is the concept of inclusive education in Bolivia. In other words, the peoples have understood that linking ourselves with the mind to the heart, we do not need to lose our mind, because that is part of the legality and we need to link it to legitimacy, which is the sensitivity of the heart.

This case study highlights the importance of indigenous beliefs and culture in education and the decolonisation of education in Bolivia. This is supported by the change in the constitution described before that acknowledged the indigenous rights. The concepts of duality, complementarity and reciprocity seen as the ordering principles of the Aymara cosmos are unique to the culture. In theory this model supports a more inclusive education for groups who have been marginalised such as indigenous people and people with disability, who have been discriminated and face social barriers and victims of prejudice. Local initiatives such as this one can serve as a springboard for changes at the National level.

CONCLUSION

Considering the need for Bolivia to align with the global movement towards Education for All, '... since the 1990s, and with the return of democracy, education policies in Bolivia have shifted from historically homogenising and modernising types of schooling to a more emancipatory form of education' (Lopes Cardozo, 2013, p. 21). Nevertheless, defining itself as a multi-ethnic and pluricultural nation, Bolivia's focus on educational inclusion remains mainly centred on indigenous communities. Unlike explanations of inclusion in many countries, which focus on a broader and more encompassing understanding, including people with a range of diverse needs and disabilities, other forms of diversity are not so strongly consolidated in Bolivia (Muyor-Rodríguez et al., 2021).

Although a more consistent approach to teacher preparation has been established in Bolivia, there remains concern regarding the lack of appropriately locally trained and experienced educators who can prepare teachers for inclusion. The case study by Mr Luis M. provides an important insight into the practical challenges faced by schools in Bolivia when attempting to upskill teachers. He identifies issues that pose significant challenges to principals aiming to improve staff attitudes, understandings, and skills for implementing inclusive education in their schools. One of the major challenges he highlights continues to be reliance on external 'experts'. Being widely used to train or up skill teachers, with limited knowledge of schools in Bolivia, the type of practices that occur and the understanding of teachers' expectation regarding inclusive education, it is difficult for these overseas presenters to provide appropriate contextualised training. This is further heightened by the emphasis on training teachers to include the bicultural population of learners in Bolivia, to the extent of almost ignoring other groups of potentially excluded or disenfranchised children. Even though the rights of people with disability were established in Law in 2006, with the expectation that all children should be able to attend a mainstream school, this has not been widely enacted. Minimal attention has been given to identifying and removing social and physical barriers to schools and higher education.

The current Law in Bolivia would seem to provide the necessary guidelines to achieve the ultimate aim of valuing unity, equity and inclusion for all. To date there has been a dedicated emphasis on establishing a plurinational educational system to overcome the previous colonial discriminatory and exclusive system. Nevertheless, the focus remains on including the major group of indigenous learners. As this has become better established, it is critical now to consider other groups such as children with disabilities and learning difficulties, who are still experiencing major and widely spread forms of exclusion.

REFERENCES

Andersen, L. E., Medinaceli, A., Maldonado, C., & Hernani-Limarino, W. (2020). *A country at risk of being left behind: Bolivia's quest for quality education.* Occasional Paper Series (63).

Bohoslavsky, J. P. (2020). Development and human rights in Bolivia: Advances, contradictions, and challenges. *Latin American Policy, 11*(1), 126–147. https://doi.org/10.1111/lamp.12181

Bürgi, J. (2019). *KOF Education System Factbook: Bolivia.* https://www.dcdualvet.org/wp-content/uploads/2019_KOF_Factbook-Education-System-BOLIVIA.pdf

Cajías de la Vega, B. (2013). Las propuestas de cambio educativo en Bolivia (1994–2010). *Revista Ciencia y Cultura, 17,* 9–34. http://www.scielo.org.bo/scielo.php?script=sci_arttext&pid=S2077-33232013000100002&nrm=iso

Callisaya Argani, J. I. (2021). Historias de vida para sensibilizar el aprendizaje de la Educación Inclusiva en la carrera de Educación. *Fides et Ratio - Revista de Difusión cultural y científica de la Universidad La Salle en Bolivia, 22,* 129–143. http://www.scielo.org.bo/scielo.php?script=sci_arttext&pid=S2071-081X2021000200008&nrm=iso

Carvajal, C. R., Rodríguez, M. A., & Cuartas, B. M. (2019). Determinants of income inequality reduction in the Latin American countries. *CEPAL Review No. 126, December 2018, 79.* https://hdl.handle.net/11362/44559

Cordeiro, N., Sebastián-Heredero, E., & Mirandola-Garcia, P. H. (2021). Panorama social y educativo de las personas con discapacidad en Bolivia. *Educação em debate em novos tempos: políticas e práticas.*

Cortina, R., & Earl, A. K. (2020). Advancing professional development for teachers in intercultural education. *Education Sciences, 10*(12).

de la Cruz Aliaga, C. (2021). La educación especial e inclusiva desde la educación popular. *Padres y Maestros/Journal of Parents and Teachers, 388,* 60–66.

Defensoría del Pueblo Bolivia. (2022). *Informe Defensorial - La exclusion y segregacion de las personas con discapacidad en el sistema educativo plurinacional.* Adjuntoria para la defensa y cumplimiento de los derechos humanos. https://www.defensoria.gob.bo/uploads/files/informe-defensorial-la-exclusion-y-segregacion-de-las-personas-con-discapacidad-en-el-sistema-educativo-plurinacional.pdf

Estado Plurinacional de Bolivia. Asamblea Legislativa Plurinacional. (2012). *Ley No 223: Ley General para Personas con Discapacidad.* https://www.comunicacion.gob.bo/sites/default/files/dale_vida_a_tus_derechos/archivos/LEY%20223%20ACTUALIZACION%202018%20WEB.pdf

Hincapié, D., Duryea, S., & Hincapié, I. (2019). *Education for all: Advancing disability inclusion in Latin America and the Caribbean.* Inter-American Development Bank. http://doi.org/10.18235/0001673.

Kindernothilfe. (2022). Aurelio is on his way to a brighter future. *Kindernothilfe.* https://www.kindernothilfe.org/Worldwide+Programming/Projects+and+Countries/Latin+America+and+the+Caribbean/Bolivia/Project+Example_+Children+with+disabilities-p-958.html. Accessed on November 21.

Klein, H. S. (2022). *A concise history of Bolivia* (3rd ed.). Cambridge University Press.

Lopes Cardozo, M. T. A. (2012). Transforming pre-service teacher education in Bolivia: From indigenous denial to decolonisation? *Compare: A Journal of Comparative and International Education, 42*(5), 751–772. https://doi.org/10.1080/03057925.2012.696040

Lopes Cardozo, M. T. A. (2013). Turbulence in Bolivia's normales: Teacher education as a socio-political battlefield. *Prospects, 43*(1), 17–34. https://doi.org/10.1007/s11125-012-9256-4

Ministerio de Educación -Estado Plurinacional de Bolivia. (2018). *Ministerio de Educación del Estado Plurinacional de Bolivia.* Ministerio de Educación. http://www.minedu.gob.bo/pages/ministeriode-educacion-bolivia.html. Accessed on December 13.

Ministerio de Salud y Deportes (MSyD). (2012). *Metodología e Instrumentos Oficiales del Programa de Registro Único Nacional de Personas con Discapacidad.* http://www.siprunpcd.sns.gob.bo

Ministerio de Educación -Estado Plurinacional de Bolivia. (2020). *Ministerio de Educación garantiza la regularización de Centros Privados de Educación Especial.* https://www.minedu.gob.bo/index.php?option=com_content&view=article&id=4444&catid=182&Itemid=854

Ministerio de Educación -Estado Plurinacional de Bolivia. (2010). *Ley no. 70 de Educación ASEP - Revolucion en la Education.* https://siteal.iiep.unesco.org/sites/default/files/sit_accion_files/ley_70-2010.pdf

Ministerio de Educación -Estado Plurinacional de Bolivia. (2012). *La Educación Especial en Bolivia Un estudio sobre su situación actual.* https://www.minedu.gob.bo/files/publicaciones/veaye/LIBRO-ESPECIAL.pdf

Murillo Lafuente, E., & Sherry, M. (2021). Disability in Bolivia: A feminist global south perspective. In C. Figueroa & D. I. Hernández-Saca (Eds.), *Dis/ability in the Americas: The intersections of education, power, and identity* (pp. 135–165). Springer International Publishing. https://doi.org/10.1007/978-3-030-56942-6_7

Muyor-Rodríguez, J., Fuentes-Gutiérrez, V., De la Fuente-Robles, Y. M., & Amezcua-Aguilar, T. (2021). Inclusive university education in Bolivia: The Actors and their discourses. *Sustainability, 13*(19), 10818. https://www.mdpi.com/2071-1050/13/19/10818

Radhuber, I. M. (2012). Indigenous struggles for a Plurinational State: An analysis of Indigenous rights and competences in Bolivia. *Journal of Latin American Geography, 11*(2), 167–193. https://doi.org/10.1353/lag.2012.0035

Ramírez, I., Maldonado, C., & Villacorta, R. (2020). De la Jaula al Aula abierta: Niños con discapacidad. *Infancias: Discapacidad e interseccionalidades, 3*(3), 1–7.

Stang Alva, M. F. (2011). *Las personas con discapacidad en América Latina: del reconocimiento jurídico a la desigualdad real.* Cepal.

The World Bank. (2021a). *GDP (current US$) - Latin America & Caribbean.* https://data.worldbank.org/indicator/NY.GDP.MKTP.CD?locations=ZJ

The World Bank. (2021b). *Population total - Bolivia.* https://data.worldbank.org/country/BO

Tockman, J., & Cameron, J. (2014). Indigenous autonomy and the contradictions of Plurinationalism in Bolivia. *Latin American Politics and Society*, *56*(3), 46–69. https://doi.org/10.1111/j.1548-2456.2014.00239.x

UN Committee on the Rights of Persons with Disabilities (CRPD). (2011). *Consideration of reports submitted by States parties under article 35 of the convention, initial reports of States parties due in 2011: Plurinational State of Bolivia*. https://documents-dds-ny.un.org/doc/UNDOC/GEN/G15/219/61/PDF/G1521961.pdf?OpenElement

UNDP. (2022). *Human development report 2021–22*. UNDP (United Nations Development Programme. http://report.hdr.undp.org

World Bank. (2018). *Poverty and shared prosperity 2018: Piecing together the poverty puzzle* (1464813302) https://documents1.worldbank.org/curated/en/104451542202552048/pdf/Poverty-and-Shared-Prosperity-2018-Piecing-Together-the-Poverty-Puzzle.pdf

World Data Atlas. (n.d.). *Bolivia - Current expenditure on education as a share of gross national income, 1960–2021*. https://knoema.com/atlas/Bolivia/topics/Education/Expenditures-on-Education/Expenditure-on-education-as-a-share-of-GNI

TRAINING TEACHERS FOR INCLUSIVE EDUCATION IN COLOMBIA: FROM POLICY TO PRACTICE

Gloria Calvo

National Pedagogical University, Colombia

ABSTRACT

A teacher for educational inclusion requires training to cater for difference and competences to identify and remove barriers in order to guarantee the right to education for their students. Thus, this chapter initially addresses the relationship between education, inclusion and teaching in order, in the second section, to show the main guidelines that Colombian regulations propose for social inclusion and teacher training for social inclusion through education. The third section presents three cases that illustrate innovative proposals for teacher training for educational inclusion and ends by analysing the main teaching competences for this purpose.

Keywords: Inclusive education; teacher training; education case study; education Colombia; legislation Colombia; pedagogical innovation

FROM INCLUSIVE EDUCATION TO QUALITY EDUCATION FOR ALL

Colombia is a country with great economic inequality and high social segregation, making it one of the most unequal countries in the world and the second most unequal in Latin America, a situation exacerbated by the massive migration of foreigners, the increase in climate change and the Covid-19 pandemic (World Bank, 2022). Although for several decades there have been policy formulations aimed at social and educational inclusion, exclusion associated with regional differences by educational sectors among other multiple factors – social, cultural and economic – is present in Colombian society (Camargo Muñoz, 2018).[1]

An education for all people without exception requires a broader understanding of the diversity of communities and contexts, their magnitude and complexity with respect to guaranteeing the right to education and its educational relevance, as well as ensuring complete, timely and diverse educational trajectories for all.[2] In this perspective, inclusion and equity processes are the way to make structural and systemic changes that guarantee the right to education for all people in the country.

This power to be and to do from education leads to the recognition that inclusion is a process, and that inclusive education is the path to a better future in order to transform ways of thinking and acting in diversity. From the perspective of inclusive education, the Colombian education system needs not only clear definitions of what inclusion and equity mean, but also attitudes and responses to diversity. If the paradigm is that all students count equally, the purpose is to learn to capitalise on difference.

Colombia has made significant progress in this regard by moving from a policy of attention to populations, understood as isolated actions for native ethnic groups, Afro-descendants, the Rom and people in vulnerable situations, to one that proposes quality education as a right in a perspective of the development of human capacities. Similarly, it has policies that seek territorial integration to guarantee this right to address the specific conditions of each region of the country, so that all regions have budgets allocated for educational inclusion programmes. However, there are still major inequalities that prevent the Sustainable Development Goals (SDGs) from being fully met (United Nations [UN], 2022a, 2022b), specifically the fourth goal, which calls for highly qualified teachers to guarantee education as a right for all regardless of their origin. In this context, teacher competences for inclusive education are of great importance.

The interest of this chapter is to show how in Colombia there are conditions that make it possible to advance in the training of teacher competences for educational inclusion based on educational standards and innovation; however, there is a lack of a national educational policy to explicitly formulate this purpose. Returning to some innovations related to teacher training for educational inclusion makes it possible to recover lessons learnt for this purpose.

Methodologically, this chapter is a qualitative analysis based on a documentary review of both the regulations on inclusion in the country and some research reports carried out by the author on teacher training for educational inclusion in the last decade (Orealc/Unesco, 2018). The cases are constructed as an alternative to recover innovative experiences in order to illustrate other responses to educational exclusion from local proposals that can inspire policy guidelines for all regions of the country in order to guarantee the right to education.[3]

REGULATIONS ON INCLUSIVE EDUCATION IN COLOMBIA

Colombia is a clear example of the existence of advanced legislation to provide education that includes its entire population. However, as is the case in most Latin American countries, it has great difficulty in translating legislation into sectoral policies and, even more so, into pedagogical practices that guarantee quality education for all school-age children and young people. In order to illustrate this assertion, the following sections present the main regulations in this regard.

The Political Constitution of Colombia (1991) recognises education as a fundamental right and as a public service with a social orientation. Education is a guarantee for the enjoyment of future benefits, both individual and collective. The two fundamental principles of the Constitutional Charter serve as a general framework for a more situated understanding of the meaning of inclusion and equity in education in the Colombian social rule of law. The first of these is equality before the law, without any discrimination and with the recognition of the dignity of every human being (Article 13), and the second is the plurality of the State, which recognises ethnic and cultural diversity, and obliges its protection (Articles 7 and 8).

The universality of education for all people empowers them to fully exercise other social, economic, cultural and environmental rights, and is a basic condition for the recognition of their dignity and for the establishment of social justice. Finally, education is a guarantee for the enjoyment of both individual and collective future benefits. In this sense, Ruling T881 of 2002 of the Constitutional Court contributes to specifying that education is a fundamental condition for each person to be able to design a life plan in accordance with their characteristics (to live as they wish) and to maintain their physical and moral integrity, that is, to live without humiliation.

Inclusion and equity in education can therefore be developed as principles (statements), approaches (perspectives) or strategies (means) of education policy. However, they are best defined as processes, i.e. as sets of phases, operations or tasks that are closely related and developed continuously, systematically and in co-responsibility of the state with society for the transformation of the education system as a whole.

Education Policy on Inclusion

In 2020, the Ministry of National Education (MEN) issued Circular 020 (MEN, 2020), which expresses the National Government's intention that children, adolescents, young people and adults should have a quality education in an education system that promotes complete educational trajectories, comprehensive development and the achievement of learning, as well as social mobility and the consolidation of life projects.

Circular 020 takes up what is defined in Decree 1421 (MEN, 2017) and Sentence T-051 2011 of the Constitutional Court of Colombia (2011) by indicating that the country must move from segregated education to inclusive education where all girls, boys, adolescents, young people and adults can study, learn and live together, without any exclusion, so that teaching processes are adapted to students and not students to teaching, and that educational establishments respond in a relevant way to the characteristics of their development.

These actions are consistent with the Guidelines of the Policy of Inclusion and Equity in Education – Education for all people without exception (Saldarriaga Concha Foundation, 2021), presented in July 2021 to transform policies, practices and cultures so that all people enjoy the right to education under equal conditions and opportunities. Although this document is not about teacher training, it points out elements of relevance for teacher training, in aspects such as the dimension of practices, as it concretises policies in situated and contextualised interventions, mediated by culture.

In general terms, all regulations oriented towards diversity stipulate that teacher training is a priority for its implementation and whose main interest is to combat the exclusionary and discriminatory logics and dynamics that have been naturalised in social, cultural and, of course, educational contexts, a situation referred to in the previous footnotes.

Education Policy on Inclusion in Teacher Education

More specifically, the Quality Guidelines for bachelor's degrees in education (MEN, 2014) establish conceptual foundations, policy guidelines and strategies, which are based on the understanding of inclusive education as the ability to enhance and value diversity (understanding and protecting the particularities of all students), promote respect for being different and guarantee the participation of the community within an intercultural structure in educational processes. Inclusive education transcends the strictly academic and curricular to focus on the very constitution of the social, with the central aim of examining barriers to learning and participation across the education system.

With regard to the curricula for initial teacher training, Resolution 02041 of Ministry of National Education, 2016 specifically states that, in the didactics of disciplines, teachers must be familiar with the preconceptions and difficulties that students tend to have in the appropriation of specific disciplinary subjects. The pedagogy and educational sciences component specify as a requirement an understanding of the context and the physical, intellectual and sociocultural characteristics of the students. On the other hand, with regard to assessment, it establishes knowledge of the different ways of valuing, knowing and learning of children, adolescents, young people and adults. It also establishes the need to have the competences to develop relevant pedagogical strategies to meet the educational needs of students in specific cultural, local, institutional and class-room contexts. Finally, the resolution calls for the use of assessment information to enhance student learning and, in terms of practices, to include conceptual components to support them.

It could be argued, based on these regulations, that in Colombia the legal frameworks for teacher training facilitate educational inclusion through institutional policies and the curricula of Bachelor's degrees in Education. However, in practice, learning results show exclusions associated with the large regional

GLORIA CALVO

differences in the country, exclusions in terms of access to technologies and large differences between the education of the elites and public education.[4,5]

On the other hand, when initial teacher training curricula are analysed from the perspective of pedagogies for inclusion, it is observed that the regulations translate into the existence of courses specifically dedicated to the topics of diversity and inclusion as cross-cutting content at postgraduate or in-service training levels (Orealc/Unesco, 2018, pp. 52–54). These courses are training spaces in which the topics are addressed, but they do not nurture discussions or reflections in other spaces or in the experiences of practice.[6] In this sense, there is no evidence of a relationship between these contents and the development of teaching competences for educational inclusion. In conclusion, it could be stated that teacher training for inclusion in Colombia is at a level of pedagogical innovations – illustrated by the cases presented below – that would require greater visibility in order to situate within educational policies the different learning that can be derived from them for the training of teaching competences for educational inclusion.

In this regard, Colombia is in the process of developing an education policy strategy to articulate guidelines for initial teacher training in pedagogies for inclusion and the development of competences through a Framework for Good Teaching (MBE) such as the Chilean one that specifically includes them (Centro de Perfeccionamiento, Experimentación e Investigaciones Pedagógicas [CPEIP], 2021). Unfortunately, the country has favoured guidelines and regulations in general that can be interpreted by teacher training institutions through curricula, but has not translated them into guidelines for inclusive pedagogies. Nevertheless, the country has experiences that allow lessons learnt in this field to be derived. Cases that illustrate this claim are presented in the following section.

THREE CASES IN TEACHER TRAINING FOR INCLUSIVE EDUCATION

In this section, three cases are constructed with regard to teacher training in Colombia. They illustrate different possibilities of working with future teachers from explicit proposals for their training in inclusive pedagogies, as in the case of the Escuela Normal Superior de Ubaté (ENSUBATÉ) and the different programmes of the Faculty of Education of the Corporación Educativa 'El Minuto de Dios' (Uniminuto) to programmes that involve urban education policies to guarantee the right to education, such as the 'Escuela busca al niño' (EBN) in the Colombian city of Medellín. They are based on qualitative research and, with the exception of the latter, do not have publications or evaluations that systematise them.

Case 1: Training Teachers for Non-exclusion

In Colombia, initial teacher training is carried out in teacher training colleges and faculties of education. The Escuela Normal Superior de Ubaté (ENSUBATÉ) was committed to a process of teacher training for non-exclusion based on the awareness of the different logics that prevailed in that educational institution.[7,8]

For example, the *logic of normality* considers all subjects as equal, favouring homogeneous pedagogical practices. The *logic of disability* favours a view of deficiencies. The *logic of beneficence* leads to understanding education as a favour and the *positivist logic* makes teachers assume their worldview as the only valid one, ignoring the possibility of others.

In order to recognise diversity, not only in the students of the Escuela Normal Superior but also in the entire educational community, and with the aim of displacing the previous training logics, the Escuela Normal Superior de Ubaté proposed a project to re-signify diversity (Calvo, 2018).

The intention was to move from the logic of normality to the *logic of diversity*; from the logic of disability to the *logic of capacity*; from the positivist logic to the *logic of otherness*; and finally, from the logic of beneficence to the *logic of guaranteeing rights.*

For the materialisation of these approaches, the study plan was formulated on the basis of the following problem nuclei: 1. In each of the training semesters, the aim was to recover knowledge and practices in such a way that inclusion would be experienced as the permanent recognition of the existence of others in their diversity.

ENSUBATÉ understands pedagogical practice as a communicative practice par excellence. In this sense, the future normalistas know the Braille system and sign language and practise this knowledge in educational institutions in the municipality with children and adults who have not entered the education system. They are also trained to recognise exceptionality, which can be expressed in indiscipline and hyperactivity, and have pedagogical repertoires derived from the proposals of multiple intelligences to recognise other ways of being and learning.

ENSUBATÉ also works on interpersonal relationships and the classroom environment with various projects ranging from the reconceptualisation of the coexistence manual to projects on sex education and citizenship training and specific strategies to promote the ethics of caring for oneself, for others and for the environment.

With a view to opening up to other ways of being and existing, *Gender Day* is celebrated and the manifestations of new masculinities and femininities are recognised. There is also the social practice that seeks to familiarise the future teacher with the attention to different populations based on the *Pedagogies for Peace.*

In conclusion, this case shows how important it is that, in teacher training for inclusive education, teachers become aware of their exclusionary practices and reflect on their pedagogical implications in order to guarantee the right to quality education for all.

Case Two: School Seeking Child as a Reintegration Policy

The interest of presenting the programme called 'La escuela busca al niño' (EBN) (Calvo et al., 2009) in these cases that illustrate teacher training for educational

GLORIA CALVO

inclusion in Colombia is to show how an initial educational reintegration strategy highlights institutional difficulties in guaranteeing educational inclusion for marginalised populations in large Latin American cities.

The EBN is a strategy that seeks to integrate out-of-school children and young people into the educational institution. To this end, it essentially has three phases: the first is the search for and identification of those who are not in the education system; the second, in which their previous knowledge is recognised and habits for community life are created; and the third, in which an institution is sought for this population to integrate and attend school.

In the search phase, EBN Medellín identifies and motivates the out-of-school population through strategies such as parades and carnivals, which go around the sectors of the city where the Programme will be carried out.[9]

In the second phase – which aims to strengthen the individual, family, community and institutional conditions that will be a prerequisite for reintegration – two strategies are worked on. The first, called *Creative Interest Centres*, is based on play and art to work on identity, self-esteem and social relations, and involves professionals from very different disciplines: psychologists, therapists, social workers and special educators. These centres take place in open spaces that the city offers as educational environments: the football pitch, the park, and the metro station. The second, called *Integrating Learning Units*, seeks the appropriation of academic knowledge based on what the children and young people arrive with as a result of their lives and experiences. Teachers of the basic areas (language, mathematics and science) use a wide repertoire of didactic strategies in order to level the necessary knowledge for subsequent reintegration into school. These two processes last no longer than three months.

The third phase is insertion into the regular classroom. For this, an educational institution is sought that is interested in receiving children from the EBN through informative and explanatory conferences on the Programme. In the case of the EBN Medellín, it was necessary to incorporate a follow-up and accompaniment to the teachers of the educational institutions in order to guarantee the permanence of the children and young people in the educational system, since admission did not guarantee permanence in the institution. During these visits, they supported the teachers in terms of training in pedagogical strategies aimed at inclusion, and the children and young people with workshops in mathematics, language and science. Gradually, teachers began to become aware of their students' difficulties and to recognise that they were common to all students and not just those from EBN. Consequently, from the third stage onwards, there was a permanent presence of a group of professionals from different areas of training in the educational institutions that received children and young people from competency-based education (CBE).

The EBN Medellín has had a direct impact on initial teacher training in the Faculty of Education at the University of Antioquia, one of the best in the country. Future teachers carry out their pedagogical practices supporting the second phase of the EBN and their degree projects include these experiences accompanied by reflections on what it means to guarantee the right to education for vulnerable populations.[10] Likewise, the EBN Medellín has identified the importance of monitoring and pedagogical support for teachers as a guarantee of permanence in the education system and, therefore, of inclusion.

This accompaniment is not only in academic areas but in all those processes derived from living together: respect for rules, peaceful coexistence and recognition of authority, among other aspects aimed at citizenship. Unfortunately, there is still a tension between the characteristics and difficulties associated with vulnerability, which still clash with the education system. There are also no indicators to account for progress in self-esteem, secondary socialisation and recognition of one's own identity, etc., which are essential aspects of reintegration policies.

Hence, another of the greatest difficulties for children when they enter educational institutions is related to norms, rules, authority, limits in relationships, time, space and physical appearance, among others.

EBN also highlighted the importance of working with the educational community: in order to guarantee permanence, it is necessary to have an impact on the educational system, generating transformations in families, teachers, educational institutions, public policies and, finally, in teacher training in the Faculties of Education. Likewise, in order to guarantee the right to education, inter-sectoral work is needed in health, education and social development, among other areas, of the so-called social areas in public administration.

Case Three: In Search of Relevance for Inclusive Education

The Corporación Universitaria El minuto de Dios – Uniminuto – is an institution that was born with a clear social project: to *offer quality education to the less favoured sectors* (Uniminuto, n.d.).[11] It believes in the social and political function of knowledge and in its contribution to integral human development.

In harmony with the philosophical principles of Uniminuto, the Faculty of Education of this same university has as its vocation to be a relevant school in pedagogies and social innovations in education; it assumes the integral and permanent training of teachers while it is committed to educational research and innovation – pedagogical and human and social development (Calvo, 2018).

The theoretical foundation of Uniminuto's Faculty of Education is derived from social pedagogy and pedagogical praxeology (Juliao Vargas, 2011). The former refers to the social and political commitment of knowledge with the communities, not in the traditional school–community relationship, but in the recognition that the pedagogical discourse is built from the communities, from their ways of reading the world and from their epistemological constructions. Hence, the Faculty of Education expresses this conceptualisation as *pedagogies and social innovations.*

For its part, pedagogical praxeology promotes reflection on practice and delves into the understandings that result from actions. For praxeology, all action produces knowledge (Juliao Vargas, 2011). Its purpose is the transformation of the subject, its practice and its mentality. Consequently, in each of the training semesters for future teachers, pedagogical practices seek to establish opportunities for social and educational transformation in the school environments of the centres of practice.

In this order of ideas, initial teacher training at Uniminuto strengthens the capacity to design and implement educational and pedagogical experiences with a view to generating changes, transformations and alternative solutions to the various realities, needs or problems in educational environments that require the intervention of the future graduate as a pedagogue (Uniminuto, n/d).

In the conceptual horizon of the Faculty of Education is the intention to become a relevant school in pedagogies and social innovations that responds to the country's educational problems. Consequently, it envisages the creation (Calvo, 2018) of a centre on inclusion – with several postgraduate training offers such as the master's degree in social Innovations in Education, with emphasis on Social Management of Education and Educational Innovations – on the understanding that educational innovations are necessary to solve social problems.

To this end, Uniminuto's Faculty of Education has research and extension projects on the cultural diversity – musical and literary – of Colombia's regions, with a special focus on the Pacific region, one of the poorest in the country. Among them, Narrativas cantadas de la violencia política en Colombia (*Sung narratives of political violence in Colombia*) (López & Martinez, 2019) stands out, as well as extension work with schools in some municipalities and university educational institutions in that region (Uniminuto, n.d.).[12]

As noted in the first sections, Uniminuto also places the theoretical debates on inclusive pedagogies in postgraduate training, either at master's degree level or in centres of thought that will support the training of future graduates in the medium term. However, in accordance with its institutional philosophy, it insists on the recognition of the other as a being different in its specificity. It also has a deaf and blind population among the future graduates in education and supports them with scholarships or with the payment of the respective interpreters in the case of deaf students. It also defined sign language as the first language of this population with its corresponding implications for the training and development of the linguistic competences of these future graduates. In the virtual faculty, one of its teachers has designed a *mobile laboratory* (Calvo, 2018) which allows any text to be converted into Braille.

The case of Uniminuto exemplifies the social commitment to inclusive education, the recognition of the different regional, social, economic and cultural contexts for the formulation of the pedagogical projects of future teachers and illustrates the postgraduate level as a place for theoretical reflections on educational inclusion in Colombia (Orealc/Unesco, 2018).

These three cases highlight the role of pedagogical innovation in teacher training for inclusive pedagogies. They are context-sensitive teacher training proposals that seek to include rather than exclude. They emphasise reflection on practice and seek to guarantee the right to education for all. However, they are still confined to specific regional contexts with little visibility from the decision-making bodies of education policies in the country. This is why we have categorised them as pedagogical innovations. The teaching competences they develop can be seen from the postulates presented in the following section.

TEACHING COMPETENCES FOR INCLUSIVE EDUCATION

The teaching competences for educational inclusion within the framework of guaranteeing the right to quality education emphasise the *pedagogical knowledge* required by teachers about how students learn and develop; how they are educated in educational institutions and how they plan and evaluate teaching. They also start from the recognition of the teacher as a professional who not only knows the discipline he or she teaches, but has a *knowledge of teaching* and even more so knows the contexts of disadvantage and poverty and their effects on the characteristics of learners (Orealc/Unesco, 2018). Consequently, they know how to select the methods and social relations required for effective teaching to guarantee the right to quality education (Ainscow, 2019; Arnove, 2007; Darling-Hammond, 2006).

The cases presented in the previous section illustrate these competences. Emblematic is the curricular adaptation of the EBN in the sense of recognising the deficient contexts from which its students come and starting the teaching processes from strategies aimed at their socio-affective recomposition. On the other hand, it selects the best didactic proposals so that the classroom is only one of the learning spaces, favouring the street, the football pitch, the museum, on the understanding that they favour horizontal social relations and affective expressions that allow the subsequent acceptance of the school rules of great importance in the schooling processes. Learning environments within pedagogies for inclusion encompass social relations within the school community (teachers, students, administrative and service staff and families). The School Seeks the Child – EBN – favours welcoming, affection, accompaniment and coexistence dynamics, with special attention to the integration of students and training against any type of social or cultural discrimination (Ferri & Connor, 2006).

The teacher training college in Ubaté – ENSUBATÉ – has adapted its curriculum so that trainee teachers can understand the difficulties associated with certain disciplinary content – the teaching of mathematics for example – and can generate competencies to attend to the different learning rhythms of their students and thus avoid school failure and dropout, which are factors of social exclusion.

Uniminuto defines relevance as a principle for its curricular proposals that seek to be in tune with the needs of the local contexts of its teacher training programmes through each of the moments of its praxeological proposal. The recognition of cultural diversities, as well as regional inequalities, underpins the projects formulated by students in their degree programmes throughout the country. Moreover, their teaching methods are sensitive to disability.

The proposals of the Escuela Normal Superior de Ubaté have a wide repertoire of learning strategies ranging from the use of educational *software* to individual counselling for students to the reformulation of coexistence manuals and training for conflict resolution in the classroom. In the School Seeks the Child programme, the development of social competences to facilitate life together is relevant. Respect for agreements, listening and participation are

GLORIA CALVO

present in the different learning spaces and are fundamental for these children to be able to integrate later into regular classrooms in the different educational institutions of the city of Medellín.

Another competence for teachers to develop inclusive pedagogies in their pedagogical practice is their *professional commitment*. A number of considerations apply here.

The first is the importance of reflecting on practices in order to understand the causes of barriers and obstacles to inclusion and equity in education. Teachers need to develop a capacity to collectively reflect on their own prejudices and stigmatisation within schools, to analyse the situations that affect the learning of some students and the most effective strategies and methodologies to address them. In this respect, ENSUBATÉ has identified the logic of exclusion in its teaching practices and is constantly reflecting on this with its trainee teachers.

The second is related to the possibilities of learning from experience, understood as a situated practice. In this sense, systematisation opens up the possibility of finding the best strategies for all students to learn. The three cases presented have in the systematisation of experiences a source of continuous learning and, as documented, in the case of EBN, this practice has led them to rethink initial teacher training in the Faculty of Education of the University of Antioquia in the city of Medellín. However, these pedagogical innovations need to be extended to teacher training for inclusive education in the country.

A third consideration is that of fostering a common working culture and a collective will that involves all members of an educational community. Thus, in the interest of relevant training for inclusion in Uniminuto, work is carried out on the basis of community projects, participatory evaluation is encouraged and collaboration and mutual help among teachers is sought (Calvo, 2018).

The three cases analysed allow us to identify a number of constants in order to put into practice the guidelines of the Colombian education legislation for inclusive education. These include the existence of interdisciplinary support teams in schools in order to promote inter-sectoral work, training in inclusive education for all teaching staff and strengthening links with students' families in order to build trust and mutual respect. They also embrace the guidelines for teacher training in that they take into account the conditions of their students and contextualise teaching.

CODA

Education is fundamental to overcoming inequality and making Colombia a country that values the diversity of its population. To this end, public policy aims to guarantee the right to quality education for all, regardless of the conditions of origin. Education, as a right, is a public good and teachers are important for inclusive education (Fullan & Langworthy, 2011). In this sense, the country has significant experiences in teacher training for inclusive education that unfortunately have not transcended the state of pedagogical innovation, i.e. they are still reduced to small-scale programmes and projects, but they deserve to be rescued.

On the other hand, the regulations that recognise education as a right for all people, together with coverage indicators, illustrate exclusionary inclusion (Mancebo & Goyeneche, 2010). People go to school, but they do not learn what is relevant. School curricula do not take into account the interests, perspectives and needs of all sectors, despite the existence of regulations such as institutional education projects (PEI) that allow for curricular contextualisation.

Ensuring educational inclusion in Colombia requires taking into account the unequal distribution of educational opportunities and regional differences in educational attainment, among other inequities, as illustrated at the beginning of this chapter. Hence, the Ministry of Equality, created at the end of 2022, may be a window of opportunity in this regard (Congress of the Republic of Colombia, 2022).

On the other hand, schooling alone does not guarantee the restitution of the rights of individuals if it is not accompanied by policies that provide adequate, precise, relevant and timely institutional interactions regarding the situations that affect the educational trajectories of vulnerable children and adolescents (Loyo & Calvo, 2009). The new guidelines for educational inclusion proposed in 2021 facilitate access to knowledge through greater articulation between the different agencies of the Colombian state in search of a regional perspective to address population differences for the sake of social inclusion.

Educational legislation in Colombia provides a legal framework that favours quality education for all. However, there is still a long way to go before equality and equity permeate teachers' pedagogical practices for inclusion. Hence the importance of redefining the role of teachers and training them to be aware of the exclusions that mark the country, to attend to those who are at risk, to have learning strategies that respond to the diversity of learners in order to shape their minds and, in general, to develop skills for the 21st century. Showing these tensions and possibilities, to move from words to deeds, was the purpose of this chapter.

NOTES

1. *The Right to Education. Perspectives and indicators in Colombia and Bogotá* (Abadía et al., 2020). This study by the Economics of Education Laboratory of the Pontificia Universidad Javeriana in Bogotá illustrates some of these educational inequities. For example net coverage in education is 82% in primary and 71% in secondary; dropout rates are higher in official sector institutions than in private ones and are even higher in rural institutions in the official sector. In terms of regional differences, remote departments such as Vichada and Putumayo have the highest dropout rates in primary and Putumayo and Arauca in secondary. In the state evaluations, known as the Saber 11 tests, there is a 31-point difference between the results of graduates from official versus private sector educational institutions. Women score eight points lower than men in these tests.

2. The same study reports a dropout rate of 7.6 for the department of Guainía and 6.2 for Vichada, two remote regions of the country with indigenous populations that illustrate regional and population inequalities in educational attainment.

GLORIA CALVO

3. Education in Colombia is highly decentralised. Most of the departmental and municipal secretariats are 'certified' and can design programmes based on the guidelines formulated by the Ministry of National Education, but with independence in terms of policies and programmes. Hence, the limitations of the cases which, with the exception of *La Escuela Busca al Niño*, have not transcended the character of pedagogical innovation experiences.

4. Data from the Economics of Education Laboratory, to which the authors belong, put the number of students in official schools who do not have access to the internet either at school or at home at 62% (Abadía et al., 2020).

5. Abadía et al. (2020) report that 50% of the country's official institutions do not have internet access or computers, according to information from the Colombian Institute for the Promotion of Higher Education (ICFES) based on data from the 2018 SABER 11 tests, the name of the state exams at the end of secondary education in the country. These examinations give access to tertiary education.

6. Two of the cases presented in this chapter were analysed for the Orealc/Unesco (2018) study.

7. The Escuela Normal Superior de Ubaté (ENSUBATÉ https://www.ensubate.edu.co/web/) is an institution located in the municipality of Ubaté (approximately 50,000 inhabitants), in the department of Cundinamarca, in a region of high dairy production located about three hours from the city of Bogotá, capital of Colombia.

8. Inclusive education in initial teacher training: Innovation proposal for Teacher Training Colleges and Faculties of Education, 2010–2012.

9. Escuela Busca al Niño was initiated in the city of Armenia following a major earthquake in 1999. The analysis presented in this section is based on the experience of the programme in the city of Medellín, where it gained relevance for its achievements and conceptual developments Calvo (2013).

10. The term *vulnerabilised* was coined by Aurora Loyo (Loyo & Calvo, 2009) to point out that deprivations are not natural conditions that do not guarantee the rights of children and young people to a quality education, but rather they are social problems that require educational inclusion policies.

11. Uniminuto is an educational institution that is the product of the social commitment of its founder, Father Rafael García Herreros, and the congregation of Eudist priests. It serves more than a thousand students in the bachelor's degree courses of the faculty of education in Bogotá and ten thousand in the virtual faculty in 27 centres throughout the country.

12. This research addresses the pedagogical proposals that affect the imaginaries of the armed conflict. https://repository.uniminuto.edu/bitstream/10656/7609/1/TM.ISE_Lopez QuinteroDaniel_2019.pdf

REFERENCES

Abadía, L., Bernal, G., Blanco, C., Guevara, Y., Vega, C., Gómez, S., García, G., & Manzano, L. (2020). *The right to education. Perspectives and indicators in Colombia and Bogotá.* Instituto para la Investigación Educativa y el Desarrollo Pedagógico, IDEP and Laboratorio de Economía de la Educación de la Pontificia Universidad Javeriana.

Ainscow, M. (2019). *25 years after the Unesco Salamanca Statement. Creating inclusive and equitable education systems.* Discussion paper prepared for the International Forum on Inclusion and Equity in Education "Every Learner Counts". https://es.unesco.org/sites/default/files/2019-forum-inclusion-discussion-paper-es.pdf

Arnove, R. F. (2007). Teaching profession, equity and social exclusion: Challenges and responses. *Educar, 39*, 11–34.

Calvo, G. (2013). Teacher training for educational inclusion. *Páginas de Educación, 6*(1), 19–35.

Calvo, G. (2018). *Initial teacher education, inclusion policies and the development of 21st century competencies in Colombia.* Unpublished document.

Calvo, G., Ortiz, M., & Sepúlveda, E. (2009). *La Escuela Busca al Niño, EBN*. Eurosocial, OEI, Colombia.

Camargo Muñoz, A. (2018). Brief historical overview of inclusion in Colombia. *International Journal of Inclusion Support, Speech Therapy, society and Multiculturalism, 4*(4), 181–187. https://doi.org/10.17561/riai.v4.n4.16.16

Congress of the Republic of Colombia. (1991). *Constitución Política de Colombia*. https://www.suin-juriscol.gov.co/viewDocument.asp?ruta=Constitucion/1687988

Congress of the Republic of Colombia. (2022). *Bill 222 of 2022. Justification for the creation of the Ministry of Equality*. Bogotá, Colombia. https://www.camara.gov.co/sites/default/files/2022-10/P.L.261-2022C%20%28MINISTERIO%20DE%20LA%20IGUALDAD%29.pdf

Constitutional Court of Colombia. (2011). *Sentencia T- 051 2011*. https://www.suin-juriscol.gov.co/viewDocument.asp?ruta=Decretos/30033428

CPEIP. Centro de Perfeccionamiento, Experimentación e Investigaciones Pedagógicas. (2021). *Estándares para la profesión docente marco para la Buena Enseñanza*. Santiago.

Darling-Hammond, L. (2006). Constructing 21st-century teacher education. *Journal of Teacher Education, 57*(3), 300–314.

Ferri, B. A., & Connor, D. J. (2006). *Reading resistance: Discourses of exclusion in desegregation & inclusion debates* (Vol. 1). Peter Lang.

Fullan, M., & Langworthy, M. (2011). *Towards a new end: New pedagogies for deep learning*. Collaborative Impact SPC. https://michaelfullan.ca/wp-content/uploads/2013/08/New-Pedagogies-for-Deep-Learning-An-Invitation-to-Partner-2013-6-201.pdf

Juliao Vargas, C. G. (2011). *The praxeological approach*. Corporación Universitaria Minuto de Dios. Bogotá D.C., Colombia. http://hdl.handle.net/10656/1446

López, D. A., & Martinez, G. C. J. (2019). *Narrativas Cantadas del conflicto armado en Colombia capítulo FARC-EP*. Corporación Universitaria Minuto de Dios. https://repository.uniminuto.edu/bitstream/10656/7609/1/TM.ISE_LopezQuinteroDaniel_2019.pdfuniminuto.edu/bitstream/10656/7609/1/TM.ISE_LopezQuinteroDaniel_2019.pdf

Loyo, A., & Calvo, B. (2009). *Centros de transformación educativa: Mexico, D.F Mexico. Inclusive Policy Studies*. Eurosocial, Madrid.

Mancebo, M. E., & Goyeneche, G. (2010). Educational inclusion policies: Between social exclusion and pedagogical innovation. In *VI Jornadas de Sociología de la UNLP 9 y 10 de diciembre de 2010 La Plata, Argentina*. National University of La Plata. Faculty of Humanities and Educational Sciences. Department of Sociology.

MEN. Ministry of National Education. (2014). *Lineamientos de calidad para las licenciaturas en educación (Programas de Formación Inicial de Maestros)*. Bogotá. https://www.mineducacion.gov.co/1621/articles-344483_archivo_pdf.pdf

MEN. Ministry of National Education. (2016). *Resolution 02041 of 3 February 2016*. https://www.mineducacion.gov.co/portal/normativa/Resoluciones/356144:Resolucion-No-02041-de-3-de-febrero-de-2016

MEN. Ministry of National Education. (2017). *Decree 1421 of 2017 which regulates, within the framework of inclusive education, the educational attention to the population with disabilities*. https://www.suin-juriscol.gov.co/viewDocument.asp?ruta=Decretos/30033428

MEN. Ministry of National Education. (2020). *Circular N° 020*. https://www.mineducacion.gov.co/1780/articles-394018_recurso_1.pdf

Orealc/Unesco. Regional Bureau for Education in Latin America and the Caribbean. (2018). *Initial teacher training in competencies for the 21st century and pedagogies for inclusion in Latin America. Comparative analysis of seven national cases*. https://bibliotecadigital.mineduc.cl/bitstream/handle/20.500.12365/17604/Formacion%20Inicial%20Docente%20en%20competencias.pdf?sequence=1&isAllowed=y

Saldarriaga Concha Foundation. (2021). *Education for all people without exception. Policy guidelines for inclusion and equity in education*. https://www.colombiaaprende.edu.co/sites/default/files/files_public/archivos_contenidos/AF%20LINEAMIENTOS%20DE%20POLI%CC%81TICA%20ACCESIBLE.pdf

Uniminuto Corporación Universitaria Minuto de Dios Uniminuto (n/d). *Mission and vision.* https://www.uniminuto.edu/mision

UN. United Nations. (2022a). *Sustainable Development Goals.* https://www.un.org/sustainabledevelopment/es/objetivos-de-desarrollo-sostenible/

UN. United Nations. (2022b). *Goal 4: Ensure inclusive and equitable quality education and promote lifelong learning opportunities for all.* https://www.un.org/sustainabledevelopment/es/education/

World Bank. (2022). *Together for a better future. Update of the systematic diagnosis of Colombia.* https://documents1.worldbank.org/curated/en/099342006202217806/pdf/IDU09342dc7f05065045e70aa0702f3e7862222e.pdf

TEACHER TRAINING AS A MEDIATOR OF CHANGE TOWARDS INCLUSIVE EDUCATION IN COSTA RICA

Lady Meléndez Rodríguez, Rocío Deliyore Vega and Mario Segura Castillo

Universidad de Costa Rica-Instituto de Investigación en Educación (INIE), Costa Rica

ABSTRACT

Currently, schools are not born inclusive, and teachers report feeling that this approach is alien to their practical possibilities, so they constantly ask for training on the subject. However, this training is hardly transferred to the school. This chapter has therefore set out to analyse how training bodies in Costa Rica are doing, and how much of this effort is permeating the educational culture. The methodologies applied were studied, as well as the background of good practices, with the final intention of guiding more effective training to make inclusion a sine qua non *condition of being a school.*

Keywords: Inclusive school; human rights; diversity; teacher training; knowledge transfer

INTRODUCTION

Although interest in inclusive education has been growing, it is also true that many education systems are still developed based on attitudes and practices that are diametrically opposed to it '…favouring situations of exclusion, segregation and discrimination' (Montánchez et al., 2015, p. 7). This happens because under the title of inclusive education, enrolment practices for all are proposed, but, once inside, the school does not know how to generate strategies to address diversity and the old standardising practices are enthroned. Schools are established on

---

Intercultural and Inclusive Education in Latin America
International Perspectives on Inclusive Education, Volume 24, 97–112
Copyright © 2024 Lady Meléndez Rodríguez, Rocío Deliyore Vega and Mario Segura Castillo
Published under exclusive licence by Emerald Publishing Limited
ISSN: 1479-3636/doi:10.1108/S1479-363620240000024007

incongruent foundations and actions and are incapable of responding to the students in their personal and cultural differences. Therefore, the teaching staff are increasingly disoriented, exhausted and frustrated in the whirlpool of absurd dilemmas.

This is when teachers claim that they have not been trained to deal with diversity and turn to training as a mechanism to try to resolve the situation. However, it is possible to identify a large number of teachers who attend training courses without this having an impact on their practices and request more and more training in the subjects they have already studied, a fact that can be corroborated in the records of the training bodies.

As Ocampo (2015) explains, it may be necessary to define an ontology and epistemology of inclusive education; the lack of updating teacher may not be to blame, but rather the ways of educational management that are undermining this approach. Nevertheless, inclusive education is either materialised or denied in practice, as a result teachers are faced with a phenomenon that finds its ontology in doing education in a certain way, in a particular heuristic way. So, in order to be an inclusive educational centre, inclusive education must be the norm, which requires a *know-how* and, therefore, the need to be trained.

This chapter has set out to learn about training experiences on inclusive education, as well as to characterise the methods behind good practices, in order to determine the most effective means of teacher updating for the successful transfer of new knowledge to the classroom by teachers and thus ensure a more consolidated expansion of inclusive education.

INCLUSIVE EDUCATION IN A HUMAN RIGHTS FRAMEWORK

During a lesson of the Master's Degree in Education with a specialisation in Inclusive Education at the Casa Grande de Guayaquil University, the terms *inclusion* and *diversity* were discussed and also the way in which some segregationist groups and movements try to drag both concepts into a muddy terrain in order to generate mistrust around them. In this context, there was also a discussion about the closeness or otherwise of inclusive schooling to Jacques Derridà's (2007) idea of *hospitality*. And there were those who claimed this concept applied to the school from a possible meaning of equitable, supportive educational attention, adjusted to the group and individual needs to which hospitality appeals. In this colloquium, the rural teacher Horacio Vinueza made the following reflection: 'What happened to the hospitable school? At what point did the school become twisted and, with the complicity of parents, we began to see our students as supermarket products?' (Vinueza, 2019).

There would be much to say about this expression from the Theory of Education, but later on, after referring to inclusive education in the framework of human rights, we will focus on the idea of the 'crooked school', and how it undermines the right to education.

Education, in terms of human rights, has gone through different forms of classification, from being a first-generation individual right, focused on access to literacy and schooling, to a second-generation right pointing out the differences of groups excluded due to ethnic, demographic, economic or prejudicial reasons, to the definition of Sustainable Development Goal 4 (SDG4), which, in the context of the so-called 2030 Agenda (UN, 2015), aims to 'Ensure inclusive and equitable quality education and promote lifelong learning opportunities for all'.

The SDG4 is considered a third-generation human right, and in addition to reflecting the previous intentions, it also determines the way in which this education should be provided, indicating that it should be *inclusive, equitable* and *of quality.* Therefore, the signatory states must strive, through their regulations, policies, budgets, projects and activities, to comply with it in their education provision.

It is clear that failure to meet this objective will only widen the social and economic gaps in the coming years, and those most affected will be the people historically excluded from the right to quality education. And it is well known that exclusion from education brings with it censorship of the exercise of other rights, resulting in poverty, illiteracy, violence, insecurity, foreseeable illnesses, even early death and an inability to escape from this condition (Meléndez & Solano, 2017). Inclusive education is therefore not just about what happens in school but about putting people on the path to decent opportunities for human development.

Professor Vinueza's words remind us that before talking about inclusive education, the antecedents of a psychometric education erased the natural figure of the school, capable of receiving and attending to everyone regardless of their conditions, in order to build an excluding structure based on the norm, so far impossible to dismantle in Latin American education. And, when we look to the future, we find the imaginary of globalism, which pushes a person to go through school in order to perform competitively by means of an egocentric climbing to achieve a false emulation of success, also carrying families away in the process. That is why, even though it is based on a promise of a better quality of life for all and an equitable exercise of rights, inclusive education comes to the present, as a pressing need in the midst of the crisis of modern democracies (Gaete & Luna, 2019); but also, as an intrusive anomaly in the history of education, which neither teacher training nor practice understand well how to address, let alone educational management.

Then, if we are convinced that inclusive schooling is the way forward, we have to fight for the understanding that neither the normalising practices of the past nor the selfish practices of the future lead in that direction. Furthermore, it must be clear that human rights constitute the paradigm from which foundations are shaped but also do inclusive practices, and these must also be the object of learning in order to give sustainability to their realisation (Darretxe-Urrutxi et al., 2021).

THE WHYS OF INCLUSIVE SCHOOLING

Inclusive education is the result of a complex historical evolution in the search for an increasingly equitable participation of the entire student population in the same space and with the same opportunities. Thus, there is a need for a major transformation in the education system to ensure full participation, coexistence and quality learning. This requires a high sense of recognition and appreciation of diversity, in which respect and healthy interaction of all students is encouraged without further classification or exclusion.

According to Ocampo (2015), 'The inclusive education approach is one of the most important paradigms of the 21st century' (p. 18); however, we began talking about educational inclusion, as an incipient evolution of the integrationist movement, during the World Conference on Special Needs Education held in Salamanca in 1994 (UNESCO, 1994). And, as it is possible to corroborate in Castillo et al. (2018), although UNESCO begins to support the inclusive education movement within the framework of Special Education, at this point, under SDG4, it is expected to cover all populations historically excluded from the right to education, with the intention of 'leaving no one behind'.

In 2012, UNICEF began a study with the aim of understanding the different ways in which educational exclusion manifests itself in order to counteract it in the best way possible. The results identified processes ranging from the impossibility of entering school, the absence of pre-school, dropping out without completing school, to the bottleneck that prevents a transition to secondary school and working life. In addition, as a transversal axis in all processes, there are curricular and attitudinal aspects that cause barriers to learning, participation and school success (UNICEF, 2012).

People experience forms of school exclusion in an intersectional manner together with other manifestations of exclusion, such as economic and social exclusion, which are mutually reinforcing in a perverse cycle that tends to perpetuate itself throughout life and to be inherited by future generations. In Latin America, children from indigenous and Afro-descendant groups, in conditions of poverty and destitution, in situations of disability, with significant health difficulties, in dispersed demographic areas, in situations of violence, armed conflict or displacement and in sexual diversity present the highest incidence of suppression of rights and a high threat of future exclusion.

For a state to opt for inclusive education is to embark on a complex undertaking that must begin by diagnosing the forms of exclusion and the people affected and to take remedial action tailored to each situation. Avoiding this responsibility only makes the problem bigger, but just pretending to do so is worse, as it disguises a reality that will never be effectively addressed. Therefore, at this moment in time, all states are called upon to try to ensure that no one is left out of a quality education that allows them to develop competencies to improve their quality of life and that of their descendants, and this is precisely the purpose of inclusive education.

With emphasis on the principle that inclusive education is consolidated in practices, we will position ourselves in the argument that curricular and attitudinal aspects can cause barriers to learning and participation, hinder educational success and, as a consequence, push people to fall behind and drop out of school. From this argument, it is possible to assume that if we prevent or break down these barriers, we will avoid the consequences of exclusion that is generated or reinforced in the classroom. To achieve this, we should start by convincing teachers that providing equitable and quality attention to the diversity of students is not limited to the classroom or to immediate educational achievements, but that their work will transcend towards the human development of the people to whom they give an opportunity.

The National Observatory for Inclusive Education (ONEI), as a result of a series of studies on the subject and reflective exercises for share, has concluded that inclusive education is:

> Quality education in which all people are welcomed and recognised in their diversity and which is based on equity, the reduction and elimination of barriers to access, participation, permanence and successful learning at all levels, modalities, as well as educational and cultural opportunities. (ONEI, 2021, p. 48)

Starting from this new view of education requires a conscious recognition of the diversities present and the consequent positive valuation of these singularities, so that the entire educational community articulates efforts to make these diversities the essential bases of curriculum design and educational work.

For UNESCO (2020), inclusive education consists of:

> A process: measures and practices that embrace diversity and create a sense of belonging, based on the conviction that each person has value and potential and should be respected. However, inclusion is also a state of affairs, an outcome, whose multifaceted nature makes it difficult to define. (p. 12)

This multifaceted connotation of inclusive education can be further defined in the light of three fundamental dimensions put forward by Echeita (2020). The first of these is:

> The necessary presence of all students in the centres and common/regular educational spaces and, within them, in everything from classroom activities to complementary and extracurricular activities, including break times and meal times. (p. 36)

Inclusive education assumes that all learners will be together sharing educational spaces, opposing the historical segregation of students based on gender, ability, sexual orientation, culture or any other characteristic. The importance of presence is that:

> We can hardly hope that all our students learn to seriously value human diversity, to live with it in all its facets and to understand it as something valuable in society if they do not learn to cope with it daily at school. (Echeita, 2020, p. 61)

Inclusive education requires the presence of all students, without segregationist classifications, in the same space to develop their learning, but presence alone is

102   *Teacher Training as a Mediator of Change*

not enough to guarantee inclusion. It also requires ensuring the active participation of each classroom member, as well as their learning. This implies giving each participant a voice through collaborative strategies and constantly assessing the quality of the construction of learning to confirm its constant evolution.

The second dimension is participation, which, according to Echeita (2020), 'involves, first and foremost, learning with others and collaborating or cooperating with them in the course of classes and lessons' (p. 124). Participation is also about 'a necessary active engagement with what is being learned and taught' (p. 124) and consistent with the principles of Universal Design for Learning (UDL) (UNICEF, 2022). In addition, participation implies 'speaking of concern for the personal and social well-being of students, which leads us to ask about the quality and warmth of their educational experiences while at school, in the classroom or in any other space or activity' (Echeita, 2020, p. 37).

Participation should take place within a framework of respect and acceptance of diversity, so that students build a sense of well-being when they take part in educational decisions for the construction of their learning. This is so that the student achieves learning with a strengthened self-esteem and a high sense of security for their own process without comparison with others.

The third dimension of inclusive education referred to by Echeita (2020) is learning, which has to do 'with the concern that all students should have the best possible performance in the different areas of the curriculum of each of the educational stages established for all' (p. 39). To achieve this, it is necessary to:

> Pay more attention to the recognition of each student's progress in relation to the development of basic and essential competences that will facilitate inclusion in their social and working life and less to a new accreditation assessment that translates into a numerical mark. (Echeita, 2020, p. 39)

In other words, learning is closely related to participation, as it requires an interrelation between feelings of well-being, affection and academic knowledge to finally give meaning and significance to learning.

As Meléndez and Solano (2017) explain, an inclusive school is characterised by the fact that its management, planning and educational practices focus on trying to free all students from personal and social exclusion. A school with inclusive policies makes the right to education effective and also considers that participation based on difference is a fundamental right of every human being. This also means that what is done in the school must be relevant to the culture in which it is immersed. For this reason, an inclusive educational centre in Latin America needs to comply with the following features:

• Starting from an inclusive approach to educational management:

> It is not possible to achieve effective results with isolated or occasional actions for the benefit of the most disadvantaged school population. To achieve this, it is necessary to consider as an institutional culture and policy the concern for those who are inside the services as well as for those who are left out, in addition to what can be done from the school, in collaboration with other organisations, to improve the living conditions in the communities. As well as making the

necessary resources available in order to achieve equitable and quality education for all students. For this reason, it is imperative to have a management project that brings together the proposal of actions and term goals to become an increasingly inclusive school. (Meléndez & Solano, 2017, pp. 67–68)

It is essential to develop a sustained process of transformation, in which the teaching staff and school management lead a constant reflection on the practices that perpetuate exclusion and replace them with others that ensure the presence, learning and participation of the entire student body. The teaching staff must do everything together and through cooperative dialogue, covering ongoing research on practice, evaluation of actions for improvement, training or professional updating activities, the definition of educational support and other complementary projects, in addition to teaching.

- Make the school a safe place:

Children must find in school a refuge that allows them to feel safe from the contextual and sometimes familial threats they live with. Therefore, the school cannot appear as an additional threat, for example, to school performance; it cannot be negligent in the face of the abuse it discovers and even less so when it considers that information on protection and justice enforcement does not correspond to the school curriculum. (Meléndez & Solano, 2017, p. 68)

- To be a watchdog of integral development:

The school, through universal allowances or any other type of subsidy, should ensure that a canteen service is always available to provide and monitor an adequate diet for the student body. It should also coordinate with health personnel assigned to their community to constantly record the development of children in accordance with access to a basic, balanced and nutritious diet, as well as the provision of nutritional supplements that enable age-appropriate human development, which should be complemented with training for families to improve their income and invest it in planned nutrition and even organise with other families to produce their own food. (Meléndez & Solano, 2017, p. 68)

- Assume that families and the community are also schools:

As UNESCO (2015) explains in its document *Education transforms lives*, maternal education and early care can significantly prevent the effects of illiteracy and poverty on child development. For this reason, the school's extracurricular activities should include literacy proposals and training in prenatal care, neurodevelopment, child nutrition and many other topics that allow babies or those who are about to be born to arrive at school in optimal conditions to enjoy it. (Meléndez & Solano, 2017, p. 68)

- Providing relevant education for the removal of barriers to learning, participation and success in school:

Relevant education is that which adjusts to the needs and conditions of the target population and its context, allowing them to develop adequately, given that it starts from their own reality to propel them towards the next levels of personal and social progress. (Meléndez & Solano, 2017, p. 68)

- For this reason, from the curricular dimension, an inclusive educational centre must be:

> Leading everyone to be ambitious with their own learning goals; facilitating opportunities to recognise and value their identities, and their cultural and family heritages; acting as a facilitator of knowledge without losing sight of the fact that it is the learner who must take responsibility for their own learning; creating spaces and opportunities for learners to learn from each other by grouping them according to multiple criteria, depending on the occasion (interests, friendships, confidence, or perceived strengths). (Echeita et al., 2016, p. 7)

Such education must also provide specific supports for students whose personal characteristics say that they require these to ensure their success in school.

Regarding the recommended features, it is suggested to implement the UDL approach, which fulfils all of them and more conditions conducive to inclusive education (UNICEF, 2022).

TEACHER TRAINING ON INCLUSIVE EDUCATION

In the face of the transformation that inclusive education implies, teacher training is not only an opportunity to propose new perspectives that challenge the traditional school, but also to establish collaborative networks between the actors in the education system.

In Costa Rica, training differs from education in that the latter refers to formal educational processes for professionalisation purposes, such as those provided in tertiary and higher education, while training refers to short courses for professional improvement and updating.

Training, according to Huberman (2005), consists of a:

> Conscious, deliberate, participatory and ongoing process implemented by an education system or an organisation with the aim of improving performance and results; stimulating development for renewal in academic, professional or occupational fields; reinforcing the spirit of commitment of each individual to society and particularly to the community in which he or she lives. (p. 25)

It is important to consider that, given the current situation, inclusive education requires 'an approach that goes far beyond a mere question of specific support for certain students and has much more to do with a process of profound restructuring of schools' (Echeita, 2014, p. 97). Training, in this sense, 'is installed as a mediator between the real and desirable situation. It is understood as "making up" for professional and training weaknesses, either due to a deficit in their initial training or due to a mandate for change in teaching practice' (Huberman, 2005, p. 26).

Training, as a constant practice in the professional practice of teaching, is born 'as a necessity, a search for answers to new questions posed by the social reality in which the school is inserted, the transformation of contents or the modification in the orientations of pedagogical theories' (Huberman, 2005, p. 26).

In order to implement teacher training, a clear conjunction between educational theory and practice is necessary, in which research is adapted to the contextual needs of each educational centre. Therefore, teachers must have a leading role in the design and development of training, as this 'implies the analysis of their own practice in the light of theory, overcoming the theory/practice dualism; this continuous feedback approach enables the professionalisation of teachers' (Huberman, 2005, p. 27). Therefore, it is required that professionals be the ones who, in a critical and continuous way, manage to develop meaningful learning, applicable to their own practical reality and in accordance with the global proclivity.

Huberman (2005) mentions that, in terms of training, 'teachers need to be able to select among theories, develop their own theories and argue with their own theoretical foundations in order to be able to make relevant, possible and priority changes' (p. 27). This implies that training is formulated according to the context, trends and specific needs of each school.

Training processes are not an act of innovation in Costa Rican educational reality. There are several bodies that constantly offer training on various topics, including inclusive education. The National Resource Centre for Inclusive Education (CENAREC), public universities, the Ministry of Public Education (MEP) and other organisations have taken on the task of providing training through various methodologies. However, as detailed in previous sections, both teachers and families express that more training is needed in this field. This raises the question of why training does not fully deliver what it is supposed to.

Huberman (2005) explains that a constant criticism of these processes is that 'the objectives of the trainers do not always respond to the expectations (interests + desires + needs) of the participants' (p. 33), which is why prior enquiry into the context in which the learning processes will take place is necessary.

The same author points out that 'the impact of training on organisations depends on the place the trainees occupy in them and their intentions to socialize, or not, their new knowledge' (p. 33). In other words, a person can be an agent of knowledge multiplication after training in order to articulate cooperative actions for the improvement of the whole centre. However, this willingness to share knowledge is necessary. Moreover, the content learned during training must be transferable in a timely manner to the practical reality of each participant, which is why, Huberman (2005) reiterates, the context in which it takes place acquires vital importance for the success of the processes.

Another criticism of training is that 'within an organisation, not everyone wants to be trained, not everyone has the same level of training, the same interest, the same experience' (Huberman, 2005, p. 34), nor the same commitment, and this must be considered when selecting those people who can have a positive impact on the educational centre by receiving training. In other words, the body that decides who requires professional updating must select as immediate participants those potential multipliers of knowledge and managers of positive changes.

In relation to the criticisms, Huberman (2005) states that 'the instances of training of trainers are scarce and disconnected from the instances of initial training' (p. 34), which causes a massification of information that does not consider the diversity of each centre and the heterogeneity of the teaching population that receives the information. As a result, learning fails to be meaningful and to have an impact on practical reality.

Therefore, the skills that a trainer needs to demonstrate to achieve meaningful and long-term learning, according to Huberman (2005), are the following:

- Listening and being listened to.
- Identify obstacles or solve problems in order to carry out projects or satisfy individual, group or institutional needs.
- Choose strategies by assessing benefits and risks on an ongoing basis.
- Plan and implement the strategy involving other stakeholders.
- Implement the strategy according to events and their context.
- Continually reassess the situation and, if necessary, change the strategy, addressing resistance to change.
- Respect the rules of ethics, law and equal opportunities.
- Cooperate with others, in the sense of interrelating, interdisciplinary, transversalising.
- Documenting the processes and products of the teaching–learning situation and the training process. (p. 46)

These skills require that the trainer establishes a horizontal relationship with the participants, in which they give the leading role to those who develop the teaching practice so that they can apply the learning that is built together. This requires a clear diagnosis of needs and the establishment of medium- and long-term evaluation processes with timely indicators that allow for self-reflection by the teaching team in order to propose constant improvements in their professional practice.

In addition to what Huberman points out about effective forms of teacher training, if inclusive education is to be consolidated in practice, it is necessary for training to be extended to the transfer of what has been learned into school work in order to ensure its sustainability. Therefore, the evaluation of professional updating achievements through training should include the observation and recording of the exercise of renewed practices based on what has been learned. However, it is suspected that, at least so far, Costa Rican training on inclusive education is unlikely to have this scope.

RESEARCH ON TEACHER TRAINING IN INCLUSIVE EDUCATION ONEI-2022

In the year 2022, the ONEI of Costa Rica carried out a research, which started from the following background[1]:

I. During the years 2019–2021, ONEI analysed its objectives and actions in the light of Costa Rican demands for inclusive education, represented in two populations: teachers and families.

As part of this exploratory descriptive work, participants (471 teachers and 29 families) expressed, through an online questionnaire and in response to one of the questions, that one of the main functions of ONEI should be to ensure training on various topics related to inclusive education (83.86% and 93.10% respectively). (ONEI, 2021)

II. On the other hand, the Eighth Report on the State of Education in Costa Rica (CONARE, 2021) reported that[2]:

The pandemic not only increased the vulnerability of the socioeconomically disadvantaged student population with limited access to connectivity and technological resources, but also affected students with previous disadvantages associated with factors beyond their control. This is the case of the population with disabilities and learning barriers [sic] whose right to education was violated during the pandemic. (Consejo Nacional de Rectores [CONARE], 2021, p. 98)

The State of Education, in its survey about the student population with disabilities, concluded that 'the support of the teacher is highly valued by most families (72%), and it is families with low cultural capital that demand his or her presence the most and where his or her pedagogical mediation is most relevant' (CONARE, 2021, p. 100). However, despite the high need for teacher support, the report adds that about 40% of families indicated that they received feedback infrequently (once a week, once a month or a few times a month), in addition to the 10% of students who did not have access to connectivity. This implies that there is a clear disarticulation between the work of teachers and families, a situation that significantly hinders the achievement of quality education as a right.

The aforementioned background, the mission of the ONEI, as well as the difficulties already mentioned regarding the implementation of inclusive education and the lack of scope of teacher training on the subject, led the organisation to consider the need to initiate new research with the aim of answering the question: What characteristics should a training process have in order to ensure that teachers' learning about inclusive education is meaningful and sustainable over time?

To answer this question, the Observatory set out to carry out a new study titled "Training processes in inclusive education, from theory to sustainable practice" during 2022–2023. This was a mixed exploratory-descriptive type of study, which was carried out in order to identify the methodologies that best ensure the effectiveness of training in inclusive education, as well as to analyse good practices in order to find the original training that motivated them. The six trainers and the nine participating teachers completed questionnaires using the Google Forms platform, differentiated according to their group of belonging.

RESULTS OF THE STUDY 'INCLUSIVE EDUCATION TRAINING PROCESSES, FROM THEORY TO SUSTAINABLE PRACTICE' (ONEI, 2022)

The training bodies in Costa Rica that develop training processes in relation to inclusive education and that were consulted for the development of the study are the Continuing Education Project Training, Counselling and Dissemination of

Guidance and Special Education of the University of Costa Rica (UCR), the Training and Professional Development Programme of the School of Education Sciences, the Equity and Diversity Project and the Open Doors Extension Project of the State Distance University (UNED), the National Resource Centre for Inclusive Education (CENAREC), the College of Graduates and Teachers in Literature, Philosophy, Science and the Arts (COLYPRO) and the Ministry of Public Education (MEP).[3]

First of all, through the questionnaire applied, the people in charge of each training body were asked what they understood by training. They agreed that it was synonymous with 'continuous improvement'. UCR stated that training 'is a continuous and systematic process, it includes an indispensable support for constant improvement'. UNED stated that it is the 'process of acquiring knowledge, skills and attitudes for the improvement of the functions that a person performs'. And according to COLYPRO, it is 'training actions aimed at strengthening the competent exercise of the teaching profession'. These criteria are in line with what Huberman (2005) defines as teacher training. The rest of the bodies consulted referred more to didactics than to the purposes of training itself.

In order to identify training processes that support good practice in inclusive education, nine reputable teachers were consulted and stated that most of the training courses they had passed were certified by CENAREC, COLYPRO and UNED, although they had also benefited from some courses offered by MEP and UCR. The selected teachers were identified through cross-checking of information between the MEP, as the employing entity, and the teacher training centres; they work at educational levels ranging from pre-school to university and are all women with more than 10 years of professional experience.

The majority of teachers had participated in six or seven in-service courses (40/80 hours per course) in the last decade, meaning that they have spent between 240 and 560 hours in total, where the most significant topics have been on teaching strategies for overcoming barriers to learning, participation and success in school (including UDL), principles, policies, laws of inclusive education and human rights. The motivation for training, in all cases, was the desire to improve teaching practice of their own free will.

This implies that they have a self-critical attitude and are committed to constant preparation and improvement. This may be related to the success of their educational practice, as Huberman (2005), when analysing teacher training, determines that:

> Real change can only be internalised through a real awareness of its necessity, by experiencing new situations that allow teachers and professors to access other *modus vivendi,* different from those that were their own learning models. (pp. 25–26)

The training institutions agreed that they had developed the topics of teaching strategies (100%) and rights (89%) in the last 10 years, through courses or workshops, each lasting 40 hours or more.

With regard to the pedagogical mediation modality, the didactic interaction most used by the training instances is hybrid (virtual and face-to-face combined) in 55.6% and pure virtual in 44.4%. The participating teachers indicated that the

LADY MELÉNDEZ RODRÍGUEZ ET AL.

methodology that most favours them in the development of their learning is that of self-management. They also indicated that the workshop modality facilitates the construction of learning as well as collaborative learning.

Precisely, according to the training bodies, the most frequently used methodologies are workshops (89%), collaborative learning (55.6%) and, to a lesser extent, self-managed learning (44.4%).

With regard to the sustainability of the training, 55.6% of the training instances indicate that they do not follow up on the implementation of what they have learned, while 44.4% say that they do. This coincides with the answers given by the teachers: five of them stated that they had not received any follow-up in relation to the implementation of what they had learned in the training, while the rest stated that they had received this support. When the participating teachers were asked about what this support was like, they explained that, as a way of evaluating the learning acquired during the training, they had to carry out research on their practice and report on the inclusive approach they used in their teaching and the main difficulties encountered, in order to receive feedback from the trainers.

Fig. 1 illustrates some of the quotes collected in the field regarding participants' recommendations for ultimate success. The circle on the left shows the recommendations with the highest incidence expressed by the trainers, and those of the teachers appear in the circle on the right. While in the intersection area, expressions that synthesise the coincidences of both groups that characterise the features of successful teacher training on inclusive education are collected.

CONCLUSIONS

From the literature review, it is possible to conclude that the implementation of inclusive education is torn between a long and entrenched tradition of standardising education and the market's demand for globalising, competitive and dehumanising education, even though the underlying discourse speaks of inclusive education. This complexity confuses educational management and the work of teachers, as well as transgressing inclusive education in practice. As a result training is used to try to make logical and practical sense of this trend, but it seems that training has not been effective or sufficient.

According to preliminary data from the ONEI research, which also coincides with Huberman's (2005) recommendations, the most successful training in relation to good practice in inclusive education is that which, in the first instance, includes teachers as participants, who not only want to be trained but are willing to share learning with others, as well as feeling listened in regard to their specific needs for professional improvement and updating.

On the other hand, it is noted that the effectiveness of the training depends on the trainers considering the context and reality of each educational centre in which the participants work and on the trainers being truly competent in both the fundamentals and practices of inclusive education. In addition, the dynamics of the training should reflect a living model of how to do inclusive education, respect

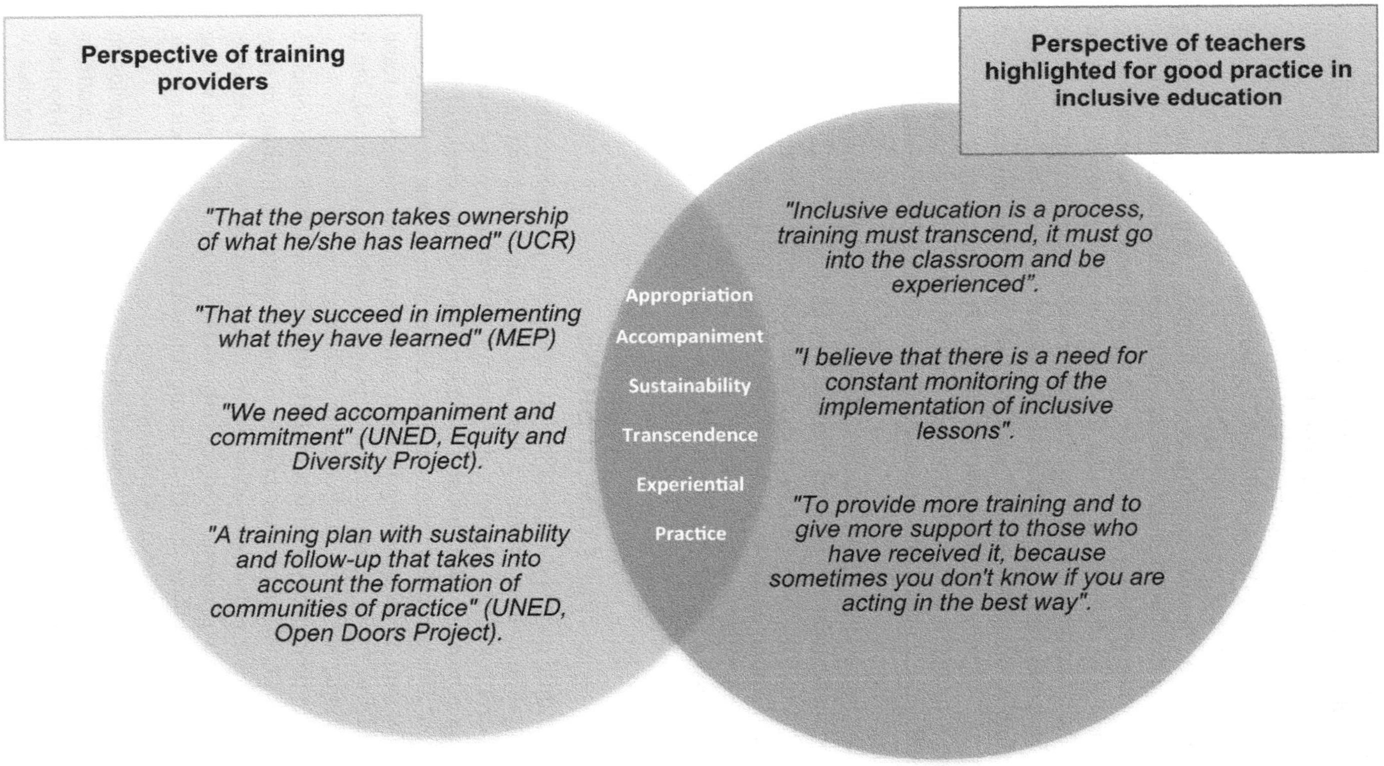

Teacher Training as a Mediator of Change

Perspective of teachers highlighted for good practice in inclusive education

"Inclusive education is a process, training must transcend, it must go into the classroom and be experienced".

"I believe that there is a need for constant monitoring of the implementation of inclusive lessons".

"To provide more training and to give more support to those who have received it, because sometimes you don't know if you are acting in the best way".

Appropriation
Accompaniment
Sustainability
Transcendence
Experiential
Practice

Perspective of training providers

"That the person takes ownership of what he/she has learned" (UCR)

"That they succeed in implementing what they have learned" (MEP)

"We need accompaniment and commitment" (UNED, Equity and Diversity Project).

"A training plan with sustainability and follow-up that takes into account the formation of communities of practice" (UNED, Open Doors Project).

Fig. 1. Overlapping Recommendations for Translating Training Into Teaching Practice. *Source:* Prepared by the authors, based on data from ONEI (2022).

LADY MELÉNDEZ RODRÍGUEZ ET AL.

and take advantage of the personal and cultural diversity of the participants and exercise SAD, collaborative and self-managed learning in their methodologies and didactic actions.

Finally, a follow-up seems to be important for the success of the training processes, since when both the organisations and the teachers were asked about the recommendations they would give so that the training received could be put into practice, the majority agreed on the need to accompany the training, through modelling and correction in situ, which would allow the transfer and consolidation of what was learned in the space in which the teaching practice is carried out.

It is therefore urgent that, in addition to monitoring the content of inclusive education itself, the training courses planned for updating teachers in this field should also note the methodology that is considered to be the most effective, and that the participant should be accompanied to ensure that inclusive education is revealed in their daily teaching practice.

NOTES

1. ONEI was created in 2015 with the purpose of monitoring and articulating knowledge and good practices at a national and international level on inclusive education and decision-making in the Costa Rican education system. The Observatory brings together various public and private bodies interested in this issue.

2. The State of Education is a programme attached to the National Council of Rectors of Public Higher Education, which is responsible for preparing a biannual report on the state of Costa Rican education, for which it develops its own diagnostic studies in addition to collecting the main enquiries that are made on the subject in universities and authorised research centres.

3. These are teacher training and updating units that operate within institutions or organisations dedicated to education and the professional development of teachers.

REFERENCES

Castillo, K., Deliyore, R., González, V., Madriz, L., Marín, M., Meléndez, L., Montenegro, F., Rodríguez, R., Segura, M., & Solórzano, J. (2018). Epistemological analysis of Special Education in Costa Rica. *Revista Actualidades Investigativas en Educación, 18*(2), 1–28.

CONARE. National Council of Rectors. (2021). *Eighth State of Education Report.* State of the Nation Programme.

Darretxe-Urrutxi, L., Alvarez-Rementería, M., Alonso-Sáez, I., & Beloki-Arizti, N. (2021). Political will in favour of inclusive and equitable education: Beginnings and development analysing its meaning. *Archivos Analíticos de Políticas Educativas, 29*(64). https://epaa.asu.edu/index.php/epaa/article/view/4976/2634

Derridà, J. (2007). *La Hospitalidad.* Ediciones La Flor.

Echeita, G. (2014). *Educación para la inclusión o Educación sin exclusiones.* Narcea.

Echeita, G. (2020). *Inclusive education. The dream of a summer night.* Octaedro.

Echeita, G., Sandoval, M., & Simón, C. (2016). *Notes for an inclusive pedagogy in the classroom. IV Iberoamerican Congress on Down Syndrome* (pp. 1–9). https://www.researchgate.net/publication/303643610_Notas_para_una_pedagogia_inclusiva_en_las_aulas

Gaete, A., & Luna, L. (2019). Inclusive education and democracy. *Revista Fuentes, 21*(2), 161–175. https://institucional.us.es/revistas/fuente/22/Educacion_inclusiva.pdf

Huberman, S. (2005). *How trainers are trained. Arte y saberes de su profesión.* Paidós.

Meléndez, L., & Solano, V. (2017). Malnutrition and stress go to school: Child poverty and neuro-development in Latin America. *Innovaciones Educativas, 27*, 55–70. https://revistas.uned.ac.cr/index.php/innovaciones/article/view/1955/2194

Montánchez, M., Ortega, S., & Moncayo, Z. (coords). (2015). *Inclusive education: Reality and challenges*. Ecuador: Pontificia Universidad Católica del Ecuador Sede Esmeraldas.

Ocampo, A. (2015). Ch. 1: The great challenge of inclusive education in the 21st century: Moving towards the construction of a theory. In V. García, S. Aquino, J. Izquierdo, & P. Santiago (coords) (Eds.), *Research and Innovation in Inclusive Education. Diagnósticos, modelos y propuestas*. Universidad Juárez Autónoma de Tabasco.

ONEI. National Observatory of Inclusive Education. (2022). *Partial Report: Training Processes in Inclusive Education, from Theory to Sustainable Practice 2022-2023. 724-C2-308.* INIE.

ONEI. National Observatory on Inclusive Education. (2021). *Informe Final. Bases teóricas y metodológicas para el observatorio temático de Educación Inclusiva en Costa Rica 724-C1-732.* INIE.

UNESCO. United Nations Educational, Scientific and Cultural Organization. (2015).

UNESCO. United Nations Educational, Scientific and Cultural Organisation. (2020). *Global education monitoring report. Inclusion and education: All without exception.* https://unesco.unesco.org/in/documentViewer.xhtml?v=2.1.196&id=p::usmarcdef_0000374817&file=/in/rest/annotationSVC/DownloadWatermarkedAttachment/attach_import_9bb5b1b1-f82e-4a5c-ad89-1bf48f561d99%3F_%3D374817spa.pdf&locale=es&multi=true&ark=/ark:/48223/pf0000374817/PDF/374817spa.pdf#p36

UNESCO. United Nations Educational, Scientific and Cultural Organization. (1994). *Salamanca statement and framework for action on special needs education.* https://unesdoc.unesco.org/ark:/48223/pf0000098427_spa

UNICEF. United Nations Children's Fund. (2022). *Universal Design for Learning and accessible digital textbooks. Find out what it is and how it can transform education.* https://www.unicef.org/lac/dise%C3%B1o-universal-para-el-aprendizaje-y-libros-de-texto-digitales-accesibles

UNICEF. United Nations Children's Fund (2012). *Global Initiative for Out-of-School Children.* Asociación Civil Educación para Todos.

UN. United Nations. (2015). *Agenda 2030 and Sustainable Development Goals.* https://www.un.org/sustainabledevelopment/es/2015/09/la-asamblea-general-adopta-la-agenda-2030-para-el-desarrollo-sostenible/

Vinueza, H. (2019). *Comunicación personal.* Casa Grande University.

INCLUSION OF FAMILIES IN BASIC EDUCATION IN MEXICO: POLICIES, PRACTICES AND CULTURES

Cristina Perales Franco

INIDE, Universidad Iberoamericana, Mexico

ABSTRACT

This chapter analyses, from the perspective of inclusion, the possibilities of participation for families in basic education schools in Mexico. Based on the analysis of articles published between 2012 and 2022, complemented by an analysis of normative instruments, the main patterns related to policies, practices and cultures were explored. The outcomes highlight a lack of recognition and appreciation of the diversity of families, restricted spaces and forms for their participation and cultural patterns that hinder their inclusion. The bases to favour inclusion are recognised and four key axes are proposed for its strengthening.

Keywords: Diverse families; inclusion and exclusion of families; basic education; index for inclusion; family participation; critical inclusion

INTRODUCTION

The involvement of families in the educational processes of students is considered a necessary pillar to guarantee the quality of education (Razeto, 2018). There is international evidence on the relevance of family support, especially parental support, in learning (Acevedo et al., 2017; Bazán Ramírez et al., 2014; Hampden-Thompson & Galindo, 2017; Park & Holloway, 2017; Valdés & Yáñez, 2013). However, this involvement is generally considered, at least in the Mexican case, as insufficient or inadequate, constantly pointing out the failures and limitations of participation (Valdés & Sánchez, 2016); the responsibility for deficiencies is placed mainly on the side of the families (Perales Franco, 2022).

Intercultural and Inclusive Education in Latin America
International Perspectives on Inclusive Education, Volume 24, 113–126
Copyright © 2024 Cristina Perales Franco
Published under exclusive licence by Emerald Publishing Limited
ISSN: 1479-3636/doi:10.1108/S1479-363620240000024008

This chapter problematises this notion through an analysis of the possibilities of families' participation in basic education schools in Mexico, based on previously conducted research from the perspective of inclusion. This analysis draws on critical perspectives of inclusion (Ocampo González, 2019; Slee, 2011) and relational approaches to school *convivencia* (Perales Franco, 2022), which contribute to a situated positioning regarding diversity. In this logic, the most common constructions about families and their participation in schools are shown in relation to policies, practices and cultures, as three central dimensions for inclusion. This work highlights the lack of recognition of the diversity of families in these dimensions, as well as the lack of appreciation of the richness and possibilities that this complexity offers.

Such approach is important, first, because it is necessary to guarantee the possibility of participation of students' families in basic education for the full inclusion of the latter and, second, because these possibilities are fundamental in a broader path of inclusion that places education as a shared and socially valued project. Furthermore, the analysis is relevant because the socio-communitarian dimension, particularly with regard to school–family relations, although recognised as fundamental, has been seldom explored in Mexico and Latin America in general (López Pereyra, 2022).

For this analysis, we conducted a systematic literature review of articles published between 2012 and 2022 in four databases: Web of Science, Scopus, SciELO and Google Scholar. Various combinations of the terms: families, diversity, schools, basic education, inclusion, participation, involvement and Mexico were used. This search yielded a total of 46 articles; four were excluded as they did not fit the purpose of the analysis.

The remaining total was analysed considering its research purpose and main findings, which were classified into three broad categories: cultures, policies and practices. These categories were explored individually; the main patterns reported in the literature were identified and complemented by reviews of current policy instruments and findings from research projects in which the author participates. Results show that the main area is forms of participation, and the most robust category is practices. The inclusion of families is only directly addressed in nine of the studies analysed (Bustos, 2011; Duarte, 2021; Jiménez Naranjo & Kreisel, 2018; Mejía-Arauz et al., 2013; Mercado Maldonado & Montaño Sánchez, 2015; Muñoz Rodríguez, 2022; Perales Franco, 2022; Schalla, 2015; Valdés & Sánchez, 2016), although other research papers provide elements to reflect on the implications of the construction of family participation in basic education.

This chapter seeks to analyse how existing policies, practices and cultures enable or hinder the inclusion of families in basic education. Although it does not pretend to account for the totality of the national reality, since its wide diversity is acknowledged, it aims to present relevant patterns for its understanding. To this end, this chapter begins with a brief presentation of the importance of the relationship between schools and families and the perspective of inclusion used. Subsequently, the findings are presented in the three dimensions mentioned: policies, practices and cultures. This chapter closes with reflections on what has been presented, including a proposal of axes to strengthen the processes of inclusion of families in formal educational spaces.

THE IMPORTANCE OF THE RELATIONSHIP BETWEEN SCHOOLS AND FAMILIES

The school–family relationship is considered a central element in the quality of education, mainly because of its link with students' learning achievement (Bazán Ramírez et al., 2014; Valdés & Yáñez, 2013), as there is evidence that greater family involvement is associated with better academic performance in general, although its effects vary depending on the context, type of involvement and characteristics of the families and those of the school (Acevedo et al., 2017; Hampden-Thompson & Galindo, 2017; Park & Holloway, 2017).

This relationship has been explored, on the one hand, by analysing 'structural factors' (Valdés Cuervo & Urías Murrieta, 2010), which correspond to the general characteristics of families that tend to favour or limit the opportunities for students' educational development. Thus, socio-demographic data, beliefs, attitudes and expectations of families can be considered as predictor or explanatory variables of school processes and outcomes (Chaparro Caso-López et al., 2014; Sheridan and Moorman Kim, 2016). On the other hand, 'processual factors' (Valdés Cuervo & Urías Murrieta, 2010) that explore the characteristics of relationships in families and with the school have been investigated, identifying, for example, more or less effective forms of participation (Martiniello, 2000; Valdés Cuervo & Urías Murrieta, 2010; Valdés Cuervo et al., 2009), the motivation it generates in students and the effects of different forms of participation for teachers and the school in general (Acevedo et al., 2017; Valdés & Sánchez, 2016).

In the analysis of this relationship, the possibility for schools to become public spaces for participation, where schooling is a socially shared experience, also stands out. Although this is a less explored aspect in Mexico, studies on social participation have redefined the importance of families in education systems (Martínez Bordon et al., 2010). Valdés and Yáñez (2013), for example, point out that, due to the social position of schools, they can be considered as mechanisms that promote exchange between educational authorities, families, students and the community in general, to foster social participation, having effects not only on school performance but also on social harmony, the reduction of violence and conflict resolution.

Finally, although it has not been a topic of educational research, the relationship between schools and families is essential in recognising and guaranteeing the rights of children and adolescents, mainly their right to education and identity, which includes 'preserving their identity including their name, nationality and cultural belonging, as well as their family relationships' (National Human Rights Commission, 2018) and their right to not to be discriminated against. A relevant, collaborative and respectful relationship between schools, families and communities is therefore considered necessary to ensure that these rights are promoted.

INCLUSION AS A FRAMEWORK FOR ANALYSING THE RELATIONSHIP BETWEEN SCHOOLS AND FAMILIES

In this chapter, the relationship between schools and families is analysed with an inclusion approach, revising the possibilities and barriers for the participation and involvement of all families. Inclusion is conceived as a systematic response to diversity, which can be understood as a 'set of processes aimed at removing or minimising barriers that limit learning and participation' (Booth & Ainscow, 2000, p. 10). Inclusion therefore implies 'the elimination of all forms of discrimination, as well as deciding what needs should be met and how; it involves addressing key issues such as social justice, equity, human rights and non-discrimination' (Barton, 2009, p. 82).

Inclusion, therefore, is used as a concept that visualises, problematises and attempts to transform the fact that there is 'a lack of participation in educational environments, as well as public and private, of diverse individuals and communities, which is associated with their physical, social, economic or cultural characteristics' (Perales Franco & Sartorello, 2023, p. 4.). In particular, critical perspectives of inclusion that recognise that processes of inclusion and exclusion are mediated by power relations that are socially, culturally and historically constructed are useful (Artiles, 2020).

This critical position questions and seeks alternatives to the deficit perspective that maintains that the social, economic, social, cultural and physical characteristics of excluded groups are the reasons for poor educational outcomes (Ocampo González, 2019) and seeks to transform educational spaces that have been exclusionary since their origin (Slee, 2011). From this framework, it seeks to 'make visible, recognise and attend to diversity in school spaces, avoid exclusion and take advantage of the particular knowledge of each family' (Muñoz Rodríguez, 2022, p. 339).

The approach is based on the recognition of the wide diversity of families in Mexico and the importance of differences in terms of type of family structure, social class, gender relations, geographic location, cultural group membership, disability and migration experiences (Capulín et al., 2016; Echeverría-Castro et al., 2021; Perales Franco & Sartorello, 2023). It also conceives that these categories combine and intersect with each other in different family formations, and that they interact in specific ways in different contexts (Muñoz Rodríguez, 2022; Perales Franco, 2022). Such diversity must be considered to understand the differences in the possibilities of participation and to problematise the ways in which it is constructed in policies, practices and cultures. A critical perspective of inclusion not only recognises diversity as something inherent to national societies but also as something that must be acknowledged and valued for the possibilities of creating fairer and more equitable societies.

In order to explore the inclusion processes of families considering their diversity, the dimensions proposed in the Index for Inclusion (Booth & Ainscow, 2000) – policies, practices and cultures – are used in this text up in a flexible way, as they provide a more complex view of how to understand inclusion at different levels. These dimensions were originally constructed to analyse and promote the inclusion of students in schools. Here, I use them only to account for three broad categories of research which will be conceptualised in the sections below.

POLICIES ON FAMILY INVOLVEMENT IN EDUCATION

In this analysis, the policy dimension corresponds to the regulatory instruments that govern the Mexican education system. For this section, we considered the laws and programmes that frame and regulate the participation of families, as well as the analyses presented in the explored academic literature, examining their implications for the possibilities of participation for the diversity of families.

The involvement of families in the national education system is nourished by two perspectives at the policy level. The first corresponds to the promotion and guarantee of human rights and, the second, to reforms around the notion of social participation. In the first one, the normative frameworks that regulate educational policies at the international and national levels and in the states of the country deal with the inclusion of the diversity of families in schools closely related to the rights of children and adolescents, under the premise that their involvement is important for children's right to education, to non-discrimination and their right to live in a family (López Pereyra, 2022).[1] In this sense, at the international and national levels, the family is recognised as the basic social unit, and the right of children and adolescents to develop in a family or similar care environment is established, as well as the right of the family itself to be protected by the State and by the society as a whole (López Pereyra, 2022).

At the national level, in instruments such as the General Law on the Rights of Children and Adolescents (Diario Oficial de la Federación [DOF], 2023) and the General Education Law (DOF, 2019), it is recognised that in order to offer equal opportunities for access, transit, permanence, academic advancement and timely graduation from the education system, it is necessary to understand the background and provide equitable attention to the diversity of characteristics, needs and contexts of students. Similarly, there is recognition of the need to protect students in conditions of vulnerability, which include those associated with 'gender, sexual preferences, marital status, social origin, circumstances of birth, family situation, (and/or) family responsibilities' (López Pereyra, 2022, p. 33). Thus, families are generally considered in relation to the contextual factors of the students.

There is also a growing recognition of the need to strengthen inclusion and equity – for example, the most recent constitutional reform recognises the need to include a gender perspective in the curriculum and emphasises the term 'families' in the plural form, whereas before it was in the singular form (López Pereyra, 2022). However, this approach is still limited because it does not identify family diversity as a characteristic of educational actors and the gender perspective focuses only on the differentiation between men and women.

The second perspective contemplates their participation in school spaces, which, although not a new issue, has moved from a clear delimitation of obligations and commitments to a closer involvement (Valdés Dávila, 2019). In the 1990s, along with the state decentralisation and democratisation reforms that Mexico underwent, the notion of social participation in education gained momentum. Its implementation began with the construction of School Councils for Social Participation, which involved not only families, principals and teachers but also broader sectors of the population (Jiménez Naranjo & Kreisel, 2018).

The 2013 education reform sought to foster participation to strengthen school autonomy, recognising parents as central figures (Valdés & Sánchez, 2016), granting them the right to organise themselves in each school: 'as observers in teacher evaluation processes', 'in dialogue mechanisms between schools and communities' and 'as members of the participation councils of each school' (Secretaría de Educación Pública [SEP], 2013, p. 5 in Valdés Dávila, 2019). The Participation Councils, however, did not manage to consolidate the democratic participation of families, as they did not become spaces for analysis, decision-making and collective action (Martin & Guzmán Flores, 2016; Perales Mejía, 2014). Their functions also overlapped with those of the longer established parents' associations, and in many schools, the need and relevance of broadening family participation were not clear.

Currently, there is a certain rethinking of the participation of families in the 'The School is Ours' programme. The new programme, in addition to encouraging social participation, collective work and decision-making, in continuity with previous approaches, proposes to deliver the resources directly to families, through the School Committees for Participatory Administration, allowing families intervene in the improvement of educational spaces and food services. The programme also prioritises those schools in indigenous communities with a high index of poverty and marginalisation, in vulnerable situations and those lacking drinking water (DOF, 2022).

The spaces for participation proposed by education policy have been subject to strong criticism. Valdés and Yáñez (2013), for example, find that the involvement of families is practically in 'peripheral aspects of the educational process' which prevents them from 'participating in decision-making related to academic and school organisation processes that really affect student learning' (p.130). Specifically in relation to inclusion, these forms of family participation allow for the involvement of a limited number of people in specific spaces and moments of the school experience, an aspect that is described in the following section.

SCHOOL PRACTICES INVOLVING FAMILIES

The dimension of practices collects the main forms of participation and involvement that are promoted in schools and analyses the way in which these promote or hinder the inclusion of families. For this analysis, the main practices that relate schools and families were identified; three of them focused on school management and two on support for learning. These have been collected in different research projects, such as those carried out by Martin and Guzmán Flores (2016), Perales Mejía and Escobedo Carrillo (2016), Valdés Dávila (2019), Valdés and Sánchez (2016), as well as the author's own (e.g. Perales Franco, 2022).

The first practice is participation in the parents' associations and participation committees mentioned above. The participation of families in these spaces is necessary for school management, as it is here that the use of resources to meet school needs is decided. The committees and associations are made up of groups of around 6–20 family representatives, mainly mothers. Their participation is voluntary and, in theory, all families can participate, through self-nomination to be elected by the families as a whole. In addition to these spaces, a mother or father can also participate as a group representative.

In the research, however, it is reported that this possibility of participation is much more restricted, as mothers who are close to teachers or managers tend to be involved and are often invited directly. Similarly, although parent representatives are positioned in the policy as the decision-makers, there is evidence that teachers and principals are the ones who propose or decide, and it is seen as good practice to have the 'support' of families, which reduces their autonomy and agency (Perales Franco, 2022; Perales Mejía & Escobedo Carrillo, 2016).

The second practice does involve all families and corresponds to their participation through financial contributions to the school. In Mexico, compulsory public education is free; however, it is a traditional practice in the vast majority of schools that families pay a fee each school year, the amount of which varies from school to school and is used to obtain even such basic things as cleaning materials and toilet paper, or for the maintenance or improvement of infrastructure. The financial contributions are administered by the parents' associations and are, in principle, voluntary. However, families are expected to cooperate financially, and there are different strategies to ensure that they do so, from asking and arguing why their money is needed to intimidation and blackmail. In many cases, families choose the school for their children depending on the type of fees they are expected to pay (Perales Franco, 2022), which turns them into mechanisms of social segregation.

The third management practice also has to do with cooperation to meet the needs of the schools but through manual cleaning or maintenance work of the school grounds and buildings, or the preparation of food to raise funds (Martin & Guzmán Flores, 2016). For these, invitations are extended to families, and participation is expected from all of them. These practices sometimes are a substitute for economic collaboration and are deeply rooted in rural communities where community education committees are responsible for supporting schools as part of their traditional *cargo* systems. In these cases, unlike the above common practices, there is community agency that appropriates the school space (Vásquez García & Gómez González, 2006). In the case of urban schools, participation in this modality is usually smaller and organised from the school (Perales Franco, 2022).

In addition to these three management practices, families are expected to be directly involved in supporting the students' learning process. To this end, the fourth and fifth practices identified are homework accompaniment and attendance at meetings called by schools (Perales Franco, 2022; Valdés & Sánchez, 2016; Valdés Cuervo & Urías Murrieta, 2010). Homework accompaniment is widespread and takes place at home. It is a recurrent request from schools and a strong differentiator in families: 'those who help with homework' and those who do not (Muñoz Rodríguez, 2022; Perales Franco, 2022). It is important to remember that this accompaniment during the COVID-19 pandemic became essential to maintain school-based learning processes (Muñoz Rodríguez, 2022).

When attending meetings convened by the school, whether general assemblies, group meetings or meetings to discuss particular issues (Valdés Dávila, 2019), schools provide information to families and make general or specific requests for support for the student. The latter occurs especially when there are conflicts in relation to their behaviour or academic difficulties (Perales Franco, 2022). Participation in these spaces is carried out at the invitation of the schools and at times that are favourable to them. The attendance of families is also an indicator of their interest and willingness to collaborate (Perales Franco, 2022; Valdés Dávila, 2019; Valdés & Sánchez, 2016).

The various research studies reviewed agree that the involvement of families in these five practices is continually considered to be deficient. Managers and teachers, as well as mothers involved in the committees, point out that, although all families are invited, few participate and a lack of interest and support is continually noted (Perales Franco, 2022; Valdés Dávila, 2019). Based on this lack of involvement, it is suggested that one strategy is to work with the families that do show willingness (Valdés & Sánchez, 2016), which in many schools means effectively excluding many others.

An analysis from the perspective of inclusion shows that this separation between school and family can hardly be attributed only to a lack of interest on the part of the latter. It is therefore important to recognise that the way in which these practices are constructed in schools restricts, firstly, the areas in which families can participate, as they can hardly be involved more broadly in relation to pedagogical processes and decision-making (Martín & Guzmán Flores, 2016; Valdés & Yáñez, 2013).

Second, the form taken by family involvement practices also facilitates the participation of some families and hinders that of others. Studies from intersectional (Muñoz Rodríguez, 2022) or relational (Perales Franco, 2022) perspectives find that the intersection of certain characteristics related to social class, schooling, gender, cultural belonging, race, disability and migration situations is fundamental to understanding the way in which families get involved in school. Thus, mothers are the ones who are generally involved, but especially those who have a higher level of schooling (Sánchez Escobedo et al., 2010), perform domestic and child-rearing work as their main occupation and have a perception that education will help their children's social mobility. These mothers also have a self-perception that they can contribute in schools and that they are valued (Perales Franco, 2022). In the pandemic, access to technology is also seen as fundamental to understanding their involvement (Muñoz Rodríguez, 2022).

In this type of relationship, families participate in the logic of what is desirable for the school, which can be understood as an 'alliance' relationship. Other types of relationships – where they question or want to influence school processes ('confrontation') or where there is a clear separation between schools and families ('disengagement') – are not valued as positive (Perales Franco, 2022; Solís

Castillo et al., 2017). In this sense, it is possible to point out that the most common practices promoted by the education system are based on a homogeneous notion of families, in which mothers are expected to support schools, their directors and teachers, without recognising the richness of the link with families from their diverse possibilities, as well as their right to participate.

There is also evidence of 'collaborative' relationships (Perales Franco, 2022) between families and schools. These construct a different way of carrying out the previous practices. Here we find, for example, an explicit recognition of the possibilities for families to participate, an openness to do so in different ways and a valuing of these participations (Duarte, 2021). We observe, for example, changes in meeting times to adapt to work schedules, telephone calls, use of family knowledge as part of the curriculum, wider invitations and accompaniment to join committees for families who 'do not dare'. These interactions also validate the ways in which families use their resources to collaborate with their children's learning, opening spaces for their involvement in pedagogical issues (Jiménez Naranjo & Kreisel, 2018; Mercado Maldonado & Montaño Sánchez, 2015), and involve different family members – such as grandmothers, older siblings, aunts – and not only mothers, as co-responsible, thus recognising diverse family constructions (Muñoz Rodríguez, 2022; Perales Franco, 2022).

CULTURES IN FAMILY–SCHOOL RELATIONSHIPS

The practices and policies explored relate to different cultures that promote or hinder the inclusion of family diversity. This dimension captures some of the principles, values and/or frameworks of meaning that guide and justify practices and policies, as well as being constructed by them. It is important to note that this dimension is not often explicitly explored in the literature analysed, but it is possible to identify four important cultural patterns.

The first corresponds to the construction of gender roles. As can be seen, the practices presented are based on a notion of the traditional family, where mothers are in charge of raising children and are therefore the main interlocutors and responsible for accompanying school processes at home, as well as for providing support to meet the needs of schools (Martin & Guzmán Flores, 2016; Perales Franco, 2022; Perales Mejía, 2014; Valdés Cuervo & Urías Murrieta, 2010). Although it is indicated that parents are also invited to participate, culturally, both in schools and families, there is an expectation that their involvement is desirable, but secondary. Along the same lines, there is a rejection of other family configurations where the responsibility for raising children is shared by new partners, in the case of reconstituted families, or by other family members in the case of extended families (Muñoz Rodríguez, 2022), since it is understood as a less relevant involvement and as a lack of responsibility on the part of fathers and mothers.

This rejection is related to a second cultural pattern, that of the 'deficit' (Baquedano-López et al., 2013), in which schools position families as lacking a series of conditions for their adequate involvement. Thus, principals, teachers and many of the same families in basic education explain the 'failures' in the involvement of the latter based on their characteristics (Valdés Dávila, 2019). Here, lack of participation or inadequate involvement is the responsibility of families and reduces the capacity of schools to make changes to strengthen inclusion.

This culture is reflected, for example, in the notion of 'dysfunctional families' (Perales Franco, 2022). This construct is used in many basic education schools to refer to families that fall outside the traditional family norm and/or whose conditions are not perceived as adequate (Bustos, 2011; Muñoz Rodríguez, 2022; Perales Mejía & Escobedo Carrillo, 2016), which mainly refer to situations of poverty, migration, lack of schooling, linguistic diversity and changes in family dynamics. The category of 'dysfunctional family' explains, from the perspective of school actors, why there are problems in schools such as school backwardness or violence, as well as lack of involvement (Perales Franco, 2022). To start from this notion as the basis for interaction between families and schools is highly problematic because it places diverse families in a condition of inferiority (Schalla, 2015), which breaks the trust between the parties, demonstrates a lack of sensitivity to the differences between family and school cultures and does not question whether the practices and policies proposed enable their participation (Razeto, 2018; Valdés & Sánchez, 2016) from their diversity of possibilities, configurations, knowledge and experiences.

These two patterns are counterbalanced by two others which, although less prevalent, open up the possibility of promoting inclusion. The first of these is the recognition and valuing of family and community knowledge and cultures, as well as their forms of involvement. It is the basis of the collaborative practices mentioned above and is also observed in pedagogical and curricular projects that are based on the relationship with communities (Jiménez Naranjo & Kreisel, 2018; Perales Franco & Sartorello, 2023). From this perspective, families and schools are peers in the pedagogical relationship and in the interest for the well-being of students. The promotion of this culture is based on the recognition of family diversity, and from this, relationships of trust and horizontal communication are built.

Finally, some features of the human rights culture can be observed, where family participation is understood as a right. This is seen, especially, in some of the elements of the social participation policies that seek to promote the involvement of families and in the general laws on children's rights and education. However, as we have seen, these policies open up participation, but the spaces for exercising this right are reduced and have not been translated into practices that change previous cultures. A more radical approach to the right of families to be involved in education and to the recognition of students' diversities is therefore necessary to effectively promote inclusive family involvement.

FINAL REFLECTIONS

The aim of this chapter was to carry out an analysis, from the critical perspective of inclusion, of the possibilities of participation for families in basic education schools in Mexico. Based on a systematic literature analysis of articles published between 2012 and 2022, complemented with a normative analysis of policy instruments, the main patterns in relation to policies, practices and cultures that construct the forms and spaces of participation and involvement of families in school spaces were explored. This final section will give a brief account of the barriers and possibilities encountered for the inclusion of families and will close by pointing out four key axes for its strengthening.

In relation to the barriers, in the policy dimension, there is no explicit recognition in the normative instruments of the diversity of families, which contemplates their characteristics or possibilities of participation. Families form a homogeneous entity whose representativeness is sought according to the needs of the education system (López Pereyra, 2022), and the orientations towards inclusion and equity seem to assume that the existence of spaces for participation is sufficient in terms of family involvement.

In these instruments, as well as in the way in which the practices explored are shaped, the spaces for participation are restricted, both because involvement in selected activities is allowed and because the forms that enable greater involvement in decision-making – such as membership of parents' committees – only accommodate a limited number of people. There is little evidence in the literature of sustained practices that seek to broaden and diversify modes of family involvement.

In practices and cultures, there is also an orientation of spaces and forms towards the participation of families with specific characteristics, especially in relation to family structures, social class and schooling, as well as a devaluation of families that fall outside the symbolic construction of families that are 'adequately' involved, which, in many cases, are in situations of greater vulnerability. Thus, it is identified that the relationship between schools and families tends to be vertical, guided by the needs and demands of the former, without considering the possibilities of families for their involvement but also the richness that a diverse participation could generate.

Although the possibilities for inclusion are more limited, in what the literature reports, the recognition in these three dimensions of the importance and positive aspects of the involvement of families in school spaces and activities stands out. Such recognition is a basis for favouring processes that are more sensitive to contextual characteristics. Similarly, the general human rights framework and the student inclusion project, increasingly recognised by schools, open up possibilities for further work along these lines. Finally, studies such as those by Bustos (2011), Duarte (2021), Jiménez Naranjo and Kreisel (2018), Mercado Maldonado and Montaño Sánchez (2015) and Perales Franco (2022) show significant experiences of collaboration between schools and families, which show real possibilities for inclusion based on the recognition and valuing of diversity, as well as the creation of a common project between schools and families.

The critical perspective of inclusion that has been developed in this chapter allows us to identify four key axes to strengthen the relationships between schools and families and to promote the 'set of processes aimed at eliminating or minimising barriers that limit learning and participation' (Booth & Ainscow, 2000, p. 10) by seeking the 'disappearance of all forms of discrimination' (Barton, 2009, p. 82). The first of these axes consists of promoting the explicit recognition of family diversity, as well as its valuation at the level of normative frameworks. This construction of policies would help to establish a framework of meanings that would make it possible to work directly on expanding the spaces and forms of recognition of diversity.

The second has to do with the deconstruction of deficit cultures that understand the characteristics of families as the cause of inadequate participation, without recognising how historically constructed practices for their active involvement exclude particular families (Baquedano-López et al., 2013; Ocampo González, 2019; Perales Franco, 2022). To this end, it is important to develop specific practices to raise awareness, value and recognise diversity. The third axis is also related to the deconstruction of deficit cultures and proposes a diversification of the forms and spaces for family participation, based on the particular identification in each context of the possibilities, interests and experiences provided by families, as well as the construction of a shared educational project between school and community.

Finally, the fourth axis corresponds to the research agenda on educational inclusion. The analysis carried out for this chapter shows the lack of systematic research in relation to the inclusion of families in school spaces. Although there is a body of research that studies the forms and meanings of family participation, there are relatively few of them, and they do not take an inclusion perspective as an explicit axis of analysis. It is therefore necessary to continue exploring school–family relations within an inclusion project, not only taking into account the barriers but also the actions, perhaps seminal, which exist and which should be supported for their development and consolidation.

NOTE

1. An important part of the analysis of the normative frameworks is based on the work of Hermida, Villaroel and Martínez in the project 'Pedagogy of hope and non-violence: an educational proposal for the inclusion of new family models' (in López Pereyra, 2022), in which the author also participated.

REFERENCES

Acevedo, C., Valenti, G., Aguiñaga, E., Valenti, G., & Aguiñaga, E. (2017). Institutional management, teacher and parent involvement in public schools in Mexico. *Calidad en la educación, 46*, 53–95. https://doi.org/10.4067/S0718-45652017000100053

Artiles, A. (2020). Inclusive education in the 21st century disruptive interventions. *The Educational Forum, 84*(4), 289–295. https://doi.org/10.1080/00131725.2020.1831821

Baquedano-López, P., Alexander, R., & Hernandez, S. (2013). Equity issues in parental and community involvement in schools: What teacher educators need to know. *Review of Research in Education, 37*(1), 149–182. https://doi.org/10.3102/0091732X12459718

Barton, L. (2009). Disability studies and the quest for inclusivity: Observations. *Journal of Education, 349*, 137–152. http://www.revistaeducacion.mec.es/re349/re349_07.pdf

Bazán Ramírez, A., Vega Alcantara, N., & Bazán Ramírez, A. (Eds.). (2014). *Family-school-community: Theories in practice* (1st ed.). UAEM.

CRISTINA PERALES FRANCO

Booth, T., & Ainscow, M. (2000). *Index of inclusion.* CSIE.

Bustos, A. (2011). Rural schools and democratic education. The opportunity for community participation. *Revista Electrónica Interuniversitaria Interuniversitaria de Formación del Profesorado, 14*(2), 105–114. https://www.redalyc.org/pdf/2170/217019031009.pdf

Capulín, R., Díaz Otero, K., & Román Reyes, R. (2016). The concept of family in Mexico: A review from an anthropological and demographic perspective. *Ciencia Ergo Sum, 23*(3), 219–228. https://www.redalyc.org/journal/104/10448076002/10448076002.pdf

Chaparro Caso-López, A., Díaz López, K., & Caso Niebla, J. (2014). Family factors, self-esteem, study strategies and orientation to academic achievement in secondary school students. In A. Bazán & N. Vega (Eds.), *Family-school-community: Theories in practice* (pp. 155–177). UAEM.

Diario Oficial de la Federación [DOF]. (2023). *Ley General de los Derechos de Niños, Niñas y Adolescentes [General Law on the Rights of Children and Adolescents].* https://www.diputados.gob.mx/LeyesBiblio/pdf/LGDNNA.pdf

Duarte, J. M. (2021). It is possible to build peace, we are doing it. Experiences of parents in primary schools in Chiapas, Mexico. *Revista de Educación, 22*, 243–262. http://fh.mdp.edu.ar/revistas/index.php/r_educ/article/view/4805/5003

Echeverría-Castro, S., Sandoval-Domínguez, R., Sotelo-Castillo, M., Barrera-Hernández, L., & Ramos-Estrada, D. (2021). Beliefs about parent participation in school activities in rural and urban areas: Validation of a scale in Mexico. *Frontiers in Psychology, 5*(1), 79–91. https://doi.org/10.3389/fpsyg.2020.00639

Hampden-Thompson, G., & Galindo, C. (2017). School-family relationships, school satisfaction and the academic achievement of young people. *Educational Review, 69*(2), 248–265. https://doi.org/10.1080/00131911.2016.1207613

Jiménez Naranjo, Y., & Kreisel, M. (2018). Community participation in education-reconfigurations of schooling and social participation. *Teoría de la Educación. Interuniversity Journal, 30*(2), 2. https://doi.org/10.14201/teoredu302223246

López Pereyra, M. (2022). *Annex 14. Other Products of Proposal 309451. Pedagogy of hope and non-violence: Educational proposal for the inclusion of new family models.* Universidad Iberoamericana.

Martin, C., & Guzmán Flores, E. (2016). Parent involvement in schools: A divorce by mutual consent. *Synectica, 46*, 46. http://sinectica.iteso.mx/index.php/SINECTICA/article/view/610

Martínez Bordon, A., Bracho González, T., & Martínez Valle, C. (2010). The councils for social participation in education and the quality schools programme: Social mechanisms for accountability? In A. Olvera (Ed.), *La democratización frustrada. Limitaciones institucionales y colonización política de las instituciones garantes de derechos y de participación ciudadana en México* (pp. 129–174). CIESAS-Universidad Veracruzana.

Martiniello, M. (2000). Parental involvement in education: Towards a taxonomy for Latin America. In J. C. Navarro, K. Taylor, A. Bernasconi, & L. Tyler (Eds.), *Perspectives on education reform* (pp. 175–210). U.S. Agency for International Development, IDB, Harvard Institute for International Development.

Mejía-Arauz, R., Keyser Ohrt, U., & Correa-Chávez, M. (2013). Cultural and generational transformations in the collaborative participation of girls and boys in a P'urhépecha community. *Revista Mexicana de Investigación Educativa, 18*(59), 1019–1045. https://www.scielo.org.mx/pdf/rmie/v18n59/v18n59a2.pdf

Mercado Maldonado, R., & Montaño Sánchez, L. (2015). *Processes of participation between kindergarten teachers and mothers in teaching activities.* https://www.comie.org.mx/revista/v2018/rmie/index.php/nrmie/article/view/130/130

Muñoz Rodríguez, É. (2022). Interaction of social categories in the family-school relationship: How do they favour or hinder participation? *Revista Latinoamericana de Estudios Educativos, 52*(3), 3. https://doi.org/10.48102/rlee.2022.52.3.519

National Human Rights Commission. (2018). *Children and adolescents have the right to Identity.* National Human Rights Commission. https://www.cndh.org.mx/sites/all/doc/Programas/Ninez_familia/Material/cuadri-identidad-ninas-ninos.pdf

Ocampo González, A. (2019). Theoretical contours of inclusive education. *Redipe Bulletin, 8*(3), 66–95. https://doi.org/10.36260/rbr.v8i3.696

126 *Inclusion of Families in Basic Education in Mexico*

Official Journal of the Federation [DOF]. (2019). *DECREE issuing the general law on education and repealing the general law on physical education infrastructure.* https://www.diputados.gob.mx/LeyesBiblio/pdf/LGDNNA.pdf

Official Journal of the Federation [DOF]. (2022). *AGREEMENT number 05/02/22 issuing the Rules of Operation of the School is Ours Programme for the 2022 fiscal year.* https://dof.gob.mx/nota_detalle.php?codigo=5643991&fecha=28/02/2022#gsc.tab=0

Park, S., & Holloway, S. D. (2017). The effects of school-based parental involvement on academic achievement at the child and elementary school level: A longitudinal study. *The Journal of Educational Research, 110*(1), 1–16. https://doi.org/10.1080/00220671.2015.1016600

Perales Franco, C. (2022). *School community relationships, a study of school coexistence in Mexico.* Universidad Iberoamericana.

Perales Franco, C., & Sartorello, S. (2023). School and community relationships in Mexico. Researching inclusion in education from critical and decolonial perspectives. *British Journal of Sociology of Education*, 1–19. https://doi.org/10.1080/01425692.2023.2219406

Perales Mejía, F., & Escobedo Carrillo, M. (2016). Social participation in education: Between innovative proposals and educational tradition. *Revista Electrónica de Investigación Educativa, 18*(1), 69–81. http://redie.uabc.mx/redie/article/view/738

Perales Mejía, F. (2014). Social participation in education: Between community habitus and administrative obligation. *CPU-e, Revista de Investigación Educativa, 19*, 86–119. https://www.redalyc.org/articulo.oa?id=283131303004

Razeto, A. (2018). Strategies to promote family participation in children's education in Chilean schools. *Educação e Pesquisa, 44.* https://doi.org/10.1590/S1678-4634201844180495

Sánchez Escobedo, P. A., Valdés Cuervo, Á. A., Reyes Mendoza, N. M., & Carlos Martínez, E. A. (2010). Involvement of parents of primary school students in their children's education in Mexico. *Liberabit, 16*(1), 71–80. http://www.scielo.org.pe/pdf/liber/v16n1/a08v16n1.pdf

Schalla, L. (2015). *Family-school collaboration in Mexico: Perspectives of teachers and parents* [Doctoral dissertation, University of Minnesota]. https://www.proquest.com/openview/6246c4d48ece97825ad9acbba58f6e69/1?pq-origsite=gscholar&cbl=18750

Sheridan, S., & Moorman Kim, E. (Eds.). (2016). *Research on family-school partnerships, Family-school partnerships in context* (Vol. 3). Springer.

Slee, R. (2011). *The extraordinary school. Exclusion, schooling and inclusive education.* Ediciones Morata.

Solís Castillo, F., Aguiar Sierra, R., Solís Castillo, F., & Aguiar Sierra, R. (2017). Analysis of the role of family involvement in secondary school and its impact on academic achievement. *Sinéctica, 49*, 1–22. https://www.scielo.org.mx/scielo.php?script=sci_arttext&pid=S1665-109X2017000200013

Valdés Cuervo, Á., Martín Pavón, M., & Sánchez Escobedo, P. (2009). Involvement of parents of primary school students in their children's academic activities. *Revista Electrónica de Investigación Educativa, 11*(1), 1–17. http://redie.uabc.mx/vol11no1/contenido-ss.html

Valdés Cuervo, Á., & Urías Murrieta, M. (2010). Creencias de padres y madres acerca de la participación en la educación de sus hijos. *Perfiles Educativos, 33*(134). https://doi.org/10.22201/iisue.24486167e.2011.134.27943

Valdés Dávila, M. (2019). Parental involvement and students' academic achievement. A case study of a primary school in Mexico. *Diálogos Pedagógicos, 17*(33), 1–17. https://doi.org/10.25529/dp.2019.17(33)01

Valdés, A. A., & Sánchez, P. A. (2016). Teachers' beliefs about family involvement in education. *Revista Electrónica de Investigación Educativa, 18*(2), 105–115. http://redie.uabc.mx/redie/article/view/1174

Valdés, Á., & Yáñez, A. (2013). Differences in the promotion of family participation in primary schools with high and low performance in the link test. *Intercontinental Journal of Psychology and Education, 15*(2), 115–133. https://www.redalyc.org/pdf/802/80228344007.pdf

Vásquez García, S., & Gómez González, G. (2006). Indigenous self-management in Tlahuitoltepec Mixe, Oaxaca, Mexico. *Ra Ximhai: Scientific Journal of Society, Culture and Sustainable Development, 2*(1), 151–169. http://www.uaim.edu.mx/webraximhai/Ej-04articulosPDF/08%202006.pdf

TEACHERS' SCIENTIFIC EXPLANATION PRACTICES: OPPORTUNITIES FOR EQUITY

Valeria M. Cabello[a] and David Geelan[b]

[a]Pontificia Universidad Católica de Chile, Chile
[b]The University of Notre Dame Australia, Australia

ABSTRACT

Teachers' explanations of scientific concepts to students are essential to science teaching. While there is potential for such explanations to perpetuate societal advantage, we argue that explanation in science education can be an emancipatory practice when considering the needs, aspirations, life experiences and background knowledge of teachers' diverse groups of students. Considering that explaining science is usually implemented as a hierarchical discourse, the purpose is to inform science education in Latin America towards teaching practices that can promote a dialogical approach to distribute the power of knowledge in the classroom. This chapter discusses research on teacher education conducted in science classrooms, focusing on how explanations in science education can offer opportunities for enhancing educational equity and access to the languages of the sciences.

Keywords: Educational equity; instructional explanation; science education; emancipatory teaching; classroom research; literacies of science; classroom discourse

INTRODUCTION

Teaching science involves providing a range of learning experiences and activities for students, and one of the principal activities of science teachers is explaining scientific concepts to students. This activity is a pedagogical strategy and a cognitive tool. It satisfies children's explanation-seeking curiosity and desire to understand the world through plausible reasons (Liquin & Lombrozo, 2020).

Intercultural and Inclusive Education in Latin America
International Perspectives on Inclusive Education, Volume 24, 127–139
Copyright © 2024 Valeria M. Cabello and David Geelan
Published under exclusive licence by Emerald Publishing Limited
ISSN: 1479-3636/doi:10.1108/S1479-363620240000024009

Thus, teacher explanations play a crucial role in promoting science learning and developing learners' ways of thinking.

Teachers also elicit explanations from students in classrooms, which enables the students to exchange scientific ideas with each other and contribute to the development of one another's understanding. Skills in developing and defending such 'science teaching explanations', however, are typically learned based on teachers' modelling.

It is plausible that science teacher explanations could be delivered in such a way that social inequities would be perpetuated (e.g. Bolger & Ecklund, 2022; Tenenbaum & Leaper, 2003). If explanations require particular intellectual and social capital on the part of students to understand them and those forms of capital are inequitably distributed among the students in a class, understanding may be facilitated more effectively for those who are already advantaged.

We would argue, however, that science teacher explanations as a teaching device – a product – and explaining in the classroom – a process – can instead become emancipatory if and when practised as intentional teaching, considering the diverse student's knowledge, interests, background, language, abilities, and social and intellectual capital.

This chapter explores science teacher explanations as an intentional teaching practice and discusses classroom-based research findings from studies conducted in Australia, Chile and Canada. It then considers ways in which science teacher explanations can more effectively serve as an emancipatory practice with the potential to enhance equity and challenge entrenched patterns of advantage and disadvantage.

EXPLANATION IN SCIENCE AND IN SCIENCE TEACHING

Explanation in the practice of science itself has been long debated within the philosophy of science, by Plato and Aristotle, followed by Hempel and Oppenheim (1948, Hempel, 1965), van Fraasen (1977), Salmon (1978, 1998, 2006) and others. Ruben (2012) offers an excellent overview of this work.

Explanation in science is typically conceived of as an explanation of causation (Salmon, 2006). Theories in science can be said to have a combination of descriptive, predictive and explanatory power. That is, they must be able to accurately describe the phenomena we observe in nature and enable us to predict the outcomes of particular interventions or occurrences. At the same time, it also offers a causal explanation for these outcomes. For instance, Kepler's laws of planetary motion offer descriptive and predictive power: they can describe past and present positions of the planets relative to one another and to the sun and predict their future motion and related events such as solar and lunar eclipses and conjunctions of the planets. Kepler developed them from empirical observations and careful mathematical analysis. They do not, however, offer explanatory power: they do not explain the causes of the motions they describe. For explanation, it is necessary to go to the theories of Newton on universal gravitation or Einstein's general relativity.

Hempel and Oppenheim (1948) proposed a 'deductive-nomological' model of explanation in science that drew on scientific laws and initial conditions to explain phenomena and events. Salmon (1978, 1984) critiqued their model on various grounds and presented a causal/mechanical account of scientific explanations.

For the purposes of this chapter, we are concerned with the different phenomena of what Treagust and Harrison (1999, 2000) called 'science teaching explanations' and Braaten and Windschitl (2011) described as 'explications of an explanation'. Whereas explanations within science are concerned with causality, science teaching explanations are focused on students' developing new understandings of scientific concepts. Science teachers aim for their students to develop a 'dynamic and fluid mental model' of concepts and phenomena (Harrison & Treagust, 1996). Treagust and Harrison (2000) summarised the differences between explanations in science and in science teaching as follows:

> There are important philosophical and epistemological differences between science explanations and science teaching explanations. Science explanations are strictly characterised as theory and evidence-driven, use the correct scientific terms and include analogical models. Science teaching explanations differ in rigour, length and detail, involve varying degrees of 'explain how' and 'explain why', are sometimes open-ended, include human agency and can raise new questions as they answer previous questions. (p. 1138)

Explanation and Explaining: A Constructivist Perspective

Explaining might be seen as a 'transmissive' activity whereby a teacher develops an explanation in their mind and delivers it to their students using an explanation as a vehicle. The students memorise it and then replicate the content in an examination or apply it in their lives as a way of understanding the world around them. Based on the work of our German colleagues Kulgemeyer and Schecker (2009, 2012), we argue that explaining in science teaching can be considered a constructivist practice (Geelan, 1997), which is learned in initial science teacher education.

Constructivism is an epistemological theory, a theory about knowledge and how we come to know (e.g. Piaget, 1972; Solomon, 1987; Vygotsky, 1978). While some learning strategies and student activities have been associated in the past with a constructivist perspective on knowledge, constructivism does not directly prescribe teaching methods. Rather, the metaphor is that of constructing a new building from the available materials and can be extended to include the idea of the 'ground' on which the new construction occurs – the student's prior understanding of the topic – and the structure of the discipline. Construction is an active process, but the critical point is that the mind is active in the processes of learning. It may or may not be accompanied by physical activity at any particular moment.

Students construct new understandings about the world based on all of their experiences with it, including but not limited to everyday play, interactions with peers and adults and media usage, as well as other classroom experiences. Teacher explanation is not a strategy that should be exclusively relied upon for learning scientific concepts – experiments and hands-on activities are also important – but explanations can provide one source of 'material' with which students can construct and test new understandings as they build more sophisticated mental models of the phenomena.

Kulgemeyer and Schecker (2012) discuss the distinction between the noun 'explanation' and the verb 'explaining' in the context of a constructivist approach. It is essential to distinguish between one and the other because one can open more possibilities for equity in the classroom than the other, which is the focus of this chapter.

An 'explanation' is a static artefact, a product of thinking converging with the structure of the discipline, which can be delivered verbally in a classroom, written in a textbook, presented on video, illustrated in an animation or communicated in a range of other ways. An explanation is designed and developed for a particular audience, but in a sense, it must be an imagined audience because, usually, the person explaining does not have direct knowledge of the audience. The terms, concepts and approaches used to explain why the sky is blue will differ depending on the age of the target audience. In one-way communications like YouTube videos, the explainer typically does not have the opportunity to receive feedback from the audience and modify the explanation to fit better the needs and interests of those who are intended to come to understand the concept.

On the other hand, *explaining* is a dynamic process whereby a teacher offers a class a 'live' explanation. With a good understanding of developmental stages and prior knowledge at both an individual and classroom level, teachers can tailor their initial explanations accordingly. However, the classroom setting allows teachers to get students' instant feedback through questions, comments, facial expressions and body language. Based on this feedback, teachers can decide to elaborate or modify their explanation while trying a different analogy or approach. During this process, teachers actively respond to the needs of the students by raising or lowering the level of complexity of their explanation, among a range of other practices.

Moreover, suppose teachers inquire about their students' initial ideas, experiences or connections with the topic. In that case, they can reshape their explanations for the classroom to contrast, link, clarify or negotiate the meaning in response to students' inputs. This approach has arguably greater potential to enhance students' construction of rich, well-elaborated concepts that coincide with the current canonical scientific concepts and can include their own experiences. In addition, while students are less likely to develop misconceptions and misunderstandings, teachers can develop and deepen their expertise in enhancing students' understanding through an active and recurrent process of delivering, sophisticating or modifying such explanations over time.

The sine qua non (without this, nothing) of effective explaining is knowledge on the part of the teacher of the diverse students' needs. As stated above, this includes not only knowledge of the current state of students' understanding of the target concept to be learned but also their thinking structure and flexibility, developing scientific reasoning, and ways of constructing new learnings. Hence, this chapter focuses on this breadth of knowledge from which the practice of teachers' scientific explanations can offer an opportunity to enhance equity in the classroom.

Explaining, Understanding and Equity

When secondary school physics students were asked about the qualities of their favourite teachers (Geelan, 2020), they identified two features (paraphrased): 'She knows her stuff, and she knows me'. That is, the teachers had a strong understanding of the content knowledge and concepts being taught, which enhanced confidence on the part of the students, and the teachers took the time and expended the interest to really come to know the students, both as learners and as people with their own backgrounds, needs, interests and abilities. In a similar exercise with Chilean students (Pontificia Universidad Católica de Valparaíso, 2010), 73.2% said 's/he knows how to explain and is willing to do it repeatedly' as one of the three most important characteristics of a good teacher, followed by 's/he listens and considers the students' opinions' and 's/he has high content knowledge'. Thus, the students in these two studies across different countries perceived that both elements were essential.

When explaining scientific concepts or phenomena as a practice within a classroom, teachers need to draw on each of these elements. Both their initial explanations and their revisions and responses to feedback are informed by the following:

- their own rich, well-elaborated understanding of the scientific concept itself, its place in the structure of the discipline and links to other scientific concepts, knowledge of common student misconceptions and how to challenge them and a range of additional content and pedagogical content knowledge (Shulman, 1986) and
- their rich, well-elaborated understanding of *these* students, *this* class and *this* year in this school.

We believe the potential for emancipatory practice arises from this second element. When teachers know who their students really are, where they come from, what their home lives and circumstances are like, what their capabilities with literacy and numeracy are, their abilities and disabilities, expectations, their hobbies, sports and interests, among other features, the process of developing and offering explanations of scientific concepts can become a practice for equity in the classrooms. Linking teachers' explanations to student experiences, receiving and interpreting student feedback, checking for understanding and revising their explanations to collectively construct meaning can be far more effective in facilitating learning for all students. Moreover, explaining can be a strategy for knowledge integration, and, from this perspective, explanations are seen as learning artefacts that embrace elements of how science and school science are constructed and reconstructed in classrooms (Bell & Linn, 2000). Nonetheless, from teacher education, we argue that teachers are typically taught to provide the 'correct explanation' rather than equipped for classroom explanation construction based on the premise that students can openly question their explanations (Charalambous et al., 2011).

Beginning Teachers' Scientific Explanations in Chilean Classrooms

In the context of Chile, students' achievements in science are measured by national and international tests. National ones are curricula based, and science curriculum is extensive in content. International tests show that one of the weakest performances of Chilean students is explaining natural phenomena based on scientific theories, concepts or ideas. Moreover, gender differences have been shown in national achievements favouring boys' performance in science over girls (Navarro & Förster, 2012). The gender gap is a crucial point to be considered because it is not a global tendency in developed countries. In this context, the results of international and national science tests are also highly dependent on the income level of the students' families (González et al., 2009; Navarro & Förster, 2012; Valencia & Taut, 2011). It is worrying because although the country seems to be doing better than other Latin American countries in general terms, it is one of the least equally distributed in terms of learning and income level (OECD, [Organization for Economic Cooperation and Development], 2018).

Teacher quality has been shown to affect students' learning in the Chilean context. A direct association between teachers' performance levels and students' learning outcomes was found in national tests (Alvarado et al., 2012). Currently, some efforts in research and practice within the field of teacher education are advancing to promote better explanations in the classroom.

Research on science pre-service and beginner teachers' explanations in Santiago de Chile has identified structural and representational elements that can be learned – some more easily than others – during initial teacher education programs. These elements are centred on pedagogical resources in general and the use of language in structuring the explanation in particular (Cabello et al., 2019; Cabello & Topping, 2018; Marzabal et al., 2019).

Studies conducted with student teachers and novice teachers show that giving students definitions with examples or images is the most common strategy used to communicate or illustrate concepts in Chilean classrooms. Learners' misconceptions or misunderstandings are not frequently employed to enrich the learning process with explanations. In fact, if misconceptions appeared, teachers immediately corrected students by providing the 'correct' information or by simply ignoring the misconceptions without inquiring about their causes or underpinning ideas. Even if the topics had available simulations or possibilities to be modelled, student teachers rarely used analogies or metaphors. They did not refer to history or the nature of science to present how the concepts or theories typically develop in a particular sociocultural context (Cabello et al., 2019).

Several aspects of teacher explanations, however, can be intentionally modified to reach diverse audiences and meet student needs:

(1) *Explaining with body gestures as a connection between scientific concepts and daily-life concepts.* Non-verbal language expressed through gestures and body movements helps students with diverse ways of processing information, or sensory impairment, to differentiate essential from peripheral details and connect the scientific concepts with their use in daily life versus in scientific fields.

(2) *Explaining using everyday words to favour level-appropriate explanations.* Considering the students' grade level, the explanation's language might need to be simplified or advanced. For instance, if the subject-specific language is introduced too early, it might not connect with what students already know, so using everyday words will be necessary to enhance comprehension. On the contrary, if the explanation overuses simple language, students with more robust prior knowledge or ones academically more advanced than others might feel that the explanation is not challenging enough for them, leaving their cognitive need to understand why the phenomenon occurs at a more sophisticated level unfulfilled.

(3) *Including scientists and female learners' voices in explanation construction.* Why did the scientist put effort into postulating an idea, probing a hypothesis or discovering a pattern? In what socio-historical context were the theories behind explanations needed and constructed? Addressing these questions and explicitly including female voices – the ideas of women scientists and girl students – in explanation construction helps to give the epistemic sense that:
- concepts in science are not final but are our best current understanding;
- scientific knowledge can be questioned;
- science is under constant scrutiny and revision.

(4) *Explaining using diverse representations and ways of constructing knowledge.* Although we have argued that redundancy in explanations might overload students' cognitive system, we believe that adding diverse, complementary and redundant representations during the process of explanation construction might actually enrich learning and promote equity in classrooms, especially in those with students who have additional learning needs. Metaphors, analogies, simulations, demonstrations, experiments and concrete or physical representations are some examples of ways to diversify students' access to knowledge construction.

These alternatives are not exhaustive. Rather, each teacher can develop different ways to transform students' ideas during lessons keeping equity at the front and centre of their practice. The practice of explanations must base itself on students' diverse needs and characteristics, as well as the discipline structure and the use of verbal and non-verbal language as teaching tools that can open access to the languages of sciences.

Physics Teachers' Explanatory Frameworks in Australian and Canadian Classrooms

Australia's education system has been described as 'high quality, low equity' (Gannon & Somerville, 2014). While, in general, Australian students perform well on international comparisons such as Trends in International Mathematics and Science Study (TIMSS) and Programme for International Student Assessment (PISA), socio-economic status is strongly correlated with academic achievement and as societal inequality grows. Indeed, as funding is increasingly directed towards those schools and students already economically advantaged, the gaps between the highest and lowest-performing students are growing, which is leading to a decrease in the aggregate performance of Australian students. Broader societal and political changes are needed to refocus on 'education for all' and adequate resourcing of the public schools serving approximately 65% of students to get to the foundations of these inequities. Nonetheless, we would argue that there are also highly effective practices available to teachers in all sectors that have the potential to address student disadvantage and offer opportunities for academic success and concomitant economic benefits.

Canada is arguably less divided on these lines, although its province-based approach to education policy means it can be challenging to make generalisable statements about approaches to education, funding and equity. The results reported here are from Edmonton in Alberta, and at the time of the study, the provincial government funded both public and religious schools in that province.

Leaving aside the economic differences between Australia and Canada for the moment, the ways in which senior secondary school physics was taught in both countries were so similar to the data from four classes in Perth, Western Australia, and 12 classes from Edmonton, Canada, which were coded as a single large data set (Geelan, 2009). Several hours of video were recorded from the back of each classroom and then coded to identify common features of teacher explanations in physics classrooms. The following features were coded:

- Appeals to earlier learning in the course.
- Knowledge from other school subjects.
- Anthropomorphic and teleological language.
- Hand gestures or body movements.
- Analogies and metaphors.
- Calculations on the whiteboard or smartboard.
- Use of diagrams.
- Electronic animations or simulations.
- Apparatus and demonstrations in explanations.
- Explicit allusions to assessment.
- Open- and closed-ended questioning.
- Jokes and humour.

These features were observed, at varying degrees, in diverse ways across different classrooms. However, differences appeared to depend more on teachers' personal teaching style and experience, the topic being studied and the time in the school year or term (early or late in the teacher's relationship with the students) than on either the country in which the teaching occurred or the socio-economic status of the school community. However, there were exceptions which are discussed in more detail below. There were striking similarities across all classrooms: the conventions of physics and physics teaching seem to have considerable 'inertia' in guiding practices.

After conducting a thematic analysis of the coded video, the following common elements of physics teacher explanations emerged:

- The 'move to mathematics' – teachers often began an explanation in a qualitative mode, describing a physical situation or using a demonstration or video to introduce students to the phenomena the explanation was intended to explain, but then often moved relatively quickly to a whiteboard or other medium to write out calculations, using mathematics as a tool for encoding and manipulating the symbols representing the physical entities being discussed. Sometimes, there was dynamic movement between equations and verbal depictions, but often the conclusion of the sequence was focused on how this calculation demonstrated the explanatory power of the scientific concept.
- Attention to the requirements of success on external exams – teachers typically spoke about exam success during their explanations, but some were more explicit than others in saying, 'This is the physics content, and here's how you will demonstrate that you understand it in an exam', whereas for others, understanding and exam success seemed to be conflated. Often, this guidance was in the form of shortcuts: 'skip a calculation at this step by combining these things to give you more time for the rest of the exam'.
- Use of analogies – analogies are pervasive in the teaching of physics and have received considerable research attention (e.g. Duit, 1991). Some teachers paid more explicit attention to the ways in which the analogical context mapped the target scientific concept, including the places in which the analogy breaks down, while others were less so, and perhaps sometimes led to the development or reinforcement of student misconceptions as the students made unintended incorrect mappings from the familiar to the new concept.
- Storytelling and references to the history of science – developments in human understanding of the world were often illustrated with anecdotes from the history of science or descriptions of 'dead ends' in science such as phlogiston and aether theories. The (probably mythical) narratives of Archimedes emerging from his bath shouting 'Eureka' when he solved the density problem, Newton observing (or in some versions being struck by) a falling apple, Galileo conducting experiments by dropping objects from the Leaning Tower of Pisa and so on were also frequently included in teacher explanations.
- Role of technology – information technologies were used in various ways to illustrate explanations and conduct experiments. Teachers were more or less explicit in discussing the 'black box' nature of electronic sensors connected to computers as a means of taking measurements and conducting experiments and talked in various ways about the dynamic relationship between science and technology.
- Humour – physics teacher humour tends to be quite deadpan and dry but was a feature in almost every classroom observed. Sometimes teachers used pop culture allusions (often outdated) to try to connect with students, but some teachers also used 'physics humour' that required understanding the physics concepts to 'get' the joke both as a means of teaching concepts and to check students' understanding.

One interesting difference noted between schools in communities of lower and higher socio-economic status was the extent to which students, and some students in particular, were included or excluded in questioning and classroom discussion.

Among schools in the wealthy independent 'grammar school' sector in Australia and in more-affluent suburbs in Canada, physics classes focused on success in the external examinations at the end of Grade 12. This focus was since these examinations are the pathway to access particular university degrees connected to relatively lucrative occupations. This meant that in these schools, more emphasis was placed on explicit attention to the requirements of examination success. The goal of the physics course was an explicit examination of success, and physics problems were assessed and analysed in terms of this criterion.

In these classrooms, the teacher typically had a small group of high-achieving students, who often sat near the classroom's front and provided the correct answer to any questions directed by the teacher to the class. The 'IRE' (initiation, response, evaluation) sequence was the most common questioning pattern: the teacher asked a factual question with a correct answer, a student offered an answer and the teacher indicated whether it was right and offered the correct answer if it was not, concluding the sequence. The focus is on correct answers.

Most students in the class did not participate in class discussions, and checking for understanding on the part of all students was not a routine feature of teacher explanations or classroom discussions. It was quite possible for a student to be attending class but not really following what was being learned, and the attitude from all involved seemed to be that success was the student's responsibility, and the exam would 'sort it all out' in terms of who would succeed and who would not. It could be argued that this teaching approach is more likely to perpetuate than challenge existing societal inequities.

Among schools in communities of lower socio-economic status, the focus was much more on understanding physics concepts for their own sake and as lenses with which to interpret experiences of the world. Typically, most or all students were actively involved in classroom discussions and were called 'back on task' by the teacher if they were not participating and paying attention. Questions were directed by name to all or most students, including those less likely to be able to provide a correct answer. Teachers often gently persisted with a student through a sequence of a few questions leading towards understanding and challenging misconceptions with evidence or arguments. Exam success was also valued and spoken about in these classrooms, but the focus was on students' understanding of the physics concepts and particularly on ensuring that no student was 'left behind' in developing understanding. Students typically saw themselves and behaved as comrades and collaborators in one another's learning rather than as competitors.

It might be clear where our values lie in these descriptions of the two kinds of classrooms, but at the same time, it is true that the students who did succeed in the more competitive, success-focused classrooms were more likely to go on to the societal advantage, relative wealth and more comfortable lives. Are there ways in which the best features of both approaches can be combined in teacher explanations to support all students to succeed in their studies? and could it be done by developing a deep understanding of the core scientific concepts to be learned rather than simply by learning to comply with assessments under exam conditions? There remains additional work to be done in exploring whether more explicit teaching of the skills of science teacher explaining might modify the processes of explaining in practicum. Likewise, more research is needed to explore the extent to which in-service teachers have the ability to enhance student learning based on constructing explanations across the spectrum of school contexts.

CONCLUSION

Explanation and explaining in science classrooms are crucial teacher skills for developing students' scientific understanding. It can potentially perpetuate societal inequity and advantage if used without carefully considering students' backgrounds and needs. This is a key point considering Latin American science education, which tends to follow more traditional approaches or construct hierarchical discourses about science and its construction. In this, Chilean science education context is more like the regional context, specifically offering finished explanations, based mainly on teacher-centred explanations compound by images and examples. As a result, the learning levels according to international and national science tests are highly dependent on the income level of the students' families and the learners' gender. Thus, this country is one of the least equally distributed in terms of learning and income level, which might change with more equitable approaches to teaching. The purpose of this chapter was to inform science education in Latin America towards teaching practices that can promote a dialogical approach. Applying such considerations will promote pathways to success among students from less-advantaged backgrounds, with learning difficulties, sensory impairments or those belonging to groups usually excluded from the scientific construction of knowledge (woman, gender minorities, etc.). We suggest this is a way to pedagogically distribute the power of knowledge in the classroom. Thus, constructing explanations in this learning setting might enhance societal equity and access to science, as a strategy for educational justice.

ACKNOWLEDGEMENTS

To Agencia Nacional de Investigación y Desarrollo ANID/FONDECYT 1221716 and ANID – Millennium Science Initiative Program – Code NCS2021_014.

REFERENCES

Alvarado, Cabezas, G., Falck, D., & Ortega, M. E. (2012). *La Evaluación Docente y sus instrumentos: discriminación del desempeño docente y asociación con los resultados de los estudiantes. Ministerio de Educación.*

138   *Teachers' Scientific Explanation Practices*

Bell, P., & Linn, M. C. (2000). Scientific arguments as learning artifacts: Designing for learning from the web with KIE. *International Journal of Science Education, 22*(8), 797–817. https://doi.org/10.1080/095006900412284

Bolger, D., & Ecklund, E. H. (2022). Seeing is achieving: Religion, embodiment, and explanations of racial inequality in STEM. *Ethnic and Racial Studies, 45*(1), 3–21.

Braaten, M., & Windschitl, M. (2011). Working toward a stronger conceptualisation of scientific explanation for science education. *Science Education, 95*(4), 639–669.

Cabello, V. M., Real, C., & Impedovo, M. A. (2019). Explanations in STEM areas: An analysis of representations through language in teacher education. *Research in Science Education, 49*(4), 1087–1106. https://doi.org/10.1007/s11165-019-9856-6

Cabello, V. M., & Topping, K. (2018). Making scientific concepts explicit through explanations: Simulations of a high-leverage practice in teacher education. *International Journal of Cognitive Research in Science, Engineering and Education, 6*(3), 35–47. https://doi.org/10.5937/ijcrsee1803035C

Charalambous, C. Y., Hill, H. C., & Ball, D. L. (2011). Prospective teachers' learning to provide instructional explanations: How does it look and what might it take? *Journal of Mathematics Teacher Education, 14*(6), 441–463. https://doi.org/10.1007/s10857-011-9182-z

Duit, R. (1991). On the role of analogies and metaphors in learning science. *Science Education, 75*(6), 649–672.

Gannon, S., & Somerville, M. (2014). *Contemporary issues of equity in education.* Cambridge Scholars Publishing.

Geelan, D. R. (1997). Epistemological anarchy and the many forms of constructivism. *Science & Education, 6*(1–2), 15–28.

Geelan, D. (2009). Explaining topics in physics: An international video study. In G. Siemens & C. Fulford (Eds.), *Proceedings of ED-MEDIA 2009—World conference on educational multimedia, hypermedia & telecommunications* (pp. 2541–2546). Association for the Advancement of Computing in Education (AACE).

Geelan, D. (2020). Physical science teacher skills in a conceptual explanation. *Education in Science, 10*(1), 23. https://doi.org/10.3390/educsci10010023

González, C., Martínez, M. T., Martínez, C., Cuevas, K., & Muñoz, L. (2009). La educación científica como apoyo a la movilidad social: Desafíos en torno al rol del profesor secundario en la implementación de la indagación científica como enfoque pedagógico. *Estudios pedagógicos (Valdivia), 35*, 63–78.

Harrison, A. G., & Treagust, D. F. (1996). Secondary students' mental models of atoms and molecules: Implications for teaching chemistry. *Science Education, 80*, 509–553.

Hempel, C. G. (1965). *Aspects of scientific explanation; and other essays in the philosophy of science.* The Free Press.

Hempel, C. G., & Oppenheim, P. (1948). Studies in the logic of explanation. *Philosophy of Science, 15*(2), 135–175.

Kulgemeyer, C., & Schecker, H. (2009). Kommunikationskompetenz in der Physik: Zur Entwicklung eines domänenspezifischen Kompetenzbegriffs [Developing a domain-specific communication model for physics]. *Zeitschrift für Didaktik der Naturwissenschaften, 15*, 131–153.

Kulgemeyer, C., & Schecker, H. (2012). Physikalische Kommunikationskompetenz - Empirische Validierung eines normativen Modells [Empirical validation of a normative model for communicating physics]. *Zeitschrift für Didaktik der Naturwissenschaften, 18*, 29–54.

Liquin, E. G., & Lombrozo, T. (2020). A functional approach to explanation-seeking curiosity. *Cognitive Psychology, 119*, 101276.

Marzabal, A., Merino, C., Moreira, P., & Delgado, V. (2019). Assessing science teaching explanations in initial teacher education: How is this teaching practice transferred across different chemistry topics? *Research in Science Education, 49*, 1107–1123.

Navarro, M. B., & Förster, C. E. (2012). Nivel de alfabetización científica y actitudes hacia la ciencia en estudiantes de secundaria: comparaciones por sexo y nivel socioeconómico. *Pensamiento Educativo, Revista de Investigación Latinoamericana (PEL), 49*(1), 1–17.

VALERIA M. CABELLO AND DAVID GEELAN

OECD. Organization for Economic Cooperation and Development. (2018). *Equity in education: Breaking down barriers to social mobility.* OECD Publishing. https://doi.org/10.1787/9789264073234-en

Piaget, J. (1972). *The principles of genetic epistemology.* Basic Books.

Pontificia Universidad Católica de Valparaíso. (2010). Encuesta mis profesores y yo. https://www.pucv.cl/uuaa/site/docs/20151019/20151019163020/mis_profesores_y_yo.pdf

Ruben, D.-H. (2012). *Explaining explanation* (Updated and extended 2nd ed.). Paradigm Press.

Salmon, W. (1978). Why ask 'why?'? An inquiry concerning scientific explanation. *Proceedings and Addresses of the American Philosophical Association, 51*(6), 683–705. Reprinted in Salmon 1998: 125–141.

Salmon, W. C. (1984). *Scientific explanation and the causal structure of the world.* Princeton University Press.

Salmon, W. (1998). *Causality and explanation.* Oxford University Press. https://doi.org/10.1093/0195108647.001.0001

Salmon, W. C. (2006). *Four decades of scientific explanation.* Pittsburgh University of Pittsburgh Press.

Shulman, L. S. (1986). Those who understand: Knowledge growth in teaching. *Education and Researcher, 15*(2), 4–14.

Solomon, J. (1987). Social influences on the construction of pupils' understanding of science. *Studies in Science Education, 14,* 63–82.

Tenenbaum, H. R., & Leaper, C. (2003). Parent-child conversations about science: The socialization of gender inequities? *Developmental Psychology, 39*(1), 34.

Treagust, D. F., & Harrison, A. G. (1999). The genesis of effective scientific explanations for the classroom. In J. Loughran (Ed.), *Researching teaching: Methodologies and practices for understanding pedagogy* (pp. 28–43). Falmer Press.

Treagust, D. F., & Harrison, A. G. (2000). In search of explanatory frameworks: An analysis of Richard Feynman's lecture 'Atoms in motion'. *International Journal of Science Education, 22*(11), 1157–1170.

Valencia, E., & Taut, S. (2011). *Evidencia de inequidad en el acceso a los docentes mejor calificados en la Enseñanza Básica chilena.* Centro de Medición MIDEUC.

Van Fraassen, B. C. (1977). The pragmatics of explanation. *American Philosophical Quarterly, 14*(2), 143–150.

Vygotsky, L. S. (1978). *Mind in society: The development of higher psychological processes* (M. Cole, V. John-Steiner, S. Scribner, & E. Souberman, Eds.). Harvard University Press.

INTERCULTURALITY AND EDUCATIONAL INCLUSION IN BRAZIL AND MEXICO: A COMPARATIVE ANALYSIS

Stefano Claudio Sartorello[a] and
Alexandre Ferraz Herbetta[b]

[a]*Iberoamerican University of Mexico City, Mexico*
[b]*Universidade Federal de Goiás (UFG), Brazil*

ABSTRACT

From a critical and decolonial perspective, a comparative analysis is made of the intercultural and inclusive education policies implemented in Mexico and Brazil during the 20th century and the first two decades of the 21st century. We observe the tendency to generate integrationist, ethnocidal, linguistic and epistemicidal educational policies, programmes and actions, generated from modern-colonial Eurocentric approaches aimed at the political, sociocultural and linguistic homogenisation of the national population. These contrast with the initiatives generated by indigenous and Afro-descendant peoples, organisations and movements which, from counter-hegemonic conceptions, are aimed at promoting autonomy and the valuation of their own ontologies, epistemologies and educations.

Keywords: Education; interculturality; inclusion; Brazil; Mexico; decoloniality

INTERCULTURAL AND INCLUSIVE EDUCATION POLICIES IN BRAZIL

Intercultural and inclusive policies have developed in Brazil since the 1980s and are intimately linked to the struggles of the Indigenous Movement and the Black

Movement in the country; they are inscribed in the perspective of reorganisation of civil society, linked to the notion of representative democracy, and begin to consolidate after experiencing more than two decades of a terrible process of civil–military dictatorship (1964–1985) that suppressed civil rights through the use of epistemological and physical violence. These policies generated actions that, in different ways, cut across and problematise centuries of racism and colonialism experienced in the country implemented with integrationist policies whose intention was to eliminate ethnic differences and other possibilities of existence. Thus, currently, they represent fundamental themes and actions for the construction of the social project of nationhood.

In these historical processes, it is important to highlight that the field of education – religious and civil – has been used strategically in the colonisation process to dismantle other epistemologies and homogenise the country. The indigenous school education proposed by the *Fundação Nacional do Índio* (FUNAI), the institution responsible for indigenist policies in Brazil since 1967 and, after 1991, by the Secretariat of Education, which assumes educational policies at the federal level, continues to be based on integrationist actions.

According to indigenous intellectual Daiara Sampaio Tukano (2018), current advances regarding the development of intercultural and inclusive public policies imply that they can be considered as policies of historical reparation.

Despite the complexities and differences inherent to the struggles of the Black and indigenous populations, this text attempts to highlight how such policies are articulated with processes of agency of these peoples, in a path saturated by tense situations and conflict, and which present advances and limits that are framed in structures and logics that are still very colonialist.[1]

It is important to note that the field of interculturality is insistently and univocally linked to the demands and situations experienced by native populations in Brazil. Inclusion policies are directly related to the affirmative actions claimed first by Black populations and later by indigenous populations, which was consolidated by Law number 12.711/2012, popularly known as the '*Lei de Cotas*' (*Quota* Law).

All intercultural and inclusive policies in the country are related to the appropriation of the education system by the aforementioned population groups and to the development of sub-areas such as 'indigenous school education', the creation of 'intercultural education courses' for the training of indigenous teachers and the access of indigenous, Afro-descendant, gypsy, trans and other populations to university, from which they have been historically excluded. It can be affirmed that these policies constitute concrete and delimited public actions for social transformation, with well-defined advances and obstacles, which, nevertheless, limit the possible transformations and innovations and hinder the valorisation of autonomous and community experiences within the same field. So far, for example, the creation of an indigenous university, which has been a project demanded by the Indigenous Movement since 2014 (Nascimento Potiguara, 2022), together with the transformation of the curricular matrix and pedagogical practices of universities and schools (Apinajé & Herbetta, 2018), as well as the creation of other alternative experiences, has not materialised.

In this context, there are great challenges and limits for the development and consolidation of more comprehensive intercultural and inclusive policies, as well as for the construction and multiplication of spaces for reflection and action that promote epistemological and political transformations in institutions that generate radical and effective inclusion. According to Professor María do Socorro Pimentel da Silva, public policies often strengthen a monocultural character that intensifies centralised decision-making mechanisms and reproduces a power structure with authoritarian decisions that exclude indigenous knowledge and that of other populations (Pimentel da Silva et al., 2021, p. 16).

HISTORICAL CONTEXT

Intercultural policies, although the term was not yet present at the time, began with the mobilisation of indigenous peoples in the 1970s and have been strengthened ever since. Attempts have been made to break with centuries of integrationist political projects based on genocide and epistemicide, which showed a cruel side also in relation to indigenous knowledge systems, attempting to eliminate and extinguish them.

In this context, in the 1990s, with the struggle of the Black Movement, organised from the *Unified Black Movement* (MNU) that originated in 1978, and based on mobilisations made by Black intellectuals since the beginning of the 20th century, such as Lélia Gonzalez, Beatriz Nascimento and Abdias Nascimento, the discussion of affirmative policies of inclusion, fundamental for the access and permanence of populations previously excluded from the academy, began. According to anthropologist Lélia Gonzalez (1988), racism plays a central role in the internalisation of a violent notion of superiority of 'colonisers' over the 'colonised', with its particular version installed at the base of Brazilian society.

The period of Brazilian re-democratisation (from 1974 to 1988) is a fundamental historical framework for understanding the aforementioned processes. It culminated in the consolidation of the 1988 Constitution, which brought important achievements for different populations in the country thanks to the actions of social movements and the reorganisation of civil society, with the prominent presence and action of the Indigenous and Black Movements and the emergence of the notion of representative democracy. Such a constitution is called '*Constituição Cidadã*' (Citizen Constitution), which aims at the insertion of a set of important ideas and postulates in search of a new project of society. Indigenous professor Luciano Baniwa (2014) argues that, despite these important constitutional changes, the idea of citizenship continues to be inspired by a modern-colonial Eurocentric perspective, without it having been possible to move towards different forms of ethnic citizenship.

The Constitution determines that the State will protect the 'manifestations of popular, indigenous and Afro-Brazilian cultures' (article 215, *Constituição 1988*, 2016) and that 'indigenous communities will also be assured the use of their mother tongues and their own learning processes' (article 210, *Constituição 1988*, 2016), in addition to 'native rights' in relation to the land and the practice of their particular customs (article 231, *Constituição 1988*, 2016). At the same time, the Constitution postulates for the first time that racism will be considered a non-bailable and imprescriptible crime (article 5, paragraph 42, Constituição 1988, 2016).

It is important to highlight that the aforementioned rights constitute an advance in relation to previous policies. Indigenist policy, for example, had as one of its legal frameworks the 1973 Statute of the Indian (Lei 6.001, 1973), which affirmed the cruel policy of integration through tutelage, and considered the indigenous person incapable of exercising their citizenship. On the other hand, the right to autonomy and the right to territory continued to be associated with the notion of Union (to the State), which indicates the concrete limits that are implicit in these intercultural and inclusive policies. In this way, the Citizens' Constitution, on the one hand, represents a fundamental moment in the process of conquering rights and, on the other, is associated with the maintenance of modern-colonial domination.

The term intercultural begins to appear in documents that refer to the indigenous struggle in the field of education, as in: *Diretrizes para a Política Nacional de Educação Escolar Indígena de* (1993), which marks an approach of public policies to the field of interculturality. At the same time, possible meanings of the concept are being consolidated, some related to a more critical stance and others to a more functional one. Thus, interculturality appears defined in the '*Lei de Diretrizes e Bases da Educação*' of 1996. The fight against racism and its practices continues to be postulated as a central theme to be dealt with in institutional spheres and state action. The Durban Conference, held in South Africa in 2001 (Durban Declaration and Programme of Action, 2001), was a milestone for the advancement of inclusive policies in the country, as it articulated and strengthened the struggle of the Black Movement in favour of affirmative action and culminated in successful and interesting experiences during the 2000s.

CURRENT SITUATION AND PROSPECTS

Intercultural and inclusive policies in Brazil gained interesting advances and momentum from the 1980s onwards, as noted above. It is interesting to note that, since then, the Indigenous Movement and the Black Movement have often, though not always, articulated in the struggle for intercultural and inclusive policies. There is a considerable increase of indigenous and Afro-descendant students in public and private universities. The profile of the previously elitist federal universities has changed considerably.

In this scenario, the indigenous intellectual of the Tuxá people, Felipe Sotto Cruz (2017), affirms that access is an important step, but an epistemic change is necessary, breaking with the monolithic knowledge matrix currently present (Sotto Cruz, 2017, p. 97).

The first courses in intercultural indigenous education were created at the '*Universidade do Estado de Mato Grosso*' (UNEMAT) in 2001 and at the '*Universidade Federal de Roraima*' (UFRR) in 2003, in order to fill the resulting gaps in the higher education of teachers working in indigenous schools. Today, there are about 25 experiences in the country. All of them are based on notions from the field of critical interculturality and the effective imprint of decoloniality. These courses continue to be supported and are dependent on the '*Programa de Apoio à Formação Superior e Licenciaturas Interculturais Indígenas*' (PROLIND), created in 2005 and which is still not very institutionalised from a formal point of view, so that its existence is threatened with each new governmental administrative policy (Herbetta, 2018).

In this way, with limited resources and processes, one of the obstacles is that it is not possible to reach and include a larger number of teachers working in indigenous schools. In addition, projects are designed and managed in federal and state institutions where the vast majority of teaching and technical staff are non-indigenous, thus reducing indigenous ownership of decision-making. In the current period, the strengthening of regional and national councils in the field of education continues at the federal, state and municipal levels, with the presence of indigenous and Black intellectuals in the Secretariat for Continuing Education, Literacy and Diversity (Secad), created in 2004 and which, as of 2012, added the term Inclusion to its name, becoming the Secretariat for Continuing Education, Literacy, Diversity and Inclusion (SECADI). SECADI, meanwhile, was extinguished in 2019 during the extreme right-wing government of Jair Bolsonaro, which caused profound damage to the entire Brazilian education system.

At the same time, the formalisation and institutionalisation of decision-making spaces in which indigenous and Black people have access and real participation are still limited. For example, it is only in the new government of Luis Inácio Lula da Silva, which begins in 2023, that the country will have two indigenous elected federal deputies for the first time: Sonia Guajajara and Celia Xacriabá; in addition, the *Ministry of Indigenous Peoples* was created, which will be coordinated by an indigenous person; and finally, the former federal deputy Joênia Wapichana is the president of FUNAI.

Rights were also recognised with regard to school education based on the specificities of each people. In this process of transformation and conquest of rights, nearly 3000 indigenous schools are key sites for recognising ethnic difference through educational policies related to the mother tongue and their own ways of learning. On the other hand, in indigenous schools, curricular disciplinary dynamics are at the centre, threatening indigenous knowledge, along with other difficulties that affect teaching and learning methods; for example, in most cases, the calendars, rituals and social organisation of each population are not respected.

In such a scenario, indigenous intellectual Daniel Munduruku argues that there is a structural problem in the development of some of the aforementioned policies and calls for reflection on inclusive pedagogies. According to him, many times, 'such policies are nothing more than a mockery in the solution of an indigenous "problem", as they further emphasise the lack of a real understanding of what an indigenous people is and their real needs' (Munduruku, 2009, p. 3).

Despite the advances in policies and experiences, it is clear that in the institutions and actions achieved so far, the epistemological and political dimensions have not been sufficiently deepened, which indicates evident limits in the progress of the processes, such as permanence in the university, the consolidation of a differentiated and intercultural education and the generation of intercultural spaces.

Such policies bring in themselves, therefore, central political and epistemic challenges for the consolidation of new educational and social paradigms and for the design of new public policies. Only intercultural policies that take into account in their principles and arguments other epistemologies, such as indigenous and Afro-descendant ones, for example, can effectively generate and sustain intercultural and inclusive processes.

INTERCULTURALITY AND EDUCATIONAL INCLUSION IN MEXICO

In Mexico, the school education that the state has imposed on indigenous populations throughout the 20th century was part of integrationist, assimilationist, paternalistic and welfarist policies (Korsbaek & Sámano, 2007) known as *indigenism* which, from a modern-colonial (Quijano, 2000) and mestizo-philic conception of Mexicanity (Rebolledo Resendiz, 1997), conceived of indigenous populations as pre-modern, backward and underdeveloped, and therefore in need of state tutelage. From a deficit conception (Hamel Rainer, 2003), their ways of life and ways of generating knowledge, their economic, political, legal, medical, etc. systems were disqualified and considered responsible for their backwardness. This racist and paternalistic conception served to exclude them from the definition and implementation of public policies, including educational policies, supposedly aimed at promoting development and modernisation which, in the end, have never been achieved. These policies are not only based on logics and rationalities that are ontologically and epistemologically alien to them but also seem to have been conceived to reproduce the relations of domination–submission (Gasché, 2008) that have historically characterised intercultural relations between the state and indigenous peoples. Indeed, it is suspicious to say the least that after having been the object of indigenist and developmentalist policies for more than a century, Mexican indigenous populations today continue to suffer from high rates of poverty and marginalisation and have educational indicators far below national standards.[2]

THE 'ATTENTION' TO DIVERSITY IN MEXICAN EDUCATION POLICIES

Since the creation of the Ministry of Public Education in 1921, the Mexican state has implemented educational policies of a civilising (Todorov, 2019) and epistemicidal (Santos De Sousa, 2009) nature towards indigenous ways of life and knowledge. Conceived from the positivist and Eurocentric evolutionist paradigm, they assumed that Mexico's progress would go hand in hand with the formation of a socioculturally homogeneous mestizo nation (Bertely Busquets, 1998). The indigenous were idealised for their glorious past as a source of national identity, but in the present, they were considered 'subjects lacking in culture and rationality, incapable of generating knowledge' (Dietz & Mateos Cortés, 2011, p. 67). Assumed as ontologically and epistemically inferior and far from the desired Eurocentric modernity, they had to develop and modernise in order to achieve capitalist, urban and mestizo ways of life.

For this purpose, public education would serve to castellanise and promote acculturation processes that would banish indigenous languages from the classroom, finally admitting them from 1964 onwards, but only as the most efficient strategy to achieve castellanisation (Bello Domínguez, 2009). This approach did not change with the implementation in 1978 of the Bilingual and Bicultural Education Programme by the General Directorate of Indigenous Education, which was supposed to promote the preservation, consolidation and development of indigenous languages and cultures within a framework of self-affirmation of ethical identity (Lezama, 1982). Nor did the nominal change to the intercultural education system implemented by the neoliberal government of Salinas de Gortari (1988–1994) change this situation, since it took place within the framework of the National Agreement for the Modernisation of Basic Education which, rather than an opening towards sociocultural diversity, was related to the slimming down of the state, the implementation of compensatory policies, the decentralisation and federalisation of education, the search for efficiency and competitiveness in educational processes.

In this context, the armed uprising of the Zapatista Army of National Liberation (EZLN) in January 1994 revealed the major contradictions of the neoliberal project in Mexico and, among other things, put the indigenous issue back on the national agenda, redefining the terms of the social, political and educational debate. However, the San Andrés Accords signed in February 1996 by the EZLN and the Mexican government, in which the demands for inclusive autonomy for indigenous peoples and communities, political representation in the Congress of the Union and in state congresses, informed participation in decision-making that affects them, and the promotion of their languages and cultures, were never implemented. The Indigenous Law enacted in March 2001 by the PAN government of Vicente Fox (2001–2006) limited itself to granting constitutional recognition of the pluricultural character of the Mexican nation and, reaffirming the indigenist spirit of yesteryear, established that it would be the state's responsibility to guarantee linguistically and culturally relevant education for indigenous peoples at all educational levels. In response to the Indigenous Movement's demands for political-administrative autonomy and recognition as subjects of law, the Mexican state offered intercultural education and the creation of new bodies and laws. These included the National Commission for the Development of Indigenous Peoples (CNDI) – which replaced the National Indigenist Institute (INI), reducing its budget and functions – and the National Institute of Indigenous Languages (INALI), the body responsible for implementing the Law on the Linguistic Rights of Indigenous Peoples (Olivera Rodríguez, 2019).

In the field of education, the General Coordination of Intercultural Bilingual Education (CGEIB) was created with the aim of mainstreaming interculturalism in the National Education System (SEN) and offering quality education of cultural and linguistic relevance for the national population at all levels of education (Schmelkes, 2013). The National Education Programme (PNE) 2001–2006 established a policy of intercultural education for all as the main tool to solve discrimination, exclusion and marginalisation of indigenous peoples. However, the PNE also gave continuity to the policy of educational modernisation initiated at the end of the 20th century aimed at achieving levels of coverage and terminal efficiency in order to be in line with the demands of international institutions. Through programmes focused on educational equity, asymmetries and social inequalities would be reduced, achieving quality education, educational federalism, social participation in education, the fight against marginalisation and poverty and, as the icing on the cake, the mainstreaming of interculturalism in the SEN would be promoted (Olivera Rodríguez, 2019).

It is worth mentioning that the interculturalisation of basic education mainly took the form of defining a diversified curriculum that was limited to adding ethnic content to the national education plan and programme, without promoting a transformation of educational purposes and processes that would facilitate a horizontal dialogue with indigenous knowledge (Jiménez Naranjo, 2011).

An example of the contradictions intrinsic to the interculturalisation of the SEN is the case of the Intercultural Universities (UIs) created by the CGEIB and installed in different indigenous regions of the country with the aim of offering socioculturally relevant higher education and improving access to university for indigenous young people, who represented 3% of the national university enrolment (Schmelkes, 2013).

In the intentions of those who designed the UI curricular model (Casillas Muñoz & Santini Villar, 2009), these would have a critical and decolonising intercultural approach that would allow for the inclusion not only of indigenous people but also of their knowledge and knowledges (Olivera Rodríguez, 2019). One of the most interesting innovations of the UIs was to offer careers related to regional labour markets and focused on professions more in line with the needs of indigenous populations, such as degrees in language and culture, intercultural communication, sustainable development, alternative tourism, intercultural health and intercultural law.

Other relevant changes were the importance given to the study and research of indigenous languages, which would be compulsory and curricular in all degree programmes and the establishment of the community linkage axis as a curricular space for the dialogue of knowledge between Western and indigenous knowledge (Casillas Muñoz & Santini Villar, 2009).

However, the UIs were born with severe structural limitations. They were separated from other higher education institutions and placed under the academic tutelage of the CGEIB and its officials, who imposed their educational model without showing much empathy for the proposals that emerged from the teaching collectives of the UIs, which reproduced a vertical relationship between centre and periphery that was not very much in line with intercultural principles.

Another factor that limited their operation was their administrative and budgetary dependence on the General Directorate of University Higher Education, whose criteria did not consider the principles of the intercultural education model (Olivera Rodríguez, 2019). Finally, it was established that the Rector of each UI would be appointed by the Governor of the entity and that the only members of the Board of Trustees with voting rights were representatives of the federal, state and municipal governments, excluding from institutional deliberations those from civil society, among whom would be indigenous leaders and intellectuals (Hernández-Loeza, 2016).

Perspectives for the 21st Century

The limited advances in the interculturalisation of the SEN resulting from the state's response to the indigenous insurgency at the end of the 20th century were not only partial but also transitory and temporary. The neoliberal governments of Calderón (2007–2012) and Peña Nieto (2013–2018) returned interculturality to education policy for indigenous peoples and replaced the paradigm of interculturality for all with that of educational inclusion. This shift reflects the persistence of the vision of deficit that has historically characterised the educational policies implemented by the Mexican state towards indigenous peoples.

Mendoza Zuany (2017) highlights that the policy of educational inclusion implied a substantial shift in attention to and for diversity. Leaving aside educational relevance and without recognising the characteristics associated with the ethno-cultural and linguistic identities of indigenous peoples, emphasis was placed on access to education for very different sectors of the population, coming from different sociocultural and economic contexts and with diverse educational needs, whose specificities were denied by being homogenised and classified as 'vulnerable': indigenous people, migrants, people with disabilities, people with outstanding aptitudes and special talents and students in telesecundarias. The limited progress made in the recognition and valuing of indigenous languages and cultures in schools was thus diluted, returning to the old paradigm of indigenist integration. The idea was promoted that the indigenous person is a vulnerable individual who has to be included in a single, homogenous and homogenising education system, whose quality is established without their participation and based on the criteria of the hegemonic urban cultural matrix. In this way, an individualising conception was fostered that does not consider the existence and relevance of indigenous peoples and community social networks; furthermore, this approach not only ignored sociocultural, territorial and community forms of education but also proposed that there is no need for differentiated attention for indigenous children, implicitly promoting the idea that a differentiated education subsystem for indigenous peoples could be dispensed with, which is ultimately functional with the reduction of public spending promoted by neoliberal policies. An example of this was the merger of seven programmes that served the aforementioned vulnerable groups in a differentiated manner, whose budget in 2014 was 59.82% lower than the sum of the programmes that previously formed part of it (Mendoza Zuany, 2017).

Finally, the new scenarios that opened up in Mexico with the federal government – avowedly anti-neoliberal – of the Fourth Transformation led by Andrés Manuel López Obrador (2019–2024), and with the late and still incomplete enactment of an educational reform that puts interculturality back at the centre of educational policies, are too recent to be analysed in depth in this chapter. It is undoubtedly interesting that the mainstreaming of inclusion and interculturality is being proposed from critical and decolonial perspectives (Walsh, 2012) that link educational processes with community territorial processes, taking up some of the proposals generated by community educational projects and independent indigenous organisations, breaking, at least discursively, with the vision of the deficit of indigenous societies and cultures that has permeated Mexican educational policy throughout contemporary history.

INTERCULTURALITY AND INCLUSION IN BRAZIL AND MEXICO: A COMPARATIVE REFLECTION

It should be pointed out that it is daring, to say the least, to compare two countries as large, populous and megadiverse as Brazil and Mexico, which are characterised by different historical, political and social processes. Furthermore, while in the Brazilian case, we are in the presence of a strong Afro-descendant population component (more than 50% of the population, including Blacks and browns) and a small part (0.4%) of a very diverse indigenous population within it (IBGE, 2012), in the case of Mexico, it is the indigenous peoples who make up the most consistent percentage of the ethnically differentiated national population, with 23.2 million people aged three years and older self-identified as indigenous (19.4 % of the total population in that age range), while those who consider themselves Afro-descendants amounted to 1.4 million, representing 1.2 % of the national population (INEGI, 2020).

However, despite these differences, as shown in the previous pages, in the case of both Brazil and Mexico, we observe that the intercultural and inclusive educational policies that have been implemented throughout the 20th century and in the first two decades of the 21st century were characterised by modern-colonial integrationist approaches (Quijano, 2000) and were directed towards the political, sociocultural and linguistic homogenisation of the national population. As we have argued, both countries have been marked by violent processes of colonisation before and of modern-colonial national integration afterwards; as in other countries of the American continent, these processes followed modernising, assimilationist, ethnocidal and epistemicidal political, economic, social and educational principles defined from the paradigm of Eurocentric capitalist modernity (Lander, 2000). In this way, they sought, but fortunately did not entirely succeed, to delegitimise, demobilise and annihilate other ontologies, epistemologies and languages, such as those of the indigenous and Afro-descendant populations living in Mexico and Brazil.

It is also important to note that, in both cases, the processes of interculturalisation in education in recent decades have not been the result either of generous government initiatives or of virtuous concerns for sociocultural diversity but were driven primarily by the struggles of indigenous and Afro-descendant social movements which, in this way, expressed their dissatisfaction with the status quo and their desire to be included, from positions of sociocultural and legal equality and equity, in truly pluricultural national states.

In Mexico, the importance of the autonomous processes generated by the EZLN and other indigenous organisations and communities is highlighted, not only in the educational sphere but also in the political, medical and economic spheres throughout the country. The autonomous educational system promoted in Zapatista communities as well as the different educational projects generated by initiatives of independent indigenous communities and organisations and/or associated with critical sectors of the indigenous teaching profession in Mexico constitute concrete examples of processes of critical and decolonial educational interculturalisation generated from below and from within (Sartorello et al., in press) whose achievements are qualitatively better than those derived from the policies and actions implemented by the state.

In Brazil, these processes have been generated by the popular struggle against the dictatorship and the process of re-democratisation that began in 1985 and led to the promulgation of the 1988 Constitution. We especially highlight the struggle of the Black Movement, later appropriated by the indigenous populations, which led to the Quota Law, and the struggle of the Indigenous Movement which, in search of political rights in relation to territory, differentiated health and education, contributed important epistemological questions and transformations in public policies and institutions, at the same time as this epistemic approach began to be part of the Afro-descendant mobilisations.

We observe that, in both countries, the institutionalisation of intercultural and inclusive education policies derived from the state's response to the social demand of Afro-descendant and Indigenous Movements, carried out by neoliberal national governments reluctant to promote structural changes that favour a deeper transformation and democratisation of national education systems, present strong political, ontological, epistemic, educational, etc. limitations, thus denoting the prevalence of systemic-functional approaches marked by the coloniality of power, being and knowledge (Walsh, 2012). As we have emphasised in this chapter, the failure to comply with the San Andrés Accords and the enactment of a neo-indigenist Indigenous Law in the case of Mexico and, as far as Brazil is concerned, the institutional limits set by the Citizens' Constitution for the achievement of profound transformations in society are a clear example of this.

In the Brazilian case, where there is an interesting articulation over time between the struggle of the Black Movement and that of the Indigenous Movement, the experiences of interculturalisation and inclusion generated by the State have focused mainly on teacher training courses for indigenous education and on the law of quotas to favour the access and permanence of the ethnically differentiated population in higher education, while the political-epistemological dimensions demanded by the Black Movement, which are related to confronting the structural racism that permeates Brazilian society, have yet to be fulfilled.

In the Mexican case, where the issue of the Afro-descendant population is just beginning to appear on the public agenda, intercultural policies for indigenous people have had greater scope, ranging from basic to higher education with the UIs and teacher training with the Intercultural Teacher Training Colleges and the programmes offered by the National Pedagogical University. This has made it possible to generate far-reaching changes at the level of institutions and educational programmes, as well as at the curricular level. Likewise, as we pointed out earlier, although this chapter has not been able to go into this in depth, for more than three decades, there have been important intercultural and community-based educational initiatives in Mexico, generated by indigenous organisations and communities themselves, which have energised the field of education in and for sociocultural and linguistic diversity, generating counter-hegemonic alternatives to governmental projects.

Finally, in both countries, recent political changes at the national level, with progressive political organisations taking power, would seem to generate a favourable environment for the generation of intercultural and inclusive policies of a critical and decolonial nature. However, history shows the strong limitations of policies generated from above without real participation and involvement of Afro-descendant and indigenous peoples, organisations and communities in their design, implementation, monitoring and evaluation.

NOTES

1. One of the interesting aspects when it comes to the indigenous issue in Brazil is its enormous diversity. Pending the publication of the 2022 Demographic Census data, the 2010 *Instituto Brasileiro de Geografia e Estatística* (IBGE) census indicates that there are 896,963 self-declared indigenous individuals in Brazil, representing 0.4% of the Brazilian population. They are present in all the states of the Federation and are divided into 305 peoples who speak around 274 languages. In relation to the Afro-descendant population, the indicators relating to the demographic dimension are striking. Of the approximately 191 million Brazilians in 2010 (IBGE, 2012), 15 million were classified as Black and 82 million as brown. It should be remembered that Brazil was one of the world's largest slave-owning centres and was the last country in the Americas to abolish slavery.

2. In Mexico, in 2020, there were 7,364,645 people over 3 years old who spoke an indigenous language (6.1% of the national population), 77% of whom were living in poverty (41.5% is the national average), 80.9% without social security and 67.4% without basic housing services (CONEVAL, 2022). 19.8% are illiterate. At the primary level, 93.6% of indigenous children aged 6–11 attend school; for adolescents aged 12–17 (secondary and upper secondary), this figure drops to 66.0%, and for young people aged 18–22 (higher education), it is only 17.2% (CONEVAL, 2022).

REFERENCES

Apinajé, J. K. R., & Herbetta, A. (2018). Cantos filosóficos e a possibilidade de uma pluriversidade. Articulando e construindo saberes. *Goiânia, 3*(1). https://doi.org/10.5216/racs.v3i1.55373

Bello Domínguez, J. (2009). The beginning of bilingual bicultural education in indigenous regions in Mexico. In *Report of the X National Congress of educational research. Area 9: History and historiography of education* (pp. 1–10). COMIE.

STEFANO CLAUDIO SARTORELLO AND ALEXANDRE FERRAZ HERBETTA 153

Bertely Busquets, M. (1998). Educación indígena del siglo XX. In L. Sarre (Coord.). *Un siglo de educación en México* (Vol. II, pp. 74–110). COMIE.

Casillas Muñoz, M. D. L., & Santini Villar, L. (2009). *Intercultural University: Educational model (Universidad Intercultural: modelo educativo)*. SEP-CGEIB.

CONEVAL - Consejo Nacional de Evaluación de la Política de Desarrollo Social (National Council for the Evaluation of Social Development Policy). (2022). *Education for the indigenous population in Mexico: The right to a bilingual intercultural education*. CONEVAL.

Constituição da República Federativa do Brasil. (2016). *Constituição da República Federativa do Brasil: Texto constitucional promulgado em 5 de outubro de 1988, com as alterações determinadas pelas Emendas Constitucionais de Revisão nos 1 a 6/94, pelas Emendas Constitucionais nos 1/92 a 91/2016 e pelo Decreto Legislativo no 186/2008*. Senado Federal, Coordenação de Edições Técnicas.

Dietz, G., & Mateos Cortés, L. S. (2011). *Interculturality and education in Mexico. Un análisis de los discursos nacionales e internacionales en su impacto en los modelos educativos mexicanos*. SEP-CGEIB.

Diretrizes para a Política Nacional de Educação Escolar|Elaborado pelo comitê de educação escolar indígena. (1993). *Cadernos de educação básica. Série institucional* (Vol. 2, p. 24). MEC/SEF/DPEF.

Durban Declaration and Programme of Action. (2001). *Adopted on 8 September 2001 in Durban, South Africa*. Ministry of Culture (MinC).

Gasché, J. (2008). La motivación política de la educación intercultural indígena y sus exigencias pedagógicas. ¿Hasta dónde abarca la interculturalidad? In M. Bertely, J. Gasché, & R. Podestá (Coords.) *Educating in diversity. Intercultural and bilingual educational research and experiences* (pp. 367–397). Abya-Yala.

Gonzalez, L. (1988). A categoria político-cultural de amefricanidade. In *Tempo Brasileiro* (issue 92/93, pp. 69–82). Universidad Fluminense, Brasil.

Hamel Rainer, E. (2003). Language policies and cultural strategies in indigenous education. In *Inclusion and diversity. Recent discussions on indigenous education in Mexico* (pp. 130–167). Fondo Editorial IEEPO.

Herbetta, A. F. (2018). Políticas de inclusão e relações com a diferença: Considerações sobre potencialidades, transformações e limites nas práticas de acesso e permanência da UFG. *Revista Horizontes Antropológicos*, *24*(50). https://doi.org/10.1590/S0104-71832018000100011

Hernández-Loeza, S. (2016). Limited by decree. The normative restrictions of official intercultural universities in Mexico. *Revista del Cisen Tramas/Maepova*, *4*(2), 95–119.

IBGE - Instituto Brasileiro de Geografia e Estatística. (2012). *Censo Brasileiro de 2010*. IBGE.

INEGI - National Institute of Geography and Statistics. (2020). *Population and housing census 2020*. INEGI.

Jiménez Naranjo, Y. (2011). Exclusion, assimilation, integration, cultural pluralism and "modernisation" in the Mexican education system: A historical approach to public education schools for indigenous people. *CPU-e, Revista de Investigación Educativa*, (12), 1–24. https://doi.org/10.25009/cpue.v0i12.46

Korsbaek, L., & Sámano, M. Á. (2007). El indigenismo en México: Antecedentes y actualidad. *Ra Ximhai*, *3*(1), 195–224.

Lander, E. (2000). La colonialidad del saber: Eurocentrismo y ciencias sociales. In *Perspectivas latinoamericanas*. CLACSO.

Law No 12.711. (2012, August 29). Câmara dos Deputados. https://www2.camara.leg.br/legin/fed/lei/2012/lei-12711-29-agosto-2012-774113-normaatualizada-pl.pdf

Lei No 6.001. (1973, Dezembro 19). Estatuto do Índio. https://www.planalto.gov.br/ccivil_03/leis/l6001.htm

Lezama, J. (1982). Theory and practice in bilingual education. In A. P. Scanlon & J. Lezama (Eds.), *Hacia un México pluricultural. De la castellanización a la educación indígena bilingüe y bicultural* (pp. 155–181). SEP.

Luciano Baniwa, G. J. D. S. (2014). *Educação para manejo do mundo. Entre a escola ideal e a escola real no Alto Rio Negro*. LACED/Contracapa.

Mendoza Zuany, R. G. (2017). Inclusión educativa por interculturalidad: Implicaciones para la educación de la niñez indígena. *Perfiles Educativos, 39*(158), 52–69. http://www.scielo.org.mx/scielo.php?script=sci_arttext&pid=S0185-26982017000400052&lng=es&tlng=es. Accessed on February 14, 2023.

Munduruku, D. (2009). A escrita e a autoria fortalecendo a identidadea-escrita-e-a-autoria. http://pib. socioambiental.org/pt/c/iniciativas-indigenas/autoriaindigena/fortalecendo-a-identidade. Accessed on December 30, 2022.

Nascimento Potiguara, R. G. d. (2022). *Povos indígenas e democratização da universidade no Brasil (2004–2016): A luta por autonomia e protagonismo.* Mórula.

Olivera Rodríguez, I. (2019). Del indigenismo a la interculturalidad: construcción e intencionalidades de la política mexicana de educación superior intercultural. In M. Lloyd (Coord.). *Las universidades interculturales en México: Historia, desafíos y actualidad* (pp. 15–42). IISUE-UNAM-PUEES.

Pimentel da Silva, M. d. S., Herbetta, A., Pocuhto, T., Guajajara, C., Jukureakireu Boe, A., Waura, A., Kayabi, M., Kemenha, M., Yudjà, J., Krikati, C., Eibajiwu, A., Kayabi, M., & Karajá, U. (2021). Histórias da Covid-19: reflexões sobre violências desveladas na pandemia e o potential das plantas-pessoas-espíritos. *Articulando E Construindo Saberes, 6.* https://doi.org/10.5216/racs.v6.69076

Quijano, A. (2000). Colonialidad del poder, eurocentrismo y América Latina. In E. Lander (Coord.) *La colonialidad del saber: Eurocentrismo y ciencias sociales. Perspectivas latinoamericanas* (pp. 201–246). CLASO.

Rebolledo Resendiz, N. (1997). Indigenous education. Between nationalist education and applied anthropology. In M. Bertely & A. Valle (Coords.). *Indígenas en la escuela. Investigación educativa 1993–1995* (pp. 15–34). COMIE.

Sampaio Tukano, D. (2018). *Ukushe kiti niishe. Direito a memória e a verdade na perspectiva da educação cerimonial de quatro mestres indígenas.* Dissertação de mestrado em direitos humanos e cidadania. University of Brasília - CEAM.

Santos De Sousa, B. (2009). *An epistemology of the South: The reinvention of knowledge and social emancipation.* CLACSO-SIGLO XXI.

Sartorello, S. C., Ortelli, P., & Gómez Álvarez, M. (in press). Community education, educational autonomy and indigenous resistance. In G. Dietz (Coord.) *Multiculturalismo, interculturalidad y educación 2012–2021. State of Knowledge.* Consejo Mexicano de Investigación Educativa (COMIE) AC.

Schmelkes, S. (2013). Education for an intercultural Mexico. *Sinéctica,* (40), 01–12. http://www.scielo.org. mx/scielo.php?script=sci_arttext&pid=S1665-109X2013000100002&lng=es&tlng=es. Accessed on February 14, 2023.

Sotto Cruz, F. (2017). Indígenas antropólogos e o espetáculo da alteridade. *Revista de Estudos e Pesquisas sobre as Américas, 11*(2). https://periodicos.unb.br/index.php/repam/article/view/15949

Todorov, T. (2019). *The conquest of America: The problem of the other.* Siglo Veintiuno Editores.

Walsh, C. (2012). *Critical interculturality and (de)coloniality. Ensayos desde Abya-Yala.* Abya-Yala.

INTERCULTURALITY IN AND OUT OF THE CLASSROOM: INDIGENOUS VOICES AND KNOWLEDGE ABOUT EQUITY

Laura Alicia Valdiviezo[a], Rukmini Becerra Lubies[b] and Dayna Andrea Moya Sepulveda[b]

[a]University of Massachusetts-Amherst, USA
[b]Pontificia Universidad Católica de Chile, Chile

ABSTRACT

The creation of intercultural education in the Quechua and Mapuche contexts, in Peru and Chile respectively, marks a milestone in the institutionalisation of equity-oriented state policies that deserves attention given the serious inequalities that still persist in these societies. In this chapter, we analyse ethnographic studies of intercultural knowledge and practices inside and outside the classroom and interpret them as catalysts for equity in education. The findings of the analysis point to the centrality of Indigenous actors as transformative agents inside and outside the classroom and the urgency of restructuring not only education but also society towards equity.

Keywords: Quechua; Mapuche; Indigenous youth; intercultural bilingual education; community; ethnography

INTRODUCTION

The creation of intercultural education in the Latin American context, particularly in the Andean context, marks an important milestone in the institutionalisation, at least in state discourse, of educational policies and practices oriented towards equity and social justice that echo global initiatives such as Education For All (UNESCO, 1990), the Universal Declaration of Linguistic Rights (Follow-up Committee, 1997), the United Nations Declaration on the Rights of

---

Intercultural and Inclusive Education in Latin America
International Perspectives on Inclusive Education, Volume 24, 155–173
Copyright © 2024 Laura Alicia Valdiviezo, Rukmini Becerra Lubies and Dayna Andrea Moya Sepulveda
Published under exclusive licence by Emerald Publishing Limited
ISSN: 1479-3636/doi:10.1108/S1479-363620240000024011

Indigenous Peoples (United Nations, 2007) and Convention 169 of the International Labour Organisation (1989) (López & Küper, 2000; Valdiviezo & O'Donnell, 2019). Although initially created as an experimental and compensatory programme (Zavala et al., 2007), intercultural education has responded to the democratisation and pluralisation efforts of state policies with respect to the Indigenous sector as a historically excluded sector (Valdiviezo, 2014).[1] Thus, the intercultural bilingual education school (IBE), unlike regular public schools where the medium of instruction is Spanish, directly serves Indigenous peoples through initial, primary and secondary education where the mother tongue and culture of each community are used in order to maintain and develop them in parallel with the learning of Spanish and the national curriculum. However, the creation of IBE confronts an education system that is the product of profoundly unequal societies whose traditional function has reinforced these inequalities both through the discourse of citizen integration and homogenisation (López, 2009) and through a history of state violence against the human rights of Indigenous peoples that still persists today (Valdiviezo, 2009b, 2014, 2020; Woodhead et al., 2009). Thus, the promise of equity in education for the Indigenous population has been both cruel and unattainable, as it has meant that education is dedicated to cultural and linguistic uprooting that aims to assimilate or erase the Indigenous in the imaginary of mestizo (non-Indigenous) national identity (Valdiviezo, 2014). This has contributed not only to justifying but also to exacerbating the ideologies of marginalisation and exclusion of the Indigenous in education, the consequences of which beyond the classroom can be seen in the reproduction of deep and violent social, economic and political inequalities.

THEORETICAL AND LEGISLATIVE FRAMEWORK OF INTERCULTURAL EDUCATION

Interculturality as a theoretical framework for IBE presents evident tensions due to its instrumental and assimilationist state function, as opposed to the critical role that challenges the state to rethink its policy towards Indigenous peoples and Afro-descendants from the perspective of social and epistemic justice (Tubino, 2019). Despite criticism of this concept, even from the Indigenous world (Figueroa, 2015), interculturality is constituted as a field of analysis of the relations between the state/national society and native peoples and also as a normative horizon for social justice, the empowerment of national minorities and the decolonial transformation of policies and epistemologies (Walsh, 2010). The decolonial perspective allows us to offer a profound critique of the hegemonic structure of relations between Indigenous peoples and state or national society, inherited from Western modernity, revealing how this hegemony has become embedded in the production of knowledge, negating the vision of Indigenous peoples and other excluded groups (Quijano, 2007; Walsh, 2010).

At the time of writing this chapter, the Peruvian state has dismantled initiatives for professional training and quality in IBE, as well as the legal platform necessary to resource and sustain the inclusion of Indigenous languages and cultures in public education (Fowks, 2022). Thus, institutional efforts and material support for equity are being discontinued. In the face of this, as recently pointed out by López (2023), various Indigenous organisations have raised their voices to advocate for the rights of their peoples to intercultural bilingual education, while denouncing officials in the Ministry of Education for being obstacles to the achievement of this educational right. In the present context of political instability and social violence, the deterioration of democratic structures and the radicalisation of political–social and educational discourse in Peru is worrying (Berríos, 2023; Política, 2022; Zavala & Almeida, 2022).

Meanwhile in Chile, although the State has a legislative framework committed to respecting the rights of groups that are minoritised in the prevailing conservative discourse – for example, the Indigenous Law 19.253 (1993), Decree 280 (2009) of the Indigenous Language Sector and the ratification, in 2008, of Convention 169 of the International Labour Organisation (1989) on Indigenous peoples – IBE has remained on the institutional sidelines and symbolically identified as important in the recognition of diversity and inclusion.[2–4] But the state has done little to implement it, and it has been rather the Indigenous community itself that has supplied the educational needs of an inclusive education of Indigenous languages and cultures (Castillo & Mayo, 2019), hence the urgency of paying fair attention to local efforts such as the pedagogical actions of teachers, students themselves and the community that build equitable intercultural teaching and learning spaces. Such efforts, voices and knowledge, as we argue in this chapter, can constitute spaces for transformation, both practical and theoretical, of the impact of education and its role in the construction of equity.

OUR METHODOLOGY

In this chapter, we analyse selected ethnographic studies on interculturality that have been conducted in Quechua educational contexts in Peru and Mapuche educational contexts in Chile from the early 2000s to the present. We select these studies based on findings about knowledge and practices inside and outside the classroom and on the centrality of those local educational actors that we conceptualise as most impacted by interculturality and equity (or lack thereof) in education: teachers, students and community members. We use two main analytical lenses: language and culture. We start from the premise that linguistic and cultural knowledge and practices by local actors, beyond the institutional political discourse, constitute generators of knowledge for the possibilities and challenges of equity in education.

To analyse the Peruvian case, we identified studies focused on different actors: teachers in IBE primary schools, Indigenous youth in secondary schools and university students and artists whose cultural and intellectual production promotes Quechua. Thus, based on the findings in the ethnographies of Sumida Huaman (2015), Sumida Huaman and Valdiviezo (2012) and Kvietok (2021), the knowledge of young people about their language and cultural practices in their community is detailed. Likewise, the ethnography of the first author of this chapter on the pedagogical practices of IBE teachers shows how they incorporate cultural aspects of the community into the school curriculum (Valdiviezo, 2009a, 2013). Among others, the work of Ames (2012) and Zavala (2019) with children and youth, respectively, expands knowledge about the possibilities of equity outside the intercultural school classroom into the social realm.

For the Mapuche case in Chile, we analyse three groups of studies that have in common being ethnographic in nature and developed in the macro-south of Chile. The first group focuses on educational centres with an intercultural approach for children, directed by the second author of this chapter. The projects included in this chapter are: (a) 'Repairing relationships: an investigation for the construction of alliances between intercultural kindergartens and Mapuche communities' and (b) 'Building, learning and sharing a place: the challenge of intercultural bilingual education for Mapuche kindergartens and communities in the Araucanía Region' (Becerra-Lubies, 2021a, 2021b; Becerra-Lubies & González, 2017). The second refers to a set of ethnographic studies carried out in elementary schools with an intercultural approach (e.g. Figueroa, 2015; Forno et al., 2009; Fuenzalida, 2014; García, 2012; Lagos, 2015; Manzo & Westerhout, 2003; Matus & Loncón, 2012; Programa Educación Intercultural Bilingüe, 2011) and finally a group of studies with a focus on teaching practices of the Mapuche people (for example: Catriquir Colipan, 2014; Ibáñez, 2010; Quilaqueo, 2007; Quilaqueo & Quintriqueo, 2008; Quintriqueo et al., 2014; Williamson et al., 2012).

It seems to us that these three emphases can bring together and make visible the experiences and knowledge that are put into practice in the different settings in which intercultural education occurs in southern Chile. In the following section, we examine intercultural practices of equity inside and outside the classroom in the Peruvian Andean context.

Discussion of Ethnographic Findings

The Context of IBE in Peru

In order to understand the intercultural experience of the Quechua population in Peru, it is important to refer to the economic, social and political disparities that concretely, and often violently, affect the lives of people of Indigenous identity. These serious disparities have been documented from various disciplines, including education and development, psychology and other social sciences (Hall & Patrinos, 2005; Rojas, 2008; Trivelli, 2005; Valdiviezo & Valdiviezo-Arista, 2008; Woodhead et al., 2009). Referring to the problem of poverty, the National Institute of Statistics and Informatics (INEI) confirms this reality and states that:

> The groups most affected by poverty are Indigenous peoples and Afro-descendants. One of the ways of approaching ethnicity is through the mother tongue learned in childhood and ethnic self-perception. The National Household Survey includes questions to identify these populations. When applying the question on mother tongue learned in childhood, it is found that the population whose mother tongue is a native language (Quechua or Aymara or Amazonian language) has poverty rates (30.5%) that are on average almost double those whose mother tongue is Spanish (17.6%). INEI (2020, p. 45)

LAURA ALICIA VALDIVIEZO ET AL.

The INEI report also highlights the historical exclusion of Indigenous and Afro-Peruvian populations from access to education, health and employment, among others, and states that in addition to being economically disadvantaged, the educational attainment of both groups is below the average of the general population (INEI, 2020).[5] It is important to note that this information shows the intersections between poverty, ethnicity and language in the exclusionary tendencies of Peruvian society and institutions. We use this information as a contextual framework from which to examine the issue of equity that impacts the Quechua Indigenous in the formal and then intercultural education sphere.

One of the central concerns at government level has been access to formal education for rural populations, many of whom are non-Spanish speakers. Data collected through multiple studies (Hall & Patrinos, 2005; Trivelli, 2005; Zambrano & Beltran, 2012) highlight the infrastructural deficiencies as well as the lack of access to services among the poorest populations, especially Indigenous peoples. Reports such as that of the INEI help to emphasise these deficiencies, which have also served to justify policies that invest in the expansion of formal education in the most remote parts of the country. However, the great emphasis on access to formal education for the Indigenous population has been part of political discourse rather than concrete action, and when it has taken place, it has been limited to infrastructure, the construction of schools, the donation of computers or even the provision of texts in Spanish that reflect the national curriculum. Thus, formal education has not responded to the reality and the cultural and linguistic characteristics of the local context and population. The promise of equity based on access to formal education has meant entering into a system that excludes non-mestizo identities and imaginaries, be they Indigenous, Afro-Peruvian and non-European immigrant minoritised sectors.

The purpose of formal education that precedes intercultural education has been to change or outright destroy one's own identity, language and culture as obstacles to education, unification and the social and economic well-being of each country. Thus, the Indigenous identity, constructed as opposed and inferior to the mestizo national identity, has been identified as the great obstacle to education (Valdiviezo, 2009b, 2014). The failure of assimilationist formal education in rural sectors and especially in Indigenous communities has allowed the continuation of classist and racist stereotypes (Pasquier-Doumer & Risso Brandon, 2015) that blame students for their culture, skin colour, language, social status or origin, while very little has been done to re-evaluate the imposing and homogenising – and certainly colonial – nature of formal education. In this context, it is worth asking how IBE has responded to the hegemony or vision of the original peoples. Next, we turn our attention to local actions of inclusion of Indigenous language and culture, specifically in the case of Quechua, which we consider to be examples of equity in intercultural education.

Quechua Cultural Practices in Education

Ethnographic research by Sumida Huaman with Quechua youth in the community (Sumida Huaman, 2015; Sumida Huaman & Valdiviezo, 2012) and by

Valdiviezo with IBE teachers in schools in three localities, respectively in the central and southern Andes (Valdiviezo, 2009a, 2009b, 2010), coincide in highlighting the necessary connection between school and community, and not the school as an entity separated from Quechua knowledge and cultural practices, a legacy of formal education where the school also represents the place of assimilation and abandonment or suppression of Indigenous language, culture and identities (Sumida Huaman & Valdiviezo, 2012). The findings of Valdiviezo's ethnography with teachers in IBE programmes (Valdiviezo, 2009a, 2010) indicate that when the learning provided by the community – such as agricultural knowledge and respectful recognition of the *pachamama* – is part of the interactions and curricular content in the classroom, students are exposed to experiences in which the IBE school – in contrast to the exclusive experience of general formal education – recognises and includes local knowledge in a genuine and explicit way (Valdiviezo, 2013).[6]

Ames' (2012) anthropological work with young children in the Quechua community as well as Zavala's (2019) sociolinguistic research with young Quechua activists outside of education have identified cultural practices of children and youth that illuminate the importance of community and out-of-school spaces, as managers of learning and new knowledge, that educators serving equity must take into account. As the work of Ames (2012) reveals, learning practices among young community members, where active observation and increased responsibilities, inside or outside the home, represent valued learning in the community for cultivating productive life skills for these young community members. The findings of Zavala's (2019) work show young people using the Quechua language to create and advocate for its revalorisation in social spheres through art and virtual platforms.

Pedagogical Promotion Versus Institutional Opposition to Quechua Culture

Findings from work with IBE teachers (Valdiviezo, 2009a, 2010) have also pointed to their work as promoters of Quechua culture in the classroom. IBE teachers identify and collect community practices to guide the curriculum development of intercultural teaching and use adults' knowledge of their daily and spiritual work as sources of learning in the IBE school. The findings of this study show that in the realisation of equity, the school space is transformed and interwoven with the knowledge and practices of the Quechua community to critically reconsider its transformation towards the inclusion of the Quechua student and their community as creators of knowledge and active contributors to the educational process. This study has also shown the successful role of IBE teachers who, without explicit intercultural training (Valdiviezo, 2010), have the capacity to generate a local curriculum inclusive of Quechua language and culture in a way that is culturally relevant and representative of local knowledge and voices. Furthermore, this work found that, without institutional support, IBE teachers strive to include students' identities as an integral part of their education (Valdiviezo, 2013). Paradoxically, the findings also showed how these educational practices, which can be identified as culturally relevant and equitable, have been negatively judged by IBE supervisors in the Peruvian Ministry of Education for not reflecting Western ways of knowing (Valdiviezo, 2009b). The complexity of equity revealed in the findings of this study shows institutional actions that undermine it in IBE programmes. These actions respond to ideologies firmly rooted in the exclusionary formal education system. Equity is generated in culturally relevant educational spaces, but also in spaces of conflict, where actors directly challenge institutional authority and injustice.

Quechua Activism Inside/Outside the Institutional Space

In this section, we analyse the use of the Quechua language separately from the discussion on culture in IBE, not because we consider language and culture to be separate entities – on the contrary, we consistently argue about the need to conceive of them as always united and in relation (Valdiviezo & Nieto, 2015) – but rather we do so in order to emphasise the importance of the use of the Quechua mother tongue within the space of education, which should encompass education inside and outside of school, as a response to the systematic and historical suppression of this and other Indigenous languages in educational institutions and society in general.

The use of the Indigenous mother tongue in IBE education already represents an important transformation of educational policies and practices, which until then had been dedicated to exterminating Quechua and other languages in order to impose Spanish (Valdiviezo, 2013). Valdiviezo's ethnography of language practices in the IBE classroom shows that these take place in a complex ideological environment where teachers struggle against the stigmatisation of the Indigenous language vis-à-vis the dominant language, Spanish, while trying to respond to the rejection or fear of some community members to teach Quechua in school due to the fear of stigmatisation (Valdiviezo, 2009b).

Kvietok's (2021) ethnographic work with Quechua youth in the context of secondary education highlights the fluidity of young people's understanding and identification with their language and culture from the perspective of their own identity in a context that still rejects Indigenous identity. Likewise, these findings (Kvietok, 2021) highlight the interest of young people in maintaining and/or learning Quechua, revaluing it. This task of revaluing the Quechua language and identity from school is extremely difficult in a society where, together with new discourses of diversity and inclusion, both the language and Indigenous cultural practices continue to be stigmatised and qualified as a major impediment to the economic, political and social progress of the country. In this context of contradictory discourses, it is worth reconsidering the educational space as that both inside and outside the institution, beyond the classroom, in the community and society (Sumida Huaman & Valdiviezo, 2012) to examine the progress and/or setbacks of equity in education.

In the context of tertiary education, Kenfield's (2021) ethnography with Indigenous university youth in Cusco, Peru, highlights the multiple efforts of students to make use of the Quechua language in a recognised and legitimate way in the university space. On their own initiative and through the cultivation of collective efforts that include ways of advocating for the use of Quechua in the university, these young people challenge institutional obstacles to the use of Quechua in the classroom, where traditionally, only Spanish, the dominant language, is used. Through the use of the *photovoice*, these students identify actions that the university can take to maintain and promote Quechua–Spanish bilingualism among its students.[7]

Studies such as Zavala's (2019) reveal social and public spaces, outside of educational institutions, where young people challenge their own inclusion initiatives in which they clearly have the capacity to identify neoliberal ideologies that represent an apparent, not real, shift towards policies of equity. In their efforts to spread the Quechua language, these young activists are redefining the language and its speakers. Likewise, the activist practice of these young people, through art in public spaces and social platforms, challenges stereotypes and ideologies that exclude non-dominant languages, cultures and identities. Among the most recognised young people who vindicate the Quechua language and culture is Renata Flores, who in an interview with the *Los Angeles Times* (Entertainment, 2021), on the occasion of her concert during the International Book Fair in Guadalajara, Mexico, said 'I want children and young people to listen to the traditional language, there are many who are losing this identity and this pride in feeling music in Quechua because their parents don't speak it...'. Renata Flores uses a varied repertoire and musical genre such as hip-hop whose lyrics in Quechua include themes of feminist and Indigenous empowerment. Like Flores, the young musician, singer and educator Liberato Kani is prolific in his artistic production and collaborations with other young Latin American Indigenous musicians and with academics in countries such as the United States where he has presented his work at several universities. Liberato Kani maintains an active presence on social platforms where one can easily find access to his musical production, characterised by the valuation of rural life and Quechua cultural practices, the wisdom of the ancestors, together with the call for social justice. These young people's will to reclaim the right to the legitimate use of the Indigenous language, in this case Quechua, in spaces where it had been made invisible or actively prohibited, show concrete actions of the use of the living language, not as a future promise but as a present reality. Thus, they constitute actions that deserve to be recognised in order to understand the urgency of equity from the local level, beyond the existence, or not, of institutional and/or state reforms that protect such actions. In the case of Peru, a country with a long history of education policies that disproportionately favour urban, capital city, private and higher education sectors, and which tends to ignore minority sectors, the current situation of state and social political conflict, has destabilised the equity platforms of public state institutions, especially programmes that had been created in recent decades that supported the access of Indigenous populations to bilingual education, that promoted educators trained in the native language and that provided educational resources to ensure cultural relevance and quality of teaching and learning.[8] But while we see it as the responsibility of the democratic state to promote equity as an objective and a constant commitment, it is necessary to recognise that although in a very fragile legal context such as the Peruvian one – equity does not cease to exist and is made possible by the will of educational actors such as young Indigenous artists who actively promote the Quechua language, culture and identity along with social justice. We move our analysis in the next section to the Chilean case, where we examine equity in education inside and outside the classroom in Mapuche communities.

Chile, IBE and Mapuche Children and Adolescents

Social science research and reports from international and Chilean organisations coincide in their assessment of the inequalities and disadvantages faced by Indigenous children and adolescents in Chile (e.g. UNESCO, 2021; UNICEF, 2014). Unfortunately, 'the Indigenous population, especially Indigenous BGT [children and adolescents], is one of the populations with the greatest socio-economic vulnerability, in relation to those who are not of indigenous descent' (Defensoría de los Derechos de la Niñez, 2019), a situation that has been maintained historically as revealed by the National Socioeconomic Characterisation Survey, CASEN (Ministry of Social Development and Family, 2017). Specifically, Indigenous children are the poorest population in Chile, facing the highest levels of overcrowding, isolation and malnutrition – for example, in the regions of La Araucanía and Los Lagos (Díaz Torres & Millapán Muñoz, 2021). This disparity is even stronger when comparing living conditions between rural and urban areas. Indigenous children living in rural areas face higher levels of poverty and more difficulties in accessing healthcare, despite the country's economic growth. In this regard, it has been recommended that the State prioritise the reduction of inequality between rural and urban areas, particularly in areas with a large Indigenous population, and continue to request technical assistance from UNICEF for this priority (Defensoría de los Derechos de la Niñez, 2019). Also of concern is the persistence of discriminatory attitudes and practices towards Indigenous children in Chilean society (Observatorio Niñez y Adolescencia, 2014). Therefore, national institutions concerned with children, such as the Defensoría de los Derechos de la Niñez and the Consejo Nacional de la Infancia, have pointed out the importance of strengthening policies and programmes aimed at combating the multiple forms of discrimination and negative attitudes to which Indigenous children are victims (Defensoría de los Derechos de la Niñez, 2019).

In addition to these social and economic disadvantages, in terms of cultural identity, studies have shown that Mapuche children tend not to identify with Mapuche culture, 'which implies that they do not know or participate in their traditions, whether in festivities or speaking their own language' (Defensoría de los Derechos de la Niñez, 2019, p. 4). And because of this, the aforementioned organisations have expressed their concern about the limitations of the right to identity of Indigenous children as part of their cultural identity and point out the need to respect their right to identity in accordance with their culture and to favour a climate of inclusion and respect in society as a whole (Defensoría de los Derechos de la Niñez, 2019).

164 *Interculturality In and Out of the Classroom*

Finally, both international (e.g. UNESCO, 2021; UNICEF, 2014) and national organisations such as the Defensoría de los Derechos de la Niñez and the Consejo Nacional de la Infancia have made explicit the urgency for the Chilean state to act to put an end to police violence of all kinds against Indigenous children and their families. In particular, children living in the context of territorial claims of the Mapuche people in Araucanía or in the context of conflict between the State and the Mapuche people find themselves in scenarios in which the Chilean police have exercised force and used weapons against Mapuche minors (Defensoría de los Derechos de la Niñez, 2021). In short, Indigenous children, and in particular Mapuche children, are still victims of inequality, discrimination and violence.

These factors hinder the educational advancement of Indigenous children (UNICEF, 2004). Therefore, States have been urged 'to ensure that Indigenous children have access to good quality education in ways that respect their cultural heritage and consolidate their identity' (UNICEF, 2004, p. 1), as well as to create and implement 'interventions for social inclusion, in order to give visibility to Mapuche children and adolescents, promote their participation and offer them an adequate response to their needs' (UNICEF, 2004, p. 1). Such actions 'must become a central axis of State intervention' (Defensoría de los Derechos de la Niñez, 2019).

Mapuche Cultural Practices

In an education system such as the Chilean one that has historically excluded and prohibited the culture of Indigenous peoples, the linking of educational centres with Mapuche communities in order to offer relevant education to Indigenous children and adolescents is a step towards equity. Although it is still necessary for the school system at all levels to have a strong and systematic cultural relevance with the knowledge and practices of the Mapuche culture, it is especially significant in the case of kindergarten education, which has intercultural education as one of its working dimensions in contexts with a larger Mapuche population and where communities or families request the presence of a kindergarten with an intercultural approach. This linkage has been possible thanks to the creation of intercultural kindergartens and the training and hiring of Indigenous language and culture educators. Particularly relevant are the Indigenous language and culture educators who speak Mapudungun, who are validated by a Mapuche community and whose role is to be a bridge between the Mapuche communities and the kindergartens where they work. These intercultural kindergartens have been built as spaces that seek to build alliances with Mapuche communities to offer an education that integrates Mapuche ancestral knowledge and current practices.

Particularly in the Araucanía region, ethnographic studies carried out between 2016 and 2022 by the second author have shown that intercultural kindergartens make efforts to create their own educational curricula with relevance to the context in which they are located (Becerra-Lubies & González, 2017). In them, pedagogical practices, ceremonies and cultural activities are carried out with the clear intention of strengthening the cultural identity of their children and of the educational centre. For example, they teach *weaving*, tell *epew* (Mapuche oral storytelling), teach *purrun* (traditional Mapuche dances), include Mapuche games and use elements from nature such as pine nuts and branches to create pedagogical materials. In these spaces, the participation of local actors and members of Mapuche communities is seen as central to the educational work of the kindergarten, therefore, *lonkos* (chief or head of the Mapuche community), *machi* (healer of evils derived from spiritual forces or transgressions of rules), grandmothers/grandfathers and other wise people are invited to contribute their knowledge to the educational space of the kindergarten. In addition, these kindergartens have an Indigenous language and culture educator, who uses her cultural knowledge to form alliances with Mapuche communities to promote relevant pedagogical processes that respect the particularities of the children and their families (Becerra-Lubies et al., 2019).

Promotion of Mapudungun Among Children and Young People

The revitalisation of Mapudungun – one of the names given to the language of the Mapuche people – is one of the demands of the Mapuche people pending before the Chilean state (Loncon, 2017). The IBE programme in Chile has favoured the creation of some measures that have enabled progress in the teaching of Mapudungun in basic education (6–13 years), the most important of which, in recent years, is the creation of the Indigenous Language Sector in the national curriculum under the responsibility of a traditional educator, who should normally be a member of the local community, knowledgeable about the culture and its linguistic variant (Figueroa, 2015). Although the implementation of the Indigenous Language Sector has not had the expected results in terms of teaching Mapudungun (Loncon, 2017), this course for elementary school students is considered a step forward in the promotion of Mapudungun and in equity towards Indigenous peoples, as it includes in schools a language that had been banned and punished a couple of decades ago in the school system. The work of Castillo and Mayo (2018) has investigated the experiences of traditional educators in schools, elders (over 45 years old) who are Mapudungun speakers and who in their school years were punished for speaking Mapudungun in the school where they now teach it.

It is important to mention that the revitalisation work carried out by Mapuche organisations aimed at young people, often self-managed, through language internships, face-to-face and online workshops, among others, is the format that has had the greatest impact in recent years (Castillo & Mayo, 2019). These Mapuche organisations, led by young activists, are characterised by being autonomous and fighting against the hegemony of the language, by generating an epistemic break where meaning is created and by the construction of a representative social framework for Mapudungun (Castillo & Mayo, 2019). This work is fundamental, as it presents instances where language is developed in a context from and for the Mapuche people that has 'contributed to the recovery of linguistic sovereignties, ... through the dissemination and vehiculisation of

166 *Interculturality In and Out of the Classroom*

Mapudungun', and that has also 'contributed to contesting its exoticisation and to breaking down its status as a minoritised language' (Castillo & Mayo, 2018, p. 16).

Among the successful strategies that have been implemented by these groups, we can mention: the creation of material in Mapudungun and the linguistic internship, as a space for teaching and immersion in Mapudungun. The internship, called *Koneltun*, offers workshops that encourage the valuation and experience of the roots of the language and culture (Castillo & Mayo, 2018) as well as the presence of Mapudungun in social networks (Castillo & Mayo, 2018). Some of these strategies are inspired by international models that have experience in promoting equity through the linguistic valuation of Indigenous peoples. All of these actions contribute to equity by rescuing the sociolinguistic value that has been depleted over the years. On the other hand, these strategies that use the language in everyday spaces can empower the new generations to revitalise the language as a living element and representative of the present culture. It would be fundamental for political bodies to use these examples, in addition to more transversal elements such as those proposed by Bustos et al. (2021) who mention how fundamental it is to talk and educate about human rights in educational contexts, with the aim of rethinking the application and practice of human rights in the local context. We believe that considering all these aspects in the public policy scenario could generate a significant advance towards cultural equity, revitalising, through the new generations, culture and language.

Innovations for the Inclusion of Voices and Knowledge

Given that IBE seeks to promote interculturality in the education system, but the Chilean education system does not focus on interculturality, the pedagogical work of educational centres interested in this proposal requires educational actors to seek or create new pedagogical forms to implement intercultural education relevant to their contexts, respecting the curricular frameworks established by the Chilean Ministry of Education (Becerra-Lubies et al., 2019; Becerra-Lubies & González, 2017). An increasingly frequent innovation is the interest in listening to the voices, opinions and experiences of traditional educators, Indigenous language and culture educators and Mapuche families. For example, in regions of Chile with a larger Mapuche population (La Araucanía, Los Ríos, Los Lagos), it is possible to find groups of Mapuche and non-Mapuche early childhood educators interested in learning about the Mapuche worldview, willing to participate in ritual ceremonies such as *Wiñol Tripantu* (the return of the sun), who want to know how to establish ties with a *lonko*, who ask and want to know if they can wear Mapuche clothing and who make efforts to learn Mapudungun to be able to use it in educational centres, among others (Becerra-Lubies & González, 2017; Becerra-Lubies et al., 2019).

It is also possible to find pedagogical teams that invite families to collaborate in joint workshops on the Mapuche cosmovision, to share the knowledge of their grandparents, co-creating educational materials with textures from the territories and collaboratively elaborating an educational curriculum that considers the

LAURA ALICIA VALDIVIEZO ET AL.

knowledge of the families and the Mapuche people. Research in Chile has also focused on this aspect and has collected and systematised the voices of Mapuche actors in the education system or community sages, who are fundamental in combating the hegemony that is promoted in educational spaces (Quintriqueo et al., 2015). Specifically, this research shows that Mapuche organisations expect reciprocity through connections with educational centres, and that it is difficult for them to collaborate with formal education entities because the education system provides little space for transformation (Becerra-Lubies, 2021a). Mapuche organisations have also highlighted the relevance of revitalising Mapudungun by showing the link between language and culture, and how fundamental it is not to disassociate them, as Western culture does, where language is only a means of communication of concrete elements and not a fundamental part of the cultural legacy (Arias-Ortega et al., 2019; Quintriqueo et al., 2015). Listening to the voices and aspirations of Mapuche sages and other Mapuche actors in charge of teaching processes is an advance towards equity, as it is an action that considers the life experiences and opinions on what the original peoples want for the education of their own children.

Another innovation that is not very common in the education system, but which has gained strength in early childhood IBE, is the link of people with the territories. Especially in the southern macro zone, it is possible to find intercultural kindergartens that conceive interculturality from the characteristics of their territories and thus take the limits of their classrooms outside the school, opening up to the teaching possibilities and resources that exist in the territories, for example, visiting sites with historical value for the Mapuche people, and forests and rivers that provide knowledge and values of the Mapuche cosmovision.

Often teachers, on their own initiative, develop processes of self-training in interculturality, as in Chile, the State does not offer teacher training in interculturality (Becerra-Lubies & González, 2017; Turra-Díaz, 2015). It is only the personal and professional commitment of teachers that can promote or not 'innovations in their pedagogical practices', and not public policies that support teachers (Catriquir Colipan, 2014, p. 6).

CONCLUSIONS: HOW TO MOVE TOWARDS EQUITY IN INTERCULTURAL EDUCATION?

The problem of equity (or lack thereof) cannot be defined solely through information on the conditions of serious educational, social and economic disadvantage affecting the Quechua and Mapuche sectors. This information is the starting point for seeking solutions but isolated from the knowledge and practices of educational actors inside and outside the classroom; it does not allow us to understand the importance of local efforts in the trajectory, perspectives and challenges of equity in the most affected sectors. Likewise, for those engaged in research, allowing the silence and invisibility of local actors in defining equity is not a neutral act but tends to favour, both in the academic and social fields, the reinsertion of the same ideologies of exclusion that impact Quechua and

Mapuche sectors and that intercultural education aims to challenge. We therefore use the findings offered by ethnographic work as an opportunity to address the complexity of equity as a problem, as well as its solutions from the voices and knowledge of local actors. Underlying the impetus for this work is our commitment to attend to these actors, not as passive recipients, but as agents of change, possessing voices and knowledge from which we urgently need to learn.

The experiences of IBE in both Peru and Chile show trajectories of progress and setbacks, as well as the protagonism of local actors, including the youngest children, young people, community elders, families and teachers. It is not our intention to idealise the situation of these actors, since, as is evident from ethnographic research, their actions have made equity a reality even in contexts of great challenges and constant struggles against violence and a fight for the most basic survival. Hence, our call to recognise the knowledge and solutions generated by local actors in situations of great vulnerability. Even more so in the present context where recent decisions by the State have made IBE programmes in Peru vulnerable and in the Chilean case where the absence of the State continues to undermine the sustainability of intercultural education, it is important to clarify that the State has a great responsibility in supporting and sustaining intercultural education and unfortunately so far, both in Peru and Chile, it has tended to create policies that have not only exempted the State from all responsibility but have also perpetuated social, economic and political exclusion and violence against Indigenous and other minority sectors. We therefore advocate for the presence of the State in the law that makes visible and recognises the centrality of equity in education – based on the knowledge of local experience and actors – and the material support that makes possible the infrastructure where such equity is implemented. Such a presence must be conceived through transformations that decolonise the relationship between the State and Indigenous groups, a great task indeed, but one that requires a first step that is more immediately achievable: dialogue, where the State can be willing to genuinely listen to the voices and learn about the knowledge of Indigenous community members, youth, elders, educators and artists. The first step of dialogue is followed by that of alliances and collaborations of the State with other sectors because the task of equity does not consist of isolated action, for an isolated entity, but requires the will and action of groups across society. In this sense, we believe that equity requires in an important way the participation of non-Indigenous sectors or those whose privilege has been built and continues to be built through the perpetuity of minority groups. As education researchers, we have explored curricular innovations in other education systems serving minority groups outside Peru and Chile that allow us to conceive of the possibility of transformations that decolonise the national curriculum, both in Peru and Chile, and that allow students to learn from a history that is not biased, whitewashed or sanitised but enriched by the existence of the experiences and contributions of all the peoples that make up society. Far from the fears instilled about the radicalisation of excluded groups, this education of equity not only cements positive experiences but opens doors, connects and unifies, all necessary elements in the process and purpose of interculturality inside and outside the classroom, in society at large.

ACKNOWLEDGEMENTS

To the Quechua communities in southern Peru and the Mapuche communities in southern Chile who have made our learning possible over the years, we will always be grateful for your time, generosity and wisdom.

NOTES

1. We write the terms Indigenous and also Afro-descendant or Afro-Peruvian with a capital letter in recognition and respect for the legitimacy of the identities, rights and collective history of native peoples and also of those peoples forced into slavery, as recipients of systemic, structural and institutional violence.

2. We use the term minoritised – rather than minorities – to emphasise the inequity in social and power relations that have led to stereotypical identification, exclusionary attitudes and poor characterisation, usually racialised and classist, of certain groups in a society (see Wingrove-Haugland & McLeod, 2021).

3. Law that regulates actions and programmes for the recognition of the cultural, economic and social rights of Indigenous peoples. For example, it commits the state to develop a bilingual intercultural education system for education in areas with a high Indigenous density.

4. This sector specifies the teaching of Indigenous language and culture from first to eighth grade in IBE. This was modified in 2021, giving rise to a new mandate from first to sixth grade that extends its coverage from four to nine of the total of 10 Indigenous peoples recognised by the Chilean State through Law 19.253.

5. See clarification of our choice of capitalisation for the term in footnote #1.

6. At the end of this chapter, we provide a glossary for Indigenous terms indicated in the text in italics.

7. A visual research method initially developed in the late 1990s by health researchers. *Photovoice* is characterised by the use of photographs taken and selected by participants, who produce an explanation of the reasons, experiences and emotions that have guided the process of image taking and selection.

8. As this chapter was being written, in 2022, Peru was suffering a deep crisis of governability, strong opposition and political, economic and social instability, where President Pedro Castillo had attempted a self-coup, suspended constitutional guarantees and initiated drastic changes towards the elimination of initiatives that included equity policies. Once Castillo was removed from the presidency in December 2022, and following protests led by the rural and Indigenous sectors of the country, his successor, the Minister of Development and Social Inclusion, Dina Boluarte, initiated a campaign of violence where peaceful marchers, including young university students, mothers, children and the elderly who were advocating for their dignity and human rights, were criminalised, killed and imprisoned.

REFERENCES

Ames, P. (2012). Language, culture and identity in the transition to primary school: Challenges to indigenous children's rights to education in Peru. *International Journal of Educational Development, 32*(3), 454–462.

Arias-Ortega, K., Quilaqueo, D., & Quintriqueo, S. (2019). Intercultural bilingual education in La Araucanía: Main epistemological limitations. *Educação e Pesquisa, 45*. https://doi.org/10.1590/S1678-4634201945192645

Becerra-Lubies, R. (2021a). Intercultural education and early childhood: Strengthening knowledge based on Indigenous communities and territory. AlterNative. *An International Journal of Indigenous Peoples, 17*(2), 326–334.

170   *Interculturality In and Out of the Classroom*

Becerra-Lubies, R. (2021b). Ways of seeing indigenous communities in urban intercultural preschools in Chile: A case study. *Diaspora, Indigenous, and Minority Education*, 1–16. Ahead-of-print.

Becerra-Lubies, R., & González, S. M. (2017). *Alliances in intercultural bilingual kindergartens and Mapuche communities in the Metropolitan Region, Chile: Negotiations in a contact zone.* Doctoral dissertation. Pontificia Universidad Catolica de Chile.

Becerra-Lubies, R., Mayo, S., & Fones, A. (2019). Revitalization of indigenous languages and cultures: Critical review of preschool bilingual educational policies in Chile (2007–2016). *International Journal of Bilingual Education and Bilingualism, 24*(8), 1147–1162.

Berríos, M. (2023, April 30). Patricia Salas: "There is a conservative and absolutely anti-democratic agenda in education". *Ojo Público.* https://ojo-publico.com/4403/patricia-salas-hay-una-ola-conservadora-muy-fuerte-la-educacion

Bustos, C., Castillo, S., Mayo, S., & Cárcamo, J. E. S. (2021). Towards a transformation of relational spaces: Case study of an experience in human rights education. *REICE: Revista Electrónica Iberoamericana sobre Calidad, Eficacia y Cambio en Educación, 19*(1), 5–24.

Castillo, S., & Mayo, S. (2018). Revitalization of indigenous languages as epistemic decolonizing processes: A look from mapuche autonomous educational experiences. In E. Del Valle (Ed.), *On decoloniality series by Walter Mignolo and Catherine Walsh.* Duke University Press.

Castillo, S., & Mayo, S. (2019). Inclusive language as a 'norm' of empathy and identity: Reflections among teachers and future teachers. *Literature and Linguistics*, (40), 377–391.

Catriquir Colipan, D. (2014). Performance of the intercultural bilingual education teacher: Evaluative criteria from the voice of the lof che. *Polis: Revista Latinoamericana, 39.* http://journals.openedition.org/polis/10514

Decree 280. (2009). *Indigenous language sector.* Ministry of Education. Library of the National Congress of Chile. https://www.bcn.cl/leychile/navegar?idNorma=1006477

Defensoría de los Derechos de la Niñez. (2019). Proposal based on a rights-based approach in public intervention with respect to Mapuche children and adolescents in the Araucanía region. https://www.camara.cl/verDoc.aspx?prmID=162752&prmTIPO=DOCUMENTOCOMISION

Díaz Torres, N., & Millapán Muñoz, D. (2021). *Vulneración de derechos a los niños, niñas y adolescentes, producto de la violencia de estado en las reducciones Mapuche.* Graduate Thesis. Universidad Academia de Humanismo Cristiano.

Entertainment. (2021, December 5). Renata Flores, the Quechua Indian who sings trap to empower herself. *Los Angeles Times.* https://www.latimes.com/espanol/articulo/2021-12-05/renata-flores-la-indigena-quechua-que-canta-trap-para-empoderarse

Figueroa, L. L. (2015). Educación Mapuche e interculturalidad: Un análisis crítico desde una etnografía escolar. *Chungará, Revista de Antropología Chilena, 47*(4), 659–667.

Follow-up Committee. (1997). *Universal declaration of linguistic rights.* Institut d'Edicions de la Diputació de Barcelona.

Forno, A., Alvarez-Santullano, P., & Rivera, R. (2009). Entre el edificio y el currículum de la interculturalidad: Una mirada antropológica a la educación actual en el territorio Mapuche-Huilliche. *Chungará, Revista de Antropología Chilena, 41*(2), 287–298. https://www.redalyc.org/articulo.oa?id=32612436009

Fowks, J. (2022, December 10). Peru defends intercultural bilingual education. *El País.* https://elpais.com/america-futura/2022-12-10/peru-defiende-la-educacion-intercultural-bilingue.html

Fuenzalida, P. (2014). Re-ethnization and decolonization: Epistemic resistances in the intercultural curriculum in the Los Lagos Region-Chile. *Polis, Revista Latinoamericana, 13*(38), 107–132.

García, S. (2012). Scope and limits of intercultural bilingual education policy in Chile: A postcolonial analysis. *Ignire, 1*(16), 1–16.

Hall, G., & Patrinos, H. A. (2005). *Indigenous peoples, poverty and human development in Latin America: 1994-2004.* World Bank. https://centroderecursos.cultura.pe/sites/default/files/rb/pdf/Pueblos%20indigenas%2C%20pobreza%20y%20desarrollo%20humano%20en%20Amrrica%20Latina%201994%20-%202004.pdf

Ibáñez, N. (2010). Pedagogical attention to diversity: A study of rural school classrooms in Mapuche communities in southern Chile. *Educacion Superior y Sociedad, 3,* 83–109.

INEI. National Institute of Statistics and Informatics. (2020). Estado de la población peruana. https://www.inei.gob.pe/media/MenuRecursivo/publicaciones_digitales/Est/Lib1743/Libro.pdf

LAURA ALICIA VALDIVIEZO ET AL.

Intercultural Bilingual Education Programme. (2011). *Education to preserve. Challenges of the implementation of the indigenous language sector in Chile.* Ministry of Education and United Nations Children's Fund, UNICEF. http://peib.mineduc.cl/wp-content/uploads/2018/05/Estudio_Implementacion_Sector_Lengua_Indigena2012.pdf

International Labour Organization. (1989). *Indigenous and Tribal Peoples Convention. No. 169.* https://www.ilo.org/dyn/normlex/es/f?p=NORMLEXPUB:12100:0::NO::P12100_INSTRUMENT_ID:312314

Kenfield, Y. (2021). *Enacting and envisioning decolonial forces while sustaining Indigenous language: Bilingual College students in the Andes.* Multilingual Matters.

Kvietok, F. (2021). Bilingualism and youth identity: Ethnographic contributions to the teaching of Quechua in urban secondary schools. *Revista Peruana de Investigación Educativa, 13*(14), 25–52.

Lagos, C. (2015). The intercultural bilingual education programme and its results: Perpetuating discrimination? *Pensamiento Educativo. Revista de Investigación Educacional Latinoamericana, 52*, 84–94. https://doi.org/10.7764/PEL.52.1.2015.7

Ley Indígena 19. (1993). *Library of the National Congress of Chile.* https://www.bcn.cl/leychile/navegar?idNorma=30620&idParte=253

Loncon, E. (2017). *Políticas públicas de lengua y cultura aplicada al mapuzugun* (pp. 375–404). Centro de Estudios Públicos Collection. https://www.plataformaconstitucionalcep.cl/wp-content/uploads/2022/11/loncon_2017_politicas_publicas_de_lengua_y_cultura_aplicada_al_mapuzugun.pdf

López, L. E. (2009). Democracy and change in Latin American education: Lessons for Peru. *CARE, 1*, 9–39.

López, L. E. (2023). Quechua, politics and public policy: Initial comments. *International Journal of the Sociology of Language, 280*, 13–25.

López, L. E., & Küper, W. (2000). *Intercultural bilingual education in Latin America: Balance and perspectives.* GTZ.

Manzo, L., & Westerhout, C. (2003). Propuesta metodológica en educación intercultural para Contextos Urbanos. *Cuadernos Interculturales y del Patrimonio, 1*, 1–50.

Matus, C., & Loncón, E. (2012). *Description and analysis of PEIB-CONADI plans and programmes.* Ministry of Education and UNICEF. https://peib.mineduc.cl/wp-content/uploads/2018/05/WDPEIB_CONADI_web-FINAL.pdf

Ministry of Social Development and Family. (2017). CASEN, informe de desarrollo social 2017. https://www.desarrollosocialyfamilia.gob.cl/pdf/upload/IDS2017_2.pdf

Observatorio Niñez y Adolescencia. (2014). Infancia cuenta en Chile. https://facso.uchile.cl/dam/jcr:7b31788e-1798-430b-88cc-17a1dc925745/infanciacuenta2014-co-autoria-1

Office for the Defence of Children's Rights. (2021). *Annual report 2021. Derechos humanos de niñas, niños y adolescentes en Chile.* https://www.defensorianinez.cl/informe-anual-2021/wp-content/uploads/2021/11/ia2021.pdf

Pasquier-Doumer, L., & Risso Brandon, F. (2015). Aspiration failure: A poverty trap for indigenous children in Peru? *World Development, 72*, 208–223.

Política. (2022, May 5). Mirtha Vásquez: "Ayer trajeron abajo la reforma universitaria, hoy la educación con enfoque de género" (Mirtha Vásquez: "Yesterday they brought down university reform, today education with a gender focus"). *La República.* https://larepublica.pe/politica/2022/05/05/mirtha-vasquez-ayer-trajeron-abajo-la-reforma-universitaria-hoy-la-educacion-con-enfoque-de-genero

Quijano, A. (2007). Coloniality and modernity/rationality. *Cultural Studies, 21*, 168–178.

Quilaqueo, D. (2007). Saberes y conocimientos indígenas en la formación de profesores de educación. *Educar, 29*, 223–229. https://doi.org/10.1590/S0104-40602007000100015

Quilaqueo, D., & Quintriqueo, S. (2008). Formación docente en educación intercultural para contexto mapuche en Chile. *Cuadernos Interculturales, 6*(10), 91–110.

Quintriqueo, D., Quilaqueo, D., Lepe-Carrión, P., Riquelme, E., Gutiérrez, M., & Peña-Cortés, F. (2014). Teacher training in intercultural education in Latin America. The case of Chile. *Revista Electrónica Interuniversitaria Interuniversitaria de Formación del Profesorado, 17*(2), 201–217.

172   *Interculturality In and Out of the Classroom*

Quintriqueo, S., Quilaqueo, D., Peña-Cortés, F., & Muñoz, G. (2015). Cultural knowledge as contents of Mapuche family education. *Alpha (Osorno)*, *40*, 131–146.

Rojas, R. M. (2008). Absence of indigenous cultures in Peruvian higher education. *ISEES: Social Inclusion and Equity in Higher Education*, *2*, 119–132.

Sumida Huaman, E. (2015). "Why can't we admire our own?": Indigenous youth, farming, and education in the Peruvian Andes. In *Indigenous innovation: Universalities and peculiarities*. Sense. https://doi.org/10.1007/978-94-6300-226-4_8

Sumida Huaman, E., & Valdiviezo, L. A. (2012). Indigenous knowledge and education from the Quechua community to school: Beyond the formal-non-formal dichotomy. *International Journal of Qualitative Studies in Education*, 1–23. https://doi.org/10.1080/09518398.2012.737041

Trivelli, C. (2005). Indigenous households and poverty in Peru: A look from quantitative information. *Economia*, *28*(55–56), 83–158.

Tubino, F. (2019). Interculturality. In C. Alegría (Ed.), *Manual de principios y problemas éticos* (pp. 203–217). Fondo Editorial Pontificia Universidad Católica del Perú.

Turra-Díaz, O. (2015). Mapuche teachers and historical-educational knowledge in history teaching. *Educare Electronic Journal*, *19*(3), 241–260.

UNESCO. (1990). *World declaration on education for all and framework for action to meet basic learning needs*. United Nations Educational, Scientific and Cultural Organization, UNESCO.

UNESCO. (2021). Reimagining our futures together: A new social contract for education. https://unesdoc.unesco.org/ark:/48223/pf0000379707

UNICEF. (2004). *Securing the rights of indigenous children. Report*. Innocenti Research Centre. https://www.unicef-irc.org/publications/pdf/digest11s.pdf

UNICEF. (2014). *UNICEF annual report 2014*. https://www.unicef.org/media/50786/file/UNICEF_Annual_Report_2014_ENG.pdf

United Nations. (2007). *United Nations declaration on the rights of indigenous peoples*. https://www.un.org/esa/socdev/unpfii/documents/DRIPS_es.pdf

Valdiviezo, L. (2009a). Bilingual intercultural education in indigenous schools: An ethnography of teacher Interpretations of government policy. *International Journal of Bilingual Education and Bilingualism*, *12*(1), 61–79. https://doi.org/10.1080/13670050802149515

Valdiviezo, L. A. (2009b). "Don't you want your child to be better than you?": Enacting ideologies and contesting intercultural policy in Peru. In F. Vavrus & L. Bartlett (Eds.), *Critical approaches to comparative education: Vertical case studies from Africa, Europe, the Middle East, and the Americas* (pp. 147–162). Palgrave Macmillan. Comparative and development education series. ISBN: 978-0-230-61597-7 (hbk) 978-1-137-36654-2 (sbk).

Valdiviezo, L. A. (2010). Indigenous worldviews in intercultural education: Teachers' construction of interculturalism in a bilingual Quechua-Spanish Program. *Intercultural Education*, *21*(1), 27–39. https://doi.org/10.1080/14675980903491866

Valdiviezo, L. A. (2013). "El niño debe aprender en su Idioma:" A Teacher's approximations to language policy in an Indigenous Peruvian School. In J. Shoba & F. Chimbutane (Eds.), *Bilingual education and language policy in the Global South* (pp. 13–29). Routledge, Taylor & Francis Group. ISBN: 978-0-415-50306-8 (hbk) 978-0-203-58794-2 (ebk).

Valdiviezo, L. A. (2014). Political discourse and school practice in multilingual Peru. In R. Cortina (Ed.), *The education of indigenous citizens in Latin America* (pp. 187–209). Multilingual Matters. ISBN: 978-1-783-09094-5.

Valdiviezo, L. A. (2020). Interculturality against the mirror; a critique from the Peruvian experience. In C. Pica, C. Veloria, & R. Manuela Contini (Eds.), *Intercultural education: Critical perspectives, pedagogical challenges and promising practices*. Nova Science Publishers. ISBN: 978-1-53616-929-4.

Valdiviezo, L. A., & Nieto, S. (2015). Culture in bilingual and multilingual education: Conflict, struggle and power. In W. E. Wright, S. Boun, & O. García (Eds.). *The handbook of bilingual and multilingual education* (Chap. 6, pp. 92–108). Wiley-Blackwell. ISBN: 978-1-118-53349-9.

Valdiviezo, L. A., & O'Donnell, J. L. (2019). "To educate for them in different ways;" defining inclusion in popular and intercultural education in Argentina and Peru. In M. Schuelka, C. Johnstone, G. Thomas, & A. Artiles (Eds.), *SAGE handbook on inclusion and diversity in education* (Chap. 34, pp. 468–480). SAGE. ISBN: 978-1-5264-3555-2.

Valdiviezo, L. A., & Valdiviezo-Arista, L. M. (2008). Política y práctica de la interculturalidad en la educación peruana: Análisis y propuesta. *Revista Iberoamericana de Educación, 45*, 1–25.

Walsh, C. (2010). Critical interculturality and intercultural education. In *Construyendo Intercultur-alidad Crítica* (pp. 75–96). III-CAB.

Williamson, G., Collia, G., Pérez, I., Modesto, F., & Rain, N. (2012). Rural teachers, Mapuche childood and adolescence. *Psicoperspectivas, 11*(2), 77–96. https://doi.org/10.5027/psicoperspectivas-Vol11-Issue2-fulltext-180

Wingrove-Haugland, E., & McLeod, J. (2021). Not "minority" but "minoritized". *Teaching Ethics, 21*(1), 1–11.

Woodhead, M., Ames, P., Vennam, U., Abebe, W., & Streuli, N. (2009). *Equity and quality? Challenges for early childhood and primary education in Ethiopia, India and Peru.* Bernard van Leer Foundation. https://files.eric.ed.gov/fulltext/ED522535.pdf

Zambrano, O., & Beltran, M. I. (2012). *Retos de desarrollo del Perú, 2012-2016.* IDB.

Zavala, V. (2019). Youth and the repoliticization of Quechua. *Language, Culture and Society, 1*(1), 59–82.

Zavala, V., & Almeida, C. (2022). "Motoso y terruco": Linguistic ideologies and racialisation in Peruvian politics. *Lexis, 46*(2), 481–521. https://doi.org/10.18800/lexis.202202.002

Zavala, V., Robles, A. M., Trapnell, L., Zariquiey, R., Ventiades, N., & Ramírez, A. (2007). *Avances y desafíos de la educación intercultural bilingüe en Bolivia, Ecuador y Perú. Case studies.* IBIS, CARE.

APPENDIX: GLOSSARY

Epew: oral storytelling used by the Mapuche people as a pedagogical tool to deliver teachings through fables.

Lonko: sociopolitical authority of the Mapuche people who heads one or more communities. Their jurisdiction is divided into territorial or family units.

Machi: physical, psychological and spiritual doctor. According to Mapuche belief, their healing capacity is granted by a superior being.

Pachamama: Quechua term meaning mother earth.

Purrun: traditional Mapuche dance, performed in religious and cultural ceremonies.

Wiñol Tripantu: ceremony performed by the Mapuche people on the winter solstice. The beginning of a new year is celebrated on this date.

INCLUSION AND EQUITY IN HIGHER EDUCATION: THE CASE OF ECUADOR, A PLURINATIONAL AND INTERCULTURAL COUNTRY

Pilar Samaniego-Santillán[a],
Verónica Gabriela Maldonado-Garcés[b] and
Mónica Delgado-Quilismal[a]

[a]*Independent Researcher, Ecuador*
[b]*Pontificia Universidad Católica del Ecuador*

ABSTRACT

This chapter was developed with the conceptual, political, structural and pragmatic dimensions promulgated by UNESCO for an inclusive and equitable education, which would be impossible without the lens of interculturality. The research was carried out in seven higher education institutions (three public and four private) located in the Andean region of Ecuador. The sample consisted of 250 pre-service and in-service teachers who responded to an online survey and 28 interviews with eight university teachers and 20 students from higher education institutions. The results show the felt needs of university students who self-identify with Indigenous peoples and nationalities, Afro-Ecuadorian or Montubian populations, which contrast with the statements of higher education teachers. Teacher training to respond to diversity poses a challenge for the academy. The ulterior aim of this work is to invite the different regional actors to contribute to quality education without exceptions, leading to the construction of fairer, more democratic, and equitable societies, maintaining as a goal the equalisation of opportunities so that no one is left behind or left out, an aspiration and commitment that we must assume jointly.

Intercultural and Inclusive Education in Latin America
International Perspectives on Inclusive Education, Volume 24, 175–196
Copyright © 2024 Pilar Samaniego-Santillán, Verónica Gabriela Maldonado-Garcés and Mónica Delgado-Quilismal
Published under exclusive licence by Emerald Publishing Limited
ISSN: 1479-3636/doi:10.1108/S1479-363620240000024012

Keywords: Inclusion; equity; interculturality; higher education; teacher education; Ecuador

INTRODUCTION

Intercultural and inclusive education is moving through shifting sands of instability and confusion, with challenges and tensions that do not provide a way out from a perspective of unity. The local and situated voices of both teachers and students speak of historical exclusions, fragmentations and invisibilities, with an evident predominance of non-indigenous and Afro-Ecuadorian groups that reflect the social model.

The analysis from an intercultural approach on the four dimensions of inclusive and equitable education: conceptual, political, structural and pragmatic (OEI-UNESCO, 2018), shows that we are still not where we have long been claiming we wanted to be. In terms of inclusion, obstacles persist that limit the presence, participation and achievements of students. The notions of social justice and equality, concomitant with the principle of equity, fall short of ensuring that the education of all students is considered of equal importance and quality. At the higher education level, inclusive, equitable and intercultural action has yet to be put into practice in the classroom due to weak structural coordination and timid inter-institutional coordination.

Progress in general terms overshadows inequalities to the detriment of the Afro-descendant and Indigenous population, as shown by the 2020 results published by the Economic Commission for Latin America and the Caribbean (ECLAC). There is a marked difference between young people aged 20–24 who have completed upper secondary education according to ethnic self-identification: 42.7% Afro-descendant and 56.6% Indigenous, compared to 77.6% of the non-indigenous or Afro-descendant population (ECLAC, 2022, p. 131); the trend increases at the higher level of education. There is a direct relationship between educational level and poverty rates, with a difference of more than 20% points between those who have completed tertiary education and those who have not completed primary education; consequently, the highest poverty rates are found among Indigenous people (47%) and Afro-descendants (43%), which contrasts with the rest of the population (25%) (ECLAC, 2022, p. 66).

Against this backdrop, we investigated the extent to which the accounts of educational trajectories reflect the international treaties signed by Ecuador, current legislation and public policies. We investigated how teachers perceive their initial and in-service training, while at the same time probing for suggestions that would help to improve the relevance and assertiveness of the educational response without leaving anyone behind or out.

When we notice from the conceptual dimension that terms that do not represent the same elements or evoke the same meaning are easily and frequently mixed, it is a challenge to make the meeting of multiple visions feasible by combining discourses, practices and resources. Inclusion, equity and interculturality are a categorical call to stop sacrificing individualities. Although the prospective vision becomes dilemmatic, within a common framework of shared duties and rights, buoyancy is possible through effective commitment leading to action.

The main objective of this work is to identify coincidences and divergences between the felt needs of university students who self-identify with peoples and nationalities, with Afro-Ecuadorian or Montubian populations, and the perception of the teaching staff in terms of their capacity to respond to cultural diversity with principles of inclusion and equity.

Our research question is: Do students who self-identify as Indigenous peoples and nationalities, Afro-Ecuadorian or Montubio peoples exercise their right to education with the support they need in terms of inclusion and equity?

This study was conducted with members of educational communities from seven universities located in the Andean region of Ecuador.

METHODOLOGICAL APPROACH

The study is framed within the hermeneutic method of the interpretative paradigm of qualitative research; it is descriptive in nature, and the intercultural approach is framed within the principles of inclusion and equity at the higher education level in Ecuador from the logic of 'purposive sampling' (Flick, 2015, p. 48). It is an atheoretical study in that it is descriptive, with no interest in making generalisations or formulating hypotheses a posteriori.

The approach to the political and structural dimensions is based on a review of documents and open access databases, among them: current regulations; 2010 census data published by the National Institute of Statistics and Censuses of Ecuador (INEC), since at the time of this study the results of the VIII Population Census, VII Housing Census and I Communities Census, rescheduled as a result of the pandemic to take place from 7 November to 18 December 2022, have not yet been published; information from the Ministry of Higher Education, Science, Technology and Innovation (SENESCYT) and its affiliated bodies such as the National Higher Education Information System (SNIESE); official reports on progress related to international treaties signed by Ecuador, as well as responses and recommendations sent by the Ministry of Higher Education to the National Institute of Statistics and Censuses (INEC); information from the Ministry of Education, Science, Technology and Innovation (SENESCYT) and its affiliated bodies such as the National System of Higher Education Information (SNIESE); official reports on progress related to international treaties signed by Ecuador, as well as responses and recommendations sent by specialised bodies of the United Nations (UN); studies prepared by international intergovernmental bodies such as the Organisation of Ibero-American States for Education, Science and Culture (OEI); multilateral organisations, international cooperation and Official Development Assistance (ODA) agencies, national and international non-governmental organisations; studies carried out by academics and independent researchers; and some minutes of the roundtables related to collective rights, education and interculturality.

For the conceptual and pragmatic dimensions, the methodology of discourse analysis is favoured, which allows 'detecting and examining symbolic relations' (Salgado, 2019), making visible the exercise of power, asymmetries and structural inequalities and their social impact based on the interrelation between key theoretical concepts and linguistic categories for the identification of which the iKeyCriteria computational tool was used (Carrión et al., 2019). The information was collected through semi-structured interviews with teachers, students and former students of higher education institutions.

In order to understand the underlying structures in the university space, such as the academic preparation of applicants, the possibilities of admission related to place of birth, economic situation or mother tongue, seven higher education institutions (three public and four private) located in Pichincha, a province with more universities in its territory and one in Chimborazo where a public university that stands out for its intercultural approach (SENESCYT, 2022) were selected based on the criterion of homogeneity. With the criterion of heterogeneity, different approaches are selected in order to get closer to the experiences that arise from the interaction between students and teachers, collected through semi-structured interviews. Given the concomitant convergence of teacher training in the practice of implementing regulations, policies and guidelines through curriculum management, we proceeded with an online consultation, open to teachers in training or in service at different educational levels. Perceptual, attitudinal categories and actual events from the interviews and the online survey are combined to better understand individual and multi-personal systems. The SPSS software platform was used to process the information obtained through the online survey. The identification of those who participated freely, voluntarily and in their personal capacity, as well as the details of the institutions to which they refer, is not publicly disclosed and will not be passed on to third parties, which is underlined by an obvious fear of retaliation. The data of both participants and institutions useful for the general analysis refer to: province, support, type, area, language and ethnicity.

The instruments used to collect information were created by the authors:

- Semi-structured interviews aimed at students or former students of higher education institutions, with the objective of identifying, making visible and positioning the needs felt because of their experiences as students studying at the higher education level. This instrument collects general data and information on student trajectory from the initial stages of schooling and their experience at university.
- Semi-structured interviews with teachers from higher education institutions with the aim of finding out the perception of the teaching staff in relation to the educational principles of inclusion and equity from the perspective of cultural and ethno-linguistic diversity. This instrument collects general data and information related to conceptual, political, structural and pragmatic dimensions.

- Online survey aimed at teachers in training or in service in Ecuador with the objective of finding out their perception of the relevance of teacher training for inclusive and intercultural education in Ecuador. This instrument collects general data and questions related to teacher training processes on issues of inclusion and interculturality.

The interviews were conducted by the authors of this research. The legitimate basis for the processing of the participants' data is informed consent. The information obtained from the interviews was recorded with codes to guarantee confidentiality. A visual guide to the interview coverage is provided in Fig. 1.

Characterisation of Participants

The university teachers who participated in the interviews belong to seven universities, public and private, located in the Sierra of Ecuador. The students interviewed self-identified as members of Indigenous peoples and nationalities, Afro-Ecuadorian peoples or Montubio peoples.

Respondents to the online survey say they have a university degree in teaching or are studying to become a teacher, have classroom experience and work at different levels of education.

The inclusion criteria for the interviews were: to be teachers, students or former students of higher education institutions located in the provinces of Pichincha or Chimborazo; to sign the Informed Consent to be interviewed.

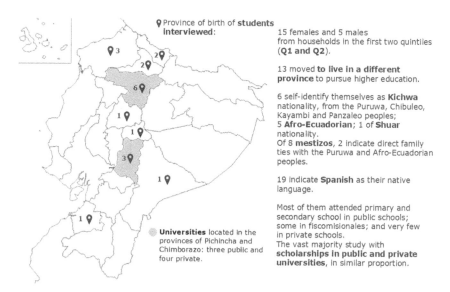

Fig. 1. Characterisation of 20 University Students Interviewed Between October and November 2022. *Source*: Prepared by the authors based on information from interviews with university students (2022).

For the online survey, the inclusion criteria were to be a trainee or current teacher, regardless of the level of education at which they are working in Ecuador.

Exclusion criteria were persons under 18 years of age; failure to sign the Informed Consent Form to be interviewed; from the online survey, incomplete questionnaires were discarded.

The variables considered were the dimensions of inclusive and equitable quality education: conceptual, political, structural and pragmatic.

Recognising that the function of language is not only referential (informative) and epistemic (interpretative) but also creative because of its 'generative capacity' (Echeverría, 2003, p. 23), during the interviews with students and teachers (p. 21), critical knots were explored in depth in accordance with the flow of conversation.

The total number of students interviewed was 20 (15 women and five men); they ranged in age from 20 to 43. Thirteen were born in a different province from the university where they study. Six self-identify as Kichwa, from the Puruwa, Chibuleo, Kayambi and Panzaleo peoples; five as Afro-Ecuadorian; one as Shuar; and of eight mestizos, two report a direct family relationship with the Puruwa and Afro-Ecuadorian peoples. For all but one, Spanish is their mother tongue.

The teachers interviewed were eight, six women and two men, aged 41–58, five self-identify as mestizo and three as white. All report Spanish as their mother tongue. Seven have a master's degree and one a doctorate. On average, they have more than 20 years of experience in education; in the institution where they currently work, they report a seniority between 1.5 and 17 years.

Given the importance of analysing the discourses generated by civil society as 'an important clue' (Garretón, 2007, p. 48), the online survey answered by trainee and in-service teachers (Fig. 2) asked about: the conceptualisation of inclusive and equitable education, the perception of the contributions provided by initial and in-service training to address diversity, the main barriers to inclusion and the topics they suggest should be incorporated into the training curriculum.

Out of 353 questionnaires submitted, 250 were completed mainly by women (78.31%) from 17 of the 24 provinces of the country, most of them from Pichincha (70.62%). Almost all the participants identified themselves as mestizo (90.36%), and Spanish was their mother tongue (99.6%). In general, they do not know the ethnic self-identification of students in the institutions where they work but state that most of them are mestizo.

Political and Structural Dimensions: Regulatory Scenario

Ecuador has progressive legal and institutional provisions in harmony with ratified international treaties that guarantee respect for diversity, the rejection of all forms of hegemony, stereotypes and prejudices; fundamentally, the Magna Carta (Constitution of the Republic of Ecuador, 2008) positions the right to quality, equitable and inclusive education as an articulating axis of inter-culturalism, pluralism and universal citizenship (UNESCO, 2022a).

A state of justice and equity, plurinational and intercultural, seeks to ensure the realisation of collective and individual rights, promoting convergence and

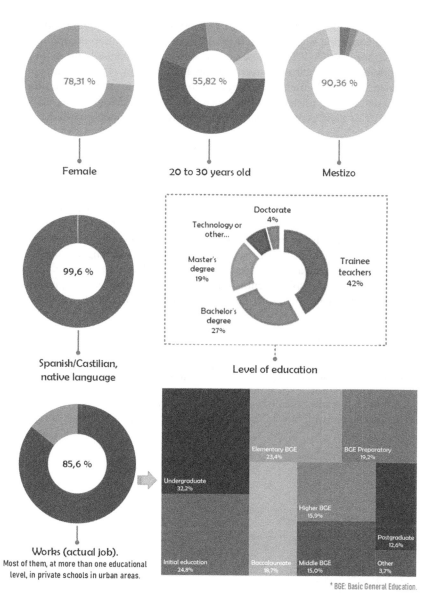

Fig. 2. Characterisation of Trainee and In-Service Teachers Who Responded to the Online Survey. November 2022. *Source*: Prepared by the authors based on the systematisation of the responses to the online survey ($n = 250$).

valuing diversity to contribute to peaceful coexistence. Although this is the ideal, historically, the pyramidal construction of citizenship has made invisible the 14 nationalities and 18 Indigenous peoples that inhabit the different geographic regions of Ecuador, as well as the Afro-Ecuadorian and Montubio peoples who, together, constitute slightly more than a fifth of the population according to the 2010 Census (INEC, 2021), whose actions should be recognised and respected as a manifestation of their customs, language and ideology (Fig. 3). The updated information from household surveys is not feasible to consider because the sample size is at the micro-data level; therefore, it is not disaggregated and leaves out remote or hard-to-reach areas whose harsh realities remain invisible, not only statistically.

The homogenisation that invisibilises by not disaggregating statistical information involves – among other abuses – disrespecting the right to use one's own language and preserve one's own culture. Spanish is positioned as the main language even though the Constitution of the Republic also recognises Kichwa and Shuar as official languages for intercultural relations, as well as the other ancestral languages, for official use by Indigenous peoples in the areas where they live. On the other hand, by misleadingly claiming that they are not useful for acquiring scientific knowledge, the inherent potential of all languages to be used in multiple communicative contexts is nullified, leading to a linguistic loss that increases the risk of displacement for their users: 522 Indigenous peoples and 420 Indigenous languages in use in Latin America (UNICEF et al., 2009), among them:

> Ecuador's Indigenous peoples comprise 14 nationalities with 13 living Indigenous languages. On the coast, we have Awapit, Cha'palaa and Tsa'fiki; in the Amazon, Achuar, Shuar, Shiwiar, Baikoka, Paikoka, Sapara, A'i and Waotededo. The Kichwa language, traditionally spoken in the Sierra, is also present in the Amazon and the Galapagos Islands. Haboud (2019, p. 3)

Although a precise estimate of the number of speakers of each of the 13 living languages is not available, it is possible to infer from the 2001 census information

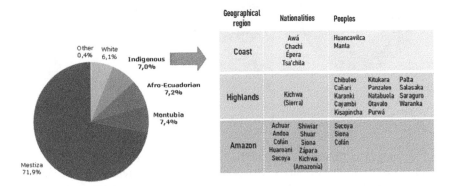

Fig. 3. Population of Ecuador by Ethnic Self-Identification. *Note:* Prepared by the authors based on data from the VII Population Census and VI Housing Census of Ecuador conducted in 2010 (INEC, 2021). Disaggregation of Indigenous population into peoples and nationalities by geographic region based on: MINEDUC (2022a), CARE Ecuador (2016) and GoRaymi (2022).

that about half of the population that defines itself as Indigenous would speak the ancestral language and "the remaining 50% would be speakers of Spanish". López and García (2009, p. 596)

The regulations have not been implemented effectively or in a relevant manner for the protection of rights, which seriously affects historically excluded populations that continue to suffer discrimination in relation to access to justice, security, land, drinking water, education, healthcare, housing and opportunities for economic growth (Hinojosa et al., 2020). In Ecuador, according to data from Antón (2020) and the UN (2019), better indicators are achieved in terms of enrolment coverage at the primary level, but the problem lies in the quality of learning, the identity relevance of the educational model, the continuity of school trajectories until the end of high school and restricted access to higher education, despite affirmative actions, such as the allocation of scholarships and additional compensating points in the admission process, due to poor learning at the primary and secondary levels.

According to the report: Educational inequalities in the context of the COVID-19 pandemic in Ecuador (INEC, 2022), despite social achievements in recent pre-pandemic years, underlying mechanisms of exclusion and multiple inequities are aggravated by the emergence of new inequalities faced by students, families and educational communities. The report reveals statistically significant differences, with curves and indices of school attendance concentration, teacher–student communication and participation in school activities, which show Indigenous and Afro-Ecuadorian populations with the least favourable educational outcomes due to social, demographic and economic factors. Thus, inequalities in teacher–student communication are the most pronounced for Indigenous students. In terms of income quintiles, there is a significant and positive difference in the attendance of students living in households in the highest economic quintile compared to those in the lowest economic quintiles.

Article 343 of the Constitution of the Republic of Ecuador (2008) organises the National Education System with an intercultural approach in accordance with the geographical, cultural and linguistic diversity of the country, and respect for the rights of Indigenous communities, peoples and nationalities, Afro-Ecuadorian and Montubio peoples, as priority groups. Legislation makes no mention of ethno-education, nor do school textbooks reflect the country's diversity as might be expected, being particularly deficient with reference to the Afro-Ecuadorian people (Mesa Nacional de Etnoeducación Afroecuatoriana, 2019). As such, the compilation of information prepared by the Office of the United Nations High Commissioner for Human Rights recommends introducing ethno-education into the national curriculum and ensuring that educational materials accurately reflect historical facts related to past tragedies and atrocities, particularly slavery (UN, 2022).

The Committee on Economic, Social and Cultural Rights (CESCR), the independent expert body that monitors the implementation of the International Covenant on Economic, Social and Cultural Rights (ICESCR) by its States Parties, is concerned about persistent disparities between rural and urban areas, as well as a higher dropout rate among low-income populations, Indigenous peoples, Afro-descendants and Montubios. Consequently, it recommends increasing social spending for education to ensure universal and equal access to quality education while strengthening policies to prevent school dropout (UN, 2022). In turn, the UN Special Rapporteur on the rights of Indigenous peoples welcomed the measures adopted by the Ecuadorian government in relation to intercultural bilingual education and recommended guaranteeing the full autonomy of the Secretariat for Intercultural Bilingual Education, as well as allocating the necessary resources for its proper functioning (UN, 2022). The national government accepted the recommendation and on 21 September 2022 signed a document accepting all the demands made by the social organisations and the organisations of Indigenous peoples and nationalities represented by the Confederation of Indigenous Nationalities of Ecuador (CONAIE), the Council of Evangelical Indigenous Peoples and Organisations of Ecuador (FEINE) and the National Confederation of Peasant, Indigenous and Black Organisations (FENOCIN). The agreements signed mark a milestone and imply a titanic challenge for the Intercultural Bilingual Education and Ethno-education System since: it will enjoy full organic and political autonomy; it will have a budget increase to provide services from early stimulation to higher education; it will redesign the curricular system; it will improve infrastructure and services; it will reopen 100 % of intercultural bilingual community education centres and rural community schools; and it will expand the staff of advisors, mentors and auditors (Mesa de Diálogo. Collective Rights. Intercultural Bilingual Education, 2022).

The act is the vindication of a plurinational state severely affected by the process of transition from community schools to Millennium Education Units. The number of schools closed or merged is imprecise. In 2013, Indigenous social organisations estimated that 14,000 out of 29,050 would be closed; in 2018, the Ministry of Education stated that 8,033 were closed; and in 2019, in relation to the gradual process of reopening, the Ministry reported around 6,200 (Cevallos, 2021; Torres, 2013). The consequences for Indigenous children, their families and communities were tragic:

> ...dismantling of interculturality and plurinationality, displacement of language, interruption of educational trajectories, impoverishment, mistreatment, difficulties to enter university, emptying of communities, among others. *Sources:* Contrato Social por la Educación [Documentary] (2016) and Contrato Social por la Educación & Ecuarunari (2017, pp. 20–29)

'Bilingual intercultural education began in the 1940s with the Cayambe schools established by Dolores Cacuango, a Kichwa-speaking woman from the region' (Haboud, 2019, p. 6). With a trajectory of agreements and dissent marked by ups and downs, in 2004, the Intercultural Community University of Indigenous Nationalities and Peoples Amawtay Wasi (Kichwa: house of knowledge) was created, closed eight years later (Sarango, 2019) and created by law in 2018 as a public higher education institution of community character. Following its own path, in 2013, the Universidad Regional Amazónica Ikiam (Shuar: jungle) was created, which proposes research as the basis for social, productive and environmental transformation (Ikiam, 2022).

The Organic Law on Intercultural Education (2011) emphasises the right to education, integrates lifelong learning and, by addressing special educational needs associated or not with disability, achieves a certain approximation to the broad umbrella of inclusion. The Organic Law on Higher Education (2018) states that, as part of the National System of Inclusion and Social Equity, it is governed by principles of universality, equality, equity, interculturality, solidarity and non-discrimination (article 12); and it establishes equalisation processes to eliminate existing educational gaps for those who have been immersed in contexts of social and cultural inequalities. The Ecuadorian System of Access to Higher Education has the responsibility to provide affirmative action measures aimed at people in situations of inequality or vulnerability (SENESCYT, 2021).

By constitutional mandate (article 356), public higher education is free up to the third level, free education linked to academic responsibility; however, it worrying that Latin America is the region with the highest number of private universities, and Ecuador does not escape this trend that reduces the role of the State to the market with overcrowded classrooms and segmentation based on family resources, calling into question equity and freedom of choice, two pillars of the right to education (UNESCO, 2022b).

In line with Sustainable Development Goal 4 (SDG4) target 4.5 (UN, 2018), it is questionable whether the policy framework is sufficient to eliminate disparities in education and ensure equal access to all levels of education and vocational training.

The implementation of the guidelines established in the legislation becomes more complex in the structural dimension that implies inter-sectoral articulation and coordination, and even more so in the possible responses from the pragmatic dimension to attend to diversity by identifying individual needs and expectations while considering the conditions in which teaching is exercised.

Pragmatic Dimension: Educational Trajectories

In the pragmatic or practical dimension are the organisational strategies of educational centres to promote the presence, participation and academic achievement of each student, in harmony with current regulations (political dimension) and the inter-sectoral coordination of actions that make the mobilisation and distribution of resources viable (structural dimension), based on the principles of equity and inclusion previously agreed as the foundation of education at the national level.

The legislation of a constitutional state that guarantees rights and justice leads to the assumption that it is easy to adapt to university life in cities with a high population rate, different rhythms and high costs as opposed to those of small, rural or remote towns; that interaction and otherness among students does not imply any difficulty; that the teaching action guarantees learning and the appreciation of a cultural richness that contributes to the teaching processes, overcoming the historical division (Hinojosa et al., 2020): all erroneous assumptions that call for looking at the journey through the different educational levels and listening attentively to the stories of both students and teachers.

186   *Inclusion and Equity in Higher Education*

The Primary School

In their school careers, regardless of the type of school, the students interviewed refer to primary school as a stage in which discipline was synonymous with physical and verbal abuse, accepted and consented to; with favouritism towards those who were related to a teacher or who came from families that could buy materials and pay fees, which are the hidden costs of free education. They say that in community schools, culture and dress were respected, but competition between communities was encouraged, with concomitant fragmentation. Parents preferred their children to study in a Hispanic school so that they would have better opportunities, but 'if you were different, as an Indigenous person, the children treated you badly, they would say "dirty Indian", "you are an Indian", they would beat you, it was difficult to make friends because of the rejection' (E13). On the other hand, special reference is made to the warm treatment of teachers who listened, supported and accompanied individual, family or community processes.

The teacher's lack of knowledge of the students' mother tongue is the most serious problem because it leads to loneliness: 'I grew up in the nursery, they only spoke Spanish, I had no one around me who spoke Shuar' (E12). Other problems mentioned are: poor learning, lack of motivation and, consequently, a greater risk of interrupting the student's learning path.

They recall with pain and helplessness situations of violence at home and at school. 'I had female classmates who were touched without their permission. Sometimes they were beaten' (E13).

The Secondary School

Entry to secondary school in urban centres is evoked as a transition marked by expectations. 'It was a time when we had to get up early to stand in long queues and fight for a place' (E7). The support of the family, which sees education as an alternative to break the intergenerational cycle of poverty, is the most frequent support from mothers to their daughters:

> We suffered a lot in the community, she went to school in boots or barefoot and without eating because her father left her alone to look after us, she was not responsible. My mum's dad didn't let her go to school, so my mum wanted us to study, to have a career. With my mother's support I studied at night and in the morning, I helped her look after my siblings, I worked in agriculture on my own land, or in community or associative mingas. There was racism from classmates and not from teachers (E11).

The depth of personal experience leads to the identification of significant relationships: family members who were protective references; friends who supported the adaptation to a new environment and shared experiences; teachers who generated trust, who helped them to level their knowledge, who defended them from mockery by classmates and from discrimination by managers or other teachers.

The primary school teacher's approach to their students is lacking, 'Teachers should be more involved with the students (...). There were drugs, they didn't even know about it, there was no control over anything' (E2). Based on painful experiences, topics that should be dealt with in depth are highlighted: violence, emotional intelligence and sex education. They suggest incorporating public speaking and writing as key tools. The importance of a stable teaching staff with a good command of content, especially mathematics, physics, chemistry and English, is raised; at the same time, it is proposed to incorporate subjects linked to the reality of the environment and those recommended by the academy based on the results of entrance exams and pre-university courses that show insufficient academic preparation received at the secondary level: 'there were light years between secondary school and university' (E13).

It is considered inescapable to stop romanticising folklore in order to move forward in terms of respect and mutual appreciation based on the knowledge of different cultures without losing identity.

Gender-based violence starts at an early age, disproportionately affects girls, deepens inequality and is intertwined with poverty, school dropout and teenage pregnancy. The risk is greatest for girls and adolescent girls who live in rural communities or belong to Indigenous or Afro-descendant communities (UNICEF, 2022).

> A classmate left because of that [pregnancy]; she stopped studying. A girl disappeared; they said she had been abused. There were teachers who abused girls, but they didn't always report it. The psychologist said it was the girl's fault because she provoked him (E17).

The University

Free higher education eliminates enrolment and tuition fees with a positive effect on access, although there is no consensus on the results (Rivera, 2019). There is no information available – by university and faculty – disaggregated by ethnic self-identification, gender, age, mother tongue; nor on repetition, absenteeism or dropout rates; even less on certification, accreditation and promotion rates; participation in student organisations; internships, teaching assistantships, pre-professional internships and research; labour market insertion and improvement of living conditions. The university professors interviewed state that they observe very few Indigenous or Afro-Ecuadorian students; they refer that in their groups of 50–60 students, occasionally, they have had a maximum of two; most of them are unaware of the difficulties they face.

The choice of career was determined by the score achieved in the standardised test or the possibility of a scholarship; in general, they indicated that they would have opted for a different career, and that it would have helped them to receive vocational guidance.

Entering university meant, in many cases, moving away from the family, facing alone an urban context in which they had to survive on a meagre budget that did not cover the minimum food and housing requirements. 'The distance from their homes is an overwhelming situation, family values are very strong for the Puruwa people. They come from other parts of the country and the biggest difficulty they face is economic' (P1).

Making friends was easier in university spaces where students from different regions come together. Not all of them self-identify with a people or nationality, some attend in their own traditional costumes and, although they use their mother tongue to converse with each other, they prefer Spanish to share knowledge. 'The university has students from different ethnic groups and also welcomes refugee students from other countries' (P8).

It is underlined that in private universities in the capital city, prejudice is frequent, and racism emerges from different fronts: 'From Indigenous people to Indigenous people, they feel they have the right to diminish those who don't have money just because they already have a degree or because they have been in the city longer' (E11); from classmates: 'Black people from the village! What are you doing here? The university shouldn't have people like you' (E14); from security guards who ask for ID if a student is Afro-Ecuadorian or wearing Indigenous clothing; from professors who declined to tutor Indigenous students' theses after the national strike (in October 2019). 'In the strikes many Indigenous people asked where the academy is. They are using us. Where is it when we need its support. We need to strengthen contact and do it more systematically. Develop diagnostics and implement intervention' (P7).

Internal policies to promote ancestral and intercultural knowledge and knowledges do not transcend paper. 'They may exist, but I don't know about them because they are not socialised. We are involved in teaching and projects; it is known when we enter politics. On social networks you see photos [of the highest authority] signing agreements' (P2). 'In a public university I saw ancestral festivals and traditions being recreated to talk about language. It was a discussion from the subject, not from the supra-faculty' (P4).

Academic excellence, honesty and compliance are pitted against pseudo-academicism, corruption and irresponsibility. 'There were professors who did not go to class. One teacher gave me four subjects, he only arrived on the first day, (...) for grading he would say: "you are going to do this consultation, minimum five pages, maximum 8", the grades were between 8 and 9' (E6). Those who teach without getting involved are identified: 'colleagues with experience in rural areas get stuck on the "no"s' instead of paying attention on the focal elements of progress or simply giving them the opportunity' (P1).

In contrast, the good work of faculty who respect diversity, do not discriminate and seek strategies for inclusion is highlighted, as well as those who provide remedial teaching, advise on academic programmes, guide students to career opportunities, help students who need income to continue at university to find employment and even support with money for someone who has suffered a mishap and with food when the need arises. It is emphasised that respect and empathy are personal characteristics, not institutional.

> The teachers are aware of these situations, and food is collected and stored in the directorate of the programme. The teachers understand the need and deliver a bag of food every month.

> Students communicate directly and confidently with the academic director. When they run out of food, they go to the directorate because they know that they are provided with food when they need it. Solidarity works, for example, in the case of a girl who disappeared because she

suffered physical violence from her partner; she was found and the help she needed was provided. Another girl was beaten by her partner so that she would have an abortion. These are very hard, strong situations that must be sustained. The academic director supports and accompanies both teachers and students (P1).

In a publication by the Spanish Agency for International Development Cooperation and the Secretariat for Higher Education, Science, Technology and Innovation, it is acknowledged that interculturality is a pending task in higher education institutions (AECID and SENESCYT, 2017). 'The university has a faculty (...) that, among other things, develops all intercultural issues, both with native populations and international relations' (P6). 'The universities have a folklorist vision, they celebrate Inti Raymi. To talk about interculturality is to talk about tolerance' (P3).

Policies related to equity are little known by the student body. 'We all paid for health insurance, but nobody informed you that you could get health care and pay only $5. I found out because I was in the student council' (E20). The procedures are cumbersome, time-consuming and there is not always a positive response: 'they say that they can have a place to sleep, but after a lot of procedures they are told that there is no way' (E17).

Nor are the policies, guidelines or protocols for safety, prevention and action in cases of violence known. The students interviewed indicate that they have not received information about violence against women from members of the university community and do not know where to turn for help if they need it. 'I don't know, and if they have them [safety policies], I didn't know about them. They must have them' (E14). 'They only teach their class. They don't know anything' (E6). 'I don't know about any policy' (E19).

Although women's leadership is seen as a positive development, gender-based violence persistently affects female students and professors in different ways, perpetrated by their partners or ex-partners, as well as by members of the university community. Macho phrases and sexist jokes are heard in the context of naturalised violence: 'There are a few teachers who say things like: what are you doing here, go cook at home; women are good for nothing' (E5). 'The guards are abusive, morbid, rude' (E17). 'There are teachers who make jokes that have a double meaning, and everyone knows who they are aimed at' (E1). 'There is violence from teachers towards female students and also from teachers towards female teachers who take advantage of the consumption of liquor in social gatherings for 'integration, for example, to celebrate Teacher's Day' (P3).

At best, incidents are reported. 'The teachers themselves advised us not to report because certain teachers had appointments and the report would turn against us' (E19). With the support of some student organisations, the problem has been made visible, but without reaching the level of incidence required to stop considering sexual violence as an administrative offence and to position it as what it really is: a crime. 'For example, in cases of harassment or attempted rape, there is nothing you can do. A professor had 17 complaints, they moved him to another faculty and campus, that was all' (E20). Institutions look after their *prestige* and complaints remain on paper.

The data from the study on the prevalence of gender-based violence against women in universities in Ecuador are outrageous: 31.2 % of female students and 19.3 % of female teachers or administrative staff have suffered some kind of violence by a member of the university community (Fig. 4). The most frequent forms of violence are harassment and stalking, manifestations of violence that are culturally considered 'mild' and reflect an unacceptable tolerance. It is disturbing that only 16 out of 59 invited universities agreed to participate in the study. From an economic perspective, the days lost by the 252,429 students and teachers affected amount to 3.13 % of the national budget for tertiary education (Vara-Horna, 2022).

Beyond institutional ideologies, publications and research driven by international policy influences, universities operate in a bubble mode from their own comfort and interests, both internally at faculty level and externally without enabling effective interoperability between higher education institutions or between higher education institutions and other educational levels. The subjugation to standardised and rigid structures strongly suggests that there is little or no faculty participation, and that everyone is working alone.

> With so many students – close to 300 students in charge – demand for publication, outreach programmes, undervaluation of teaching, demotivation and disrespect from the authorities, everyone works as best they can. As a teacher, I don't even have a chair in the classroom, let alone a desk. They focus on the *ranking*. You have to score 900 or more points, 200 of those are teaching points. If you don't, you're out. No attention is given to interculturalism or inclusion because there is no time, no support or resources. It is complex and frustrating. There are no real changes, and the law is not applied (P3).[1]

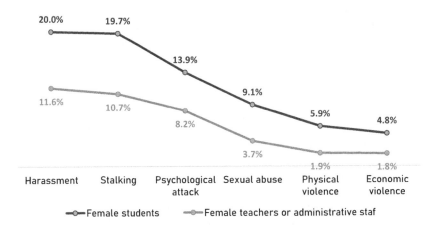

Fig. 4. Forms of Violence Perpetrated by a Member of the University Community (Student, Teacher, Administrative or Associated Staff) Against Female Students and Female Teachers or Administrative Staff. *Source:* Prepared by the authors based on Vara-Horna (2022).

Conceptual Dimension and Teacher Education

The conceptual dimension links elements, characteristics and relationships that guide and support the principles of inclusion and equity as the foundation of education. The conceptual construction of these fundamental principles with an intercultural approach requires national agreements that are clearly assumed to generate the commitment of partners in educational management. These agreements must be based on reflection and institutional research to provide qualitative and quantitative information that will lead to decision-making on environments and practices.

Teachers are key to the teaching–learning process. The shortage of teachers – with statements from the teachers' union disagreeing with the official figure – is a problem that has been dragging on for years and is expected to increase (Castillo, 2021; Machado, 2019; Torres, 2022). This deficit implies, in urban and suburban areas, a large student population per classroom to the detriment of students and teachers. In rural and border areas, there are 7,836 so-called teachers who do not have a third-level degree and who are in category J of the national teaching profession. In Zone 1 (provinces of Esmeraldas, Carchi, Imbabura and Sucumbíos), 1,793 high school graduates teach, equivalent to 22 % of hired teachers in these northern border provinces (Research Unit, 2019).

Category J: This is the entry category to the public education career when the degree is a high school, for persons who have won the merit and competitive examinations in areas of difficult access with a shortage of professionals. A maximum period of six (6) years is granted to obtain the title of teacher or bachelor's degree in education sciences, otherwise their provisional appointment will be revoked. Within the first two (2) years, they must participate in an induction programme. Promotions are only allowed for educators who have obtained at least a teaching, technologist or bachelor's degree in education (MINEDUC, 2022b).

In this scenario, the situation is aggravated by an initial training that only superficially addresses attention to diversity, understood as the capacity to generate inclusive and intercultural teaching–learning processes. In this field, the Observatory of the National University of Education (UNAE) reports that out of 30 universities offering Basic Education and 29 offering Early Education, only the University of Azuay has an inclusive education programme focused on disabilities, while intercultural education in other languages is only addressed by the National University of Chimborazo. In the curricula of Early Childhood Education and Basic Education courses, diversity-oriented subjects represent less than 10 percentage points of the curriculum (López et al., 2022), with very little being assigned to the intercultural category (Table 1).

Social change related to economic, sociopolitical and cultural transformation that affects human behavior and the conditions of our world (UNESCO IESALC, 2021) is addressed during Initial (15.8 %) and Basic Education (12.7 %) training as innovation and research through pre-professional internships and knowledge integration projects (López et al., 2022).

Table 1. Percentage of Subjects for Attention to Diversity in the Curricula of Early Childhood Education and Basic Education Courses in Ecuador.

	Initial Education	Basic Education
Attention to diversity	6.3 %	7.7 %
• Educational inclusion	4.9%	6.2 %
• Interculturality	1.4 %	1.5 %

Source: Prepared by the authors based on López et al. (2022).

The responses of trainee and in-service teachers recorded in the online survey complement and ratify the information mentioned in previous sections. No agreement was identified on the fundamental principles of inclusion and equity with an intercultural approach, but the following characteristics were noted: ensuring participation (59.7 %), promoting equal opportunities (55.6 %) and guaranteeing learning and socio-emotional skills (43.9 %).

The lowest level of compliance in initial and continuous training refers to the obligation to eliminate barriers that hinder or prevent inclusion and equity in education with an intercultural approach, mainly: poverty, exclusion, racism and violence (Fig. 5). Compliance scores are equally low with respect to consolidating the components of: plurinationality and interculturality as cross-cutting themes, strategies to prevent school dropout; intercultural coexistence relations and mental health and socio-emotional learning. The trend of low compliance is maintained in terms of the development of skills and attitudes

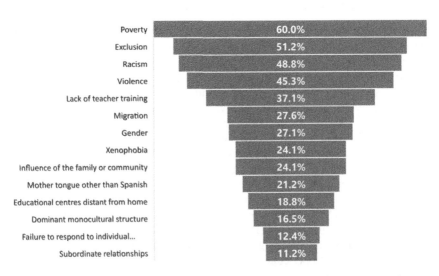

Fig. 5. Barriers to Inclusion and Equity With an Intercultural Approach.
Source: Prepared by the authors based on responses collected through online survey (*n* = 250). Participants could indicate more than one answer. November 2022.

related to: linking with the community, vision of the future, proactivity and empathy. Updating and research are highlighted as missing elements in training.

The persistence of poverty, beyond being a clearly identified barrier to achieving inclusion and equity, is a factor of inequality and discrimination that grows exponentially when added to the cultural fragmentation and segmentation of the population, resulting in profoundly disjointed societies in which fossilised hierarchies prevail and rigidities are established. The possibility of greater social inclusion depends, inevitably but not only, on ensuring full participation in education, and this requires trained teachers who have the necessary educational support for their teaching management, without neglecting to consider the system of beliefs, myths and prejudices that must be deconstructed; mastery of the subject; capacity and aptitudes; motivation and will; personality; and mental health concomitant with emotional, psychological and social well-being.

BY WAY OF COLOPHON

It is clear that inclusion and equity are processes, while interculturality is an experience suffocated by assimilation models and interventions that exacerbate discrimination and deepen asymmetries.

The greatest progress can be seen in the normative dimension, overwhelming at times, but ultimately guiding. The challenge for the government is to strengthen the structural dimension in order to guarantee an articulated and coordinated implementation at the macro and micro levels. It is necessary to combine political will with the commitment of educational institutions and the active co-participation of all actors, valuing Indigenous knowledge, wisdom and languages, building bridges to learn to live in harmony.

The stories about school trajectories are a call for attention to the pending debt of guaranteeing conditions of real equality for Indigenous, Afro-Ecuadorian and Montubio peoples, based on the understanding that the right to quality education implies meaningful and appropriate learning in accordance with what each human group defines as necessary to live with dignity. This implies, in the pragmatic dimension, favouring respect for languages and cultures, starting with the school, which is the heart of the community where citizenship is built, without neglecting impoverished populations located in suburban areas, as a result of rural–urban migration.

For a clear and mutual understanding, it is indispensable to reach agreement on the conceptual dimension. The meaning of key terms such as inclusion, equity, interculturality, justice and equality begins with teacher training, which is an essential part of the formula we must find. The academy has the floor.

Finally, we are jointly responsible for the titanic challenge that awaits the Intercultural Bilingual Education and Ethno-education System. It is to be hoped that we will rise to this challenge.

NOTES

1. The Council for Quality Assurance in Higher Education is responsible for carrying out processes that guarantee the quality of this level of education and promote the evaluation and improvement of higher education institutions (CACES, 2018). Pursuant to articles 86 to 88 of the Higher Education Teacher Career and Grading Regulations ([Reglamento de Carrera y Escalafón del Profesor de Educación Superior], 2019), each institution at this level is responsible for designing and implementing the comprehensive performance evaluation process for continuity in functions, incentives and promotions.

REFERENCES

AECID (Spanish Agency for International Development Cooperation) and SENESCYT (Secretariat for Higher Education, Science, Technology and Innovation). (2017, December). Guide for equality and environment in higher education: Steps to develop plans for mainstreaming equality and environment in higher education. https://www.educacionsuperior.gob.ec/wp-content/uploads/downloads/2018/11/Guia-para-la-igualdad-y-ambiente-en-la-Educacion-Superior_nov_2018.pdf

Antón, J. (2020). Ethnicity and education in Ecuador. La población afrodescendiente e inclusión escolar en Ecuador. https://unesdoc.unesco.org/ark:/48223/pf0000374764

CACES (Council for Quality Assurance in Higher Education). (2018). Institutional evaluation policy of universities and polytechnics in the framework of the higher education quality assurance system. https://www.caces.gob.ec/documents/20116/152061/44/4436.afsh/4436_1.0.afsh

CARE Ecuador. (2016). Ethnohistory of the native peoples and nationalities of Ecuador. https://www.care.org.ec/wp-content/uploads/2016/02/Modulo-2.pdf

Carrión-Toro, M., Aguilar, J., Santórum, M., Pérez, M., Astudillo, B., Lopez, C.-P., Nieto, M., & Acosta-Vargas, P. (2022). iKeyCriteria: A qualitative and quantitative analysis method to infer key criteria since a systematic literature review for the computing domain. *Data, 7*, 70. https://doi.org/10.3390/data7060070

Castillo, L. (2021, December 6). Deficit of 6,000 teachers in Ecuador. *El Comercio.* https://www.elcomercio.com/tendencias/sociedad/deficit-docentes-ecuador-ministerio.html

Cevallos, M. (2021). Disputes around the closure of the community school Rio Cenepa -Tauri, Ecuador. *Revista Andina de Educación, 4*(2), 83–92. https://doi.org/10.32719/26312816.2021.4.2.10

Constitution of the Republic of Ecuador. (2008). https://www.defensa.gob.ec/wp-content/uploads/downloads/2021/02/Constitucion-de-la-Republica-del-Ecuador_act_ene-2021.pdf

Dialogue Table. Collective rights. Intercultural Bilingual Education. (2022, September 21). *Acta de cierre del tema educación intercultural bilingüe. Quito, Ecuador.* https://4pelagatos.com/wp-content/uploads/2022/09/Acta-de-acuerdo.pdf

Echeverría, R. (2003). *Ontología del lenguaje.* J.C. Sáez Editor.

ECLAC (Economic Commission for Latin America and the Caribbean). (2022). *Social panorama of Latin America and the Caribbean 2022.* ECLAC. https://repositorio.cepal.org/bitstream/handle/11362/48518/1/S2200947_es.pdf

Flick, U. (2015). *The qualitative research design.* Ediciones Morata.

Garretón, M. A. (2007). *Del postpinochetismo a la sociedad democrática.* Prometeo.

GoRaymi. (2022). Cultures and nationalities in Ecuador. https://www.goraymi.com/es-ec/ecuador/culturas-nacionalidades/todas-publicaciones-eef558f5d

Haboud, M. (2019, November 18). Intercultural bilingual education in Ecuador. *ELAD-SILDA: Études de Linguistique et d'Analyse des Discours - Studies in Linguistics and Discourse Analysis, 3*, 1–20. https://doi.org/10.35562/elad-silda.579

Hinojosa, A., Orellana, M., & Toledo, C. (2022, June). Indigenous peoples' participation in higher education: A descriptive analysis. *Revista Espacios, 41*(23). https://www.revistaespacios.com/a20v41n23/20412320.html

Higher Education Teacher Career and Grading Regulations. [Reglamento de Carrera y Escalafón del Profesor de Educación Superior]. (2019). Resolution of the higher education council 265.

Institutional document 2017. https://www.ces.gob.ec/lotaip/Anexos%20Generales/a3/Reformas_febrero_2020/REGLAMENTO%20DE%20CARRERA%20Y%20ESCALAFON%20DEL%20PROFESOR%20DE%20EDUCACION%20SUPERIOR.pdf. Accessed on December 19, 2019.

Ikiam. (2022). Amazon Regional University. https://www.ikiam.edu.ec/

INEC (National Institute of Statistics and Census of Ecuador). (2022, June). Educational inequalities in the context of the COVID-19 pandemic in Ecuador. https://www.ecuadorencifras.gob.ec/documentos/web-inec/Bibliotecas/Libros/Reportes/Educacion_COVID.pdf

INEC (National Institute of Statistics and Census of Ecuador). (2021). https://www.ecuadorencifras.gob.ec/base-de-datos-censo-de-poblacion-y-vivienda-2010/

Ley Orgánica de Educación Intercultural. (2011). https://educacion.gob.ec/wp-content/uploads/downloads/2017/05/Ley-Organica-Educacion-Intercultural-Codificado.pdf

López, L., & García, F. (2009). Ecuador Andino. In UNICEF (United Nations International Children's Emergency Fund), AECID (Agencia Española de Cooperación Internacional para el Desarrollo), & FUNPROEIB (Fundación para la Educación en Contextos de Multilingüismo y Pluriculturalidad). In *Atlas Sociolingüístico de pueblos indígenas en América Latina* (Vol. 2, pp. 589–604). FUNPROEIB Andes. https://www.unicef.org/lac/media/9796/file/Atlas%20sociolinguistico%20de%20pueblos%20ind%C3%ADgenas%20en%20ALC-Tomo%202.pdf

López, M., Loaiza, K., Arias, M., & Mansutti, A. (2022, September 2). Surfing the wave: Ecuadorian universities towards 2050. *Boletín Observatorio UNAE*, (2), 49. https://revistas.unae.edu.ec/index.php/observaUNAE/article/view/780/643

Machado, J. (December 9, 2019). *Schools and colleges in the country need 79,311 teachers*. Primicias. https://www.primicias.ec/noticias/sociedad/profesores-deficir-escuelas-colegios/

Mesa Nacional de Etnoeducación Afroecuatoriana. (2019). La Etnoeducación afroecuatoriana, un aporte a la educación intercultural del país. In *Report delivered to the group of Afro-descendant experts of the United Nations carried out in Ecuador in December 2019.*

MINEDUC (Ministry of Education of Ecuador). (2022a). Intercultural bilingual education. https://educacion.gob.ec/educacion-intercultural-bilingue-princ/

MINEDUC (Ministry of Education of Ecuador). (2022b). Escalafón del magisterio nacional y sus categorías. https://educacion.gob.ec/recategorizacion/

OEI (Organization of Ibero-American States for Education, Science and Culture), & UNESCO (United Nations Educational Scientific and Cultural Organization). (2018). *Guide to ensuring inclusion and equity in education*. UNESCO.

Organic Law on Higher Education. (2018). https://www.gob.ec/sites/default/files/regulations/2021-10/Ley_educaci%C3%B3n_superior.pdf

Research Unit. (2019, January 2). 7,836 baccalaureate graduates teach in the 24 provinces. *The Telegraph*. https://www.eltelegrafo.com.ec/noticias/sociedad/6/docentes-titulotercernivel-estudiantes

Rivera, J. (2019, April). Ten years after free higher education in Ecuador: What happened to access? *Revista Chaquiñán*, (7), 58–69. http://scielo.senescyt.gob.ec/scielo.php?script=sci_arttext&pid=S2550-67222019000100058

Salgado, E. (2019). *Discourse studies in the social sciences*. National Autonomous University of Mexico.

Sarango, L. (2019, July–December). The intercultural university Amawtay Wasi of Ecuador, a project trapped in the coloniality of power. *Revista Universitaria del Caribe*, 23(2). https://doi.org/10.5377/ruc.v23i2.8929

SENESCYT (Secretariat of Higher Education, Science, Technology and Innovation). (2022). Services - Higher education institutions. https://siau.senescyt.gob.ec/instituciones-de-educacion-superior/

SENESCYT (Secretariat of Higher Education, Science, Technology and Innovation). (2021, October). Sistema Ecuatoriano de Acceso a la Educación Superior. In *General structure for the presentation of investment programmes and projects*. . https://www.educacionsuperior.gob.ec/wp-content/uploads/2022/02/PROYECTO_SEAES.pdf

Social Contract for Education [Documentary]. (2016, October 31). Se nos fue la alegría [we have lost our joy]. *Documentary*. https://www.youtube.com/watch?v=4TWtjbQBo5w

196   *Inclusion and Equity in Higher Education*

Social Contract for Education, & Ecuarunari. (2017). *Situación y propuestas en calidad de la educación e interculturalidad en las provincias de Cotopaxi y Chimborazo.* Contrato Social por la Educación; Confederación Kichwa del Ecuador -Ecuarunari. http://contratosocialecuador.org/images/publicaciones/CCE/Educacioneinterculturalidad.pdf.

Torres, R. (2013, October 15). Another education. Ecuador: Goodbye to community and alternative schools [blog entry]. https://otra-educacion.blogspot.com/2013/10/ecuador-adios-la-educacion-comunitaria.html

Torres, M. (2022, May 21). Teacher shortage aggravates the education crisis. *Expreso*. https://www.expreso.ec/guayaquil/deficit-maestros-agrava-crisis-educativa-127927.html#:~:text=La%20cifra Un%20cifra%20total%20de,educadores%20dice%20que%20faltan%207.000

UN (United Nations). (2019, December 20). OHCHR (Office of the High Commissioner for Human Rights). Statement to the media by the United Nations Working Group of Experts on Afro-descendants, at the end of its official visit to Ecuador, carried out between 16 and 20 December 2019, Quito. https://www.ohchr.org/es/2019/12/statement-media-united-nations-working-group-experts-people-african-descent-conclusion-its

UN (United Nations). (2018). Sustainable development goals. SDG 4 education indicators short guide. http://uis.unesco.org/sites/default/files/documents/quick-guide-education-indicators-sdg4-2018-sp.pdf

UN (United Nations). (2022). Ecuador. Compilation of information prepared by OHCHR (Office of the High Commissioner for Human Rights). Working group for the universal periodic review. https://www.ohchr.org/es/hr-bodies/upr/ec-index

UNESCO (United Nations Educational Scientific and Cultural Organization), in Spanish: Organización de las Naciones Unidas para la Educación, Ciencia y Cultura). (2022a). Ecuador. Overview. https://education-profiles.org/atín-america-and-the-caribbean/ecuador/~ecuador

UNESCO (United Nations Educational Scientific and Cultural Organization). (2022b). *Global education monitoring report 2021/2. Non-state actors in education: Who chooses? Who loses?* https://gem-report-2021.unesco.org/es/inicio/

UNESCO (United Nations Educational, Scientific and Cultural Organization) IESALC (UNESCO International Institute for Higher Education in Latin America and the Caribbean). (2021). Pathways to 2050 and beyond. https://www.iesalc.unesco.org/wp-content/uploads/2021/11/Pathways-to-2050-and-beyond_ESP-1.pdf

UNICEF (United Nations International Children's Emergency Fund), AECID (Agencia Española de Cooperación Internacional para el Desarrollo), & FUNPROEIB (Fundación para la Educación en Contextos de Multilingüismo y Pluriculturalidad) Andes. (2009). *Atlas sociolingüístico de pueblos indígenas en América Latina* (Vol. 1). FUNPROEIB Andes. https://www.unicef.org/lac/media/9791/file/PDF%20Atlas%20sociolinguistico%20de%20pueblos%20ind%C3%ADgenas%20en%20ALC-Tomo%201.pdf

UNICEF (United Nations International Children's Emergency Fund). (2022). Global database. https://data.unicef.org/

Vara-Horna, A. (2022). From evidence to prevention. How to prevent violence against women in Ecuadorian universities. GIZ (Deutsche Gesellschaft für Internationale Zusammenarbeit, German Technical Cooperation), Proyecto PreviMujer (Prevenir la Violencia contra las Mujeres). http://info.comvomujer.org.pe/catalogo/2021-estud-nac-univ-VCM-EC-USMP-GIZ.pdf

THE RURAL EDUCATION MODEL WITH ESCUELA NUEVA AND THE UNIVERSIDAD EN EL CAMPO IN COLOMBIA

Diego Juárez Bolaños

Universidad Iberoamericana Mexico City, Mexico

ABSTRACT

Developed collaboratively by the Caldas Coffee Growers' Committee, the Government of Caldas, university institutions, government agencies and public and private companies, the Rural Education with New School Model is a pedagogical proposal that has brought formal education from pre-school to higher education to rural inhabitants of the department of Caldas, Colombia. The model aims to be flexible and adaptable to the circumstances of children, adolescents and young people in this region of the Eje Cafetero, stimulating the construction of life projects that facilitate and promote their permanence in rural territories. This chapter aims to provide an overview of the scope and limitations of the Escuela Nueva (EN) Rural Education Model in Caldas by describing the general characteristics of the EN, identifying particularities of its implementation and examining the testimonies of graduates of the University in the field. The primary information that feeds the study comes from interviews with young people in various rural localities in the Department of Caldas. The results of the study analyse the possibilities for educational inclusion that the Universidad en el Campo has opened up for young people, as well as the achievements and challenges faced by this model, which has sought to be replicated in other Colombian departments and even in other countries. This chapter's findings highlight the importance of examining educational experiences developed at the departmental level and the fact that the Rural Education with New School Model offers continuity from pre-school to university level to rural children, adolescents and young people, following certain pedagogical principles. This is uncommon in urban and rural regions of Latin America.

Intercultural and Inclusive Education in Latin America
International Perspectives on Inclusive Education, Volume 24, 197–214
Copyright © 2024 Diego Juárez Bolaños
Published under exclusive licence by Emerald Publishing Limited
ISSN: 1479-3636/doi:10.1108/S1479-363620240000024013

Keywords: Rural education; New School; Colombia; rural youth; upper secondary education; educational models

INTRODUCTION

According to figures from the latest Population and Housing Census conducted in Colombia (Departamento Administrativo Nacional de Estadística [DANE], 2018), 48.2 million people lived in the country, of which 11 million (23% of the population) lived in rural areas. Rural areas are defined as areas that are 'not suitable for urban use, or that are used for agriculture, livestock, forestry, natural resource exploitation and similar activities' (Ramírez & de Aguas, 2017, p. 4).

However, there are other ways to quantify the rural population. The National Human Development Report for Colombia (United Nations Development Programme [UNDP], 2011) defines rurality based on the size of settlements, population density and distance from urban centres. Under this indicator, which is broader than DANE's, 32% of the Colombian national population lived in rural territories. A study by the Economic Commission for Latin America and the Caribbean (ECLAC) found that 'two thirds (65.5%) of [Colombia's] provinces are rural (Ramírez & de Aguas, 2017). They comprise 80% of the national territory and are home to a quarter of the national population', defining 'rural' on the basis of demographic criteria, spatial distributions and relations of proximity and connections between territories and cities.

These Colombian territories have faced structural challenges for decades, such as violence caused by guerrilla, paramilitary, governmental and criminal armed groups, which has led to forced displacement of population, assassinations of social leaders, forced recruitment of children, adolescents and young people by armed groups and sexual abuse, to name a few. This has been compounded by the lack or limited presence of non-military government institutions in various regions of the country, where armed groups control the economic and social aspects of the territories.[1] As a result, the provision of public services (roads, highways, river transport, electrification, drinking water, drainage and hospitals) in certain rural regions is very limited.

The Final Agreement for the Termination of the Conflict and the Construction of a Stable and Lasting Peace (Special Jurisdiction for Peace, 2016) signed between the Colombian government and the Revolutionary Armed Forces of Colombia (FARC), recognised the inequitable distribution of land and its grabbing by agricultural and mining companies/large estates as one of the fundamental aspects of the countryside. For this reason, the Agreement established the commitment to promote access to land for peasants who had been dispossessed of it through five operations: adjudication, formalisation, subsidies for access, promotion of Peasant Reserve Zones and land restitution.

Reports on compliance with the Agreement (Observatorio de Tierras, 2022; República de Colombia, 2022) attest to the limited progress on this issue, which is fundamental in the search for a definitive peace with social equity in Colombia.

The first of the points of the Peace Agreement is the Integral Rural Reform, which has as one of its components the construction of a Special Plan for National Rural Education (PEER). By the end of 2022, barely 30% of the total number of strategies proposed in the PEER had been achieved (National Planning Department, 2022).

The challenges facing rural education in Colombia are issues that have been diagnosed for decades. In a report prepared in the late 1990s in Caldas, it was identified that the existing universities in that department had little commitment to rural areas, and that there was a lack of coordination between different bodies involved in education, such as municipal and departmental governments, universities and companies (Contreras, 2006).

According to national legislation, the Ministry of National Education (MEN) will provide guidelines for the Education Secretariats of the 32 departments of the country to define flexible education models, which 'are formal education proposals that allow attending diverse populations or in conditions of vulnerability, which present difficulties to participate in the traditional educational offer' (MEN, 2016) and seek to be options to expand school coverage, preferably in rural areas; offer relevant, contextualised and quality models; strengthen school–community relations and support peaceful conflict resolution, among other objectives (Contreras, 2006, p. 54).

The flexible models, according to the MEN, are as follows:

- *Active Secondary:* aimed at students in rural and marginalised urban areas; it promotes know-how and learning to learn.
- *Accelerated Learning:* a school-based model of formal education in a regular school classroom, aimed at enabling extracurricular students to complete their basic primary education studies in one school year.
- *Post-Primary:* aimed at school-age young people in the rural sector; it addresses the compulsory areas of the curriculum, as well as pedagogical projects and productive pedagogical projects.
- *Escuela Nueva (EN):* a multigrade rural primary school model, composed of curricular strategies, teacher training, administrative management and community participation.

Ríos et al. (2020) note the existence of other flexible models (these are no longer mentioned on the MEN website) and include the following: Telesecundaria (strategy to increase school coverage from grades 6 to 8), Servicio Educativo Rural – SER (targeting out-of-school young people and adults in rural areas), Programa de Educación Continuada de la Caja de Compensación Familiar – Cafam (adult education) and Sistema de Aprendizaje Tutorial – SAT (out-of-school formal education programme).

The EN programme's predecessor was the Escuela Unitaria, a model developed by the University of Pamplona (department of Norte de Santander, Colombia) during the 1960s. This methodology was intended to be relevant to the characteristics of rural areas with low population density, respecting the learning rhythms of the students. Self-instructional materials (worksheets) were constructed for students and teachers based on guides and guides, rather than lecturers on topics.[2]

The model had problems in transferring to teachers 'a product and not the process'; it did not respect students' learning rhythms; it encouraged the filling out of worksheets (elaborated under urban standards) and not the development of problem-solving and critical thinking skills, as well as weak teacher training (Contreras, 2006, p. 85).

The evaluation of this model facilitated the creation of the EN methodology during the first five years of the 1970s by the MEN. According to the Fundación Volvamos a la Gente (2023), the components of the EN are four:

(1) Curricular seeks to be a relevant model for diverse social and educational contexts, promoting active pedagogies, with the support of learning guides for students and teaching manuals.
(2) Management seeks to ensure that the organisation of school processes complements or is aligned with the EN educational model and does not become an obstacle.
(3) In teacher training, the teacher is a facilitator of processes, so their preparation in the components of EN, in didactic and evaluative strategies, as well as knowledge of specific materials, is central.
(4) Community-based, seeks to involve members of the localities in educational processes, beyond operational issues related to the functioning of the school.

Another component in the functioning of the EN are the microcentres. These are spaces for two or more teachers from nearby schools to meet and exchange ideas, share problems and solutions on school management and pedagogical issues. Microcentres are intended to be spaces that facilitate horizontal dialogue between peers, as opposed to traditional models of school supervision, which are not adapted to the characteristics of rural areas (population dispersion, difficult access, limited means of transport, large number of schools to supervise, among others), so that a constant feature of rural schools is that they are poorly accompanied by external agents. Microcentres aim to fill this gap.

Another EN strategy is the Demonstration Schools, schools identified by the teachers themselves, in which a certain component of the EN is developed in a significant way. In these schools, teacher meetings are scheduled in which the development of the relevant strategies is visualised, followed by feedback and group reflections on what has been observed.

Another particularity of the EN model is to respect the learning pace of the student body, allowing for flexible promotion. In its foundations (as we know that this has not been fully implemented due to the lack of flexibility of the administrations and educational bureaucracies), it is established that students do not fail the school year. Instead, students are taught through modules and, if for some reason they cannot attend school for long periods of time or do not show understanding of the module, they must continue their studies where they left off and not repeat all the school contents of the grade.

Other features of the EN include working in a multigrade mode, the use of self-managed materials and the creation of a student government.

Some criticisms that have been made of the EN model include the difficulty in training teachers to work through a multigrade and active pedagogy, something that has not been achieved, largely because of the high turnover rate of teachers in rural schools. In addition, the uncritical use of self-learning guides by teachers, who sometimes ask students to copy instructions rather than to critically solve the challenges and problems posed by the materials, has been noted. A mother's testimony collected by Parra (1996, p. 187) mentions this issue clearly: 'My daughter, for example, is in 3rd grade and she comes [home] with a full notebook, I don't know if it is from what she copies on the board, all written letter by letter, but I send her to read and she is not able to do it'.

Insufficient resources (infrastructure, furniture, libraries, books, guides, school materials) have also been mentioned in the literature as a limitation in the model, in addition to the absence of specific strategies that allow for relevant and contextualised teaching of literacy in first- and second-grade students (Gómez, 1995; Parra, 1996). Urrea and Figueredo (2018, p. 1), after conducting an analysis of the self-learning guides used by students in EN, conclude that:

> (...) the New Schools were conceived considering the rural as a harmonious scenario, free of contradictions and conflicts, traditional, the peasant's own space, to silence a rurality perceived as an element of potential subversion, thus constructing a pragmatic methodology and a curriculum that, adapting to the countryside in terms of didactics, content and aims, would form a subject willing to work in the rural, without questioning the existing social problems.

During the almost 50 years that have passed since the EN model was created, it has followed various paths. Its implementation has not been linear, but several institutional experiences have been developed, among which we can highlight three:

(1) The model we have mentioned as a flexible modality and which has been promoted by the MEN, through the design of self-learning guides for the areas of mathematics, language, social sciences and natural sciences, aimed at the primary level (grades 1–5).
(2) The EN Activa model promoted by the Fundación Volvamos a la Gente, created in 1987. The Foundation has developed courses, projects, conferences and materials, such as self-learning guides aimed at primary and secondary school students – grades 1–9 – as well as a virtual campus.[3]
(3) The model promoted by the Federation of Coffee Growers of Caldas together with the Secretary of Education of that department, which will be discussed in more detail in this chapter.

The EN model began to be developed in Caldas around 1982, with majority financing (80%) by the Departmental Committee of Coffee Growers, together with the Caldas Secretariat of Education (Contreras, 2006, p. 168). Since then, this alliance between Coffee Growers and Government/Secretariat of Education of Caldas has been extended to university institutions, business, civil and productive organisations,

(...) Escuela Nueva has been extended to university education in most rural schools in Caldas and has added other complementary education programmes that respond to the needs of local communities with the objective that all rural inhabitants, especially children and young people, obtain a sufficient and adequate education that provides them with the skills to generate their own well-being and contribute to the social and economic development of the rural region and partly counteract situations that can generate conditions of vulnerability and inequality present in the rural sector. Comité de Cafeteros de Caldas (2023)

According to data from the Caldas Coffee Growers Committee (2023), EN serves 16,325 pre-school and primary students in Caldas, 12,988 post-primary students (grades 6–9), 3,281 middle school students and 7,747 students in the University in the Countryside (UC).

The existence of specific university models is relevant for rural territories, where educational coverage in Colombia only covers primary education.[4] It decreases at secondary level (13.8% of children and adolescents between 12 and 15 years old in rural areas did not attend secondary school (MEN, 2018a)), and gaps are accentuated at middle school (where only 60% of rural youth had access to schools (MEN, 2018a)) and higher education levels. To enter the latter two levels, rural adolescents and young people generally have to migrate or commute to school (as there are no schools in most rural populations), which means that their families have to pay for transport, food and accommodation costs.

There are no clear data estimating higher education coverage in Colombia. But the little information that does exist indicates that, by 2016, only 15% of rural secondary school graduates were enroled in higher education institutions, and that, of 740,000 young people living in dispersed rural areas, only 84,000 (equivalent to 11.5%) claimed to be attending a higher education institution – based on data from the 2014 National Agricultural Census (MEN, 2018b, pp. 12–13).

In addition to the difficulties rural young people face in accessing school, there are also challenges in remaining in the institutions for various reasons: economic, discriminatory, gender, social violence and lack of relevance of school content. Furthermore, those who access educational institutions do so through educational models designed for urban populations, which do not recognise the characteristics, particularities and diversity of rural youth.

This is why it is relevant to look at specific educational models for rural areas that aim to offer contextualised, relevant and specific quality education. Therefore, the objective of this chapter is to offer an overview of the scope and limitations of the EN Rural Education Model in Caldas, through the description of the general characteristics of the EN, the identification of the particularities of its implementation and the analysis of testimonies of graduates of the UC.

There are three parts to the text, in addition to this introductory section. This is followed by a description of the general characteristics of the UC. This is

DIEGO JUÁREZ BOLAÑOS

followed by the testimonies of five young graduates of the University and ends with a reflective section.

THE RURAL EDUCATION WITH NEW SCHOOL MODEL IN CALDAS

Located in the Andean region, Caldas is one of the 32 departments that make up the Republic of Colombia as shown in Fig. 1. Only four departments are smaller than this one, with a territorial extension of 7,900 km^2, where, by 2018, almost one million inhabitants lived. Of these, 434 thousand lived in the departmental capital, Manizales (DANE, 2019).

Together with the neighbouring departments of Quindío and Risaralda, it forms part of a region known as the Eje Cafetero. The departmental economy is supported by the agricultural sector (led by livestock and coffee, which accounts for almost 70% of Caldas' exports), as well as the metal-mechanical industry, textile production, mining and tourism (Gobierno de Caldas, 2017).

In this context, and as we have pointed out, the so-called Rural Education with New School Model has been developed, where the UC offers, since 2009, free on-site education in the rural localities themselves, through a 100 Rural Educational Institutions. The UC offers vocational technical studies for secondary school students, and if they complete an extra year, they obtain a degree as a technologist.

To obtain one of these degrees, the students take courses with teachers from the partner universities, who travel to the Rural Educational Institutions on certain days of the week, and the universities award the corresponding degrees.

To sustain and develop the model, the Cafeteros Committee has generated alliances with governmental organisations (Government of Caldas, mayors' offices), public companies (Central Hidroeléctrica de Caldas, Banco Agrario de Colombia) and private companies (Nestlé Nespresso), educational institutions (Servicio Nacional de Aprendizaje, Universidades Católica de Manizales, de Manizales, de Caldas) and foundations (Fundación Colombia).

One axis of the model are the productive pedagogical projects. As with other components of the programme, this is linked to other educational levels: during grades 1–9 (primary and post-primary), students develop supervised and directed projects, at the end of which they must deliver a business idea. At the intermediate level (grades 10 and 11), they implement a business model articulated to technical education, and the product is a business model. In UC, they continue with a business plan linked to technological education and at the end of this level, students must submit a business plan. In this way, from primary to higher education, students build productive projects.

It is intended that some of the businesses planned by the students will be implemented, for which there is a competition fund to obtain financing. The enterprises built by the students can be of different topics: technological, scientific, cultural, social, productive and sporting.

Fig. 1. Location of the Department of Caldas Highlighted. *Source:* WikiCommons Media, used via Creative Commons Licence.

The training approach in the model is based on competencies (basic, citizenship, labour and professional), and the means to assess them are specific subjects that are developed between the primary and higher levels, which are School and Coffee and School and Food Security.

The Rural Education with New School Model aims to support the construction of plans for the future of rural youth. It does not seek a relay, but rather a generational link, so that their life projects consider personal, family and community aspects. The internal evaluations of the UC establish that 59% of the graduates are employed in the rural sector, and 89.6% continue to live in Caldas.

We will now look at the experiences of University graduates in the field in order to explore the characteristics and effects of the model in greater depth.

EXPERIENCES OF UNIVERSITY GRADUATES IN THE FIELD

The data for this section come from three interviews conducted in March 2019 with five young people (two women and three men) who graduated from the UC. Two talks were conducted individually in the young people's homes and one was collective, involving three people gathered in a home. To access these spaces, it was necessary to travel through unpaved roads in the mountains located in the municipalities of Anserma and Riosucio and to walk, as the two of the three villages visited had no roads to reach them. In order to protect the anonymity of the interviewees, their names are not mentioned (they are replaced by other names), nor are the names of the localities where they lived.

The interviews were transcribed with the support of assistant Natalia Leyte, to whom we are grateful for this task. The ideas were then organised in order to include some of their parts in this document.

The identification of the young people interviewed was made by colleagues working in the Social-Educational Axis of the Caldas Coffee Growers' Committee, who have designed, implemented and evaluated the Rural Education with New School Model.

It should be noted that, during the research, several challenging situations were faced and solved: obtaining funding to travel from Mexico to Manizales, establishing contact and obtaining the support of the Caldas Coffee Growers' Committee, as well as travelling to the veredas (small isolated and dispersed localities) in mountainous Andean regions of Caldas to interview the young people.

The following is a summary of the main aspects of the testimonies of the graduates of the UC, which are intended to complement the information mentioned so far about the Rural Education Model with EN, through testimonies that describe the operation, scope and challenges of this educational programme.

Josephine. Grandmother's Legacy

Aged 22, Josefina lives in a small hamlet, nestled on the slopes of the mountains, where the only access is an hour's walk from the nearest unpaved road (Figs. 2 and 3).

Figs. 2 and 3. Road to the Pavement Where Josefina Lives and, in the Distance, Her Home. *Source:* Photographs taken by the author.

She was educated at EN from pre-school to the Universidad en el Campo where he obtained a degree as a Professional Technician in Agro-industrial Processes. When she attended secondary school, she did so from Monday to Friday and, on Saturdays from 7 a.m. to 4 p.m., she developed the educational processes of the Universidad en el Campo with the support of teachers from Manizales: 'They gave us a homologation of credits, that is, subjects that we had already seen at school we no longer had to see at the university because we already had the necessary content to continue with the other subjects'.

Subsequently, after an extra year of studies, she obtained the degree of Technologist in Quality Assurance of Agro-industrial Companies:

> The school where I studied is agro-industrial. It had a plant to do the whole process of food transformation, to give added value to the products we had in the same area. Apart from that, the vast majority of young people, all of us lived on coffee farms. Not only did we grow coffee, but we also had bananas, there were many young people who had chickens. .... We all had a different project, but we were all focused on the same thing: to generate sustainable development within the same community and to have an impact. To show our parents, then, that with education processes and new technologies, change can be generated.

The productive project that Josefina developed at the UC is related to coffee:

> Let's say that at that time we knew how to grow coffee (...). The problem was that good processes and good agricultural practices were not being applied (...) We were left with a very basic, very empirical knowledge and we were not in the process of change, of new methodologies, new processes.

To implement this project, her grandmother lent her a piece of land cultivated with coffee trees. Josefina set up a germinator and had to convince her grandmother not to sell the farm:

> There came a time when the grandmother was afraid that she was going to sell the farm. So, we didn't want the grandmother to sell. It was like showing her that we could implement other practices, that we could bring about a change within the family itself. It was not easy, because the grandparents say: "You are so young and how can you come to teach me how to make children".

She obtained an economic loan, as seed capital, of $8 million Colombian pesos (the equivalent at the time of $3,200 USD), within the UC's competitive fund, which was forgiven after five years, once its efficient use was demonstrated. With this resource, Josefina rented a larger plot of land to her grandmother, 3,300 m². She also had the soil analysed for its characteristics and bought and planted 2,500 coffee trees. Later, he bought a coffee pulping machine. At the same time, he produced natural fertiliser (vermicompost), something he learned at UC.

In relation to the first harvest she obtained, Josefina mentioned:

> I remember that the first crop I picked was a handful of coffee. And I said to my mum: "Ma, a handful...! She said to me: "Mija, you have to pick it because if you don't, you'll get the berry borer [a pest], so don't be sad".

The third harvest was 180 kilos and from then on, Josefina set herself the goal of processing the product. Together with other EN students, she created an association with which they gained access to machinery to process the coffee. She participated in a workshop competition for productive projects and won. With the prize, she invested in the creation of a coffee brand (registration of the name, permits, packaging, labelling):

> Before we knew how to pick [harvest] coffee, we knew how coffee was produced, but we didn't know what kind of coffee we were producing. Now we don't. My brand has three quality seals, we produce speciality coffee, it's called 'Legendario Café Especial: El legado de la abuela' (Legendary Speciality Coffee: Grandmother's Legacy).

It should be noted that Josefina was raised and educated in a female household, with her grandmother, mother and sisters, and therefore, taking into consideration the challenges and few structural opportunities for women in Latin American societies, especially in rural areas, it is to be recognised that, with the support of the EN, she has achieved the above-mentioned goals.

The Twins' Muleteering

David and Oscar are twin brothers, aged 24:

> We graduated in 2011 and when we left the institution at that time there was no University in the Countryside programme: two years later they gave us the opportunity for some graduates to start a career. I [David] started, I began a degree in Project Formulation. Then I studied Agricultural Technology and I am currently studying Agricultural Business Administration.

They competed and won a prize of $8 million Colombian pesos, which they used to create a mule-teaming business. How did the idea come about? Since I was a little boy [Oscar], I have always liked horses because of tradition, because of my father. He was like the one who gave me those lights so that I was inclined towards that side.

They started from a social and geographical need to move goods in a mountainous area, where mule-driving activity was being lost. That is, moving goods between villages using mules: 'We formed the company, which started to become a family business (...) in search of personal and family stability'.

This is an example of how projects can recover activities that have been displaced by economic processes, but which have a deep sociocultural meaning and contextual and territorial relevance: 'At the moment we have 16 animals, including the stallion and the brood mares'.

Joseph's Apiaries

Aged 23, José lives in a small village, which can only be reached on foot (Figs. 4 and 5). He studied at the UC as a professional technician in agro-industrial processes. Like the other interviewees, he obtained funding of $8 million Colombian pesos, with which he has developed his project related to the production of bees and honey:

> We started a family business in which we worked with my father, who was the one who provided us with the knowledge about beekeeping. Because I didn't know that much about it. So, we started with those 12 hives. We started producing honey and doing research to see how they could be technified and not work them in such a traditional way. With the financial support, we increased the number of hives to 30.

The brand name of their honey is taken from the Emberá language (indigenous group of the region) and means native flower or ancestral flower:

> We now have 45 hives and our touch or added value that we are giving to the project to differentiate ourselves from other beekeepers and other beekeeping companies is that we are

Figs. 4 and 5. Access Road and House Where José Lives. *Source:* Photographs taken by the author.

DIEGO JUÁREZ BOLAÑOS

working on the line of native bees or meliponiculture [stingless bees]. So, we are rescuing all the native bee breeds, because it is well known that they were not introduced by Europeans to the continent, but are native to the Americas.

He has managed to have a shop where they sell their products in the town centre: 'We are in partnership, with my brother and a cousin'.

The three of us are rotating between the three of us to attend to the shop (...). It would even be good to be able to export because honey is of very good quality, so it would be a good idea and I think we are getting a good production. At the moment we are talking about half a tonne so far this year.

At the time of the interview, it was producing honey and wax, as well as chicha and guarapo de miel (fermented beverages) and selling queen bees or nucs: 'What we do is to take smaller hives from our apiaries and people who want to start beekeeping. Then we go and sell them the small colonies'.

José shows us that a productive project that began in the UC has elements of great value: a profound environmental perspective (by recovering and promoting a native bee), involving family members, attending not only to the production of honey but also diversifying the products and their commercialisation.

Julia's Political Project

Julia, 18 years old, decided to develop a political and non-productive project in her educational process at the UC:

There are supervised projects and directed projects. The supervised ones are the ones that each student must have at home and the directed ones are the ones that are in the institution. Throughout my life I have lived in this community which, in fact, is located in an indigenous reservation[5] (...) From pre-school to eleventh grade, which I graduated last year, I had the opportunity to share and enjoy, to participate, I say it like this, in the same educational model (...), it is a very comprehensive education because it puts knowledge and the personal part, the values, on a balance.

Describe why you chose the type of project you are developing:

We need two factors in life: something that nourishes our pockets, that gives us economic stability (...) and another very important factor, which is like what fills our souls or what gives us the feeling of being useful in society, which is the moral part, the spiritual part. In my case, I am talking about the fact that we need to participate in society, because we don't just need to survive, we need to live and help in beautiful things and in things that benefit me and other people. In the educational institution, you were the president of the student government: Later, this was reflected at the community level. So, I started to be a leader in the community and now I was able to sign a contract with the Mayor's Office to be the Youth Coordinator for the municipality.

We continue to give the voice to Julia, who expresses herself very clearly:

I hope to contribute from the vitality of youth to different processes. I participated in the construction of the public youth policy of my municipality. And as the Youth Coordination is in the hands of a young rural woman, I hope to be able to contribute as much as possible to improve the quality here. I am totally convinced that it is not enough to have knowledge, but that you have to strengthen the personal part, the spiritual part, and that is what brings many more people to join in with what you want to do.

This testimony is an example of the diversity of projects that can be built and developed by young people, when opportunities are provided and educational options that encourage them are generated. Visual displays of the working environments are provided in Fig. 6a–c below.

Fig. 6. Apiaries, Production and Interview With José. *Source:* Photographs taken by the author.

DIEGO JUÁREZ BOLAÑOS   211

FINAL REMARKS

Since its inception, the Rural Education with New School Model has been supported financially and operationally by national (Federation of Coffee Growers, energy companies, educational institutions) and international organisations.[6] This characteristic has been maintained in the UC, which has helped it to remain over the years.

As has been pointed out throughout this chapter, the EN has not been a single or homogeneous model, and during its history, it has travelled along various paths in the hands of different bodies. Rodrigo Parra (1996, p. 155) pointed this out more than five decades ago:

> (...) one cannot speak of the New School as something homogeneous: the New School is not the same everywhere (...) Some New Schools operate under critical circumstances (...). In these areas their effectiveness has been significantly diminished. New Schools operating in highly developed rural areas such as the coffee-growing zone show a higher level of efficiency and quality in their performance.

In a Colombian context of highly centralised decision-making in education, the case examined is an example of alternative actions developed at the departmental level, which allows to broaden the focus beyond what happens and is decided in Bogotá and in the departments with the largest number of inhabitants (such as Antioquia and Valle del Cauca).

Another aspect to highlight has been the implementation of a model derived from the EN, but which has been enriched from regional, national and international experiences, and to attend to educational levels (secondary and higher), where other EN derivations have not been present.[7]

Some examples that show the enrichment of the original EN model that have been developed in Caldas are:

- The project subject, by extending the theme of School and Coffee, towards Food Security.
- Explicitly, the model has proposed as one of its objectives to support the permanence of young people in rural territories, that is, the possibility of building life projects that do not imply their migration to national and international urban centres. This has enormous merit in a global context where processes of depopulation or rural population ageing are taking place, as shown by the organisation *España Vaciada*.[8]

Some of the challenges facing the UC are to expand the model so that students can obtain a university degree without having to leave their territories; to try to expand the dissemination and implementation of the model in urban and not only rural areas; to strengthen the processes of external accompaniment of schools (beyond the Microcentres); not to saturate schools with the arrival of multiple projects, but rather to consolidate existing ones; to train its own graduates so that they can become future EN teachers, for which it would be useful to design a Bachelor's Degree in Rural, Multigrade and/or Peasant Education, which would bring together the knowledge and experiences developed over 40 years (Ossa, A., A., 'The New School', personal communication, 2022).

Other areas of opportunity for the Rural Education with New School Model are: achieving educational laicism (Catholic religion classes are taught in public schools), expanding the range of technical careers offered to rural youth and that the model can 'bring' other types of job opportunities, and not only productive projects.

In relation to the testimonies of the graduates of the University in the Field programme, we can examine them through the concept of agency, which, together with structure, is a central notion in social theory. While structure refers to the regular, relatively fixed, objective and generalised features of social life, agency refers to action (Merton, 2002). Social theorists (Weber, Marx, Parsons – see Ritzer, 2005) argue that social structure is reproduced by the actions of individuals through the mediation of rules, roles and other resources, which we call 'culture'. However, the concept of agency recognises that although individuals are constrained by the realities of their world, they are capable of choosing alternative courses of action. In this sense, schooling is a tool that can generate agency capabilities in individuals, as we have tried to show in the chapter.

It is important to emphasise that the testimonies of the graduates should not be understood only in terms of their studies at the UC. The Rural Education with New School Model is precisely that: a model that aims to be congruent in its pedagogical, community and school management principles throughout the entire educational journey of children, adolescents and young people, that is, from their primary studies to higher education. It is difficult to identify any similar educational case, not only in other rural regions of Latin America but also in urban areas. It is quite atypical for students' educational trajectories to follow a single pedagogical model at all levels. Building this has taken decades of effort on the part of agents from various bodies, as well as the inhabitants of the Caldas territories.

The EN-Universidad en el Campo experience shows that many pedagogical innovations are occurring in rural territories, without the attention of the mass media, social networks and academia itself. This neglect has probably allowed a greater margin of autonomy and leeway to design and implement these alternative experiences. This chapter aims to contribute to the recognition and reflection on these experiences that, with their challenges and achievements, have been developed in Latin American rural spaces.[9]

NOTES

1. Currently, the challenges in terms of territorial control by armed and criminal groups are most evident in the border regions with Venezuela, Ecuador, Panama and in the country's coastal areas.

2. The development of this model took place in the international context in which the Conference of Ministers of Education held in Switzerland, at the request of the United Nations Educational, Scientific and Cultural Organisation (UNESCO), suggested attending to rural primary education in areas of low population density (Contreras, 2006, p. 94).

DIEGO JUÁREZ BOLAÑOS

3. The existing guides are those for the subjects of Language, Mathematics, Natural Sciences and Environmental Education, Social Sciences and Citizenship Skills, Technology, Ethics and Peace Education, Entrepreneurship and Economic and Financial Education.

4. Overall, the rural population has 6 years of schooling on average, compared to 9.6 years of education on average in urban areas (MEN, 2018a).

5. 'The indigenous reserves are the collective property of the indigenous communities in favour of which they are constituted and, in accordance with the Political Constitution of Colombia, they are inalienable, imprescriptible and unseizable (....).) The resguardos are a legal and sociopolitical institution of a special character, made up of one or more indigenous communities, which, with a collective property title that enjoys the guarantees of private property, possess their territory and are governed for the management of this and their internal life by an autonomous organisation protected by the indigenous jurisdiction and their own normative system' (Ministry of Agriculture and Rural Development, 2015, p. 319).

6. Such as the United States Agency for International Development (USAID), the Inter-American Development Bank, UNICEF and the World Bank.

7. A technical education team from the Federation of Coffee Growers of Caldas collaborated in the adaptation, training and development of the New School in Vietnam (Le, 2018).

8. See: https://españavaciada.org.

9. We would like to thank Elisa Ramírez and Alexander Ossa (educational area of the Comité Departamental de Cafeteros) for the facilities and support provided to develop this study. Without them, it would have been impossible to learn about the Universidad en el Campo programme.

REFERENCES

Caldas Coffee Growers Committee. (2023). Social axis. https://caldas.federaciondecafeteros.org/sostenibilidad/eje-social/

Contreras, C. (2006). *Educación Rural en Caldas. El Proyecto de Escuela Nueva*. Universidad Nacional de Colombia.

DANE. Administrative Department of Statistics. (2019). Results of the national population and housing Census 2018. Caldas. https://www.dane.gov.co/index.php?option=com_search&searchword=caldas

DANE. Administrative Department of Statistics. (2018). Where are we?. https://www.dane.gov.co/index.php/estadisticas-por-tema/demografia-y-poblacion/censo-nacional-de-poblacion-y-vivenda-2018/donde-estamos

Gómez, V. (1995). A critical view of the Escuela Nueva in Colombia. *Revista Educación y Pedagogía, 14 and 15*, 280–304.

Government of Caldas. (2017). Economy of Caldas. https://caldas.gov.co/

Land Observatory. (2022). *Report Las deudas de la paz. Agrarian dimensions*. https://www.observatoriodetierras.org/wp-content/uploads/2022/08/Las-deudas-de-la-paz-dimensiones-agrarias-1.pdf

Le, H. (2018). Another textbook project? The implementation of *Escuela Nueva* in Vietnam. *Educational Research for Policy and Practice, 17*, 223–239. https://doi.org/10.1007/s10671-018-9230-x

MEN, Ministry of National Education. (2016). Modelos Educativos Flexibles. https://www.mineducacion.gov.co/portal/Preescolar-basica-y-media/Modelos-Educativos-Flexibles/340087: Introduccion

MEN, Ministry of National Education. (2018a). *Special rural education plan. Towards rural development and peace building*. Government of Colombia.

MEN, Ministry of National Education. (2018b). *Rural higher education plan. Capacity building strategies for territorial development*. Government of Colombia.

Merton, R. (2002). *Teoría y estructura sociales.* Fondo de Cultura Económica.

Ministry of Agriculture and Rural Development. (2015). *Decree 1071-2015. Sole regulatory decree of the agriculture, livestock, fisheries and rural development administrative sector.*

National Planning Department. (2022). Sistema integrado de información para el posconflicto. Rural education. https://siipo.dnp.gov.co/

Parra, R. (1996). *La Escuela Rural. Escuela y modernidad en Colombia. Tomo II.* Fundación FES.

Ríos, E., Franco, J. C., & Pérez, F. (2020). La educación en territorios rurales de Colombia: entre desigualdades y potencialidades. In D. Juárez, A. Olmos, & E. Ríos (Coords.). *Education in rural territories in Ibero-America.* Universidad Católica de Oriente.

Ramírez, J. C., & de Aguas, J. (2017). *Territorial configuration of the provinces of Colombia: Rurality and networks.* Office of the Economic Commission for Latin America and the Caribbean in Bogotá. https://repositorio.cepal.org/bitstream/handle/11362/40852/4/S1700637_es.pdf

Republic of Colombia. (2022). Complete report on the agricultural sector. Diagnosis and Recommendations for the agricultural sector. *Presidential Transition.* https://vertov14.files.wordpress.com/2022/07/wp-1659125176120.pdf

Ritzer, G. (2005). *Classic sociological theory.* MCGraw Hill.

Special Jurisdiction for Peace. (2016). Final agreement for the termination of the conflict and the construction of a stable and lasting peace. https://www.jep.gov.co/Normativa/Paginas/Acuerdo-Final.aspx

UNDP. United Nations Development Programme. (2011). *National human development report 2011: Rural Colombia, reasons for hope.* UNDP.

Urrea, S., & Figueredo, E. (2018). Escuela Nueva colombiana: Analysis of its learning guides. *Acta Scientiarum. Education, 40*(3). https://doi.org/10.4025/actascieduc.v40i3.39727

Volvamos a la Gente Foundation. (2023). Components. https://escuelanueva.org/componentes/

SCHOOLS AS LEARNING COMMUNITIES: CRITICAL INTERCULTURALITY AND INCLUSION IN ACTION

Luz María Moreno-Medrano

Universidad Iberoamericana, Mexico

ABSTRACT

Working in schools as learning communities (ECA) is an effective way to make visible the articulating axes of critical interculturality and inclusion proposed in the latest Mexican Education Reform of 2022. This chapter presents an experience in a teacher training college in the south of Mexico that has begun to work as ECAs and which, despite its incipient efforts, shows how it is possible to problematise the relations of inclusion/exclusion through the collaborative learning of the students and the active listening of the teacher.

Keywords: Critical interculturality; inclusion; decoloniality; schools as learning communities; inclusion/exclusion

INTRODUCTION

The aim of this chapter is to present some elements of a case study of teaching collectives that are beginning to work with the philosophy of schools as learning communities (SLC). The experience of a teacher training college in the south of Mexico is presented in order to analyse the possibilities that these approaches have for putting into practice the articulating axes of critical interculturality and inclusion in Mexican classrooms. This chapter begins by briefly explaining the set of visions of lesson study and SLC; in a second moment, the concepts of critical interculturality and inclusion within the Mexican Education Reform are presented, followed by the experience in a teacher training college and the final reflections on the possibilities of SLC as trigger for implementing critical intercultural and inclusive education in the classroom.

Intercultural and Inclusive Education in Latin America
International Perspectives on Inclusive Education, Volume 24, 215–226
Copyright © 2024 Luz María Moreno-Medrano
Published under exclusive licence by Emerald Publishing Limited
ISSN: 1479-3636/doi:10.1108/S1479-363620240000024014

Lesson Studies as a Trigger for Reflective Teacher Professionalisation

The learning gap is generally visible through the results of international standardised tests such as the Organisation for Economic Co-operation and Development's Programme for International Student Assessment (OECD, 2024), known as PISA. However, this level of analysis does not account for the dynamics of inclusion/exclusion that occur within the classroom and that can provide valuable information for teachers to develop more relevant strategies for their students, especially from an approach that identifies differences in class, ethnicity, gender and disability. Several teacher collectives have made important efforts to overcome these gaps, such as the International Teachers' Network of Schools as Learning Communities founded by Professor Manabu Sato of the University of Tokyo. This is part of the teacher professionalisation initiatives that have been carried out in several Southeast Asian countries for more than 20 years (Thailand, Cambodia, Vietnam, Indonesia Korea, Singapore, among others.), in schools with socio-economic conditions very similar to those in Mexico (Tsukui, 2020; Tsukui and Saito, 2022).

Learning communities are based on lesson study, a pedagogical approach created in Japan more than 40 years ago, which is a system of activities that emphasises collaborative learning to solve learning challenges with different levels of complexity, where a group of teachers observes the learning processes, and from an action-research approach, reflects collegially on the ways in which students learn. It is a way of thinking about educational reforms that are built from the grassroots, from the learning of each student, from each classroom and from each school, paying special attention to the dynamics of gender, social class, ethnicity, etc. in order to approach the goal of inclusive and intercultural education for all. This philosophy is understood as a shared vision, a philosophy that creates a way of working collectively, with autonomy, professionalism and collegiality.

This philosophy is based on an approach called lesson study that has been widely used in various parts of the world and emerged in Japan as early as 1870. Lesson study, for example, has been used in the United Kingdom (Dudley, 2012, 2014) where it has been shown to have successful results in student collaboration, enquiry and problem-solving, as well as promoting a classroom climate where close support, teacher collectivism, respect, help-seeking and joy in learning are also present. These dynamics imply a change in the school culture because they do not work in isolation, with the classroom closed, but rather work collectively on the innovative design of the lessons of study, often using the results of educational research to understand what works best in certain subjects, to then collectively observe the implementation in the classroom and achieve a collective reflection on the process.

This pedagogical approach, which Dr Sato considers to be more of a philosophy than a methodology, bases its principles on three pillars: public philosophy, the philosophy of democracy and the philosophy of excellence (Sato, 2018). These pillars underpin a practice of teacher professionalisation in which collegiality and collective reflection are a fundamental part. Opening classrooms at least three times a year is one of the most powerful strategies to promote that what we observe as teachers is not only focused on the practices and their forms of instruction but on the interactions and learning processes of the student body. This, in Dr Sato's words 'is like changing skin' (Sato, 2024, p. 4) because it turns upside down the educational paradigm on which the traditional school is based, where the figure of the teacher is still centred on their role as an instructor and the discussion of what happens among the students. To achieve this, the teaching collective co-designs the lessons of study in such a way that the learning challenges are at the centre. This is a revolutionary change as well. As education specialists, we have been trained to make structured lesson plans based on learning objectives, expected learning, etc. which follow a deductive model that goes from the general to the particular, such as the dosage of time and materials used in instruction processes. In this approach, learning revolves around collaborative learning challenges that are shared in teams of four students, which are organised by the teaching collective to be as diverse as possible: by gender, class, academic skills, ethnicity, etc. (Sato, 2018, 2024). The learning challenges include very simple (easily solved by the students) to very complex ones that may not be solved but work to incentivise students to continue to seek their solution at a later stage.

The format is extremely simple:

- A shared activity that fosters the joy of collaboration and enables a sense of achievement.
- A jumping activity, i.e. a learning challenge that allows the group of students to solve a problem in a specific time. The aim is for them to ask for help when necessary and to investigate on their own. This learning leap is designed at a level of difficulty of the knowledge proposed in the curriculum, i.e. in the contents presented in a textbook.
- A second jumping activity designed to challenge the students, as their answer will not necessarily be in a textbook and most of the students will probably not be able to answer it, but the intention is for them to question what they know and identify what they do not understand or know so that, in the next exercise, they can take it from there. In addition, the aim is that the students who manage to respond to the challenge can 'pull' the rest of the group.

While this interaction takes place in each of the teams of four students, the teachers gather around them, not only the teacher in charge of the class but a group of teachers who participate in this network of collective reflection. Thus, teachers observe, take pictures and videos of what happens in each team and take notes of the reactions and dialogues. What is to be observed is the students' ability to actively participate in the resolution of the challenges, the ability to ask questions and ask for help. This observation material is the raw material for the collective reflection that preferably takes place at the end of this open classroom exercise. In this session, the teaching collective discusses what happened in each classroom and reports on the dynamics of inclusion/exclusion that took place in each of the teams (Sato, 2018, 2024).

CRITICAL INTERCULTURALITY AND INCLUSION IN THE MEXICAN EDUCATIONAL REFORM

The concept of interculturality in Latin America is a product of the social struggles of indigenous peoples since the 1970s and has become a demand to guarantee the rights that have been denied since colonial times (Dietz, 2012). The concept of intercultural education was incorporated into public policies along with the possibility of offering bilingual education that was relevant and pertinent to indigenous groups, leading to the implementation of Intercultural Bilingual Education (EIB) in several Latin American countries. However, during the implementation of these educational policies, interculturality was limited to programmes aimed at indigenous peoples and left aside education for the majority social groups, without questioning the racist and classist structures that are strongly installed in Latin American societies, as a product of the history of colonisation that has led to the naturalisation of social and economic inequalities of many social groups, such as indigenous peoples and Afro-descendants, for example, and more specifically women. According to the Social Rights Information System report, elaborated by the National Council for the Evaluation of Social Development Policy (CONEVAL): 'The percentage of employed indigenous women with labour income equal to or greater than the Income Poverty Line was 33.8%, while for non-indigenous women it was 62.8% in 2022' (2023, p. 3).

In the New Curricular Framework and Curriculum 2022 (DOF, 2022), interculturality and inclusion are two axes of the educational proposal that sought to reform the educational model in a profound way. The articulating axes of the current Mexican educational proposal are: inclusion, critical thinking, critical interculturality, gender equality, healthy life, arts and aesthetic experiences, appropriation of cultures through reading and writing. These axes are designed to provide an ethical-political direction to the curriculum, so that the contents are linked to democratic values of social justice and community building (MEJOREDU, 2022). In the 2013 Mexican education reform, interculturality was blurred from the cultural and sociolinguistic needs of the country's native peoples and was understood from a limited inclusive perspective that sought integration rather than the recognition of historical debts and the need to repair the damage caused by assimilationist policies since the revolutionary eras (Mendoza-Zuany, 2017; Sriprakash, 2022).

In the current Mexican Education Reform (DOF, 2022), intercultural education appears not only as bilingual but also as a critical intercultural education with a strong decolonial focus because it seeks to concentrate efforts on groups that have been historically invisible (indigenous peoples, Afro-descendants, gender diversity, people with disabilities, etc.). It is an education that seeks to eradicate classism and racism from the roots of Latin American societies (Dussel, 2011; López, 2022; Walsh, 2013, 2017). Many countries in Latin America follow patterns of oppression that are legitimised through a symbolic order:

> ...the justification of discriminatory practices is rarely made in the name of group interests and power relations, i.e. in the universe of stereotypes, beliefs and prejudices that attribute to discriminated groups an inferior position and thus legitimise the unequal work they receive. Thus, for example, racism reproduces asymmetrical power relations of one racial group over another, but it is not usually justified on the basis of these relations, but rather in a symbolic order that attributes to discriminated racial groups traits of inferiority that justify their domination and exclusion. Solis (2017, p. 35)

Inclusion, on the other hand, has a fundamental role as an articulating axis of the basic education curriculum 2022, far from being considered a synonym of education for students with disabilities; it opens up the debate on colonial and even pre-colonial relations (DOF, 2022) that cut across the different dimensions of social spheres in Mexico.

From different feminist paradigms (Cubillos, 2017; Lugones, 2010; Viveros, 2023), the need to break with the binarism of modern-colonial logics that position a universalist value system that has historically privileged the experiences of white, heterosexual, middle-class men over other ways of knowing and inhabiting the world has been pointed out. Inclusive education from more critical perspectives is seen as a political, not just a theoretical, positioning from special education (Cruz Vadillo, 2018). Therefore, the concept of inclusion when it is not intrinsically associated with the concept of exclusion does not allow us to question the mechanisms in which power operates through its different local and state political facets. Cruz Vadillo (2018) argues the need for diverse theoretical approaches to special education because in many ways, it has pathologised the subjects and made the logics of power invisible. This approach to inclusion, from deficit and stigmatisation or superficial integration, has also been seen in approaches to intercultural education from uncritical and ahistorical positions. Interculturality from an assimilationist point of view lacks a systemic perspective that emphasises the recognition of the subjects and does not question the oppressive and historical structures that they have had to resist.

From a more complex analysis of the relations of inclusion/exclusion, the Cartesian logics of the modern-colonial model lead us to think of binarism of health/illness, woman/man, goodness/evilness, effort/conformism and, in the case in question, lead us to think of sociocultural diversity from a deficit point of view, where both people from native peoples and people with disabilities are part of the same search to integrate or assimilate them into the dominant social system. Thus, Cruz Vadillo (2018) warns that it is necessary to position oneself from a political demand not to pathologise the subjects but to strengthen subjectivities from the agency and the denunciation of the power structures that exclude and oppress.

From a feminist theoretical approach, for example, Cubillos (2017) proposes to define public policies of inclusion/exclusion as 'a dynamic process of multidimensional rupture/strengthening of social relations (given by specific power systems), which links certain subjects and collectives with society (its representative practices and institutions)' (p. 357). The consideration of inclusion/exclusion as a dynamic process of rupture/strengthening allows us to look at the continuum of social and political structures in which the subjects and collectives are inserted in a process of constant analysis of privileges and oppressions, as proposed by the theories of intersectionality (Curiel, 2010).

Intersectionality is conceived on three levels (Curiel, 2010):

(1) Structural, from the local to the global, where the same geopolitical and economic structures reproduce oppressions in terms of ethnicity, class and gender, among others.
(2) Representational, the way in which the imaginaries of certain groups and individuals have been constructed and from which the racist, classist and sexist ideologies of our Latin American and Caribbean societies stem.
(3) Political, with respect to the design and implementation of public policies.

The concept of decoloniality has been central to understanding these processes of inclusion/exclusion. Since the New Mexican School (DOF, 2022), decoloniality is understood as the need to recover the logics of being, knowledge and power from the knowledge that has been made invisible by the modern-colonial logics of domination that have been present in our histories as Latin Americans. Thus, the decolonial perspective on inclusion raises the need to incorporate other ways of approaching knowledge, from social practices and political movements. The domains of colonial logic are identified in the economic, political, social and epistemic spheres:

> Colonial logic operates in at least four domains that we have learned in all educational experiences, formal and non-formal, and include: the economic domain as land appropriation and human exploitation; the political domain, comprising control of authorities; the social domain, represented by control of gender, class, sexuality, ethnicity; the epistemic domain, dedicated to the control of knowledge and subjectivities. DOF (2022, p. 94)

These domains have filtered through as part of teaching processes that have moved away from the recognition of students' own socio-historical contexts and the possibility of re-evaluating their own in the face of other knowledge that has managed to position itself as universal and plural scientific knowledge. Mignolo (2011) argues that these logics have also achieved a mental colonialism, in which groups that have been historically marginalised have been left without representation in the construction of knowledge, in the face of the power that Eurocentric approaches have taken.

> After independence in the Americas in the 19th century, when anthropology was created, and after colonisation in Asia and Africa after World War II, the colonial matrix mutated to create the conditions for internal colonialism: that is, the very structure of management and control was now in the hands of the natives rather than in the hands of French or British officials. Both nineteenth-century anthropologists and Third World anthropologists in the second half of the

twentieth century ran the risk of reproducing in their own regions what First World anthropologists were doing. (2011, p. 135)

Mignolo (2011) makes a strong critique of the anthropological approaches that have been carried out in developing countries. This also occurs in the educational sphere where we reproduce these forms of control with colonialist legacies. Colonisation has played the role of naturalising ethnic, gender and social class differences, so that in Mexico, for example, they are hidden under the concept of equality and mestizaje. Education in Mexico and other Latin American countries has been, together with the Christian religion, the most powerful instrument for installing a version of history of assimilation, integration and cultural mixing, leaving aside the recognition of the contributions of cultural groups such as indigenous and Afro-Mexican peoples (Batalla, 1987).

Both inclusion and interculturality are polysemous concepts that have been adapted in education policy intentions; however, there has been no evidence of policy implementation and its impact in terms of improving the quality of learning for historically disadvantaged groups. In Mexico, there is a significant gap between educational discourse and practice, and the most evident form of the gap can be seen in the dramatic statistics of inequality in the country between rich and poor (OXFAM, 2024).

The challenge for education in Mexico, and in most Latin American countries, continues to be closing the learning gaps between those who are better off and those with fewer resources in order to achieve truly equitable education for all. Education policies and programmes have not focused their efforts on the most vulnerable groups so that they can achieve learning outcomes comparable to those of other groups; on the contrary, the most vulnerable groups continue to be those who have the least and who receive the least support.

HOW TO OBSERVE INCLUSION/EXCLUSION DYNAMICS WITHIN CLASSROOMS?

The dynamics of inclusion/exclusion can be clearly seen in the processes in which students relate to and through the learning tasks, in the dialogues that take place in the classroom and in the way in which teaching collectives address sociocultural diversity based on a deep knowledge of each and every one of their students through reflective teaching practice.

In Mexico, in 2023, we started a pilot project in one of the southern states of the Mexican Republic, almost on the border with Guatemala. With the support of the education authorities, schools that wanted to undertake this challenge as a collective were invited to participate. The invitation was made in the framework of the implementation of the curriculum for pre-school, primary and secondary education 2022, which proposes the creation of synthetic, analytical programmes and a co-design process that aims to promote autonomy and collegiality in teaching collectives. This proposal, to create schools as communities for learning, undoubtedly responded directly to the challenges presented by the new

Fig. 1. Implementation Process on the First Cycle of Lesson Studies in Mexico. *Source:* Prepared by the author based on Sato (2018).

educational reform, and so it was presented to a school zone in each state. The teaching collectives in each zone agreed to participate in the pilot project for two sessions during the school year and to fulfil three key moments in the process (Fig. 1).

This dynamic, as previously explained, aims to create a collaborative learning environment not only among the students but also among the teaching staff, where the management, supervisory and technical-pedagogical advisory staff played a fundamental role in accompanying them. The observations made by the teaching staff in which they identified which students remained silent or were excluded from the team dynamics led them to reflect on the articulating axes of the new educational proposal of inclusion and interculturality. In this way, discourses that sometimes seemed theoretical and highly abstract about inclusion/exclusion could be seen directly in the reactions, bodily expressions and dialogues among the students, which allowed us to ask concrete questions such as: why did the girl with a darker skin colour remain silent during the activity? why is there a boy who always participates in the mathematics class and no one else from his team takes the floor? Why did one of the children in the fourth grade classroom seem sad during the activity? how did the girl with Down syndrome feel during the activity, and how did her team support her in the process? how many questions did the students have, what kind of help did they ask for, could they see joy in the learning process, what kind of looks were there in the team, who did and who did not seem motivated by the activities, who achieved the challenge and who did not, who did and who did not?

The work began with a first open lesson, where school ethnography and action research are an essential part of the methodology for collective reflection on student learning, not on the role of the teacher, from a traditional point of view.

THE PIONEERING CASE OF A TEACHER TRAINING COLLEGE IN SOUTHERN MEXICO

The first case study was implemented in a teacher training college in the south of the country, which is not located in the capital, but a few kilometres from the border with Guatemala. The following is a brief presentation of the experience of the community for learning case study in this teacher training college in the first phase of collective observations:

The interest in working in learning communities came from an energetic and proactive supervisor who was able to motivate her teaching groups to participate.

One of the teachers showed a strong interest in participating with his groups of students in initial teacher training.

Thus, this case, although still very incipient, managed to have a successful implementation process in a very short time, where the students of the teacher training college experienced in their own classrooms how to work in a learning community, in order to implement it in their classrooms.

In November 2023, the supervisor and the teacher organised an open class to observe how learning communities work. The whole school zone was invited to participate in the classroom observation which took place in the courtyard of the teacher training college. The educational authorities were invited and we even took advantage of the visit of Dr Sato and Dr Yoshiko Kitada, Japanese academics, to do a collective classroom observation, coordinated by the group teacher. Thus, we had the opportunity to see how the students of the teacher training college approached the lessons of study through learning challenges, starting from the problems and contexts closest to their students and making use of the analytical programmes of the official curriculum.

A mathematical thinking class was chosen where they would work on addition and subtraction and their relationship as inverse operations. The tasks as challenges set by the teacher were the following: Design a problem situation linked to their context involving addition or subtraction of natural numbers up to four digits using conventional algorithms, which first has a shared task and then two activities with two jumps of complexity or challenges.

The students discussed for several minutes the socio-cultural context of their community. As they worked in small teams, there was a large group of people watching around their tables, listening and getting closer to what they were discussing. The small teams talked about the possibility of raising issues around the prices of the Coppel shop in their community and the costs of clothing, the credit they offer and the debts this causes for families. They also talked about the nearest lake and the livestock in the area, the corner shops in the village and the kind of healthy and unhealthy items they sell. And so, little by little, they designed activities that had a direct link to the lives of their students and that also had profound political implications for the life of the community, which is embedded in very specific economic dynamics, such as limited access to credit and the limited supply of goods and services created by monopolies like Coppel.

The teacher sat patiently in each of the teams listening to his students' ideas; he did not interrupt, he just listened attentively. After that session, the students took their activities to the groups in the primary school attached to the Normal, where they were able to implement their collective design experience and now see its application in learning communities (author's field notes, November 2023).

The possibilities for collective reflection in this type of approach are important, for example, one of the students from the Normal shared:

This space, with this new model we are working with, helped my colleagues and me to feel freer and more participative, because with all due respect, there were colleagues I had never listened to before. And after some time working in this way, we have seen an evolution in the class. Classmates who didn't participate before, now do, like my classmate X, who is very creative and we didn't know it. This model has helped us all, both women and men, to learn to respect each other, to work in community and to know what they think. And this is how the articulating axes become present, such as inclusion, healthy living, etc. (student from the Normal School, 17 November 2023).

As it is possible to note in the testimony of this young man, the articulating axes can be seen in operationalisation through dialogue in small work teams and in collaborative work through learning challenges. The joy of working in community and the possibility of learning from the skills of each member of the team lead to a much deeper reflection on the archaic models of education that sought the docility of the body, obedience and silence as conditions for teaching–learning to take place. Through exercises such as this, learning processes become visible, amid tensions, shared questions and the search for help. Thus, in the dialogue and the silences of the small group, critical and decolonial intercultural relations can become visible, as it is possible to dismantle the power dynamics represented by gender, class, or ethnicity, for example.

FINAL REFLECTIONS

Positioning intercultural education in Latin America has been the product of a constant struggle to make visible the sociocultural diversity of historically forgotten communities that have been systematically excluded, especially since the colonial processes. On the other hand, inclusion as an ideal to make social justice possible has also gone through a series of epistemological debates in order to situate it from a much broader ethical-political position, within the framework of the most fundamental human rights. Unfortunately, these concepts have remained largely confined to educational discourse, and it has been difficult to see them put into practice in the classroom. Both interculturality and inclusion are shown more as points of arrival but have failed to be seen as an essential part of the learning process, where the diversity of student contexts must be recognised, from an intersectional perspective, where gender, social class, different abilities, ethnicity, sexuality, religion, etc. have a profoundly valuable place in designing more effective ways of learning.

A profound educational change that modifies the historical dynamics of inclusion/exclusion is not an easy task, but it must be at the heart of an education system. Despite the good intentions of educational policies and programmes, it has not been possible to combat inequalities in learning processes, especially in populations that have been historically marginalised, such as children and adolescents of different origins, genders, abilities, etc. Undoubtedly, these populations have concentrated most of the experiences of discrimination and, therefore, have also received a lower quality education. SLC make it possible to realise that teaching–learning processes cannot be centred on the individual efforts of each teacher, but rather on the construction of an educational community that accompanies each student in a personalised way, according to their own contexts and specific needs. In this way, inclusion and interculturality are made possible, by innovatively and collectively proposing lessons that are relevant and pertinent to each context and by ensuring that learning outcomes are equitable for all students.

Despite efforts to promote interculturality and inclusion in education, significant challenges remain. As this chapter has made evident, interculturality and inclusion have historically been approached from assimilationist to integrationist perspectives, and now a critical and decolonial approach is being proposed.

However, transcending discourse and good intentions remains a challenge. A deep and close approach to learning tasks is needed, observing and attending to the dynamics of inclusion/exclusion in the classroom so that mechanisms can be individually named, while at the same time understanding and combating racism, classism and sexism at a structural level, to challenge dominant narratives and promote equity and social justice. SLC are a concrete way to make these ideals possible, in a way that fosters an environment where every teacher and every student has possibilities to collaborate, reflect and learn together, challenging also the individualistic and meritocratic ideas that have accompanied traditional education systems.

REFERENCES

Batalla, B. (1987). *México profundo: Una civilización negada*. Grijalbo.

CONEVAL. (2023, Diciembre 11). *El Coneval actualiza los indicadores del sistema de información de derechos sociales*. https://www.coneval.org.mx/SalaPrensa/Comunicadosprensa/Documents/2023/Comunicado_12_Sistema-Informacion-Derechos-Sociales.pdf

Cruz Vadillo, R. (2018). ¿Debemos ir de la educación especial a la educación inclusiva? Perspectivas y posibilidades de avance. *Alteridad*, *13*(2), 251–261.

Cubillos, J. (2017). Reflexiones sobre el concepto de inclusión social. Una propuesta desde la teoría feminista para el estudio de las políticas públicas. *Política y Sociedad*, *54*, 353–375.

Curiel, O. (2010). *Hacia la construcción de un feminismo descolonizado. A propósito de la realización del Encuentro Feminista Autónomo: haciendo comunidad en la casa de las diferencias*. Universidad del Cauca.

Dietz, G. (2012). *Multiculturalismo, interculturalidad y diversidad. Una aproximación antropológica*. Fondo de Cultura Económica.

DOF. (2022). *ACUERDO número 14/08/22 por el que se establece el Plan de Estudio para la educación preescolar, primaria y secundaria*. https://www.dof.gob.mx/nota_detalle.php?codigo=5661845&fecha=19/08/2022#gsc.tab=0

Dudley, P. (2012). Lesson study in England: From school networks to national policy. *International Journal of Lesson and Learning Studies*, *1*(1), 85–100.

Dudley, P. (2014). *Lesson study: A handbook*. University of Cambridge.

Dussel, E. (2011). *Filosofía de la Liberación*. Fondo de Cultura Económica.

López, L. E. (2022). Hacia una educación digna desde nuevos horizontes de sentido. In A. L. Gallardo & C. Rosa (Eds), *Epistemologías e interculturalidad en educación*. ISSUE. UNAM.

Lugones, M. (2010). Hacia un feminismo descolonial. *Hypatia*, *25*.

MEJOREDU. (2022). *La mejora continua de la educación. Principios, marcos de referencia y ejes de actuación*. MEJOREDU.

Mendoza-Zuany, R. G. (2017). *Evaluación de la Política Educativa Dirigida a la Población Indígena en Educación Básica*. INEE.

Mignolo, W. D. (2011). *The darker side of western modernity. Global futures, decolonial options*. Duke University Press.

OECD. (2024). *Programa Internacional para la Evaluación Internacional de Alumnos*. https://www.oecd.org/pisa/pisa-es/

OXFAM. (2024). *Desigualdad S.A.* https://oi-files-d8-prod.s3.eu-west-2.amazonaws.com/s3fs-public/2024-01/Davos%202024%20Report%20-%20Spanish.pdf

Sato, M. (2018). *El desafío de la escuela. Crear una comunidad para el aprendizaje*. El Colegio de México.

Sato, M. (2024). *Transformar la escuela. Planeación y práctica de la comunidad para el aprendizaje*. Ediciones Ibero.

Solis, P. (2017). *Discriminación estructural y desigualdad social: con casos ilustrativos para jóvenes indígenas, mujeres y personas con discapacidad*. SEGOB, CONAPRED, CEPAL.

Sriprakash, A. (2022). Reparations: Theorising just futures of education. *Discourse: Studies in the Cultural Politics of Education.* https://doi.org/10.1080/01596306.2022.2144141

Tsukui, A. (2020). School reform and democracy in East Asia. In M. Ueno (Ed.), *Shapes of liberty. From the biographies of Vietnamese socialist teachers* (pp. 131–173). Routledge.

Tsukui, A. S., & Saito, E. (2022). History of subjectivity in dispositif: Changing arrangements of Vietnamese teachers' meeting through lesson study for learning community. *Asian Pacific Journal of Education, 42*(1), 109–123.

Viveros, M. (2023). *Interseccionalidad. Giro Decolonial y Comunitario.* CLACSO.

Walsh, C. (Ed.). (2013). *Pedagogias Decoloniales. Prácticas insurgentes, de resistir, (re)existir y (re) vivir. Tomo I.* Ediciones Abya Yala.

Walsh, C. (Ed.). (2017). *Pedagogías Decoloniales. Prácticas insurgentes, de resistir, (re)existir y (re) vivir. Tomo II.* Ediciones Abya Yala.

THE IMPLICATIONS OF EPISTEMIC JUSTICE FOR INTERCULTURAL AND INCLUSIVE EDUCATION

Sylvia Schmelkes del Valle

Universidad Iberoamericana, Mexico

ABSTRACT

In this chapter, we propose to explore the paradigm of epistemic justice in education as an approach to inclusive and truly intercultural education among indigenous peoples, as a key element to foster epistemological dialogue in all educational spaces and as an indispensable component to dismantle racism among new generations. We explore some examples of indigenous knowledge around nature, governance, equity and education, and advance the need to promote the participation of indigenous peoples in this endeavour.

Keywords: Intercultural education; inclusive education; epistemic justice; indigenous knowledge; indigenous epistemology; indigenous education

INTRODUCTION

Inclusive education seeks to ensure that learning objectives – both universal and specific – are achieved with all students, based on the premise that they are different and require different processes that take into account their personal, social and cultural characteristics. Inclusive education aims to overcome simplistic conceptions of educational equity understood as equal opportunities (Cuenca, 2012) and also compensatory strategies based on the conception that certain students are deficient and need to be compensated in order to become more like those with more advantageous conditions (Aguerrondo, 2008). It understands educational equity not as offering the same to everyone but as giving everyone what they need and giving more, and differently, to those who have less. For its part, intercultural education, in one of its strands, proposes that education that truly includes minoritised cultural sectors is that which offers, on the one

---

Intercultural and Inclusive Education in Latin America
International Perspectives on Inclusive Education, Volume 24, 227–240
Copyright © 2024 Sylvia Schmelkes del Valle
Published under exclusive licence by Emerald Publishing Limited
ISSN: 1479-3636/doi:10.1108/S1479-363620240000024015

228   *The Implications of Epistemic Justice*

hand, a school and classroom environment free of discrimination and prejudice and, on the other, educational content that is culturally and linguistically relevant to the group in question (Schmelkes, 2004).

In this chapter, we will reflect on the meaning and implications of the cultural relevance of education for indigenous peoples, as well as intercultural education for the whole population, one of whose purposes is to educate people who respect and value cultural diversity, which necessarily implies knowing and recognising it. We will do so from the perspective of epistemic justice. By this, we mean the inclusion of indigenous peoples' knowledge and ways of knowing on an equal footing with Western knowledge and the scientific way of constructing it. This is considered justifiable in itself, since in the history of education in our societies, indigenous knowledge and their epistemologies have been denied and have been absent from educational content. Additionally, including other knowledge and other ways of knowing, on equal terms, is what allows for respectful and potentially fruitful epistemic dialogue, which we believe can lead to a more complete understanding of the world and probably also to solving problems that affect our societies. As Santos points out:

> The response to this situation of epistemological crisis involves a double process of internal debate within the field of science itself and the opening of a dialogue between forms of knowledge and knowledge that allows the emergence of ecologies of knowledge in which science can dialogue and articulate with other forms of knowledge, avoiding mutual disqualification and seeking new configurations of knowledge. Santos and Meneses (2014, p. 4)

The need to promote epistemic justice, which some call curricular, in our education systems has been demanded by indigenous peoples themselves, backed by the rights granted to them by ILO Convention 169 and the Universal Declaration on the Rights of Indigenous Peoples (International Labour Organisation [ILO], 2014, p. 130) in the field of education. The education authorities, however, have responded in a lukewarm and clearly incomplete manner to this demand, partly due to a lack of political will to do so and partly due to the national society's ignorance of the enormous wealth of worldviews, epistemologies, knowledge and approaches to learning of the continent's indigenous peoples.

In the case of Mexico, in 2004, the General Coordination of Intercultural and Bilingual Education carried out 10 consultation forums with representatives of indigenous peoples so that they could say what they would like to see incorporated into the national curriculum from their culture. The purpose of these forums was to remedy the general lack of acknowledgement of indigenous knowledge in order to be able to incorporate what the indigenous people themselves recommended into the national curriculum and the specific contents of education for each indigenous people. The results of four of these consultation forums were systematised and are published (see Loncón, 2006a, 2006b, 2006c, 2006d), and some of their contents will be referred to in what follows. With the results of these forums, an attempt was made to mainstream indigenous knowledge in the process of secondary education curriculum reform in 2005. Very little was achieved.

SYLVIA SCHMELKES DEL VALLE

The New Mexican School claims to be based, among other things, on Boaventura de Sousa Santos' epistemologies of the South (Santos & Meneses, 2014; Santos et al., 2005) and to be oriented towards critical interculturality (based on the writings of Catherine Walsh (2012)).[1] In order to make cultural relevance a reality, it proposes the contextualisation of synthetic programmes through a 'co-design' work of teachers to develop the analytical programme for each school. However, there are no procedures in place to objectify and systematise local knowledge. The defined strategy does not foresee epistemic justice understood as the incorporation of other knowledge and epistemologies, in equal circumstances in the educational purposes for the whole population.

This chapter aims to introduce the reader to some examples of indigenous knowledge. The purpose is to demonstrate the depth and richness of this very broad and diverse knowledge, as well as to generate reflection on what it means to move towards achieving true epistemic justice in our education programmes. This is done with a view to their possible incorporation into the curricula of schools for indigenous peoples so that they can, on equal terms, dialogue with Western knowledge. It is also intended to contribute to its inclusion in the curriculum of the entire educational system in order to achieve respect, understanding and appreciation of other ways of knowing and, through epistemological dialogue, to be enriched by them.

WHY IS EPISTEMIC JUSTICE IN EDUCATION IMPORTANT?

Epistemic injustice is one of the causes of educational inequality experienced by indigenous peoples in Mexico and has been widely documented (Instituto Nacional para la Evaluación de la Educación [INEE], 2015, 2017). This is in addition to the economic and social injustice that particularly affects indigenous peoples. According to the National Council for the Evaluation of Social Policy [CONEVAL] (2019), in 2018, 69.5% of the indigenous population lived in conditions of poverty, in contrast to 39% of the non-indigenous population. This condition is aggravated by the racism and discrimination that prevails in our country. According to the 2017 National Survey on Discrimination (INEGI, 2018), 40.3% of the indigenous population aged 18 and over reported having experienced at least one situation of discrimination in the last 5 years (National Institute of Statistics and Geography [INEGI], 2018).

In large part, the environmental crisis has allowed the world to look to indigenous peoples and the knowledge they have generated because it is in their territories that biodiversity has been best conserved. The relationship between cultural diversity and biodiversity has been demonstrated: of the nine biologically megadiverse countries, eight are also culturally megadiverse. It is the relationship of indigenous peoples with nature that seems to explain this phenomenon and may provide answers to the greatest threat to life on the planet today.

Inequality is another serious problem in today's societies (Organisation for Economic Co-operation and Development [OECD], 2015). In Organisation for Economic Co-operation and Development (OECD) countries, in 1980, the richest

10% earned 7.5 times more than the poorest 10%. In 2015, the richest 10% earn 10 times more and account for half of all property. Mexico is one of the worst cases. The richest 1% concentrate 47% of the wealth, while the poorest 50% receive just 0.03% (Aguilar Nava, 2019). Indigenous peoples have developed mechanisms over the centuries that prevent economic inequality within their communities from escalating, the most important of which is the *mayordomia*.[2]

In general, there is a disenchantment with electoral democracy in societies, largely due, according to Woldenberg (2017), to a distrust of a state that does not provide social welfare. This is linked to the crisis of social fabric aggravated by structural and criminal violence that leads citizens to live in uncertainty and fear. Indigenous peoples are careful about community cohesion, sanction harmful and violent acts, and many of them exercise a democracy based on consensus and, therefore, on argumentation and conviction, which keeps their social organisation in force.

Thus, epistemic justice matters for two powerful reasons: it addresses one of the causes of the educational inequity suffered by indigenous peoples, and it brings visions, values, knowledge and solutions to society in general that can enable it to better face its major problems and dismantle prejudice, discrimination and racism. This will be the result of a dialogue of knowledge, ways of knowing, values and world views. It is not a question of adopting one or the other; it is a question of enriching ourselves as humanity with what humanity itself has generated.

THE CONTRIBUTION OF INDIGENOUS KNOWLEDGE

The Relationship with Nature and the Understanding of the Cosmos

For all indigenous peoples in Mexico and elsewhere, the land is Mother, and it is sacred, as the aforementioned chief of the Duwanish and Squamish of Puget Sound said: 'the land is not ours, we are of the land' (quoted in Díaz, 2007). The Andean people thus conceive of themselves as part of the land, as daughters and sons of the land. At the same time, they conceive of the land as a *sentient* being (Illicachi Guzñay, 2014). For the Tsotsiles, the land is a gift from God (Pérez Pérez, 2003). Among the Mixe, the land:

> ...is a mother who gives birth to us, nourishes us and gathers us in her womb. We belong to her, that is why we are not owners of any land... Our mother is sacred, because of her we are sacred. Díaz (2007, pp. 45, 51)

The sacredness of the land extends to all living beings that inhabit it: animals and plants, but also water and hills, lightning, air and night (Loncón, 2006b). The Nahua express that the land has no owner: it belongs to everyone and is the sustenance of humanity and all the living beings that inhabit it. Land among the indigenous people can be kept in the family for generations, but it cannot be sold or separated from communal land (Navarrete, 2008). The Mazahua are clear that if humans destroy nature, they destroy themselves (Loncón, 2006a). The Comca'ac (Seri), like the Ikoot (Huave), maintain a spiritual relationship with Mother Nature, with great respect for both the land and the sea (Loncón, 2006c). The Purh'epechas venerate and care for nature, the forests, the springs because otherwise the environment deteriorates, and life is threatened. The land is not harmed; neither the air nor the water is polluted because everything is related, and we are interdependent on each other (Loncón, 2006a).

This is the big difference with Western philosophy, which holds that human beings are the pinnacle of creation and are made to dominate nature. The pan-indigenous worldview explains why there is biodiversity in their territories. And yet, despite the fact that education for sustainability has been part of the natural sciences curriculum for basic education for at least 30 years, these ways of conceiving respect for nature, which are specific to the indigenous peoples belonging to our country, are absent or at most only mentioned.

Indigenous Peoples' Conception of Community, Governance and Style of Democracy

Indigenous peoples are originally settled in communities with a territory in which they live and work and from which they take advantage of natural resources. These communities can be relatively large or very small. In the first case, indigenous communities are subdivided into barrios, sections, rancherías, in order to ensure adequate governance, but there are mechanisms for belonging to and participating in a larger community. The Rarámuri and Wixaritari, for example, generally live in small dispersed settlements (rancherías), which allows them to take advantage of the resources of the highlands, but they are grouped into larger networks that constitute communities, and meet every Sunday to make decisions collectively. In many Mesoamerican villages, the larger community is divided into neighbourhoods, each dedicated to a different patron saint but integrated as a whole community. The affairs of daily life are decided as a community. Land and territory are an inseparable part of the indigenous community. The notion of territory includes soil and subsoil. That is why communal ownership has been their main form of organisation. In general, each family grows what it consumes, and the assigned lands are kept for generations, but they cannot sell them. The struggles for the defence of their territories are collective. The indigenous communities have their own authorities who are elected according to their own customs, which differ among the peoples but whose function is to resolve internal affairs and to represent the community before external authorities (Navarrete, 2008). For the Mixes, according to Díaz (2007), the community is not the sum of individuals but the land that *brings* them *together*. In his words, 'our community is geometric, not arithmetic' (p. 29), and this is what gives it the right to its own organisation.

For Díaz and the Mixes, community has two fundamental axes: decision-making in a community assembly and the free service of authority. The indigenous people have practised democracy for centuries, but not Western democracy, rather, what is conceptualised as 'communality'. From this conception, dissent is allowed, and the contributions of the dissenters are always sought to complement the word of the majority. Communality also contains 'collective work as an act of recreation; rites and ceremonies as an expression of the communal gift' (Díaz, 2007, p. 40). Among the Tojolabales and among the Tseltales, as Lenkersdorf (2002) tells us, language itself contains this notion of community: the '*tic*', the 'we', which is heard tinkling in every assembly, plays the role of an organising principle. This concept of 'we' excludes the concept of the individual as *ego*. The individual must be incorporated into the 'we', which demands the contribution of each and every one of us to the *nososteric* group. It does not erase the individual; on the contrary, it gives them space to develop their full potential. The 'we' is translated into the life, the actions and the way of being of the people. The language and culture of these peoples are built on this key word.

In general, assemblies seek to reach consensus, for which dissent must be heard. Among the Tsotsiles, consensus is congruent with their concept of harmony because it makes all inhabitants act in favour of the community, 'thinking of others before thinking of themselves' (Pérez Pérez, 2003, p. 43). They do not decide with a show of hands, but by whispering in small groups, they know when consensus is reached: when a single voice, that of the elders, prevails. The elders are charged with passing the message on to the authorities, who collect the opinions. They return to the assembly with the coinciding and dissenting proposals – which enrich the first ones – and consensus is reached (Pérez Pérez, 2003).

Among the Tseltales, the person in authority is called *j'a'tel*, which means 'the one who does the work'. This is the essence of their concept of authority: it is not about commanding but about serving the community. Authorities are respected and recognised because they are elected by the citizens of the community. The notion of authority as service makes it inconceivable for a servant to receive a salary (Maurer Ávalos, 1983).

Among the Nahua (consulted from 13 entities), it is the duty of the elected authorities:

> To show good conduct, be honest and have proven to have been responsible in the offices they have held before. [They must also] trust in the wisdom of the elders, act with respect, abide by the agreements of the assembly and exercise dialogue among citizens without discrimination and with humility, maintaining an attitude that serves as an example to the new generations. Loncón (2006b, p. 70)

Elders play a key role in the governance of indigenous communities. They have a history of service to the community because they have held unpaid positions throughout their lives, and because of this, as well as their life experience, they are respected. They are consulted by the authorities, individually or as a Council of Elders – among the Purh'epechas, for example – when there are sensitive issues to be resolved. In this way, indigenous wisdom is preserved, as in the case of the Nahua of Michoacán, for whom it is also important to respect the opinion and wisdom of indigenous women because they give life and take care of their children. They are the ones who possess fundamental elements of the culture and who maintain the mother tongue (Loncón, 2006a). Among the Tseltales, those who have completed all the positions are released from service and become *trensipal* (principal). They no longer have to perform physical labour. The

SYLVIA SCHMELKES DEL VALLE

supreme authority is the *trensipaltik* group. They are fit to rule because they knew how to serve (Maurer Ávalos, 1983).

He who has attained the degree of *Trensipal* is not only prepared to rule, but also to play the role of high priest for the benefit of the Community. It is his task, therefore, to see to the preservation and promotion of the harmony of the Community itself, and of the Community with the higher world. Maurer Ávalos (1983, p. 80)

These forms of governance have proved their worth for centuries. The imposition of the political party system disrupts and destroys these traditions and with it often also the governance of the community. Many communities have fought for respect for their customs and traditions, and in some states, such as Oaxaca, several of them have succeeded.

Collective work and solidarity are pillars of community governance and essential elements for maintaining community cohesion. Participation is seen both as an obligation and as a requirement of belonging to the community. Among the Nahua, for example, families help each other during the most arduous phases of agricultural work. People in Otomi communities organise themselves to finance religious festivals that are coordinated by the *cargueros*. Work such as reforestation, fighting forest fires, maintenance of schools, roads, irrigation canals, the cemetery, care of the forests and water collection are done collectively and without remuneration. Among the Pur'hépechas and other groups, the construction of houses, public buildings and streets is also solidarity work. Disinterested help is also given in the cornfield, and at harvest time, there is a distribution among those who helped. Among the Nahua, it manifests itself in support for those who lack the resources to build their houses (Loncón, 2006a). Among the Pur'hépechas, the faena is divided into two: the one that occurs when there is an outstanding debt between families and the one that constitutes a system of exchange. The faenas, the tequio, the mano vuelta, the gozona, are present in the way of life of practically all indigenous communities.[3] *Nostradic* culture implies collaboration and solidarity, which become a way of life.

Community governance is also manifested in traditional forms of justice, which differ from those of the West and have little to do with positive law. Among the Andeans, for example, indigenous justice seeks to 'purify' the person who acts contrary to the Pacha Mama (Mother Earth), which dictates not to be idle, not to lie, not to steal. The process is clear: the case is known, the facts are ascertained, the truth is found in the word of those responsible, sanctions are determined and the sanctions are carried out. Sanctions range from counselling, through financial and physical punishment, to temporary or permanent expulsion from the community (Belkis, 2020). The administration of justice has a restorative character because when possible, the sanction consists of restoring the damage and returning harmony to the community (Maurer Ávalos, 1983). Among the Cucapás, as among several other peoples, land disputes are resolved in a community assembly (Loncón, 2006c). Indigenous peoples are subject to the administration of state or federal justice in serious cases, but everyday situations that are not serious, but do affect community coexistence, are resolved by resorting to their own uses and customs or by 'customary' law (Navarrete, 2008).

Recourse to democracy by consensus – as opposed to democracy by majority vote – collective work and solidarity, and an administration of restorative and 'cleansing' justice are all ideal types and are achieved to a greater or lesser extent in the course of community life. Nevertheless, they represent mechanisms for maintaining and strengthening the social fabric, leading to trust in their own institutions and among neighbours in the community. It is a different way of understanding community governance, using manageable territorial groupings that allow everyone to be heard and that are based on collaboration and mutual help. We would do well to take these ways of understanding life in common into account in order to bring them into dialogue with the dominant ones.

Containing Inequality

The vast majority of indigenous peoples have mechanisms to limit the possibility of excessive accumulation by individuals and to promote the greatest possible equality among community members. Navarrete (2008) says that many indigenous peoples believe that people who enrich themselves individually, without sharing with others, have made a pact with the devil because this contravenes the moral rules of their community. Among the Tseltales, the excess of goods offends poor people and jeopardises community harmony, which is for them the most precious thing (Maurer Ávalos, 1983).

The mechanisms and institutions that prevent excessive enrichment by individual subjects in communities are of various kinds. Collective work and mutual support, discussed in the previous section, are undoubtedly one of them, as they allow the richest and most prestigious to be equalised with the poorest (Navarrete, 2008). Among several other approaches, *Sumak Kausay*, the philosophy and sociopolitical stance of the Andean world regarding Buen Vivir, openly criticises the excessive accumulation of goods and encourages the conscious consumption of natural resources (Illicachi Guzñay, 2014).

Another fundamental mechanism revolves around religious festivals, especially those dedicated to the patron saint of each community and the institution of the *mayordomia*. The mayordomo in turn is chosen because they are the ones who have accumulated the most during the year. Community festivals involve a large investment of money in music, rituals, food and decorations that are destined to benefit the entire community and those who visit it during the festivity, and as such, it is a redistributive mechanism that puts a limit on economic differentiation. It is, as Navarrete (2008) says, a ceremonial economy that is essential to indigenous identity. Moreover, ceremonies and festivities are an essential part of communality (Díaz, 2007) and indispensable in defining and maintaining community identity.

Among the Mayan peoples of Chiapas, the 'we' (Lenkersdorf, 2002) is also a great leveller. In decision-making, the social, political or economic status of the individual does not count. Everyone has the same right to express their opinion and also to dissent. Equality is rooted in the word, in the *tic*, in the 'we'.

Indigenous peoples defend equal rights, from access to land for farming and survival to health and education services (Loncón, 2006a).

SYLVIA SCHMELKES DEL VALLE

Now that inequality – between people, between regions, between countries – has become one of the main problems of the modern world, when the mechanisms we have given ourselves to ensure the fulfilment of fundamental rights through taxation are no longer sufficient, it does no harm to consider other ways of understanding coexistence, concrete ways of ensuring equality, solidarity-based paths to redistribution and a strong moral questioning of excessive accumulation when it is not shared. This higher value of indigenous communities must be taught in their schools, counterposed in dialogue to the brutal competition that leads to excessive wealth and the exploitation that explains poverty. There is none of that in our curricula.

The Concept of Educating and Learning

There are other ways of educating and learning in indigenous communities. The fact that they are not taken into account in the schools that offer them services has been identified as an important cause of the lack of learning and school dropout. The mestizo population in our country has not had the opportunity to learn about these other ways of teaching and learning that are devoid of competition and punishment, that are flexible and that focus on the effective implementation of what has been learned. Rogoff (2003) has documented extensively with indigenous people from Guatemala and Quintana Roo these different and effective ways of learning what is necessary to live in community and to perform expected roles, and how children learn by doing things together with experienced adults, engaging in the task.

Among the Tseltal, there is no word for *teacher*. The closest word is *jnopteshuajej*, which is the one who brings knowledge closer, the one who makes or helps to understand (Maurer Ávalos, 2011). Learning takes place through observation and practice. Tseltal children never say that someone taught them how to do something, but rather 'I learned from my mother'. Maurer argues that the Tseltal way of learning can be understood through the phrase 'wisdom of the heart', which means that learning is acquired through lived experience. Among the Tsotsiles, learning also takes place through work, but according to Pérez Pérez (2003), also through words (grandfather's advice). Pérez masterfully explains Tsotsil pedagogy in four principles of deep pedagogical significance: the first is giving and receiving advice, which is necessary to reach the soul, to make the head and hands 'intelligent', and to straighten the heart. Pérez explains that receiving advice is an intentional mechanism of the community educational process. The advice is always accompanied by stories, tales or examples and revolves around learning to work, respecting things, becoming humble in front of others; learning to work the land and respect the life of the things on it; working hard; not disturbing, not mistreating plants or animals. The second principle is to bring the soul, the *ch'ulel*. This *ch'ulel* can be strengthened through practical exercises and advice, and this is what traditional pedagogy is all about. The soul comes when the child knows what their duties and responsibilities are, and when it comes, it is not easy for others to deceive them because the child can discriminate the good from the bad. It can come at any age. The third principle is to train the head, hands and feet: to make the former intelligent and the latter skilful. It consists in the 'training of creative reasoning: thinking, listening, agreeing, advising, problem

236   *The Implications of Epistemic Justice*

solving' (p. 79) and to handle working tools. The fourth principle is to straighten (or soften) the heart, which involves consciously understanding the values of respect, esteem, mutual support and honesty.

> Someone has a *tuk yo'onton*, a right heart, when he or she understands the feelings, sufferings and pains of others and helps to correct the mistakes of others. People who are "right-hearted" are those who are not quick to get upset, who do not get angry easily or often; they understand other people's attitude and are kind to others...All human beings are capable of straightening their hearts, but the process should be started at an early age when the heart is not yet hard. Education plays an important role in softening the small heart and making it bigger, kinder, friendlier. Let's start loving each other. Pérez Pérez (2003, p. 82)

For the Nahua, the most authentic form of transmission of culture is rooted in the word, which transmits knowledge, wisdom, values and traditions (Loncón, 2006a). Among the Pur'hépechas, there is a term for the rootedness of their worldview, *shirangua*, which means root and is deeper than *suruca*, which is tradition. The basis of the children's upbringing is to participate in the community tradition as dancers in the dance of 'los monos' or 'los viejitos'. From an early age, they are appointed as captains to help with the patron saint's feast. The father does all the activities involved in this role with his son so that when he is older he can take them on himself.

Village festivals are educational events *par excellence* because they are a time to thank the gods for life, planting and culture. The festivals unite people from all the villages and help them to leave their conflicts behind. It is there that they experience being 'children of a community' (Loncón, 2006a).

For the Nahua, participating in the activities of community life is also a way of learning. Children are rarely excluded from adult activities. Children closely observe events related to life and death, work and play. Observation is more important than verbal expression, questions and answers. The child learns by observing and practising the observed activity until they master it and can perform it independently, without time pressure. 'The purpose is that they master important tasks for the community and that they feel proud of their work, because work implies *respect*, which is the ethical word of the people' (Loncón, 2006a, p. 147). It is similar among the Tseltales: when people take on a new position, it is not necessary to teach them how to perform it, as they have participated in the festivities and complicated dialogues since they were children, and the prayers 'they already know them in their hearts' (Maurer Ávalos, 2011, p. 4).

It would be desirable to adapt classroom pedagogies to those of indigenous peoples when they are the students and to enrich the pedagogies in use in the education system as such with some of these valuable concepts – such as softening the heart. This would certainly contribute to inclusion and to a higher quality and warmth of the teaching and learning processes.

FINAL REMARKS

The knowledge of indigenous peoples is immeasurable. Here, I have given just a few examples on four subjects chosen for their potential contribution to the great

SYLVIA SCHMELKES DEL VALLE

problems afflicting humanity today. Astronomical, medicinal, agricultural, climatological, obstetric and hydraulic knowledge, to mention but a few, are vast and profound, and too little explored and systematised. The many indigenous languages (68 with 364 variants in Mexico alone) signify objects, events and beliefs, unknown to the West. In Mesoamerican languages, numbers and their relations are named in base 20, not in base 10. As this is not taught in school and as all transactions are in decimal system, the naming of numbers in the languages has been dropped, and Spanish is now used as a loanword. Sociolinguistic studies, such as those by Lenkersdorf and Maurer Ávalos mentioned here, are unfortunately scarce, but they clearly show how the study of languages reveals the depth of worldviews. Indigenous peoples' ways of knowing also differ from orthodox scientific ones and can enrich them.

> Among indigenous peoples, reality is not divided into "disciplines", but is analysed as an interrelated whole. For these peoples, time does not pass linearly, as in our worldview, but in a spiral: it is a circle that repeats itself with the seasons of the year, but each time it is different because it is built on the experience of previous years. Festivals are important for indigenous peoples because they reaffirm community cohesion and set limits to excessive accumulation. Festivals are also key moments for transmitting history and knowledge to new generations. Schmelkes (2023, p. 47)

Intercultural education, in its deepest sense, demands epistemic justice. Inclusive education must presuppose this, as indigenous peoples have the right to relevant, pertinent, culturally meaningful education and also to education that strengthens their language. This necessarily implies that the knowledge and ways of knowing of their culture are incorporated into the school content, and that from them, it is possible to engage in fruitful dialogues with other knowledge and ways of knowing. Epistemic justice also means educational inclusion for the general population, which to date has been deprived of discovering the enormous diversity of knowledge and ways of knowing of indigenous peoples, of which we have given just a few examples here. Intercultural education thus understood opens horizons, illuminates realities and, above all, allows us to value and appreciate others who are different in their richness.

Mexico has not taken this step in the intercultural education offered by the state. Despite the fact that Article 3 of the Political Constitution of the United Mexican States (Chamber of Deputies of the Congress of the Union, 2023) already defines national education, among other characteristics, as intercultural, and that the New Mexican School claims to base its pedagogical approaches on critical interculturality, no processes in this direction have been initiated. The purpose of the co-curricular design that teachers must carry out is to adapt the synthetic programmes to the realities of the students, including curricular realities. This is undoubtedly an important step, but it is clearly insufficient and runs the risk of trivialising the contributions of indigenous peoples because teachers have not been trained to carry out a process as complex as that which would involve recovering the knowledge of indigenous peoples. Nor are there any processes aimed at promoting epistemological dialogue as an educational proposal for the general population. It would be essential to promote the participation of the indigenous peoples themselves, who are also the ones who must decide what they want to extend to the entire population, what should strengthen their own educational processes and what knowledge should continue to be transmitted through their own educational institutions.

To get closer to doing epistemic justice, teachers in indigenous communities will have to draw from the community culture: live with them, participate in their important moments, visit their sacred places, talk to the elders – women and men – ask about the deep meanings of rites, traditions, ways of doing things, daily practices. It is important to use what your students know and know how to do as a starting point for new learning and for dialogue between your own and outsiders. Community members – women and men – should be invited to participate in some classes to offer their own knowledge. Girls, boys and young people should be able to attend field work, funerals, community festivities, baptisms, visits to sacred sites because that is where they learn about their culture. Their experiences should be brought to class and discussed. The curricular content can then enter into dialogue with the knowledge of the culture in question, and everyone, students and teachers, will be enriched.

It is also important that teachers have the possibility to observe how children learn in their community: what they already know how to do and how they learned it, what they want to know and how they access this knowledge. They can experiment in the classroom with pedagogical strategies that take them into account, such as the importance of practice until it becomes effective, learning by observation and imitation, play as a source of new knowledge, advice illustrated with stories and legends, to give a few examples.

Above all, teachers must be humbled by the incommensurability of community knowledge and recognise that they will never finish learning about it. This will motivate them to continue researching and learning about the culture in its depth.

If all or a significant part of the above can be done in the language spoken in the community, the language itself will also become a vehicle of culture and a facilitator of epistemological dialogue. When this is not possible, it is important to let the language into the classroom by inviting members of the community to talk to the learners.

In other writings, I have called epistemic justice a paradigm shift (Schmelkes, 2023). To move towards it, education is fundamental. What we know so far is strong enough to expect from its development an enrichment of our understanding of the world, a powerful tool for dismantling racism and a new pool of possible solutions to the problems that we as humanity have brought about and that affect us all.

NOTES

1. The New Mexican School is the name of the Education Reform of the 2018–2024 Administration of the Mexican government. Its main manifestation is curricular and is operationalised in new plans and programmes and new free textbooks that have been in force in schools since August 2023.

SYLVIA SCHMELKES DEL VALLE

2. *Mayordomía* is an institution that involves a temporary nomination within a community to care for an important saint or religions figure and to take charge of the festivity on the day the saint is celebrated. The festivity usually involves organizing and paying for music and a meal for the whole community, and it usually lasts one year. It is customary to elect asl *mayordomo*, the person who has accumulated the most wealth during the previous year.

3. *Tequio* is a Nahuatlism and refers to 'work performed by each member of a community for collective needs, without pay ... also called faena, faina or fajina' (Montemayor, 2009). Mano vuelta is voluntary reciprocal work, generally for agricultural work. The term 'gozona' refers to a faena that ends in a celebration.

REFERENCES

Aguerrondo, I. (2008). Revisiting the model: A challenge to achieve inclusion. *Perspectives, 38*(1), 61–80.

Aguilar Nava, A. (2019). From inequality to poverty. A brief map of the issue. *Sign of the Times, 36*(331), 3–8.

Belkis, A. (2020). The administration of indigenous justice in Ecuador. An approach from their cosmovision. *Revista Científica UISRAEL, 7*(2), 57–74.

Chamber of Deputies of the H. Congress of the Union. (2023). *Political constitution of the united Mexican states*. Chamber of Deputies of the H. Congress of the Union.

CONEVAL, Consejo Nacional de Evaluación de la Política de Desarrollo Social (National Council for the Evaluation of Social Development Policy). (2019). *La pobreza en la población indígena de México 2008-2018*. https://www.coneval.org.mx/Medicion/MP/Documents/Pobreza_Poblacion_indigena_2008-2018.pdf

Cuenca, R. (2012). On social justice and its relation to education in times of inequality. *International Journal of Education for Social Justice, 1*(1), 79–93.

Díaz, F. (2007). Comunidad y comunalidad. In Universidad Nacional Autónoma de México (Ed.), *Floriberto Díaz escrito*. UNAM.

Illicachi Guzñay, J. (2014). Religion, education and subjectivities. *Alteridad: Revista de Educación, 9*(2), 118–130.

INEE. National Institute for the Evaluation of Education in Mexico. (2015). *Panorama Educativo de la Población Indígena 2015*. INEE.

INEE. National Institute for the Evaluation of Education in Mexico. (2017). *Panorama Educativo de la Población Indígena y Afrodescendiente 2017*. INEE.

INEGI. National Institute of Statistics and Geography. (2018). *National survey on discrimination (ENADIS) 2017*. https://www.inegi.org.mx/contenidos/programas/enadis/2017/doc/enadis2017_resultados.pdf

International Labour Organization (ILO). (2014). *ILO convention no. 169 concerning indigenous and tribal peoples in independent countries. United Nations Declaration on the Rights of Indigenous Peoples* (p. 130). ILO/Regional Office for Latin America and the Caribbean.

Lenkersdorf, C. (2002). *Filosofar en clave tojolabal*. http://elzenzontle.org/archivo/lenkensdorf.pdf

Loncón, E. (2006a). *Memoria del Foro de Consulta sobre los conocimientos y valores de los pueblos originarios de Michoacán. Hacia la construcción de una educación intercultural*. CGEIB.

Loncón, E. (2006b). *Memoria del Foro de Consulta sobre los conocimientos y valores del pueblo nauatl_ Hacia la construcción de una educación intercultural*. CGEIB.

Loncón, E. (2006c). *Memoria del Foro de Consulta sobre los conocimientos y valores de los pueblos originarios de Chihuahua, Sonora y Sinaloa. Hacia la construcción de una educación intercultural*. CGEIB.

Loncón, E. (2006d). *Memoria del Foro de Consulta sobre los conocimientos y valores de los pueblos originarios de Veracruz. Hacia la construcción de una educación intercultural*. CGEIB.

Maurer Ávalos, E. (1983). *Los Tseltales*. Centro de Estudios Educativos.

Maurer Ávalos, E. (2011). The Tzeltal learn without teaching! *Latin American Journal of Educational Studies, XLI*(3 and 4), 65–71.

240 *The Implications of Epistemic Justice*

Montemayor, C. (2009). *Dictionary of Nahuatl in the Spanish of Mexico*. UNAM.

Navarrete, F. (2008). *Los pueblos indígenas del México contemporáneo*. National Commission for the Development of Indigenous Peoples (CDI).

Organisation for Economic Co-operation and Development (OECD). (2015). *In it together: Why less inequality benefits all*. OECD Publishing.

Pérez Pérez, E. (2003). *The crisis of indigenous education in the Tzotzil area. Los Altos de Chiapas*. Universidad Pedagógica Nacional and Porrúa.

Rogoff, B. (2003). *The cultural nature of human development*. Oxford University Press.

Santos, B. d. S., & Meneses, M. P. (2014). *Epistemologías del sur* (Vol. 75). Ediciones Akal.

Santos, B. d. S., Meneses, M. P., & Nunez, J. A. (2005). Introdução: para ampliar o cânone da ciência: a diversidade epistemológica do mundo. In *Semear outras soluções: os caminhos da biodiversidade e dos conhecimentos rivais* (pp. 23–105). Civilizacao Brasileira.

Schmelkes, S. (2004). Intercultural education: Reflections in the light of recent experiences. *Sinética Revista del Departamento de Educación y Valores del ITESO, 23,* 26–34.

Schmelkes, S. (2023). *De Cabeza: Repensar la Educación*. Open Door.

Walsh, C. (2012). *Critical interculturality and (de)coloniality. Essays from Abya Yala*. Abya Yala.

Woldenberg, J. (2017). Reasons and reasons for democratic disenchantment. *Andamios, 14*(35). https://www.scielo.org.mx/scielo.php?script=sci_arttext&pid=S1870-006320170003

INDEX

Academic barriers, 19
Academic excellence, 188
Academic trajectories, 23
Accelerated learning, 199
Access, 7, 72
Access barriers, 6
Active Secondary, 199
Activities, 75, 99
Admission process, 18
Afro-descendant population, 152, 156
America, 9, 220–221
ANADIME Corporation, 54, 61
ANADIME Educational Centre (CEA), 47
  impact of CEA at community level, 56–61
  collaborative work and early detection, 53–54
  evolution of student enrolment in CEA's inclusion project, 54–56
  inclusive model, 50–61
  methodological characteristics, 51–53
  perception of protagonists, 59–61
  user families' perceptions of inclusion, 56–58
Analogies, 134–135
Anthropological approaches, 221
Assessment, 4, 19, 49
Assistive educational devices, 38
Assistive technologies, 39
Australia's education system, 133–134
Australian classrooms, physics teachers' explanatory frameworks in, 133–137
Autonomous educational system, 151

Autonomous processes, 151
Avelino Sinani Elizardo Perez (ASEP) education reform, 68, 71–72

Barriers, 6
Barriers to learning, 22, 49, 108
Barriers to learning and participation (BAP), 6, 51, 53, 62
Barriers to learning and participation/ barriers to learning, 6, 22, 49, 51, 53, 62, 108
Basic education, 114
  schools, 114
Bilingual intercultural education, 184
Bilingualism, 161–162
Black Movement, 141–143, 151
Bolivia, 5
  education in, 68–69
  special education centres in, 71
Bolivian Constitution, 69
Brazil
  inclusive education in, 35–36
  intercultural and inclusive education policies in, 141–143
  interculturality and inclusion in, 150–152
  schooling system in, 34–35
  supports and barriers to inclusive education in, 36–38
  technology use in, 39–40
Brazilian Law on the Inclusion of Persons with Disabilities, 36
Brazilian re-democratisation, 143

Caldas, rural education with new school model in, 203–205

242 INDEX

Caldas Coffee Growers Committee, 202
Canadian classrooms, physics teachers' explanatory frameworks in, 133–137
Centrode Perfeccionamiento, Experimentación e Investigaciones Pedagógicas (CPEIP), 85
Century, 146
Child, 2, 46, 51, 53, 236
Children, promotion of Mapudungun among, 165–166
Children's rights, 122
Chile, 163–164
  analysis of existing education policies in, 26–27
  challenge of inclusive model in, 48–50
  challenges of practice, 18–19
  conceptualisation of disability in Chilean context, 20–21
  diversity and social justice in higher education, 19–20
  educational trajectories, 23–24
  participation of people with disabilities in higher vocational technical education, 26
  policy challenges, 16–18
  public policy, 21–23
  reflections and policy recommendations, 27–28
  relevance of inclusion in higher education, 15–16
  SEN, 21
  theoretical framework, 19–23
  transition to university, 24–27
  university access policies and opportunities for people with disabilities, 25
Chilean classrooms, teachers' scientific explanations in, 132–133
Chilean education policy, 21
Chilean education system, 166

Chilean public policies, 19
Citizen, 68
Citizens' Constitution/Citizens Constitution, 144
Citizenship, 88, 143, 180, 182
Classrooms, 3, 39
  inclusion/exclusion dynamics within, 221–222
  pedagogies, 236
  research, 128
  speech, 38
Co-design process, 221–222
Coda, 91–92
Collaboration, 46, 63, 234
Collective work, 233
College of Graduates and Teachers in Literature, Philosophy, Science and the Arts (COLYPRO), 107–108
Colombia
  Coda, 91–92
  education policy on inclusion, 83–84
  education policy on inclusion in teacher education, 84–85
  from inclusive education to quality education for all, 81–82
  regulations on inclusive education in Colombia, 82–85
  rural education in, 199
  teaching competences for inclusive education, 90–91
  three cases in teacher training for inclusive education, 85–89
Colombian government, 198
Colombian territories, 198
Colonisation, 221
Colophon, 193
COLYPRO, 108
Committee on Economic, Social and Cultural Rights, The (CESCR), 183–184
Committee on the Rights of Persons with Disabilities (CRPD), 5
Communality, 231–232

Index 243

Community Rehabilitation Centre (CCR), 53–54, 60–61
Community/communities, 49–50, 155–156, 158, 231–232
  impact of CEA at community level, 56–61
  festivals, 234
  governance, 233
  indigenous peoples' conception of, 231–234
  members, 238
  model of intervention, 53
Competences, 25, 85
Competency-based education (CBE), 87
Concepts, 72, 76
Conceptual dimension, 176, 191, 193
Conceptualisation of disability in Chilean context, 20–21
Confederation of Indigenous Nationalities of Ecuador (CONAIE), 183–184
'Constituição Cidadã', 143
Constitution (1988), 143
Constitution (2009), 67–68
Constitution of the Republic of Ecuador, 183
Constitution/unconstitutional/ constitutional, 36, 117, 143
Constitutional Charter, 83
Constitutional mandate, 185
Constructivism/constructivist, 129–130
Continuous assessment, 52
Convention 169 of the International Labour Organisation, 155–157
Convention on the Rights of Persons with Disabilities (CRPD), 7–8, 17, 22, 33–36, 41
Cosmos, relationship with nature and understanding of, 230–231
Council of Evangelical Indigenous Peoples and Organisations of Ecuador (FEINE), 183–184

COVID-19 pandemic, 37
Critical interculturality, 10–11
  and inclusion in Mexican educational reform, 218–221
Criticisms, 105–106
Cultural diversity, 83, 89
Cultural identity, 163
Cultural transformation, 191
Cultures in family–school relationships, 121–122
Curricular adaptations, 6, 21–22

Deaf community, 9
Decoloniality/decolonial, 150, 220
'Deductive-nomological' model of explanation in science, 129
Democracy/democratic/democracies, 156–157, 231, 234
Demonstration Schools, 200
Departamento Administrativo Nacional de Estadística (DANE), 198
Department of Evaluation, Measurement and Educational Registry (DEMRE), 17
Design, 223
Detection, 62
Detection and prevention of learning difficulties, 21
Development, 2, 10
Dialogue, 168
Diario Oficial de la Federación (DOF), 117
Didactic, 84
Digital, 38
Digital technology, 38
  in Brazilian schools, 39–40
Disabilities/disability
  in Bolivia, 72
  conceptualisation of disability in Chilean context, 20–21
Discrimination/discriminated, 68

Diverse families, 122
Diversity, 72, 98
  in higher education, 19–20
Dropout, 90
Dual education system, 37
Durban Conference, 144

Early Childhood Education/Early
  Childhood educator,
  46–47, 50–51
Early detection, 49, 53–54
  of alterations, 49
Ecological model of intervention, 53
Economic Commission for Latin
  America and the Caribbean
  (ECLAC), 2, 5, 176, 198
Economic exclusion, 100
Ecuador, 180, 183
Educating, concept of, 235–236
Education, 83, 91–92, 99, 142
  in Bolivia, 68–69
  in Brazil, 38
  epistemic justice in, 229–230
  in LATAM, 3–5
  policies on family involvement in,
    117–118
  Quechua cultural practices in,
    159–160
  regulations in Colombia, 82–85
  researchers, 168
  systems, 6, 143, 148, 164
Education For All, 155–156
Education policy/education policies,
  118
  analysis of existing education
    policies in Chile, 26–27
  on inclusion, 83–84
  on inclusion in teacher education,
    84–85
Education reform (2013), 118
  inclusion, 71–72
Educational
  agents, 59
  dropout, 90
  equity, 148
  exclusion, 82

experiences, 102
  inequalities, 183
  innovation, 89
  integration, 5
  legislation in Colombia, 92
  models, 202
  policies, 27
  research, 115
  team, 53
  technology, 38
  transformation, 88–89
Educational inclusion
  attention' to diversity in Mexican
    education policies,
    146–150
  current situation and prospects,
    144–146
  historical context, 143–144
  in Mexico, 146
  perspectives for 21st Century,
    149–150
Educational trajectories, 23–24, 185
  students with disabilities in school
    establishments, 23–24
Elders, 232–233
Emancipatory practice, 131
EN Activa model, 201
EN model, 201–202
EN strategy, 200
EN-Universidad en el Campo
  experience, 212
ENSUBATÉ, 90
Entrance examination, participation
  in, 24
Environmental crisis, 229
Epistemic, 151
Epistemic injustice, 229
Epistemic justice, 228, 238
  in education, 229–230
Epistemological, 10
Epistemological theory, 129
Epistemology, 9
Equality, 6–7, 69
Equitable education, 176
Equity, 6–7, 72, 77, 193
  in education, 83

Index

explaining, understanding and, 131
in intercultural education, 167–168
and social justice, 155–156
Escuela busca al niño (EBN), 85, 87
Escuela Normal Superior de Ubaté
(ENSUBATÉ), 85–86
Escuela Nueva (EN), 199
Rural Education Model in Caldas,
202
Ethnographic research, 159–160
Ethnography, 157–158, 161–162
European Commission, 38
Exclusion, 68
criteria, 180
dynamics within classrooms,
221–222
Experiences, 205–210
of students with disabilities, 219
Explaining, 129–130
understanding and equity, 131
Explanation, 129–130
in science and in science teaching,
128–137
Extracurricular, 199
Extracurricular activities, 101

Faculty of Education, 89
Family/families
cultures in family–school
relationships, 121–122
importance of relationship between
schools and, 115
inclusion as framework for
analysing relationship
between schools and,
115–116
involvement practices, 120
participation/school parental
participation, 118, 122, 124
policies on family involvement in
education, 117–118
school practices involving, 118–121
Federal Administration, 36
Feminist theoretical approach,
219–220

Field, experiences of university
graduates in, 205–210
Flexible education models, 199
Flexible models, 199
Formal education, 159
Framework, 19–23
Framework for good teaching,
85
Fundação Nacional do Índio
(FUNAI), 142

Gender-based violence, 187
General Coordination of Intercultural
Bilingual Education
(CGEIB), 148, 228
General Law for Persons with
Disabilities, The, 69, 73
General Law on the Rights of
Children and Adolescents,
117
Goals, 102–103
'Good Living' concept, 75
Google Scholar, 114
'Governance, indigenous peoples'
conception of, 231–234
Gross Domestic Product (GDP), 5,
37, 67–68

Hermeneutic method, 177
Higher, 2–3, 26
Higher education, 22, 28
access to, 72
characterisation of participants,
179–180
Colophon, 193
conceptual dimension and teacher
education, 191–193
diversity and social justice in,
19–20
methodological approach, 177–193
policies, 20
political and structural dimensions,
180–185
pragmatic dimension, 185
primary school, 186
relevance of inclusion in, 15–16

secondary school, 186–187
university, 187–190
Higher vocational technical
    education, participation of
    people with disabilities in,
    26
Historical processes, 142
Homogenisation, 182
Homogenising education system, 149
Homogenous education system, 149
Human, 76
Human rights, 7
    culture, 122
    inclusive education in human rights
        framework, 98–99
    movements, 41

IBE, 157, 168
    context of IBE in Peru, 158–159
Identity, 87
In-service, 136–137
In-service teacher training, 176
Inclusion, 6–7, 82, 98, 193, 219, 221
    in Brazil and Mexico, 150–152
    criteria, 179–180
    in education, 83, 224–225
    education policy on, 83–84
    education policy on inclusion in
        teacher education, 84–85
    education reform, 71–72
    and exclusion of families, 114
    of families, 114
    as framework for analysing
        relationship between
        schools and families,
        115–116
    in higher education, 15–16
    index, 116
    innovations for inclusion of voices
        and knowledge, 166–167
    policies, 48–49
    process, 7–8
    teacher preparation for, 72–74
    technology for, 38–39
    'user families' perceptions of,
        56–58

Inclusion/exclusion dynamics within
    classrooms, 221–222
Inclusive approach, 46, 49, 51
Inclusive education (*see also* Higher
    education), 5, 9, 11, 53, 63,
    97–102, 176, 227–228, 237
    access to higher education, 72
    in Brazil, 35–36
    education in Bolivia, 68–69
    education reform towards
        inclusion, 71–72
    in human rights framework, 98–99
    legislation in Brazil, 36–37
    National plan for equality and
        equalisation of
        opportunities for persons
        with disabilities, 69
    people with disability, 69–70
    policies in Brazil, 141–143
    to quality education for all,
        81–82
    regulations on inclusive education
        in Colombia, 82–85
    research on teacher training in
        inclusive education
        ONEI-2022, 106–107
    schooling system in Brazil,
        34–35
    in search of relevance for,
        88–89
    special education centres in
        Bolivia, 71
    supports and barriers to inclusive
        education in Brazil, 36–38
    teacher preparation for inclusion,
        72–74
    teacher training on, 104–106
    teaching competences for, 90–91
    technology for inclusion, 38–39
    technology use in Brazil, 39–40
    from theory to sustainable
        practice', results of study,
        107–109
    three cases in teacher training for,
        85–89

Index 247

Unidad Educativa 'Sagrada
Familia' Huajchilla
principal Mr Luis Adolfo
Machicado pizarro, 74–76
Inclusive Education Network, 17
Inclusive experience in Chile
ANADIME-CEA educational
centre inclusive model,
50–61
challenge of inclusive model in
Chile, 48–50
Inclusive policies, 142
in Brazil, 144
Inclusive school, 102–103
Inclusive schooling, 99–100, 104
Income quintiles, 183
Index, 118
Indigenism, 146
Indigenist policy, 144
Indigenous education, 144–145, 151
Indigenous identity, 159
Indigenous knowledge
concept of educating and learning,
235–236
containing inequality, 234–235
contribution of, 230–236
indigenous peoples' conception of
community, governance
and style of democracy,
231–234
relationship with nature and
understanding of cosmos,
230–231
Indigenous Law, The, 147
Indigenous Movements, 141–143,
151
Indigenous peoples, 2–4, 9, 71–72, 74,
155–156, 234
conception of community,
governance and style of
democracy, 231–234
Indigenous school education, 142
Indigenous youth, 157–158
Inequality, 229–230, 234–235
Information technologies, 134–135

Initiation, response, evaluation (IRE),
136
Innovation, 21–22, 166–167
Institutional education projects (PEI),
91–92
Institutional ideologies, 190
Institutional opposition to Quechua
culture, 160–161
Institutional policies, 25
Institutional practices, 18
Institutionalisation of intercultural
and inclusive education
policies, 151
Institutionalised diagnosis, 54
Instituto Nacional para la Evaluación
de la Educación (INEE),
229
Integration, 6
Integrative model, 46
Interactive Virtual Education
Network (RIVED), 39–40
Intercultural Bilingual Education
(EIB), 9, 11, 155–156,
163–164, 218
programme in Chile, 165
teachers, 160–161
Intercultural education, 159, 224–225,
227–228, 237
equity in, 167–168
in Latin America, 155–156, 224
policies in Brazil, 141–143
theoretical and legislative
framework of, 156–157
Intercultural policies, 142–143
in Brazil, 144
Intercultural Universities (UIs),
148
Intercultural/interculturality, 156,
176, 221
approach, 176
bilingual education, 9–11
in Brazil and Mexico, 150–152
Chile, EIB and Mapuche Children
and Adolescents, 163–164
context of IBE in Peru, 158–159

current situation and prospects, 144–146
equity in intercultural education, 167–168
ethnographic findings, 158–159
historical context, 143–144
indigenous education, 144–145
innovations for inclusion of voices and knowledge, 166–167
in Latin America, 218
Mapuche cultural practices, 164–165
methodology, 157–167
in Mexico, 146
pedagogical promotion *vs.* institutional opposition to Quechua culture, 160–161
perspectives for 21st Century, 149–150
promotion of Mapudungun among children and young people, 165–166
Quechua activism inside/outside institutional space, 161–163
Quechua cultural practices in education, 159–160
theoretical and legislative framework of intercultural education, 156–157
Interculturalisation
of basic education, 148
of SEN, 149
Internal policies, 188
International Covenant on Economic, Social and Cultural Rights (ICESCR), 183–184
International intergovernmental bodies, 177
International Labour Organisation (ILO), 228
International organizations, 16–17
International Teachers' Network of Schools as Learning Communities, 216
Intersectionality, 220

Intervention, 17
Issue, 19, 115–116

Japan International Cooperation Agency (JICA), 69, 73–74
Joseph's Apiaries, 208–209
Julia's political project, 209–210
Junta Nacional de Jardines Infantiles (JUNJI), 46–47, 50–51
Justice, 233

Kepler's laws of planetary motion, 128
Knowledge, innovations for inclusion of, 166–167
Koneltun, 166

Language, 9, 46
Latin, 1
Latin America (LATAM), 1
education in, 3–5
inclusive education, 5–9
intercultural bilingual education, 9–11
Law on Labour Inclusion, 27
Learning
communities, 216
concept of, 235–236
difficulties, 21
experiences, 21
process, 222
strategies, 90–91
Legislation, 27
Legislation Colombia, 82–83
Literacy, 99

Mapuche
case in Chile, 158
Children and Adolescents, 163–164
cultural practices, 164–165
organizations, 165–166
Mapudungun among children and young people, promotion of, 165–166
Maternal, 34

Index

Maternal education, 103
Medical model, 20–21
Methodological approach, 177–193
Mexican education policies, attention' to diversity in, 146–150
Mexican Education Reform (2013), 215, 218–219
  critical interculturality and inclusion in, 218–221
Mexico
  interculturality and educational inclusion in, 146
  interculturality and inclusion in, 150–152
Ministerio de Educación de Chile (MINEDUC), 21
Ministry of Education, 22, 39–40, 73–74
Ministry of Education, Science, Technology and Innovation (SENESCYT), 177
Ministry of Equality, 92
Ministry of Indigenous Peoples, 145
Ministry of National Education (MEN), 83, 199
Ministry of Public Education (MEP), 105, 107–108, 146–147
Models, 19
Modes, 39
Multicultural, 67–68

National Center for Educational Statistics (NCES), 16
National Commission for the Development of Indigenous Peoples (CNDI), 147
National Confederation of Peasant, Indigenous and Black Organisations (FENOCIN), 183–184
National Congress of Universities, 72
National Council for the Evaluation of Social Development Policy (CONEVAL), 218, 229

National Disability Service (SENADIS), 17
National Education Programme (PNE), 148
National Education System (SEN), 117, 148, 183
National Educational Technology Programme (ProInfo), 39–40
National Higher Education Information System (SNIESE), 177
National Indigenist Institute (INI), 147
National Institute of Indigenous Languages (INALI), 147
National Institute of Statistics and Censuses (INEC), 177
National Institute of Statistics and Geography (INEGI), 229
National Institute of Statistics and Informatics (INEI), 158–159
National legislation, 199
National Observatory for Inclusive Education (ONEI), 101
National plan for equality and equalisation of opportunities for persons with disabilities (PNIEO), 69
National Policy on Special Education (2006–2010), 22
National Resource Centre for Inclusive Education (CENAREC), 107–108
National Special Education Policy, 35–36
National Survey on Discrimination (ENADIS), 229
National System of Higher Education Information (SNIESE), 177
National System of Inclusion and Social Equity, 185
Networks, 47

Neurodevelopment, 103
New Mexican School, 220, 229
New school model in Caldas, rural
education with, 203–205
Non-exclusion, training teachers for,
85–86
Non-government organisations
(NGOs), 71
Nutrition, 103

Observatory of the National
University of Education
(UNAE), 191
Official Development Assistance
agencies (ODA agencies),
177
ONEI research, 109
Organic Law on Higher Education,
The, 185
Organic Law on Intercultural
Education, The, 185
Organisation of Ibero-American
States for Education,
Science and Culture (OEI),
177
Organization for Economic
Co-operation and
Development (OECD),
3–4, 229–230
Programme for International
Student Assessment, 216

Pan American Health Organization
(PAHO), 2
Parental education, 2
Participation of people with
disabilities in higher
vocational technical
education, 26
Peace Agreement, 198–199
Pedagogical approach, 216–217
Pedagogical innovations, 85
in teacher training, 89
Pedagogical intervention work, 54
Pedagogical knowledge, 90

Pedagogical mediation modality,
108–109
Pedagogical praxeology, 88–89
Pedagogical process of children, 49
Pedagogical promotion to Quechua
culture, 160–161
Pedagogies, 10
Pedagogy, 84
People, 10, 100
People with disabilities, 69–70
participation of people with
disabilities in higher
vocational technical
education, 26
university access policies and
opportunities for, 25
Perception of protagonists, 59–61
Persons, 17
Peru, context of IBE in, 158–159
Photovoice, 161–162
Physical barriers, 19
Physical disability, 24
Physics teachers' explanatory
frameworks in Australian
and Canadian classrooms,
133–137
Plurinational Education System
(SEP), 68
Policy/policies, 189
cultures in family–school
relationships, 121–122
dimension, 122
on family involvement in
education, 117–118
school practices involving families,
118–121
Political, 2, 10
Political Constitution of Colombia,
The, 83
Political violence, 89
Post-Primary, 199
Poverty, 2, 35
Practices, 3, 114
Pragmatic dimension, 185
Primary school, 186
teacher's approach, 186–187

Index 251

Professional Institutes (IP), 26
Programa de Apoio àFormação
 Superior e Licenciaturas
 Interculturais Indígenas
 (PROLIND), 144–145
Programme for International Student
 Assessment (PISA), 3–4,
 68–69, 133–134, 216
Promoting, 8, 122
Promoting family participation, 124
Protagonists, perception of, 59–61
PRUNPCD, 70
Public education, 38, 147
Public policy, 21–23

Qualified, 161
Qualified teachers, 82
Qualitative interpretative approach,
 59
Quality, 102
Quality education, 101
Quechua
 activism inside/outside institutional
 space, 161–163
 cultural practices in education,
 159–160
 pedagogical promotion *vs.*
 institutional opposition to,
 160–161
Quota Law, 151

Racism, 141–143
Re-democratisation, 151
Recognition, 123
Reflective teacher professionalization,
 lesson studies as trigger for,
 216–217
Regulations on inclusive education in
 Colombia, 82–85
Regulatory scenario, 180–185
Reintegration policy, school seeking
 child as, 86–88
Relations, 146, 219
Research, 19

Research on teacher training in
 inclusive education
 ONEI-2022, 106–107
Revolutionary Armed Forces of
 Colombia (FARC), 198
Right to education, 17, 185
Rights, 145
Rights of persons with disabilities, 5
Rural education model
 experiences of university graduates
 in field, 205–210
 Joseph's apiaries, 208–209
 Josephine, 205–207
 Julia's political project, 209–210
 rural education with new school
 model in Caldas, 203–205
 Twins' muleteering, 207–208
Rural Education with New School
 Model, 211
Rural youth, 202, 212

School Committees for Participatory
 Administration, 118
School Integration Programme (PIE),
 23–24
School/schools, 136
 education, 146
 importance of relationship between
 families and, 115
 inclusión, 22
 inclusion as framework for
 analysing relationship
 between families and,
 115–116
 practices involving families,
 118–121
 school-family relations, 114
 school–family relationship, 115
 seeking child as reintegration
 policy, 86–88
Schooling, 92
 system in Brazil, 34–35
Schools as learning communities
 (SLC), 215
 critical interculturality and
 inclusion in Mexican

educational reform, 218–221

inclusion/exclusion dynamics within classrooms, 221–222

lesson studies as trigger for reflective teacher professionalization, 216–217

pioneering case of teacher training college in Southern Mexico, 222–224

SciELO, 114

Science and in science teaching, explanation in, 128–137

Science education in Latin America, 137

Science teachers, 127–128

Science teaching, explanation in science and in, 128–137

Scientific concepts, 127–129

Scopus, 114

Second Regional Comparative and Explanatory Study, 3

Secondary school, 186–187
physics students, 131

Secretaría de Educación Pública (SEP), 118

Secretariat for Continuing Education, Literacy, Diversity and Inclusion (SECADI), 145

Secretariat for Higher Education, Science, Technology and Innovation, 189

Segregation, 5

Semi-structured interviews, 178–179

Servicio Educativo Rural (SER), 199

Servicio Nacional de la Discapacidad (SENADIS), 46–47
Early Attention Programme, 60

Sign, 179–180

Sign language, 9

Sistema de Aprendizaje Tutorial (SAT), 199

Skills, 128

Skills for the 21st century, 92

Social change, 191

Social exclusion, 100

Social inclusion, 164

Social Integration of Persons with Disabilities, 21–22

Social justice in higher education, 19–20

Social model, 20–21

Social participation, 115

Social Rights Information System report, 218

Social science research, 163

Social theorists, 212

Sociolinguistic studies, 236–237

Solidarity, 233

Southern Mexico, pioneering case of teacher training college in, 222–224

Spanish Agency for International Development Cooperation, 189

Special education centres in Bolivia, 71

Special educational needs (SEN) /special needs, 6, 8, 17, 21

Special needs, 8

Special Plan for National Rural Education (PEER), 198–199

Speech, 59–60

State of Education, 107

Strategies, 7–8, 83

Student/students, 6, 24
activities, 129
with disabilities in school establishments, 23–24
evolution of student enrolment in CEA's inclusion project, 54–56
learning, 4
welfare, 5

Support, 16

Support networks, 53

Sustainable, 107

Sustainable development, 148

Sustainable Development Goals (SDGs), 33–34, 82

Index

SDG4, 99, 185
Systematisation, 91

Teacher education (*see also* Intercultural education), 73, 191, 193
in Bolivia, 73
education policy on inclusion in, 84–85
Teacher training
on inclusive education, 104–106
inclusive education in human rights framework, 98–99
inclusive schooling, 100–104
pioneering case of teacher training college in Southern Mexico, 222–224
research on teacher training in inclusive education ONEI-2022, 106–107
results of study 'inclusive education training processes, from theory to sustainable practice', 107–109
school seeking child as reintegration policy, 86–88
in search of relevance for inclusive education, 88–89
three cases in teacher training for inclusive education, 85–89
training teachers for non-exclusion, 85–86
Teacher/teachers, 40, 128, 191
beginning teachers' scientific explanations in Chilean classrooms, 132–133
explaining, understanding and equity, 131
explanation and explaining, 129–130
explanation in science and in science teaching, 128–137
physics teachers' explanatory frameworks in Australian and Canadian classrooms, 133–137
preparation for inclusion, 72–74
quality, 132
Teaching, 4, 6
competences for inclusive education, 90–91
practices, 91
teaching-learning strategies, 62
teaching–learning process, 191
Technical Training Centres (CFT), 26
Technology
for inclusion, 38–39
use in Brazil, 39–40
Territorial, 149
Territorial integration, 82
Tertiary education, 27, 161–162
Textbooks, 183
Thematic analysis of coded video, 134–135
Theoretical framework, 19–23
Theories in science, 128
Theory of Education, 98
Theory of Social Justice, 20
Third Regional Comparative and Explanatory Study (TERCE), 3
Training approach, 204
Transfer, 106
Transformation, 7–8, 35–36
Transition, 24–27
Trends in International Mathematics & Science Study (TIMSS), 68–69, 133–134
'Twins' muleteering, 207–208

UI curricular model, 148
Understanding, 8
UNICEF, 100
Unidad Educativa 'Sagrada Familia' Huajchilla principal Mr Luis Adolfo Machicado pizarro, case of, 74–76
Unified Black Movement (MNU), 143
Uniminuto, 90

United Nations (UN), 177
United Nations Declaration on the
    Rights of Indigenous
    Peoples, 155–156
United Nations Development
    Programme (UNDP), 2,
    198
United Nations Educational,
    Scientific and Cultural
    Organization (UNESCO),
    4, 6–7, 49–50
Universal Declaration of Linguistic
    Rights, 155–156
Universal Design for Learning
    (UDL), 21, 102
Universidade do Estado de Mato
    Grosso (UNEMAT),
    144–145
Universidade Federal de Roraima
    (UFRR), 144–145
University, 187–190
    access policies and opportunities
        for people with disabilities,
        25
    experiences of university graduates
        in field, 205–210
    in Field programme, 212
    teachers, 179
    transition to, 24–27

University in the Countryside (UC),
    202
University of Costa Rica (UCR),
    107–108
Upper, 56
Upper secondary education, 34
'User families' perceptions of
    inclusion, 56–58

Village festivals, 236
Violence, 99
Vocational technical education, 26
Voices, innovations for inclusion of,
    166–167

Web of Science, 114
Welfare, 5
Western philosophy, 231
World Conference on Special Needs
    Education, 100

Young people, promotion of
    Mapudungun among
    children and, 165–166
Youth, 157–158

Zapatista Army of National
    Liberation (EZLN), 147